The Performance Arts in Africa

The Performance Arts in Africa is the first anthology with key writings on African performance drawn from many parts of the continent.

As well as articles on play texts, comedy routines and masquerades, this exciting collection encompasses community-based drama, tourist presentations, soap operas, puppet theatres, dance, song, and ceremonial ritualized performances. The articles are presented under the following themes:

- Theory
- Performers and performing
- Voice, language and words
- Spectators, space and time.

Frances Harding's radical introduction examines and globalises some of the crucial debates, past and present, surrounding African performance.

The Performance Arts in Africa is an essential guide for those new to the field and is an invaluable reference source for those already familiar with African performance.

Contributors: Oga S. Abah, Mary Jo Arnoldi, Rene A. Bravmann, Herbert M. Cole, E. J. Collins, Stewart Crehan, M. J. C. Echeruo, Laura Edmonson, Ossie Enekwe, Andrew Horn, Robin Horton, Sam Kasule, David Kerr, Asheri Kilo, Loren Kruger, Paul J. Lane, Zakes Mda, John Nunley, Ruth B. Phillips, John Picton, Julius Spencer, Paul Stoller, Emmanuel Yewah, Kenji Yoshida

Frances Harding is Lecturer in African Drama at the School of Oriental and African Studies, London. She has taught in many different countries in Africa and is the author of a range of articles on African theatre.

The Performance Arts in Africa

A reader

Edited by
Frances Harding

London and New York

First published 2002 by Routledge
11 New Fetter Lane, London EC4P 4EE

Simultaneously published in the USA and Canada
by Routledge
29 West 35th Street, New York, NY 10001

Routledge is an imprint of the Taylor & Francis Group

© editorial matter 2002 Frances Harding

Typeset in Baskerville by Exe Valley Dataset Ltd, Exeter
Printed and bound in Great Britain by The Cromwell Press, Trowbridge, Wiltshire

British Library Cataloguing in Publication Data
A catalogue record for this book is available from the British Library

Library of Congress Cataloging in Publication Data
A catalog record for this book has been requested

ISBN 0–415–26197–X (hbk)
ISBN 0–415–26198–8 (pbk)

For Connie, Christina and our families

Contents

PART II
Performers and performing   **95**

PART III
Voice, language and words in performance   **187**

Acknowledgements

I thank the many people who have helped to bring about this book.

To the many friends and colleagues in theatre companies and academic institutions whose insight has deepened my understanding of performance over the years, I owe my thanks.

I especially want to thank the contributors to the volume whose articles have been so important over the years in bringing an all round view of performance arts in Africa to many readers. I hope this volume will extend their readership.

Most of all, however, I want to thank the performers and spectators I have talked to and held discussions with over many years in several countries of Africa. I have watched many performers, marvelled at their skills and laughed, wept at, praised, challenged and feared their characters. Without them the world would be a less self-aware and a more dreary place indeed. Thank you all.

I also thank the anonymous readers of the manuscript to whose helpful suggestions I trust I have responded. At Routledge, I thank Talia Rodgers, Commissioning Editor for Drama, whose perception and support were in evidence from the start. I also thank Rosie Waters for continuing support and Kate Trench, Richard Willis and Sünje Redies for answering my questions.

Finally I want to thank my husband and our family for their support and help throughout. We can do little without our families and it is from them that we first learn about what is best in life. In order to honour the memory of our Scottish ancestors, near and distant, I have dedicated the volume to my late beloved sister and both our families and to my younger sister, a performer.

List of authors and sources

Arnoldi, Mary Jo, 'Playing the Puppets: Innovation and Rivalry in Barnana Youth Theatre of Mali' *TDR/The Drama Review* 32: 2 © 1988 New York University and the Massachusetts Institute of Technology.

Bravmann, René A., 'Gyinna-Gyinna: Making the *djinn* Manifest' *African Arts* 10: 3 (April 1977).

Cole, Herbert M., 'The Art of Festival in Ghana' *African Arts* 8: 3 (Spring 1975).

Collins, E. J. 'Comic Opera in Ghana' *African Arts* 9: 2 (1976).

Crehan, Stewart, 'Fathers and Sons: Politics and Myth in Recent Zambian Drama' *New Theatre Quarterly* 3: 9 (February 1987), © Stewart Crehan, published by Cambridge University Press.

Echeruo, M. J. C. 'The Dramatic Limits of Igbo Ritual' from *Drama and Theatre in Nigeria* (ed. Ogunbiyi) (Nigeria Magazine Publishing, Lagos, 1981).

Edmondson, Laura, 'National Erotica' *TDR/The Drama Review* 45: 1 (Spring 2001) © 2001 by New York University and the Massachusetts Institute of Technology.

Enekwe, Ossie, 'Myth, Ritual and Drama' from *Drama and Theatre in Nigeria* (ed. Ogunbiyi) (Nigeria Magazine Publishing, Lagos, 1981).

Horn, Andrew, 'Individualism and Community in the Theatre of Serumaga' *African Literature Today* 12: 2 (1982) Africana Publishing, New York.

Horton, Robin, 'The Gods as Guests' from *Drama and Theatre in Nigeria* (ed. Ogunbiyi) (Nigeria Magazine Publishing, Lagos, 1981).

Kasule, Sam, 'Folklore and Tradition in the Drama of Cliff Lubwa p'Chong', *African Literature Today* 20 (1996). Africana Publishing, New York.

Kerr, David, 'Theatre and Social Issues in Malawi: Performers, Audiences, Aesthetics' *New Theatre Quarterly* 4: 14 (May 1988) © David Kerr, published by Cambridge University Press.

Kruger, Loren, 'Acting Africa' *Theatre Research International* 21: 2 (1996) © International Federation for Theatre Research published by Cambridge University Press.

Lane, Paul, J., 'Tourism and Social Change among the Dogon' *African Arts* 21: 4 (August 1988).

Nunley, John, 'Purity and Pollution in Freetown Masked Performance' *TDR/The Drama Review* 32: 2 (Summer 1988) © 1988 by New York University and the Massachusetts Institute of Technology.

Phillips, Ruth B., 'Masking in Mende Sande Society Initiation Rituals' *Africa* 48: 3 (1978).

Picton, John, 'What's in a Mask' *African Languages and Cultures* 3: 2 (1990).

Spencer, Julius, 'Storytelling in Sierra Leone: The Example of Lele Gbomba' *New Theatre Quarterly* 6: 24 (November 1990) © Julius Spencer, published by Cambridge University Press.

Stoller, Paul, 'Horrific Comedy: Cultural Resistance and the Hauka Movement in Niger' *Ethos* 12: 2 (Summer 1984).

Yewah, Emmanuel, 'Congolese Playwrights as Cultural Revisionists' *Theatre Research International* 21: 3 (1996) © International Federation for Theatre Research published by Cambridge University Press.

Yoshida, Kenji, 'Masks and Secrecy Among the Chewa' *African Arts* 26: 2 (April 1993).

Every attempt has been made to secure permission for copyright material. If any copyright holder has been inadvertently omitted, please apply in writing to the publisher.

Preface

Focusing the collection

Using criteria generated from within the experience of performing in Africa, the papers in this volume have been selected to give an understanding of some of the particular qualities of performance in rural and urban Africa. Because I want to draw attention to the performer as a creative artist and to performance as a creative art,[1] I have sought to include papers which make direct reference to the experience of choice within a performance – either in the creation of characters as Kruger describes for South Africa, Lane for the Dogon of Mali, Arnoldi for the puppeteers of Mali, and Kerr in Malawi or else in the choice of language as Kilo describes in Cameroon, Stoller in Niger, or in acting style as Horn describes for Uganda and Abah for Nigeria or in a new context of occasion and spectatorship as Nunley describes in Freetown, Edmondson in Tanzania or Crehan in Zambia.

I have tried to arrange articles in a manner that helps readers to approach what may be new or only partly familiar material to them. None of the categories is watertight and many articles found themselves shifted several times before finding an appropriate niche in one. Below I describe how I came to the arrangement as it now stands.

I have arranged the articles in a number of key discursive arenas within the performance arts in Africa: theorizing the performance arts, the performer and the experience of performing; voice, language and words, whether oral or written; and lastly, along with spectators, time and space in African performance.

Each article had to meet three criteria:

(a) it had to address the creativity inherent in performing;
(b) it had to extend understanding of the complexity and range of performance in Africa; to do this, key articles across a wide historical range, some almost forty years old, and which I consider to be classics, some newly written, were selected;
(c) where possible, it had to reflect the geography of Africa; but I was not prepared to favour geography at the expense of comprehensive cover of modes, forms or genres.

Part I contains five articles which, whilst describing actual performance practices, also draw the reader's attention to the complexities of conceptualising practice and I have expanded on this in my Introduction. Through this arrangement, I hope to give a preliminary sweep of some of the issues that present themselves for debate throughout the subsequent articles. In this part, I have placed the two seminal articles which constitute the 'Echeruo/Enekwe' debate because these encapsulate an approach to the performance arts in Africa, about which, by the end of the volume, readers may have formed their own opinions. In this section, along with Loren Kruger's splendid and thought-provoking article on 'Acting Africa' and Laura Edmondson's superb and much needed analysis and critique on 'National erotica', I have also placed John Picton's excellent article 'What's in a mask' which focuses specifically on the role of masks in performance. Each of the articles by Kruger and Edmondson presents a perspective on the tensions and contradictions which arise in the transformations of *genres*, issues which resonate throughout the volume. These five initial articles deliberately steer the reader towards some particularly significant theoretical issues, but without confining the parameters of theory within the collection.

This is not a chronological account suggesting either a single trajectory or multiple parallel trajectories of performance in Africa, nor is there a distinction between those forms which rely on the printed word – 'playtexts' – and those which are orally transmitted. *All* efforts to be creative are equally applauded.

As the written playtext anticipates a performance, I have included an account, by Sam Kasule, of the work of the Ugandan playwright Lubwa p'Chong as well as a more broadly based description of the works of the Congolese playwrights writing for radio, both taking as they do familiar or historic icons of sacrality or power as a palimpsest onto which they can lay contemporary figures and their ideologies.

In the Introduction I have discussed some important aspects in the performance arts in Africa, some specific to Africa, but have also aimed to contextualize the African experience within an international experience of performance in order to highlight Africa's global contribution.

It has been the evidence or exploration of creativity in performance that I have sought to address. The articles are indicative of theatre people – performers, playwrights, playmakers and activists – responding imaginatively to specific situations as they occur in their experience.

Note

1 I am using the term 'art' to refer to a clearly discernible field of human activity, identified in relation to particular human-specific endeavours such as creativity, imagination, skill, aesthetics and innovation. 'Art' seeks to articulate a diverse range of experiences and concepts through the creation of form and ultimately to realize the best in human imagination. Conversely, in whatever form, music, visual, performance, at its most banal, repetitive or unimaginative, whilst remaining in some degree, pictorial, aural or an entertainment, some such formulations are not 'art'.

Introduction

[*The group begins to dirge, softly as if singing to themselves. A short silence. Samson's face begins to show horror and he gasps as he realizes what he has been doing.*]

SAMSON [*tearing off the clothes.*]: – God forgive me! Oh God, forgive me. Just see, I have been fooling around pretending to be a dead man. Oh God I was only playing I hope you realize. I was only playing.

(Wole Soyinka, *The Road*, 1965: 83)

[*The dance of the masquerade becomes wilder, racked by spasms, the gradual build-up of possession.*]

SAY T.: – I say stop playing along with this sacrilege.

…

[*The egungun*[1] *has become thoroughly possessed.*]

(Wole Soyinka, *The Road*, 1965: 95)

1

Performance and performing

In the last scene of *The Road*, one of the best known plays by Wole Soyinka, the hapless and mute Murano emerges unexpectedly from inside the covered lorry, wearing the costume of the *egungun*,[2] the Yoruba ancestral spirits. As Murano seems increasingly to *become* the *egungun* spirit, so his companion, Say Tokyo Kid ('Say T.') is increasingly terrified of the supernatural power immanent in the impromptu masquerade figure. Say T.'s pleas for an end to the sacrilegious behaviour, however, fall on ears en-tranced and deafened by possession. Suddenly, in furious retaliation for his stabbing of Professor, the *egungun* masquerade, with superhuman strength, grabs Say T. and smashes him down.

In the play, Soyinka reflects both the physical and sacred power of the *egungun* masquerade, for the actual, ceremonial, ritual *egungun* masquerade festivals, similarly anticipate fear of violent action – even death.

During a 1978 Egungun festival … one young warrior with glazed bloodshot eyes ran up … He was mounted by the spirit of a deceased warrior. Blood streamed down the side of his mouth. People scattered including myself, but the young man seemed oblivious … The confrontation was frightening …

(Drewal 1992: 98)

In the stage play the actor is playing Murano, a character who becomes an *egungun*. The actor is then impersonating or *pretending to be* an *egungun*. The actor acquires none of the sacred power of the *egungun* ancestral spirit performing in an *egungun* performance such as that described by Drewal. In the stage play the fear, the possession, the spirit, the killing, the death, is simulation, acting. In spite of this distinction between the sacred presence and the secular representation of the spirit, at the sight of the masked figure during the play, some spectators experience feelings of *real* fear, for in Yoruba society it is not always acceptable, under the threat of physical sanctions such as a miscarriage or lifelong childlessness, for women to look upon certain *egungun*.[3] Whenever *The Road* is performed then, some women spectators find it threatening or frightening to look at even an actor dressed up in the costume of the *egungun* spirit. Unlike the performer in the stage play, the masked figure in the ceremonial *egungun* masquerades is described as having *become* the ancestral spirit. He is not 'pretending to be' an ancestral spirit but has, temporarily, become its physical manifestation.

In another of his plays, *Death and the King's Horseman*, Soyinka again uses the *egungun* figure and its putative immanent power. Jane Pilkings and her husband Simon, the District Officer, have 'dressed up' for the fancy dress ball in costumes confiscated from the ancestral *egungun* masquerade performance. Thus when Amusa, the sergeant, comes to Pilkings to report the King's death, he is confronted by the ancestors – the dead. Shocked and scared by this sacrilege, he hesitates to impart the news for, he fearfully asks: 'How can man talk against death to person in uniform of death?' (Soyinka 1975: 25) or as he says later: 'This dress get power of dead' (ibid.: 49). Again the fear and the shock is simulated, acted. Again the *egungun* which appears is *an imitation* of the *egungun* spirits who appear at appropriate ceremonies.

The evanescent cusp between the imaginary and the real is inherent in performing. In Africa, and throughout the world, performing makes visible the unseen and makes present that which is in the past or in the future, manipulating space and time and challenging social and natural order. Each form of performance is, for its duration, an interface between a revealed reality and a revealed unreality, for that which is seen is what cannot ordinarily be seen, that which may not ordinarily exist. Within a staged context, illusion and reality become equal.

Notions of exaggerating, condensing, highlighting, revealing, concealing, of guise and disguise, of social, political and spiritual boundary-crossing, of transgressive behaviour, are common to all forms of performance. The acrobat stretches the body beyond ordinary limits, achieving extraordinary feats, challenging gravity; the clown and the comedian make death a laughing matter and relieve sorrow; cross-gender performing makes the male, female, the female, male; the powerless performer becomes an entranced other – powerful, central and dynamic.[4] The dancer makes time and space palpable and visible; the singer makes intellect and emotion audible. The puppeteer animates the inanimate; the mask, by concealing the wearer, reveals another – across boundaries of gender, the supernatural, the human and animal world. In many performance contexts in Africa, these boundaries cannot be crossed either in ordinary guise, nor permanently, without invoking life-threatening sanctions of death, social ostracization or physical affliction, as Samson in the opening quotation realizes.

To begin, one must identify the art and the artist. In the plastic and literary arts – painting, sculpture, literature – the 'art' is a material object, taking form separately from the physical self of the artist and can be assessed without the presence of the artist. In performance, it is quite different, for the art is produced in *the self of the artist*, and the entity thus produced each time is defined temporally '*in vivo*', produced in and by the performer as both artist and art object. It is seen and heard through presence, voice and movement and its temporary existence verified by the presence of spectators. The quality of its temporality is physical, embodied in the performer, and *only* in the performer, and because of its immateriality outside of the performer, it is rendered *forever ephemeral*, existing only *for as long as the performer performs*. Each 'reality' which appears – *seems* – to exist and which appears *in order* to exist, does so only for the duration of a performance. After the performance, there remains only the memory of a performance. Each performance is unique, each perhaps a 'subsequent performance' (Miller 1986) of a familiar text, each neither an original nor a final product, but a reproduction, a representation of previous actions: 'Performance means: never for the first time. It means: for the second to the *n*th time' (Schechner 1985: 36). With such absolute centrality of the living self in a never original, never completed and always to be repeated act, what is the experience of performing for the performer?

Performers

There is a two-layered presentation of the self as performer: firstly as 'body' (i.e. the physical presence) and secondly either as a 'character' (a fictional persona) or as an extension of one's own persona (non-fictional). A distinction therefore can be made between the extent to which performers *are* the performance and the extent to which it is what they *do* that is the performance. As well as this, we can ask, to what extent do performers present the *self* and to what extent do they present an *other*? Within the presentation of self, in ceremonial performances such as the installation of a chief, or a wedding, the central figures are fulfilling a role, designed to mark their special status. As Margaret Drewal and others have shown, imaginative interpretation and reinterpretation – creativity – is not absent in these performances.

Apart from ceremonial roles, other performance genres also focus primarily on presenting the self in a specific role – 'an extension of personality' (Cosentino 1980: 55) – which demonstrates particular skills rather than a special status. These include storytelling, singing, dancing, poetry recitations and oratory. However at the same time as presenting the self, the performer also creates a separate, but immaterial, entity: story, poem, song, dance, acrobatics, melody or oration.

Performers and their acts are judged by spectators at multiple levels: as part of the repertoire of the performer, as part of the performer's whole performance on any one occasion, and, in comparison with other like artefacts, as part of a *genre*. Thus the heightened sense of self which is displayed advantageously in these *genres* is bound up with *what* is being rendered and *how* it is being delivered. In

Sierra Leone, the master storyteller, the late Lele Gbomba, whose consummate skill enabled him to play many roles within the span of his storytelling, would, for his performances, strip down to his bare chest and legs thus ostentatiously displaying his physical self as if to reinforce that the plethora of characters which the audience will see before them, are all quite definitely *him* in different guises. In this type of performance, then, the emphasis is on the person-performers and on their own identity being evident in the performances and as a dimension of their performance.

In contrast to this display of self, performing in dialogue dramas, in masked events, in puppet theatre and in trance, emphazises the presentation of the 'other' and deliberately disguises the self thereby diminishing the degree to which the personal self is presented. In some cases this extends even to total effacement, where the performer is not seen, may not be seen and is not officially acknowledged even to be present.

Spectating

The role of the audience is vital in creating the conditions for performance and Julius Spencer in his article on Lele Gbomba, notes how Gbomba prepares for and draws in the audience:

> ... he not only faces in all directions so that the audience can fully appreciate his performance regardless of their own location, but also moves about in such a way that each segment of the audience is fully involved ... the audience are drawn into the world of the *domei* as active participants and Lele Gbomba establishes an actor–audience relationship ... (p. 193)

Spencer also describes Gbomba's other procedures for staging his storytelling performances: costuming, words, song and how he constructs the stage (a circular arena, central mat and surrounding space) which he sets up wherever he performs. Gbomba thus ensures a theatrical ambience conducive to his stepping out of his everyday role as father, farmer and neighbour and into one which requires him to display selected, specific skills as a storyteller.

The expectations of the audience are triggered by the visual and/or aural presentation, by their knowledge of the history of that character and by their own personal circumstances, needs and preferences. David Kerr draws attention to an instance of an audience in which there was 'active and sometimes acrimonious participation' and where the vigorous input of 'the traders' and villagers' viewpoints [were] being debated with a frankness unimaginable outside the context of theatrical role-play'. This interaction takes place within Theatre-for-Development, a genre of performance described more fully later. Paul Stoller describes how spectators are literally and physically dragged into the performance arena in order to meet the spirits. The word *hauka* means 'madness' and is considered to bring the men of '*hauka*'[5] closer to the world of the spirits and enable them, more easily than most other people, to communicate with the visiting spirits, the *tooru*.

In his early novel, *Things Fall Apart*, the writer Chinua Achebe gives a vivid description of the relationship between the spectators and the masked performers:

> ... And then the *egwugwu* appeared. The women and children sent up a great shout and took to their heels ...
>
> Okonkwo's wives, and perhaps other women as well, might have noticed that the second *egwugwu* had the springy walk of Okonkwo. And they might also have noticed that Okonkwo was not among the titled men and elders who sat behind the row of *egwugwu*. But if they thought these things, they kept them within themselves. The *egwugwu* with the springy walk was one of the dead fathers of the clan. He looked terrible with the smoked raffia body, a huge wooden face painted white except for the round hollow eyes and the charred teeth that were as big as a man's fingers. On his head were two powerful horns ...
>
> (Achebe 1958: 64)

This records the transformation of the performer from private individual to sacred icon by juxtaposing the anticipated and institutionalized response of the women and children to the appearance of the masks (the *egwugwu*) with just how the individual masquerade performer can actually be identified by his walk and by his absence from amongst his peers, the elders. In this way Achebe establishes for the reader the power and complicity of spectators in sustaining belief in the transformation of the performer into spirit.

I have already noted how women are sometimes constrained in their viewing, and elsewhere I note how the Tallensi men in northern Ghana lay down strict sartorial conditions for participation in certain sections of particular ceremonies. Participation, that much vaunted attribute of performance in African societies, is not a policy of open admission to all. 'Do you want to go blind from things you shouldn't see?' asks Say Tokyo Kid in *The Road* (1965: 94).

Performances are differently determined by access to, and use of, such resources as materials, performers, audience and venue. The form is determined in the first instance by the presence in a community of potential performers, for however impelling the context, however sweet the formulations for action, without the performer, there is no performance. In Kenya, as Ngũgĩ notes, the community of workers at Kamiriithu had become a community of audience-performers, poised, already desirous of professional or specialist help to articulate their concerns and consolidate their activities into a performance: 'We hear you have a lot of education and that you write books. Why don't you and others of your kind give some of that education to the village?' (Ngũgĩ wa Thiong'o 1986: 34). How communities are poised ready to become willing, receptive audiences for new forms of drama is described in Yemi Ogunbiyi's description of the drama-oriented atmosphere in Ibadan, Nigeria, in the late fifties and sixties which eventuated in the formation of Soyinka's theatre group 'The 1960 Masks' (Ogunbiyi 1981: 27). He gives a picture of a dialectic, mutually beneficial relationship between a particular cluster of eager audiences and imaginative performers. The audience is a creative force in a dyadic relationship, where they may either suggest, inform or encourage performers to incorporate new elements in their acts, address new issues, approach new audiences and adopt new forms.

This continual creativity is typical of many forms of performance which respond to new contexts by adapting existing forms or adopting new ones to meet different demands and different experiences in people's lives. So as to understand the different contexts and genres, socially and historically, it will be helpful to consider some of the literature on the performance arts in Africa and some of the debates they have raised on performing and the performers.

Some literature about performances in Africa

Much of the writing on the performance arts in Africa has focused on masquerades and masking, or on trance and dance (Spencer 1985, Jedrej 1986) and some incorporate direct reference to the processes of creativity (Messenger 1962, 1971, Jeyifo 1985, Ngũgĩ 1986, Drewal 1992). Performances which rely only on orally transmitted information about choreography, kinetics, costuming, narrative and characterization, and whose primary stimulus has been the multi-dimensional experience of urban living have attracted growing attention in publications which emphasize the verbal alongside the visual (Clark 1979, Bame 1981, Jeyifo 1984, Barber, Collins and Ricard, 1997). Other critical works on theatre include those which have focused on a particular geographical area or else a particular *genre* within an area and given a full account of it (Coplan 1985, Kavanagh 1985, Kofoworola and Lateef 1987, Orkin 1991, Hagher 1990, Arnoldi 1995, Plastow 1996, Birch de Aguilar 1996, Kruger 1999). There have also been several works on the *genre* of contemporary, issue-based community drama now often known as Theatre-for-Development (Eyoh 1986, Mlama 1991, Breitinger 1994, Frank 1995, Salhi 1998, Abah 1997). These volumes have begun the process of documenting the range, practices, techniques and usefulness of the *genre*. David Kerr's geographically comprehensive book *African Popular Theatre* (1995) gives an account of many forms of performance – film, radio drama, playtexts, masquerade and many more – particularly documenting their response to social change.

However, in spite of this relative proliferation of books on the subject, many questions, arising from what Schechner calls the 'living performance event' (1985: 32), remain unasked. In this respect, publications which combine photography with text are useful to give the reader some idea of what is actually taking place kinesthetically, spatially and physically. Amongst the best of these publications, both textually and photographically, are *Moving with the Face of the Devil* (1987) by John Nunley, *Masked Rituals of Afikpo* (1975) by Simon Ottenberg, *African Art in Motion* (1974) by Robert Farris Thompson, *Gelede* (1983) by H. Drewal and M. T. Drewal, while Mary Jo Arnoldi's book *Playing with Time* (1995) is a rich account of the puppet theatre of Mali and a source of wonderful images.

2

Debating the performance arts in Africa

The two Nigerian writers whose seminal essays are reproduced in this volume, Michael J. C. Echeruo and Ossie Enekwe, kickstart the early debate about the scholarly perception of performance in Africa regardless of country: is African performance a ritual or is it drama?

Citing performances from his own Igbo cultural context, Echeruo proposed that in much performance in Africa lie the seeds of 'drama'. He also however, takes his referents for form in performance from the Greek, and even Sumerian, context. He describes the Igbo Odo festival and concludes that its many festival and ritual characteristics, however pleasurable and certainly 'effective' in materializing in a 'propitious July thunderstorm', do not constitute 'drama' because its 'dramatic content' is 'buried in the ritual purity of the festival'. Famously he avers that the 'Igbo should do what the Greeks did: expand ritual into life and give that life a secular base'. Originally presented in 1971 at a seminar at the University of Nigeria, Nsukka, practice and theory have overtaken this approach since then. At the time however, many scholars fiercely entered into a debate on the viability of this argument and amongst the earliest and most direct responses was that from Ossie Enekwe, also Igbo, and who also uses performances from his own culture to support his refutation of Echeruo's position.

Enekwe points out that the importance which Echeruo attaches to the presence of 'story' reveals his Aristotlean tendencies to seek a 'unified plot-structure, with logical cause-and-effect progression in time'. He goes on to assert that there is a basic difference between the 'European theatrical tradition' and the 'traditional African one': amongst other things, the first being 'intellectual', the latter 'religious ... and sensuous'. Few scholars of theatre in Africa now would support this essentialist distinction because in practice each has, or can have, all of these elements. Enekwe's final point however is that 'Igbo theatre' as practised meets the needs of Igbo society, so there is no need to 'develop a form similar to the Greeks' ... Igbo drama is already flourishing all over Igboland'.

This debate presupposes an identifiable form of performance – 'drama' – against which to distinguish another form, designated 'ritual'. Whilst these two concepts of performance activity have many theatrical characteristics in common (communication, display, movement, costuming), Horn has suggested that amongst their distinguishing features are their differing intended spectatorships: 'The ultimate end of ritual is to have an effect of the spirits ... But it is an effect only on man that drama works towards: to stimulate thought, feeling, perhaps even action in the human world alone (Horn 1981: 196). However, not all rituals address spirits. Rituals, such as Drewal (1992, Chapter 8) describes, foreground display and entertainment and seek to reconfigurate or re-align (but not radically alter) the social order, rather than directly address spirits.

Performance is a preferred *form* of iteration, explication and reinforcement of social order in a primarily oralate[6] society. Spectators must confirm their adherence to, or dissension from, the social order by their presence – or absence

– at the performance and by their appropriate applause. It is also a primary *forum* for the exploration of new ideas, a new order. Setting aside for a moment the aesthetic and entertainment dimensions, sociologically it may emerge from the readings that *all* performance is ultimately about pitting established order against the challenges of change. Ngũgĩ and Ngũgĩ's work was considered subversive (Ngũgĩ and Ngũgĩ 1982, Ngũgĩ 1986 and Bjorkman 1989).

A second distinction is proposed between 'ritual' and 'popular' theatre. Ogunbiyi (1981) defines his use of 'popular' as being in 'its usual sense – that is art intended to be popular, art that is commonly approved and widely liked by the "common" people in an ever-growing urban culture'. In this usage, with the exception of the 'urban' factor, it is difficult to see anything contrary to this in, for example, the historic Lo-Gue masquerades described by Bravmann (Chapter 9) as these also embrace notions of broad accessibility and entertainment. In their form, as well as socially and iconically, such long-established performances as those described by, amongst others, Horton, Phillips and Yoshida (Chapters 7, 8 and 20 respectively) reiterate the familiar and are conservative in their ideology, while performances such as Comic Opera, the Freetown masquerades, and most playwriting, more confidently explore the relationship between form, content and the iconic elements, frequently placing social change, rather than the *status quo*, as central. Yewah (Chapter 14) specifically charts this in the work of the Congolese playwrights, as does Horn in his article (Chapter 6) on Serumaga's work – acting styles, language, silence and content.

The more accessible a quality or experience is, the less it may be valued by society: thus, intentionally or not, the word 'popular' can imply work of lesser quality. 'Popular' refers to the broad, social base of the art-making, to the easy accessibility of the skills involved in its creation and to its ready reception. However, taken together, a problem arises because these meanings of 'popular' also suggest a qualitative element whose aesthetics and worth are often defined implicitly in opposition to the unseen but ever-present canon of establishment arts:

> A great deal of the difficulty arises from the absent/present *other* which always haunts any definition we might use. It is never enough to speak of popular culture, we always have to acknowledge that with which it is being contrasted.
>
> (Storey 1993: 17)[7]

'Common' is a far from neutral word in this context with its connotations stretching far beyond that of 'ordinary' or 'familiar' to a more negative 'vulgar, low class, inferior'. That Ogunbiyi (1981) recognizes this is implicit in his use of the word '"common"', and the apologia contained in the inverted commas around it. 'Popular', in Ogunbiyi's 'usual sense' of 'widely liked' then, often simply reflects the most superficial and easily absorbed art and can as readily be distinguished by its *adherence* or even *indifference* to mainstream ideology, as by its *difference* from or *resistance* to it. Where the former imply a conservative and often populist perspective, the latter are alternative.

The several street performers in Nairobi attest to the dynamic quality of improvised, off-the-cuff repartee as a popular form of entertainment and dialogue whilst at the same time contributing to an ultimately conservative agenda. On one occasion, some very poor young street boys were watching street performers when, as usual, one performer addressed the members of the audience, asking them to look at the boys and to be sure not to let their own children get into such a condition. Singled out for special reproof were parents, as if they somehow were independent of an encompassing poverty, and simply made 'wrong' choices, or casually and thoughtlessly failed to provide homes for their children.[8]

The extent to which 'popular' (i.e. well liked, easily understood and readily appreciated) art practices have the power to effectively critique government, and thus to effect change in the lives of ordinary people, is often illusory or, at best, marginal. Like national lotteries, however, they may offer just enough hope ('to be a millionaire, think like a millionaire', Saro-Wiwa 1988: 46) and enough of an illusion of control to assuage people and redirect discontent away from government, and to that extent are 'effective'. A chorus of protesting voices, however many, varied and entertaining, is not, alone, effective action for social or political change *in spite of* being perceived by the practitioners, and some critics, as the assertion of control, articulated and experienced through art practice, over a bewildering array of socio-economic pressures. Such practice has more in common with a process of catharsis than a process of analysis, deconstruction and reconstruction. Ngũgĩ and Ngũgĩ's (1982) experiment at Kamiriithu resulted in the theatre's violent closure and their eventual exile, because it had the power to *generate* political action. Although it was not given the chance to become 'popular' in any sense of *widespread* practice beyond Kamiriithu, as Ngũgĩ wa Thiong'o points out, 'On 12 March 1982 three truckloads of armed policeman were sent to Kamiriithu Community Education and Cultural Centre and razed the open-air theatre to the ground. By so doing it ensured the immortality of the Kamiriithu experiments … (1986: 59).'

The limited extent to which 'naming' an oppression or retaining a residual, cultural space within which to articulate oppression is anything more than creating a personal psychological space (like making a prison cell more 'comfortable') for dealing with one's oppression needs to be recognized. The extent to which any form of 'popular' culture which is not directly political initiates social change, which improves the daily conditions of the disempowered, is likely to be minimal and localized. Ironically, through its satirical and comedic trope, it may in fact sustain the inequality in the distribution of resources by making them daily more bearable. Inevitably and paradoxically this moderating process deflects outright social rebellion against conditions of injustice and thus can be considered a process of 'domestication' rather than 'liberation'.

Paulo Freire quotes Fromm: 'By [this] symbolic participation in another person's life, [men have] the illusion of acting, when in reality [they] only submit to and become part of those who act' (1972: 51). Here of course 'acting' means 'behaving politically', and Freire then comments: 'Populist manifestations perhaps best exemplify this type of behaviour by the oppressed, who, by identifying with charismatic leaders, come to feel that they themselves are active and effective' (1972: 51). Just as 'charismatic leaders' may 'stand in' for others, so too can (theatre) actors. In crediting expressions of popular culture with more than an appropriate and realistic degree of political efficacy, it is essential in practice not to be promoting a range of 'bread and circuses' which, while they may assuage economically disadvantaged people by allowing frustrations to be entertainingly vented, do nothing to alter the poverty of the informing social conditions.

It is possible to go further and state that it is because of the opportunities *permitted* by authorities and *tolerated* by them for populist expression that the social order favouring the politically and economically dominant group is sustained. This is the 'safety valve' syndrome in action.

If these are some of the debates concerning the nomenclature of perception and change in the array of performance in Africa, it is to the nature of the personal change from performer to character that I now turn: spectacular and spiritual, skilful and politicized.

Disguise and transformation(s)

There are two ways in which performers alter their quotidian identity as they enter or prepare to enter a state of performing: one is through disguise of the self, and the other through the psychological transformation of the self which may or may not include physical disguise.

In describing masked performance, John Picton (Chapter 3) takes the reader into the complex possibilities of mask use and the degree of metaphysical transformation experienced in the masked figure. He proposes a four-part schema where he notes, firstly, a category in which no 'metaphysical transformation' has taken place and in which, because it is 'representing no other reality', the distance created between performer and audience by masking is 'for dramatic effect only'. This category is closest to 'dressing up' and is likely to seek to entertain rather than to be *affective*. His second category incorporates the idea of the 'denial of human agency' in which the performer is 'metaphysically re-identified and in the most extreme cases the mask in effect effaces his very existence'. Picton suggests that the masked person is 'no mere animator of the mask, nor is he just an actor in a play' because, in masking, he has 'entered a space that belongs to and is held to be, in itself, something other'. This is the most widely held perception of the masked performer and is the focus of numerous ethnographic accounts (Morton-Williams 1956 and Kasfir 1988) as well as being used effectively in fiction by Chinua Achebe and Wole Soyinka amongst others.

Picton's third category places the onus of sacrality on the artefact itself so that the wearer is rather more of a privileged bearer than a transformed performer for 'there is nothing in the space enclosed by the mask for the performer to become ...'. In his final category, Picton refers to masks such as the ivory belt masks of Benin which are designed as sacred mnemonics or icons, not as devices for disguising.

Turning from the masked figure to the costumed, and partially disguised, figure, Loren Kruger (Chapter 4) uses material spanning fifty years to give an account of the graphic choice of images for 'Acting Africa' available to South African performers in the early part of the twentieth century. Pursuing the implications of a dichotomized perception of 'modern metropolitan drama' and those found in 'praisesongs, folk-tales and community dancing', she identifies a 'strategic *retraditionalisation*' (p. 71) though not a 'return to a lost past, but ... an alternative modernity that ... would respect African agency'. The article describes 'African agency' in the work of groups such as the Zulu group 'Lucky Stars', the 'African Own Entertainers', and the 'Darktown Strutters' who, severally, sought to present 'a critical embodiment' which refused the 'disabling dichotomy between "European" civilization and its colonial other' (p. 75).

Kruger's article draws attention to the deep contradiction of performing the collective-self as the collective 'non-self' i.e. a *pre-determined* collective other, *as viewed by* outsider-others. In a context in which the opportunities for performing a self-selected or self-constructed image of the collective-self was politically fraught in South Africa, using minstrelsy and its variants[9] as the tool by which to challenge (mis)perceptions freed the performers to the possibility of their re-appropriation (Anderson 1996 and Cole 1996), but at the same time limited the exploration of the 'real' self, the truly known self, the 'desired' self. Later, as Zakes Mda shows in his article (Chapter 19), the contradictions in a hidden collective self emerge.

Transformation of existing performative material also provides the focus for the perceptive analysis of the 'national' dancing in contemporary Tanzania by Laura Edmondson (Chapter 5). She addresses the tensions and contradictions encountered in using gendered performance material to present a politically acceptable image of the country. Edmondson explores the process of inventing, counter-inventing and 'reinventing' the 'traditional' and 'erotic' (p. 79) and 'authentic' (p. 82) *ngoma* range of dances as more or less erotic depending on the specificities of both the performance troupe and the anticipated audience. She notes the influence of the commercial urban troupes, of the Bagamoyo College of Arts, of the schools and of the differing spectatorships, urban and rural, indigenous and international. The ideal of national identity has had to be created initially in response (again) to the outsider's perception of the nation's people – men and women. This agenda sought to subsume different ethnicities and different specificities of context, to an *always gendered*, public imaging of the nation state.

Correcting the representation of a collective self to a poorly or wrongly informed spectatorship continues to provide a stimulus for performers today. I touch on this briefly below (p. 22) in reference to the Tallensi people of northern Ghana, and Paul Lane (Chapter 21) describes it fully in a Dogon context where he disputes Imperato's (1971) 'lost world' perception, as does Sam Kasule (Chapter 17) in p'Chong's works, and Emmanuel Yewah (Chapter 14) on the Congolese playwrights. John Collins' (Chapter 16) classic article on the 'Comic Opera in Ghana', like Kruger's (Chapter 4) on the South African performers, also describes a lively international counterpoint in the growth and practice of the Ghana Comic Opera genre. Andrew Horn's article (Chapter 6) provides further insight into the struggle that the international performer–director–writer, Robert Serumaga had to encompass new characters, new issues and new styles of acting in performance whilst retaining sufficient familiar characteristics in ways that would still draw in an audience.

Just how an individual prepares for and achieves a move from his everyday self to the character he seeks to present, is described in Robin Horton's article (Chapter 7). Horton describes how human actors are thought to "bring the gods into the village" and how there is a fine line ('a small distance') from the presence of the god to possession by it. He goes on to describe the experience of preparation for performing, the entry into the performance arena and the tension involved in sustaining a performance. More satisfactorily than many writers and certainly in greater detail, Horton records the transformation of the performer to a point where:

> It is not hard for elation to blur the boundary of his identity a little, and not far to go before his everyday consciousness gives place altogether to some-thing quite alien to it (p. 128).

Horton's article demonstrates the range of creative interpretation available from within one complex of belief for bringing in the 'gods as guests'.

While Horton includes an account of pre-performance techniques, Kenji Yoshida (Chapter 20) offers substantial insight into the training processes of the young men's initiation. He also focuses on the funerary ritual at which the *nyau* masquerades perform and where young initiates, *namwali*, have it revealed to them that the *nyau* are human, not animals. Yoshida asserts that the *nyau* dance is no 'mere' performance, for the dancers consider themselves to be possessed by spirits portrayed in the masks they wear. Richard Schechner's (1977: 120) 'efficacy–entertainment braid' is helpful in approaching this account so that readers understand that an emphasis on one aspect – efficacious action – does not exclude the presence of the other – entertainment – within a single performance. Nor need readers be caught up endlessly in a sterile debate on the reality/unreality of the 'human-performer' v. the 'spirit-character' for, as we saw above, by the act of costuming and other preparations, the human performer can be temporarily *transformed* in his or her own perception and that of the spectators, into a spirit character. There is no contradiction here, no suspension of *disbelief* but rather the confirmation of, and participation in, a dominant, informing *belief*. The power to transform in perception without altering bodily allows the physical presence of a human mask-wearer *to be one with* the supernatural presence of a spirit: a human-performer/a spirit-character without division of identity.

Bravmann (Chapter 9) too selects a single event, the masked performances of the Zara of Burkina-Faso, and gives a dramatic and graphic account of the Lo-Gue masked characters which emerge at the funerals of notables and at one other occasion in the year. He focuses on the appearance and performance of the character in the night light and describes how the dramatic costumes of the performers are 'starkly articulated' so as to highlight their 'almost ethereal manner' and thus serve to reinforce the popular perceptions of the *djinn* (spirits). Bravmann then gives a detailed account of the gestures and movements of these characters, thereby demonstrating how very disciplined a performer must be in order to correctly portray a specific character, and thus vividly evokes the drama-turgy of the all-night performance.

Visual image alone does not make a performance. The specific actions or speech of performers as well as movement and gesture also create physical and psychological transformation of the performer into character. Each of these actions, taken individually or along with the others, effects a distance between the guise of the everyday persona of an individual and the disguise of the persona so as to bring about the presence of the 'character'. Just how these components of a performance can also be exploited comically is described in one of the rare instances of female masking – that of the Mende of Sierra Leone – by Ruth Phillips (Chapter 8).

Costuming and disguise are amongst key actions in the visible and perceptual transformation of the performer-into-character. In the two quotations from *The Road*, which open this Introduction, Soyinka draws attention to performance both as 'play' and as awe-inspiring and in both instances indicates the vulnerability of the performer to the character once they have donned the costume of an other. Salubi's fear is that even 'playing' – that is the fun of 'dressing-up' – intended as light-hearted entertainment could become *affective*, while Say T.'s fear is of the supernatural power putatively *inherent* – already and permanently – in the *egungun* masquerade figure.

By tearing the clothes of the dead man off himself, Salubi frees himself from the putative immanent power of the dead; in donning the mask of the *egungun* Murano causes (perhaps) the *egungun* to appear. Having identified the gait of the *egwugwu* as that of Okonkwo, Achebe then details the costume of the masked figure in order, as we have seen, to establish the ferocity of the *egwugwu*, and the contrast with Okonkwo and his endearing 'springy walk'.

The casual, playful mimicry of such as Salubi, the awesome power of the masked performer and the complicit role of the audience are amongst several aspects of performance which are considered in this volume. Whilst the majority of the pieces emphasize the performer, elements of performance such as disguise – extended to puppetry as in Mary Jo Arnoldi's article (Chapter 11) on the puppetry of Mali, the *most* 'othering' form of disguise – the use to which language is put (Kilo, Stoller, Chapters 13 and 18 respectively) and the mechanics of sustaining and mounting a performance, have been flagged, and to this end several pieces describe the preparation and organization which go into pre-performance arrangements as well as the ethics, pragmatics and economics of performing in a radically altered context (Nunley, Mda, Chapters 15 and 19 respectively).

Mda's article on South African theatre in a post-reconciliation era brings an understanding of the multi-facetted possibilities of a response in theatre practice through performers, playwrights and dramatists to a public discourse replete with strong emotions of anger, revenge, forgiveness and grief. He documents how the different theatre artists working from their own perspective on the same national and individual sensitivities enable others – spectators, readers, bystanders – to enter the mindset of other people. This article provides one of the most powerful testimonies to the power of theatre, especially when it is confronted by a reality far more dramatic than any imagined adversary.

In a different context, Stewart Crehan (Chapter 23) addresses the educational institutions of a country and shows how, within the formal structure of the

Zambia National Theatre Arts Association competition – almost the very antithesis of the loosely structured *hauka* performances described by Stoller (Chapter 18) – young people were struggling to find ways of articulating their own inter-generational difficulties. Many of the plays explored the 'crux of an ideological and political dilemma', wherein the possibility of fundamental social change brought with it a challenge to patriarchal authority and the distant hint of parricide – for, Crehan suggests, 'social justice implies parricide'. The articulation of this theme had a subversive meaning which threatened to overturn the normal father/son relationship and which therefore gave the plays an importance beyond mere 'end-of-term'-style entertainment. Crehan demonstrates the mythic and ritual links implied in the plays' theme and suggests that ultimately, from within a political present which, for them, was bleak, they pointed perhaps to a future for the youth of Zambia. Under cover of one of the most formal settings – the schools' competition – the boys stake their claim to future ideological and geographical space.

The global context: more practices, more debates

In the new millenium, the increasing gap between the rich and the poor in Africa becomes ever more conspicuous and entrenched. The wealthy few can afford to vacation, visit or shop anywhere in the world, whilst the poor can neither afford a home in an urban area nor to return to, or stay in, their villages.

Demographic displacement and its consequences are everywhere evident on the continent: a sense of insecurity, of being poised ready for the next crisis, pervades the air of places as far apart as Nairobi and Freetown. There is a sense of trying to control, but not stop, the tide of change in places like Zanzibar as the tourists, conservation workers, aid agencies and international conferences arrive and the hotels smarten up and the traders and taxi-drivers raise their prices. The impact of intercontinental interaction is felt everywhere: exiles in north America e-mail their relatives at home in Ethiopia and order goats for delivery to the family at home for specific festivals – a sort of 'Intergoat' service – paying for them across continents on their credit cards.

Meanwhile adverse social phenomena continually reveal themselves. People's initial fear of AIDS/HIV infection is being replaced with contemptuous disregard for it in a continent where they perceive hunger, drought, war or road accidents as more likely to cause early death. The plight of the 'street children' of the cities, the effects of international drug trafficking, the popularization and even glorification of brutality and robbery, particularly in the wake of civil wars, have variously affected the reception, the direction, the content and the form of theatre in Africa.

Television has brought intercontinental and national televangelism to Africa on a big scale, producing a wealthy few leaders and a mass of impoverished aspirants. Taking this as one of its influences, an untrammelled and burgeoning video movie industry produces endless narratives of economic betterment. These video dramas display ostentatious wealth in the clothes, houses and cars of the characters, and often posit a connection between desperate physical violence in a brutal pseudo-historicized ideology of human sacrifice and the acquisition of personal wealth. They find a ready market in providing vicarious pleasure through fashion, lifestyle and sexual models. Hundreds of new video dramas are produced each month. However, in a teeming urban milieu where people's whereabouts are not always known and many meet death unidentified, they also reflect – and create – the widespread fear of anonymously 'disappearing', trapped in a murderous net of conspiracy and sacrifice. Because Africa has never shunned either new ideas, new influences or new technologies in the performance arts, their use invariably creates new *genres*; and for the performers, the directors and producers, the endless video dramas provide well paid work in this thriving new consumer-oriented industry.

Alongside the internet, international and local gigs, video and television, film and radio, in this technological era the international publisher is seen as only one option for communication. Many new forms of local performance have no immediate external agency and all activity – creativity, funding, recruitment, training, rehearsal and production – is initiated from within the group.

In the early 1960s the Tiv people of central Nigeria created a new puppet and masquerade theatre, *kwagh-hir* (meaning a 'wonderful thing'), which incorporated song, dance, movement, music, acrobatics, masquerade and puppetry. The appeal of *kwagh-hir* was its originality in form and concept, its (relatively) democratic ideology and practice, and its contemporary relevance (Hagher 1990 and Harding 1998).

Kwagh-hir was not alone in not having a written text. Much of the alternative theatre did not rely on a written playtext, but experimented with the collectively improvised text. Raymond De Souza George's thoughtful play *Boboh Lef* from Sierra Leone and its production by the Tabuleh Company from Freetown, came to London in 1983 during the LIFT[10] festival for a very successful run of performances.

Referring to the days before widespread international travel or electronic communication, David Kerr has drawn attention to the importance of the 'question of personnel'. He suggests that the spread of experimental theatre, such as the Travelling Theatre *genre* of Zambia, owed something to the random processes of change in staff appointments, citing the experiences of teachers who moved between Ghana, Uganda and Zambia, taking their commitment to alternative theatre with them from place to place (Kerr 1995: 135).

Just as the spread of ideas and the implementation of experimentation in theatre during the 1960s and 1970s was not confined to the Travelling Theatre, at the same time creative, non-formal, theatre activity distinct in its practice from established performance was not exclusively African, but rather worldwide. Africa was a vital part of a period of global experimentation in theatre form and content:

> As the decade [1960s] drew to a close, the new theatrical movement became increasingly important to the counter-culture's sense of cohesion and identity in Britain and it began too to make tentative forays into alien territory, to a widening variety of communities. Not all of this work was overtly opposi-tional, of course. However there can be no doubt that the alternative theatre

movement as a whole had its roots in a fundamentally radical response to the hegemony of the Western status quo.

(Kershaw 1992: 99)

During the 1960s, there was widespread interest in gaining recognition for the *right* to articulate personal and sectional concerns through the arts and thus to bring about political, social and economic change. In the west, performance went outdoors and it went informal. Performances took place in the streets, in the village square, in the new towns, in the shopping centres, in the pubs, in the church halls and in the school halls. In Africa, it took place in the market place, the village, meeting halls and – at least partly – in the auditorium, rather than on the stage.

The rise of thriving *genres* of counter-theatre formed part of an international movement wresting control of the arts from an elite of highly trained practitioners who were part of the established institutions – colleges, universities, national companies and theatres. These institutions adjudicated quality in the arts and thus sought to exercise substantial commercial, creative and aesthetic control over new work. Crystallized in 'the octopine symbol of the Arts Theatre' (Soyinka 1981: 459), they fostered agents and critics who gave or withheld the *imprimatur* to new works so that they could qualify (or not) for the appellation 'art' and the possibility of subsequent successful professional and even some commercial viability. Yet critics were often inherently conservative and certainly not always sufficiently ready for the new. Soyinka recalls a critic who, on seeing an instance of mildly experimental use of theatre space, wrote that it was 'very amateurish for actors to run in and out of the audience!' and who went on to say: '... admittedly the Museum grounds are not very suitable for a dramatic performance, in that case it would have been simpler for this group to find a hall in Lagos where their plays can be staged more conveniently' (Soyinka 1981: 460). At the time, the playtext, the playwright and playwriting, was seen as the key to new work – devising collectively and orally was virtually unknown. Soyinka was part of the Royal Court's programme for new young writers in 1959/60.[11] Writing in the style of the classics of Africa (Aidoo 1987, Clark 1966, Okot p'Bitek 1969, 1970, and Sutherland 1975) or Europe (Rotimi 1971 and Soyinka 1973) or those addressing contemporary issues (Ruganda 1972) was preferred to the 'widely-liked' literature of the fifties and early sixties which was perceived as smacking of the 'non-educated', rather than of the skilful (Henshaw 1956 and Olagoke 1962) so that even in 1981, Ogunbiyi wrote that while Henshaw provided

> *badly needed texts* in schools and colleges ... the moment that demand for texts started to be filled by the *more competent artists* who emerged at the dawn of Nigeria's independence, critical attention turned away from Henshaw to *more serious drama*.
>
> (1981: 27 (my emphasis))

Although Henshaw was doing no more than fixing in print what others such as the Ghana Concert Party, described by Collins (Chapter 16), were presenting or the South African performers, described by Kruger (Chapter 4), had presented transiently in performance, these early written plays were destined to be locked negatively into a system of stratified criteria of *literary* evaluation which rested on a putatively more sophisticated style of language, until a more confident appreciation of their worth began to emerge in the 1980s (Nwamuo 1988: 112). The rise to pre-eminence of the playtext had placed more and more people into passive roles as non-participatory audiences whose task was to applaud the writer and the performers, and stay out of the performing. Eventually however, devising plays which were *not* designed to end up as published literature, and whose avowed aim was to engage directly with spectators, was to become a widespread practice as more and more people realized that performance was about *doing* and *saying aloud* and not the silent, foetal word on the printed page.

With economic and social disparity increasingly salient in almost everyone's daily life, it is not surprising to find that newer forms of performance in African countries, like elsewhere in the world, are distinguished by their meagre investment in material resources. New forms eschew elaborate sets, locations and costumes. Training resources too are scarce, so new performance relies heavily on innate personal skills: comic, acrobatic and musical. Flexibility and adaptability are essential attributes in this kind of performance. Although most of these features are in sharp contrast to the measured preparation, training and rehearsal of long-established forms of performance such as the *nyau* described by Yoshida (Chapter 20), even in these historicized and highly contextualized local performances, new acts and characters were continuously introduced. Nor, as John Nunley (Chapter 15) shows, were these new forms impromptu work, but either followed existing rules of form and iconography or developed new ones. The new themes or styles of performance arose from a combination of inspiration, re-generation of existing forms, intellectual decision and direct influences felt from a new source, but they did not replace the series of festivals and ceremonies which married efficaceous ritual practices with a pervasive ethos of entertainment and which retained their status and role within the life of the home communities. Although the new urbanized young people had not been excluded from participating in such ceremonies and festivals as they had the right and the means to attend, nevertheless, many found themselves no longer satisfied with only these opportunities for performing.

In African countries, as elsewhere, theatre forged new forms, new meanings, new performers, new audiences, finding the interstices and the links between the familiar and the unfamiliar. In his assessment of contemporary Dogon performance, Lane (Chapter 21) asserts that young Dogon men are *not* passively and disadvantageously subject to the incoming forces of tourism but are turning those very forces to their own economic advantage, whilst at the same time retaining the historic forms of performance for their own community's ritual use. This 'cut and paste' style of transformation of existing forms of performance aimed at tourists or else gestating as an 'official' enterprise is different to the many theatres of resistance born of poverty and dissatisfaction with the status quo. Edmondson (Chapter 5) notes for Tanzania, however, that even the official performance can discreetly incorporate some gestures of resistance.

Away from 'official' performances, practitioners of many new forms of theatre were frustrated by the artistic and aesthetic limitations of mainstream performance, whatever its home location, whether it be village or street, national theatre or university. In content, the 'new forms' addressed issues of political and economic concern to a majority of people; for human resources, as performers and spectators, they drew on the skilful, the creative, the imaginative, the powerless, the formally uneducated, the poor, the untrained. The economic base was their own contributions and earnings; their own economic betterment would have been welcomed. Such performers required few material resources and, adopting an *art-trouvé* approach, such props and costuming as were needed were provided by the rejected items of the well-to-do.

The performances are themselves of course susceptible to the effects of time and familiarity. Performance, for a time, can be new in content, form, dialogue, costume, language and performers, but none is a fixed entity. Each feature can be renewed, recreated. Where Freetown masquerades once flourished, few now operate; where Theatre-for-Development was once potentially radical, it is now becoming a favoured tool of international aid agencies and government instruction for 'domestication'; where Tiv *kwagh-hir* was once iconic of 'Tiv-ness', it now operates as a 'national' theatre.

Many long-established, indigenous forms of performance are conservative in their intent, while alternative theatre looks to broad political issues, but Zakes Mda specifically addresses the use of the word 'alternative' in its South African context, rightly asking alternative to what? (Mda 1993: 197). He names 'indigenous modes' (ibid. 1995: 198) as a starting point, breaking it down from a single cover-all category into several historical practices and concluding in current Theatre-for-Development practices as a vital and meaningful contemporary theatre movement for strategizing resistance to unwanted dominance.

In response to new conditions, the newer, contemporary forms of orally-transmitted community-based drama, known as Theatre-for-Development, are burgeoning. Initially supported and funded by international and national agencies, local groups increasingly maintain or initiate their own Theatre-for-Development. Many of these are thoughtful, politically focused forms of performance designed for spectatorships ranging from intensely localized rural or urban communities, to national and international ones. Few, however, as we shall see, sustain a radical political agenda.

Radical moves: decentralized and empowering

Theatre-for-Development is a particular form of theatrical practice which has established itself in several countries of Africa since the 1970s: politicized community theatre – not, of course, addressing any national party politics – but politicizing socially. This is not a 'grassroots' type of theatre which has evolved organically from a process of increased awareness within society, but nevertheless, far from rejecting or ignoring the historic forms of performance in the communities where it operates, it seeks to expand their use and application to address contemporary issues. It deliberately interpellates existing forms of performance in order to encourage the introduction of techniques of analysis and drama-building as part of a new approach to the use of familiar forms. In its ideal form, the prioritization and utilization of existing forms of performance as the basic building block of communication is this theatre's most innovative move. Usually initiated by core groups of practitioners based mainly in the universities of different African countries, it has as its basic, informing agenda, the socio-political empowerment of the disempowered. It is unashamedly interventionist in form and intent.

The most radical aspect of its approach is its aim to assist people, already capable of identifying aspects of their unequal relationship to the resources of contemporary Africa, to analyse more fully the conditions of their disempowerment and to seek ways in which it could be altered. The most radical features in its form are the extensive use of individual characterization and of dramatic dialogue in the performance. For its radical content, it focuses on issues selected by the community in which the drama is taking place and which directly affect their lives.

The new theatrical techniques offer the participation of any and/or all members of the host communities, whether rural village, urban street or a discrete social sector, in each stage of a process of drama building. Taken as a whole, this process gives people an opportunity to create their own drama which reflects their concerns, in which they perform and whose real life stories and crises, in fictional form, they address. The participation is neither superficial nor token, but is continuously realized in a connected process of issue identification, analysis and drama-building and, finally, by the community trying out in performance various strategies for resolution of the fictionalized crisis posed in the drama.

Among the key elements of this participatory theatre are: firstly, the actors are neither trained specialists nor outsiders but ordinary people from the community in which the drama is being devised; secondly, the narratives are based on accounts of real life situations which are then fictionalized; thirdly, the resolution to the dramatic crisis within the drama is arrived at by 'trying out' ways, suggested by either spectators or actors, of responding to the fictionalized characters, their relationships and their narratives. In these ways people gain some experience of the emotions and mechanics of challenging an unequal relationship (e.g. an unjust authority) and thereby 'empower' themselves to bring about change in their everyday life. This mode of drama performs on the intersection of reality and fiction.

All over the world (Habib Tanvir in India, 'Sistren' in Jamaica) these radical forms of performance arose throughout the 1960s, 1970s and into the 1980s in numerous ways all tenuously related in a broad church of theatrical activity operating independent of institutionalized, 'formal' theatre (McGrath 1981, Brecht 1988, Cameron 1993, Kershaw 1992 and Mason 1992). In Latin America, and largely in response to the education-based initiative of Paulo Freire, his fellow Latin American Augusto Boal, was grinding out his bible of theatre practice, *Theatre of the Oppressed* (1979), part diary, part workshop manual, part history.[12] Boal's formulation was disseminated through his book and through international workshops and the individuals who participated in them. His approach combined his own experience with a compilation and distillation of what was *already happening* in many countries: politicized analytical community theatre designed to enable people to engage more forcefully and more directly in a steamrolling development industry and the more disempowering practices of its ideology.

In Africa, individuals such as Robert Serumaga, Ngũgĩ wa Thiong'o and Ngũgĩ wa Mirii, Dickson Mwansa, Rose Mbowa, Iyorwuese H. Hagher, Chris Kamolongera and Stephen Chifunyise made early contributions to a nascent Theatre-for-Development critical practice which were to be picked up on through published accounts of work and shared workshops by a generation of (then) student practitioners: Oga S. Abah, Salihu Bappa, Jenkeri Okwori, Mapopa Mtonga, Walter Chakela, Prosper Kampaore, Gonche Materego, Penina Muhondo Mlama, Julius Spencer, Ndumbe Eyoh, Asheri Kilo, Frederick Borbor and many others.

Where Brecht had directed his energies to revealing the mechanics of production, performance and characterization, others[13] sought to make 'people play people' by performing their own lives, as Zaks Mda has put it so aptly in his title *When People Play People* (1993) and later Oga S. Abah in *Performing Life* (1997).

Broadly, this form emphasizes collective rather than individual action in relation to issues of social change. Everywhere people realized that performance was not the prerogative of the few, but was accessible to many. Sometimes the content or practice reflected people's own experiences and circumstances; sometimes folk tales were retold in ways that gave them contemporary relevance; old skills and old people were involved, not as peripheral to a performance, but as central to it, as 70-year-old Njoki wa Njikira, states:

> When the Kamiriithu Theatre group started … we old people found we could be useful by teaching the young some of the things they did not know. I felt I was doing something important to the nation by teaching the songs that we used in *Ngaahika Ndeenda* and that is why I am involved in *Maitu Njugira*.
>
> (Ngugi 1986: 60)

Oga S. Abah (1997) describes a much later, similar experience of building dialogue drama in a specific locale. He, as a local man himself, was able to minutely interpret the significance of the engagement of local performers and their incorporation of local performance practice into the dialogue drama so as to empower rather than overpower people with forms that are new to them. Throughout many forms of performance, the element of creativity, the new-in-the-old, is manifest differently. Oga S. Abah describes how, during a Theatre-for-Development workshop on the environment, one of the most powerful moments in a performance came when the lyrics sung by a local singer, Etta, triggered a dramatized confrontation on taxation within the village. Then, unrehearsed, the people called in the 'two powerful masquerades, Ikyahoho and Egede' who are 'masquerades of war'. Reinforced and strengthened by their presence, the village people stuck to their resolution not to pay tax for unmade roads – not a fiction, but for real! Creativity may lie in recontextualising familiar figures in just such a way so that it is the juxtaposition conveyed by the context which is the dynamic transformation. The key factor in this experience was the choice that local people were able to make based on their intimate knowledge of local performance forms. Here they put familiar masquerade figures to a new use.

Whilst the commercial forms of theatre operating in urban centres (Jeyifo 1984 and Barber, Collins and Ricard 1997) reveal and highlight, but do not seek to change, the conditions of oppression, Theatre-for-Development is deliberately directed towards enabling people to challenge, modify and even change local circumstances of injustice and oppression. It is intended to give people a technique of fictionalizing reality by 'rehearsing' a range of responses to social and political situations which favour the rich and powerful at the expense of the poor and in this way to make the poor more politically effective in their own lives.

However, as with all forms of 'art-making', yet another shift within the *genre* has taken place. Selected aspects of Theatre-for-Development have been utilized by many government and international aid agencies to enable them to pass on to different communities messages about health, water, etc. The meaning of 'for Development' has shifted away yet again from being the people's own agenda of 'development' and all too often reverted to meaning those aspects which have been identified by the funding agency rather than the host community. The extent – and even the idea – of 'participation', a key 'buzz-word' of the nineties, has been watered down to infer any representation of a community in any aspect or in any stage of the process. 'Participation' may mean as little as an approving spectatorship, when a visiting drama group comes into a community to perform a didactic play on a given topic. There may be limited or no analysis of the processes of issue-identification or drama-building. Regrettably, this too gets called Theatre-for-Development by its supporters, practitioners and funders.

In spite of this hijacking of the techniques without the accompanying political or ideological approach, a Theatre-for-Development which *does* focus on people's own priorities in development, which *does* seek to self-liberate, continues to grow in strength and usage throughout many countries of Africa.

Conclusion – performance and creativity

In performance, creativity is most often associated with the original presentation of a work. Mary Jo Arnoldi's article (Chapter 11) on the Bamana Youth Theatre of Mali demonstrates how the ability of individuals and their creativity is an essential part of any performance and is 'the very core of their definition of youth and the function of art'.

During the festive and entertaining sections of the celebrations of the harvest festival of the Tallensi people in the Tongo hills, northern Ghana, new and eclectic elements in movement, costume and props are incorporated in the dances. Towels in a specific range of colours (orange and bright electric blue) have extended choice alongside the beautifully elaborate beaded and decorated costumes of former days; plastic dolls as well as handmade fly whisks are brandished as props; heavy boots and unlaced trainers add to the range of the heavy ankle bangles worn by young men. Along with these acts of re-presenting their visual image in keeping with the availability of contemporary items, people have also recognized that certain elements in the performance are not open to interpretation and innovation, at key points in the lengthy rituals, elders and some others depart from the central performance arena in order to fulfil specific ritual obligations in a more secluded location. These sacred acts are carried out away from the gaze of the general public. In order to even be allowed to accompany the central performers in this, a strict dress code is applied to all participants – visitors and locals alike. Those not appropriately dressed *were not permitted to walk with the elders*. Tallensi people, like people everywhere, incorporate the new into the familiar, comfortably gradating and stratifying, combining and separating sacred and secular acts and artefacts.

About one hundred miles further south, but still in northern Ghana, the Dagomba people hold frequent commemorative funerary dances throughout the dry season each year. In one performance which I attended, the dancers, all men, danced on each of four days for a period of about two hours in the afternoon. Set dances were performed each day, but the dancers, working along with the musicians, selected the sequence, the costumes, how to dance and how many dances to perform. On each of the days, every dancer in the group was given an opportunity to dance solo accompanied by the master drummer and a master praise singer. The individuality of each performer was given full scope: some chose to dance in a dignified manner, aloof from the eager spectators who pressed forward to place money on the dancer's forehead as a mark of appreciation; others devised new steps which made the audience gasp with delight while some chose to play the fool, making the audience laugh; others again devised a tantalising interaction with the musicians, retreating from and advancing on them as they followed the dancer around the performing area. It is difficult to suggest criteria by which this creativity might be considered qualitatively less than that afforded by a written text and the production of a series of performances from it. Ghana offers a rich array of performance and this volume concludes with Cole's account (Chapter 24) of a performance which takes place in the town of Akropom in Ghana, temporarily transforming it into a theatre.

If the text of the theatrical experience is performance in all its manifestations, no wonder then that it is the performer – embodying ability, style, talent, imagination and skill – who, as the understudy for each scrap of individual humanity, takes the limelight in the fleeting and ephemeral arc, a luminous bridge to what Soyinka has called the 'transitional yet inchoate matrix of death and becoming' (1976: 142).

Notes

1 'Egungun masks are regarded as physical representations of ancestral spirits' (Drewal 1992: 90).
2 See Chapter 6 in Drewal 1992.

3 See Chapter 7 in Drewal 1992. See also for example: 'Should a masquerader's characteristic gruff voice be heard in the village at night, women must flee to their homes, as
the sight of the uncostumed porter who is nude, would render a woman sterile' in
Adams (1986). See also Harding 1997 and Amali 1985.

4 This is the experience of Murano in *The Road*.

5 *Hauka* is the common name for mental illness or insanity in the Hausa language. In this
Introduction it has been loosely translated as 'madman' or 'mad people'. In Hausa this
would be *mahaukaci* (madman) *mahaukata* [mad people] *mahaukaciya* [madwoman]. With
thanks to Aliyu Muhammed Bunza (1998) and to my colleagues Phil Jaggar and Malami
Buba.

6 As distinct from 'literate'.

7 See also Stalleybrass and White 1986: pp. 6–26.

8 Anne Mungai, the Kenyan filmmaker, has set up a children's home for homeless young
people. The children are nearly all performers: acrobats, singers, comediennes, etc.

9 Here I use the same word 'transformation' to mean converting and utilising differently,
not the metaphysical or psychological transformation of the performer into spirit or
character.

10 LIFT: London International Festival of Theatre.

11 Since 1995, the Royal Court in collaboration with the British Council and other
sponsors have reintroduced a programme of playwriting for new African writers,
concentrating in 2001 on Ugandan playwrights.

12 For a trenchant criticism of Boal's works, see Milling and Ley 2001.

13 The much publicized trip through Africa of Peter Brook empowered his troupe rather
than the people they encountered. See *The Conference of the Birds* by John Heilpern. For
Brook's trips to India, see *Peter Brook and 'The Mahabharata'*, ed. David Williams 1991
and *Theatre and the World: Performance and the politics of culture*, ed. Rustom Barucha
1993, *inter alia*.

Bibliography

Abah, Oga Steve (1997) *Performing Life: Case Studies in Theatre-for-Development*, Zaria,
Nigeria: Shekut Books.

Achebe, Chinua (1958) *Things Fall Apart*, London: Heinemann.

—— (1960) *No Longer at Ease*, London: Heinemann.

Adams, Monni (1986) 'Women and masks among the Western We of Ivory Coast', *African
Arts* 19.

Adedeji, J. A. (1981) '"Alarinjo": the traditional Yoruba travelling theatre', in Yemi
Ogunbiyi (ed.) *Drama and Theatre in Nigeria: A Critical Source Book*, Lagos: Nigeria
Magazine Publications.

Aidoo, Ama Ata (1987) *The Dilemma of a Ghost* and *Anowa*, London: Longman African
Classics.

Amali, S. O. (1985) 'An ancient Nigerian drama', *Studien zur Kulturkunde* 71: Franz Steiner
Verlag, Wiesbaden–Stuttgart.

Anderson, Lisa (1996) 'From blackface to "genuine negroes": nineteenth-century
minstrelsy and the icon of the "negro"', in *Theatre Research International* 21 (1).

Arnoldi, Mary Jo (1995) *Playing with Time*, Bloomington and Indianapolis: Indiana
University Press.

Bame, Kwabena N. (1981) *Come to Laugh: African Traditional Theatre in Ghana*, New York:
Lilian Barber Press.

Banham, Martin (1981) *Wole Soyinka's 'The Lion and the Jewel'*, London: Collins.

—— (1985) *John Pepper Clark, Three Plays*, London: Collins.

Banham, Martin, Hill, Errol and Woodyard, George (1994) (eds) *The Cambridge Guide to
African and Caribbean Theatre*, Cambridge: Cambridge University Press.

Barber, Karin (1987) 'Popular arts in Africa' *African Studies Review* 30: 3.

Barber, Karin, Collins, John and Ricard, Alain (1997) *West African Popular Theatre*, Oxford: James Currey, Bloomington and Indianapolis: Indiana University Press.

Bharucha, Rustom (1990) *Theatre and the World Performance and the Politics of Culture*, Routledge.

Birch de Aguilar, Laurel (1996) *Inscribing the Mask: Interpretation of Nyau Masks and Ritual Performance among the Chewa of Central Malawi*, Fribourg, Switzerland: University Press.

Bjorkman, Ingrid (1989) *Mother Sing for Me*, London and New Jersey: Zed Books.

Blumberg M. and Walder, D. (eds) (1999) *South African Theatre As/And Intervention*, Amsterdam: Rodopi.

Boal, Augusto (1979) *Theatre of the Oppressed*, London: Pluto Press.

Brecht, Stefan (1988) *Peter Schumann's Breed and Puppet Theatre*, London: Methuen, New York: Routledge.

Breitinger, Eckhard (ed.) (1994) *Theatre and Performance in Africa*, Bayreuth African Studies no. 31, Bayreuth: Bayreuth University.

Bunza, Muhammed Aliyu (1998) in 'Mahaukaci: a mad man in Hausa society', in *The Beam*, Journal of Arts and Sciences, Vol. iv.

Cameron, Neil (1993) *Fire on the Water: A Personal View of Theatre in the Community*, Sydney, Australia: Currency Press.

Clark, Ebun (1979) *Hubert Ogunde: The Making of Nigerian Theatre*, Oxford: Oxford University Press.

Clark, J. P. (1966) *Ozidi*, Oxford: Oxford University Press.

Cole, Catherine, M. (1996) 'Reading blackface in west Africa: wonders taken for signs', *Critical Inquiry* 23.

Collins, E. J. (1976a) 'Comic opera in Ghana', *African Arts* 9 (2).

Collins, E. J. (1976b) 'Ghanaian highlife', *African Arts* 10 (1).

Coplan, David B. (1985) *In Township Tonight!* London and New York: Longman.

Cosentino, Donald, J. (1980) 'Lele Gbomba and the style of Mende Baroque', *African Arts* 13 (3).

Drewal, H. and Drewal, M. T. (1975) 'Gelede dance of the western Yoruba', *African Arts* 8 (2).

—— 1983 *Gelede*, Bloomington and Indianapolis: Indiana University Press.

Drewal, M. T. (1992) *Yoruba Ritual Performers, Play, Agency*, Bloomington and Indianapolis: Indiana University Press.

Etherton, Michael (1982) *The Development of African Drama*, London: Hutchinson.

Eyoh, Ndumbe (1986) *Hammocks to Bridges*, Yaounde: BET publications.

Faris, James C. (1972) *Nuba Personal Art*, London: Duckworth.

Farris Thompson, R. (1974) *African Art in Motion*, Berkeley: University of California Press.

Frank, M. (1995) *AIDS-education Through Theatre*, Bayreuth African Studies no. 35, Bayreuth: Bayreuth University.

Freire, Paulo (1972) *Pedagogy of the Oppressed*, Harmondsworth: Penguin.

Gibbs, James (1986) *Wole Soyinka*, London: Macmillan Modern Dramatists.

Gilbert, Michelle (1994) 'Aesthetic strategies: the politics of a royal ritual', *Africa* 64 (10).

Hagher, I. H. (1990) *The Tiv Kwagh-Hir*, Lagos: Centre for Black and African Arts and Civilisation, National Theatre.

Harding, Frances (1991) 'Soyinka and power: language and imagery in "Madmen and Specialists"', *African Languages and Cultures* 4 (1).

—— (1996) 'Actor and character in masked performance', *Theatre Research International* 21 (1).

—— (1997) 'Challenging Aristotle', *Journal of Comparative Poetics, alif*, no. 17, special issue: Literature and Anthropology in Africa.

—— (1998) 'To present the self in a special way: disguise and display in Tiv Kwagh hir performance', *African Arts* 31 (1).

Harper, Peggy (1967/8) 'Dance in a changing society', *African Arts* 1.

Heilpern, John (1977) *Conference of the Birds. The Story of Peter Brook in Africa*, Faber & Faber, 1977; reprint Methuen 1989.

Horn, Andrew (1981) 'Ritual, drama and the theatrical: the case of Bori spirit mediumship', in Yemi Ogunbiyi (ed.) *Drama and Theatre in Nigeria: A Critical Source Book*, Lagos, Nigeria: Magazine Publications.

Huet, Michel (1954) *Art, Dance and Ritual: Les Hommes de la Danse*, Lausanne: La Guilde du Livre.

Imperato, Pascal James (1971) 'Contemporary adapted dances of the Dogon' *African Arts* 5 (1).

Jedrej, M. C. (1986) 'Dan and Mende masks: a structural comparison' *Africa* 56 (1).

Jeyifo, Biodun (1984) *The Yoruba Popular Travelling Theatre of Nigeria*, Lagos: Nigeria Magazine Publications.

—— (1985) *The Truthful Lie*, London: New Beacon Books.

Kasfir, Sydney, L. (1988) *West African Masks and Cultural Systems*, Belgium: Tervuren.

Kavanagh, Robert Mshengu (1985) *Theatre and Cultural Struggle in South Africa*, London: Zed Books.

Kerr, David (1995) *African Popular Theatre: From Precolonial Times to the Present Day*, London: James Currey.

—— (1998) *Dance, Media Entertainment and Popular Theatre in South East Africa*, Bayreuth African Studies no. 43, Bayreuth: Bayreuth University.

Kershaw, Baz (1992) *The Politics of Performance: Radical Theatre as Cultural Intervention*, London: Routledge.

Kofoworola, Ziky O. and Lateef, Yusef (1987) *Hausa Performing Arts and Music*, Lagos: Nigeria Magazine Publications.

Kruger, Loren (1999) *The Drama of South Africa*, London: Routledge.

Lifschitz, E. (1988) 'Hearing is believing: acoustic masks and spirit manifestation', in Kasfir, S. L. (ed.) *West African Masks and Cultural Systems*, Tervuren: Musée Royal de L'Afrique Centrale.

Mason, Bim (1992) *Street Theatre and Other Outdoor Performance*, London: Routledge.

McGrath, John (1981) *A Good Night Out: Popular Theatre: Audience, Class and Form*, London: Eyre Methuen.

Mda, Zakes (1993) *When People Play People: Development Communication Through Theatre*, London: Zed Books.

—— (1995) 'Politics and the theatre: current trends in South Africa', in Geoffrey V. Davis and Anne Fuchs (eds) *Theatre and Change in South Africa*, Harwood: Academic Publishers.

Messenger, John C. (1962) 'Anang art, drama and social control', *African Studies Bulletin* 5 (2).

—— (1971) 'Ibibio drama', *Africa* 61 (13).

Miller, Jonathan (1986) *Subsequent Performances*, London: Faber & Faber.

Milling, Jane and Ley, Graham (2001) *Modern Theories of Performance*, London and Basingstoke: Palgrave.

Mlama, Penina Muhando (1991) *Culture and Development: The Popular Theatre Approach in Africa*, Uppsala, Sweden: The Scandinavian Institute of African Studies.

Morton-Williams, Peter (1956) *Proceedings: The Third Annual Conference of the West African Institute of Social and Economic Research (March 1954)*, Ibadan.

Ngũgĩ wa Thiong'o (1986) *Decolonising the Mind*, London: Heinemann.

Ngũgĩ wa Thiong'o and Ngũgĩ wa Mirii (1982) *I will Marry When I Want*, London: Heinemann.

Nunley, John (1987) *Moving with the Face of the Devil: Art and Politics in Urban West Africa*, Urbana and Chicago: University of Illinois Press.

Nwamuo, Chris (1988) 'James Ene Henshaw', in Yemi Ogunbiyi (ed.) *Perspectives on Nigerian Literature: 1700 to the present*, vol. 2, Lagos: Guardian Books.

Ogunbiyi, Yemi (ed.) (1981) *Drama and Theatre in Nigeria: A Critical Source Book*, Lagos: Nigeria Magazine Publications.

—— (ed.) (1988) *Perspectives on Nigerian Literature: 1700 to the present*, vol. 2, Lagos: Guardian Books.

Olagoke, D. Olu (1962) *The Incorruptible Judge*, Nigeria: Evans Africa Plays.

Orkin, Martin (1991) *Drama and the South African State*, Manchester and New York: Manchester University Press.

Ottenberg, Simon (1975) *Masked Rituals of Afikpo*, Washington: University of Washington Press.

p'Bitek, Okot (1969) *Song of Lawino*, Nairobi: East Africa Publishing House.

—— (1970) *Song of Ocol*, Nairobi: East Africa Publishing House.

Plastow J. (1996) *The Evolution of Theatre in Ethiopia, Tanzania and Zimbabwe: A Comparative Study*, Amsterdam: Rodopi.

Ranger, Terence (1975) *Dance and Society in Eastern Africa* 1890–1970: *The Beni Ngoma*, London: Heinemann Educational Books.

Richards, Sandra L. (1996) *Ancient Songs Set Ablaze: The Theatre of Femi Osofisan*, Washington: Howard University Press.

Rotimi, Ola (1971) *The Gods are not to Blame*, Oxford: Oxford University Press.

Ruganda, John (1972) *The Burdens*, Nairobi and New York: Oxford University Press.

Salhi, Kamal (ed.) (1998) *African Theatre for Development: Art for Self-Determination*, Exeter: Intellect Books.

Saro-Wiwa, Ken (1988) *Basi and Company*, Lagos: Saros International Publishers.

Schechner, Richard (1977) *Performance Theory*, New York: Drama Book Specialists.

Schechner, Richard (1985) *Between Theater and Anthropology*, Philadelphia: University of Pennsylvania Press.

Schechner, R. and Appel, W. (eds) (1990) *By Means of Performance*, Cambridge: Cambridge University Press.

Soyinka, Wole (1965) *The Road*, Oxford: Oxford University Press.

—— (1973) *The Bacchae of Euripides*, London: Eyre Methuen Ltd.

—— (1975) *Death and the King's Horseman*, London: Eyre Methuen Ltd.

—— (1976) *Myth, Literature and the African World*, Cambridge: Cambridge University Press.

—— (1981) 'Towards a True Theatre', in Yemi Ogunbiyi (ed.) *Drama and Theatre in Nigeria: A Critical Source Book*, Lagos: Nigeria Magazine Publications.

Spencer, Paul (1985) *Society and the Dance*, Cambridge: Cambridge University Press.

Stalleybrass, Peter and White, Allon (1986) *The Politics and Poetics of Transgression*, London: Methuen.

Storey, John (1993) *An Introductory Guide to Cultural Theory and Popular Culture*, London: Harvester Wheatsheaf.

Sutherland, Efua T. (1975) *The Marriage of Anansewa*, London: Longman; reprint Longman Drumbeat 1980.

Thompson, Robert Farris (1974) *African Art in Motion*, Berkeley: University of California Press.

Vansina, Jan (1985) *Oral Tradition as History*, London: Heinemann.

Williams, David (ed.) (1991) *Peter Brook and the Mahabharata: Critical Perspectives*, Routledge.

Part I
Theory

1 The dramatic limits of Igbo ritual

M. J. C. Echeruo

Introduction

This paper is a very tentative statement of a view which I have held for some time but which I have hesitated to advance because more extensive field research than I have been able to undertake seemed required for its full validation. I present it now because this seems to be as good an opportunity as one could ever want for securing the reaction of those who have been engaged in Igbo and related studies for a much longer time than myself.* I should hope, in any event, that my argument will be found not only valid for the study of Igbo traditional literature but also helpful to our creative writers who may wish to exploit our traditions for contemporary uses.

My approach has been inevitably determined by my interest in myth-criticism, that is in the archetypal meaning derivable from the structure of ideas and action in a given work of art. Accordingly, I have tended to look at the Igbo Festival in gross, as an event whose structure has meaning in itself. Drama lends itself very naturally to this critical approach because its outlines of action are usually clear and the sequence of its events invariably of a deliberate kind.[1] For this reason, also, I have not concerned myself at this stage with the language of the festivals, nor with Igbo dramaturgy – that is with the Igbo *style* of presenting action. These are important aspects of the subject which, for me, follow only after the more general and theoretical argument has been established.

African drama

It is generally agreed these days that drama is an important element in traditional African culture. In Nigeria, the Yorubas, Ijaws, and sometimes the Efiks, are usually singled out as illustrating this contention.[2] In these studies, attention is drawn to the elements of song, dance, and costuming which in various combinations have resulted in such dramatic forms as heroic drama, burlesque, satire and ribald comedy. 'The Ijaws, perhaps more than any other people in Nigeria', one writer has argued, 'have developed over the centuries a form of

---

* This paper was read to the Seminar on Igbo Language and Literature organized by the Institute of African Studies, University of Nigeria, Nsukka, November 24–7, 1971.

dramatic art which is religious in purpose but which has become weighted heavily on the side of skilful performance and artistic values'.[3] Similar studies have not been carried out in detail among the Igbo, but from the evidence already in print, indications are that the same conclusions are likely to be reached with regard to the place of drama in Igbo culture.[4] It will also be found that the Igbo do not lack adequate mythologies, that they have a keen sense of stylized representational action, and that they certainly do not lack a feeling ceremony.

While asserting this, we should not lose sight of the argument recently advanced by Ruth Finnegan that 'it would be truer to say' that 'there are certain dramatic and quasi-dramatic phenomena to be found' in African traditional festivals. This is important, she holds, in view of what she regards as the absence of 'linguistic content, plot, represented interaction of several characters, specialized scenery', etc. in these indigenous dramas.[5] Her argument is borne out, in part, by statements made by some of those who champion the idea of a fully-developed indigenous drama. Writing of the *Ekine* dramas, for example, Robin Horton says that 'the masquerade is not intended as the enactment of verbal narrative. Its dominant symbols are those of rhythmic gesture, dictated by the drum; and in so far as its verbal commentaries have a use, it is one of directing attention to the broad area in which the meaning of the dance gestures lies ... it is left to the language of dance to fill in the detail which makes the masquerade rich and satisfying to its audience.'[6] If this is true, then, there is reason to re-examine our use of the word 'drama' to describe these events, since for example, the 'recitation' and 'performance' of epic poetry in chorus can also have most of the characteristics of the indigenous festival and still not be drama.

Drama and society

Drama, in its very many manifestations, including its ritual manifestations, is very specifically communal in character. More than any of the other arts, it requires a group audience at all stages of enactment; quite often, in fact, it demands the participation of the audience in the action of song. For this reason, some theorists have argued, quite convincingly, that drama flourishes most in a society that has developed a strong consciousness of itself *as a community*.[7] We should, however, add that drama flourishes best in a community which has satisfactorily transformed ritual into celebration and converted the mythic structure of action from the religious and priestly to the secular plane.

On the level of theory, this is the explanation often advanced for the development of Greek drama. It is maintained that the plays depended on the identification of Greek civilization with its common religious and cultural roots and the transformation of that identity from its strictly Dionysian or Apollonian origins to the equivalent secular experience which, nevertheless, still retained something of the original religious implications.[8]

Where this happens, drama becomes the ideal festival, communal feast which features re-enactment and rededication for every individual in the community. In

Greek and similar societies, drama, as festival, reinforces common values, shared bonds and common taboos. It re-establishes links with the past and compels the living to participate in hilarity and comradeship of a communal happening.

Drama, ritual and myth

If, therefore, the festival is a celebration, drama is a re-enactment of life. Drama is to the society what ritual is to religion: a public affirmation of an idea; a translation into action of a *mythos* or plot just as ritual is the translation of a faith into external action.[9] A divination scene, for example, is not in itself drama, though it may be dramatic. It is ritualistic or liturgical. That is to say, it is a representation in action of a faith or a dream, like communion or baptism. The pattern of action does not tell a story; it reasserts the essence of the faith in *symbolic* terms. Drama, on the other hand, allows for the reinterpretation of life through a pattern of ordered events, through that fragment of history we usually call plot.[10] Hence it is that myth gives substance to narrative just as faith gives substance to ritual. It is myth – i.e., plot – that gives mass and duration to ritual (and thence to faith), and leads it ultimately to drama.

Anthropologists have not been very helpful in sorting out these interrelationships. The so-called Cambridge School which argues that 'myth arises out of rite rather than the reverse', that myth is 'the spoken correlative of the acted rite' has misled many investigators by encouraging them to assume that rituals, especially among the so-called primitive peoples, have yet to evolve a conceptual embodiment in myth. Accordingly, they see ritual action simply as unorganized and perhaps spontaneous reaction of primitive peoples to the mystery of life. Other investigators, however, have tended to deny the relevance of any distinction between ritual and myth and identify them fully with the idea of the festival. They thereby, quite unjustifiably, give the impression that there is no special and important limit to the interpenetration of drama into the festival. A New Yam Festival, for example, is a great ritual and festive event. Behind the ritual activities of the festival is almost certainly a *mythos* of a returning and beneficent god who is both welcomed and propitiated. But the festival itself, together with its associated ritual acts, is not drama which only emerges from the selective elaboration, re-enactment and reinterpretation of significant aspects of the festival myth.

We need, therefore, to distinguish between drama and festival, not on the basis of their external 'dramatic' characteristics (including dance, song and costume) but their elaboration of action, whether or not this action is supported with dialogue (as distinct from speech). The masquerade, for example, which has strong roots in Igboland[11] is drama only to the extent that its mime element carries with it a narrative or plot content. But, basically, the force of action of the masquerade is ritual or symbolic. Behind the masquerade is a dream of faith.[12]

Greek and ancient Sumerian analogies

Analogies with Greek tradition are common in discussions of the nature and origins of drama. Some of the analogies can be misleading. Arthur Koestler argues that dramatic art has its origins in ceremonial rites – dances, songs, and mime – which enacted important past or desired future events: rain, a successful hunt, an abundant harvest. The gods, demons, ancestors and animals participating in the event were impersonated with the aid of masks, costumes, tatooings and make-up. The shaman who danced the part of the rain-god *was* the rain-god, and yet remained the shaman at the same time.[13]

Speaking of the origins of Nigerian drama, J. P. Clark says 'they lie where they have been found among other peoples of the earth, deep in the past of the race. We believe that as the roots of European drama go back to the Egyptian Osiris and the Greek Dionysius, so are the origins of the Nigerian drama likely to be found in the early religious and magical ceremonies and festivals of the peoples of the country.'[14] It is true enough that there are close analogies between, say, the Nigerian New Year (February) Festivals and early Greek Dionysian festivals which usually preceded the planting season and lasted 5–6 days. (J. P. Clark says 'seven is the magic number!') But there the comparison ends, because early Greek dramas were, in fact, *one* item in the programme of the festivals. In their dramas, the Greeks provided for a special presentation or enactment of a *mythos* within the framework of the larger (and generally ritualistic) festive event. In other words, the early Greek play was a dramatization of a myth undertaken as part of a festival. The play was never synonymous with the festival itself. As Cornelius Loew has put it, the dramatists resurrected the rich tradition of myth that all the people held in common and through a free manipulation of familiar themes they contributed more than any other group to the Greek Awakening.[15]

The difference being emphasized here becomes even clearer in the case of the ancient Sumerian New Year Festival which lasted some twelve days between March and April and again between September and October each year. This festival never led to drama, as was the case in Greece, in spite of the presence of ritual, dance and song. In the Sumerian Festival, the first four days are devoted to the purification of the entire community in readiness for the general atonement or cleansing which takes place on the fifth day of the Festival. The next five days are taken up with the arrival of the gods, the liberation and subsequent coronation of their Supreme God, Marduk, his triumphal entry to the city and the consummation of his return in a sacred ritual sexual orgy. The last two days of the festival are devoted to the blessing of the community by the gods who return on the twelfth day to the other world.[16]

There is, thus, no lack of event, even of dramatic event, in the Sumerian Festival. But unlike the Greek Festival, the enactment, for example, of the arrival of Marduk is embodied in the Festival itself as a ritual incident. That is to say, the drama is absorbed in ritual action and the *mythos* is subsumed in ritual. Hence, though the Festival has a great deal of dialogue, action, music, dance and decor, it does not crystallize in drama.[17]

The Igbo Festival

The Igbo Festival, it seems to me, is at present structured in Sumerian rather than Greek lines. If this is so, then the emergence of Igbo drama based on our indigenous traditions will depend on how effectively it can be moved beyond the rich but ritual character of the festivals themselves.

The **Mbom Ama** *Festival*

I take my first illustration from the *Mbom Ama* Festival in my own town, Umunumo. The festival is held between the first and second weeks of October each year and lasts about eight days. There is the usual feasting, dancing, and drinking; the invocations, propitiations and sacrifice. But the heart of the festival is the clearing of all footpaths leading from every homestead to the shrine of *Ebu*, the ancestral god of the town. In general, the festival has the following features:

i   All paths in the town are weeded and swept clean in anticipation of the sixth moon and the departure of Ebu from the town.

ii The chief-priest of *Ebu* announces the sixth moon and fixes a day for the celebration.

iii Led by the chief-priest and his assistants, the town makes communal offerings at the *Ebu* shrine; families specially favoured by Him also make their offerings.

iv On the appointed *Afo* market day, which is also the eighth day of the festival, the town gathers at the market square for dances, wrestling competitions and various masquerades. There is general merriment and out-of-town guests are particularly well-catered for.

v   The merriment becomes ecstatic and unruly as evening approaches. The day ends with a bitter verbal contest of insults. This takes place by the river separating the two sections of the town and is said to represent one way of accusing and chastising each section of the own for its crimes of the previous year.

vi Ebu leaves town with his consort, Lolo, during the thunderstorm which is expected to follow the end of the festival.

The overall structure of the *Mbom Ama* Festival is thus essentially ritual in character. Behind this ritual action is a suppressed (or at least, an unexpressed) *mythos*. When one unscrambles the rites, one finds that the Festival, in fact, celebrates the departure from the town of the ancestral god with his mate, *Lolo*. *Ebu* is the bringer of good fortune, not only of wealth but also of offspring. The special gifts presented to him are tokens of appreciation from those whose children born in the preceding year were divined to be reincarnations of one of *Ebu*'s two principal subordinates *Oparannu* and *Oparaocha*. It becomes evident, then, that the preliminary clearing of the paths is an anticipatory rite to make the path ready should the god and his queen choose to dwell with any of the suppliants in their several homes.

Implied or suppressed in the *Mbom Ama* Festival is the entire mythology of the town: the ancestry of *Ebu*, of his consort, *Lolo*; the circumstances of their domestication in the town; the crises of the past; the circumstances surrounding their annual departure from the town; the reason for propitiatory and thanksgiving sacrifices. Each detail is a plot or the germ of drama; each is liable to a thousand varying interpretations and reinterpretations, depending on the choice of fact and detail. Without this elaboration of the hidden myth, there can be no drama; only ritual and spectacle.

The Odo Festival

A more elaborate festival is the *Odo* Festival in Aku, a small farming and trading community some fourteen miles from Nsukka. The festival is held between February and July every two years. In a sense, this festival is not unique to the Aku community but it is to be found all over Udi and Nsukka Divisions where it is sometimes called the *Omabe* Festival and is then held every four years. Nevertheless, there is no ritual link between the Aku *Odo* and other *Odo* in the Nsukka area, perhaps because for each community, the *Odo* (in spite of the common name) is a local phenomenon.

This is all the more important because the *Odo* is not a god, but the spirit of the departed returning for a six-month stay of communion with the living. Hence, there is no reverence and no worship of the *Odo*, but instead a kind of respectful familiarity. There is good explanation, perhaps, for this. The Aku people, though a very republican community, accept a common ancestral god, *Diewa*, who is quite clearly distinguished from that supreme Igbo deity *Chukwu* whom the Aku people (like most other Nsukka people) call *Ezechitoke*. But even so, *Diewa* is only a supervisory god in Aku. Most of the active gods are located in the thirteen village units of the town, and the only one for whom there is an Aku-wide festival is *Ojiyi*, the local or paternal god of Use, one of the six villages in the Eka-Ibute complex. Even the professional gods of Aku (war-god, *Nshi*; god of justice, *Egwu*; god of agriculture, *Fejoku*; goddess of the hearth, *Usere*, and of water, *Ujere*) belong, in the first instance, to one of the village units. The *Odo* Festival is thus not even a festival of worship or even of propitiation of a god even though the ceremonies take place just after the planting season. It is, nevertheless, of sufficient importance for the community to bestow on the non-god, *Odo*, the second most respected festival in the town.

The Ojiyi Fertility Festival

The next thing to notice is that the *Odo* Festival is not a fertility rite. By a fertility rite I mean a ceremony designed primarily to ask the gods for children and good harvests. A fertility festival is usually associated with some actual or symbolic consummation of a union between male and female, earth and sky, benefactor-god and consecrated suppliant. Such ceremonies are accordingly Bacchanalian in character and feature orgies of one kind or another. There is a period of apparent sexual licence in the ritual pattern of these ceremonies deliberately meant to anticipate the hoped-for abundance of Nature and the gods.[18] Such a festival is the *Ojiyi* Festival in Aku, held during the 'eighth month' of the Aku year.[19] The *Ojiyi* Festival begins with a long procession of children, women, young men (with guns), priests, sword-bearers who receive the *Ojiyi* and move with him along the dried-up valleys to the accompaniment of heroic *Ikpa* music through every village unit of Aku. But the crucial act of the festival is the offering and dedication to the god of several young women. Through these women *Ojiyi* bears children the next year in confirmation of His continued interest in the community. These children are fully respected as *Ojiyi*'s offspring, and though they are not regarded as sacred, they are admitted to all assemblies as freeborn.[20] This sexual consummation (or marriage) ritualizes the meaning of the festival and is followed by general merriment.

The *Odo* as an Apollonian festival

In the *Odo* Festival, then, the emphasis is not on consummation but on communion. This communion is, in the first place, between two levels of existence: between this and the 'other' world; between the living and their departed kinsmen. There is thus a spiritual quality to the festival which is why it may be described, even if a little inaccurately, as an Apollonian event in order to distinguish it from a Dionysiac festival which usually commemorates the death of a hero, a god or a kinsmen (Prometheus, Orpheus, Christ). The *Odo* Festival celebrates the return of a lost or wandering hero, god or kinsman (Easter Sunday). The mood is that of rejoicing though, inevitably, this is associated with holy fear. It is important to appreciate this because it explains why every village unit of the Aku community has its own *Odo*, one of its own sons returning from the spirit world.

Broadly speaking, there are five distinct structural divisions in the festival: (i) Preparation, (ii) Welcome and Return, (iii) Communion, (iv) Dedication, and (v) Departure and Blessing.

i *Preparation:*
  This actually begins early in January with the preliminary celebrations known in Aku as the *Egorigo* Festival. The *Egorigo* is a light-hearted festival which ushers in the first *Odo*, called the *Ovuruzo*, a scout spirit whose arrival on the last but one *Afo* day in the 'eleventh month' marks the beginning of festivities.

ii *Welcome and Return:*
  Following the successful return of the *Ovuruzo*, the other twelve *Odo* begin to return. They are welcomed on successive *Afo* days with drumming, feasting and dancing. At this stage, though the people speak of the *Odo* in the singular, there are in fact as many *Odo* as there are village units and each village organizes its own additional reception festivities at the local level.

iii *Communion:*
  The *Odo* now withdraw to the sacred groves said to be under the protection of a kind of conservative but vigilant and well-meaning god, called *Uhamu*. From here the *Odo* maintain contact with the living. First some chosen young people take specially prepared food from the women and rarest palmwine from the men to the *Odo* in their several forest or hillside shrines. Secondly, in return, the *Odo* visit each household very early each morning in a gesture of reciprocation and communion. The *Odo* do threaten violence but this is generally understood to be playfully meant and to be their way of re-

establishing communion without too much familiarity. During these visits, the womenfolk again prepare very delicious meals for the *Odo* and their escorts.

iv *Dedication:*

The dedication precedes the return of the *Odo* to the spirit world. The ceremony takes place this time before a massed gathering of all the village units of Aku. One *Odo* now represents all the others. The main shrine at Umudiku is specially decorated and the entire community, including women and children this time, are allowed to take part or witness. The official *Odo* drummers and trumpeters are on hand and there is most impressive singing of *Odo* praise chants by the womenfolk. The climactic event is the *Odo's* first race: a part playful, part deadly-serious contest between the spirit and a representative group of able-bodied males (between the ages of 14 and 30) from all the thirteen village units. It is a gesture of solidarity, the *Odo's* last act of identification with the community.

v *Departure and Blessing:*

The departure of the *Odo* begins on another *Afo* market day. Its significance is to be seen quite clearly in the ritual character of the events. First comes the *Odo's* meeting with the oldest woman of the town. This meeting takes place about midnight under a bridge across a very deep gully at a village called Legelege (Lelege). This old woman presents the *Odo*, now fully naked and stripped of his heavy six-foot-high headpiece, with a symbolic gift of fish (the *Odo's* favourite) and a piece of white cloth. After this, the *Odo* makes his round of visits to all thirteen units in Aku. At each stop, the host village provides a young man to replace the previous 'spirit'. The new *Odo* then stages a competition with youthful runners from the next village. This is a highly stylized event designed to generate a lot of bad blood but also structured to end in a free-for-all race of both *Odo* and people to the next village. At the end of these visits, the *Odo* retires again to the grove, waiting for the final all-night drumming and vigil which will precede his being escorted out of the town by a choice group of youths on his way back to the other world. It is at this point that the *Odo* gives his final blessing which usually materializes in a propitious July thunderstorm.

Conclusion

This structure is the vehicle for the meaning of the festival. It will be noticed that the narrative line is that of the festivity, not of the events provoking or sustaining it. Behind the ritual meeting of the *Odo* with the oldest woman of Lelege, for example, there is a story. But that story is not dramatized, and one can only derive the meaning of that action through older men or kind interpreters. The dramatic content is, in other words, buried in the ritual purity of the festival. What is needed then, it seems to me, is to force that ritual to yield its story; to cut through the overlay of ceremony to the primary events of the *mythos*. Ritual is, and has always been, a dead end, it cannot grow. It only shrinks steadily into inevitably inaccessible (though powerful) symbolism. The Igbo should do what the Greeks did: expand ritual into life and give that life a secular base. That way, we may be able to interpret and reinterpret that serious view of life which is now only so dimly manifested in our festivals.

Notes

1 Friedrich Nietzsche, *Philosophy in the Tragic Age of the Greeks*, tr. Marianne Cowan, Chicago, 1962, *passim*.
2 J. P. Clark, 'Some Aspects of Nigerian Drama', *Nigerian Magazine*, No. 89, 1966; Robin Horton, 'The Kalabari Ekine Society', *Africa*, 2, 1962; Ulli Beier, 'Yoruba Folk Operas', *African Music*, 1, 1954; 'The Oba's Festival at Ondo', *Nigeria Magazine*, No. 50, 1956; 'The Egungun Cult', *Nigeria Magazine*, No. 51, 1956; 'The Oshun Festival', *Nigeria Magazine*, No. 53, 1957; S. A. Babalola, *The Content and Form of Yoruba Ijala*, Oxford, 1966; O. Ogunba, *Ritual Drama of the Ijebu people: a study of indigenous festivals*, Ph.D. Thesis, Ibadan, 1967.
3 Margaret Laurence, *Long Drums and Cannons*, London, 1968, p. 79. See also pp. 12, 18, 78–80.
4 G. I. Jones, 'Masked Plays of South-Eastern Nigeria', *Geographical Magazine*, 18, 1945; J. S. Boston, 'Some Northern Ibo Masquerades', *Journal of the Royal African Institute*, 90, 1960; J. P. Clark, *op. cit.*; Ruth Finnegan, *Oral Literature in Africa*, Oxford, 1970.
5 Finnegan, pp. 500, 501.
6 Horton, p. 98.
7 Northrop Frye, *Anatomy of Criticism*, Princeton, 1957, p. 249.
8 Cf. Arthur Koestler, *The Act of Creation: A study of the Conscious and Unconscious in Science and Art*, New York, 1967, p. 309: ' ... though modern theatre hardly betrays its religious ancestry, the magic illusion still serves essentially the same emotional needs: it enables the spectator to transcend the narrow confines of his personal identity, and to participate in other forms of existence.
9 Frye, p. 107.
10 Cf. J. Melville and Frances S. Herskovits, *Dahomean Narrative: A Cross-Cultural Analysis* Evanston, Illinois, 1958, p. 106: 'A rite is – it must never be forgotten – an action redone (commemorative) or predone (anticipatory and magical).'
11 Finnegan, p. 510, G. I. Jones, p. 191; J. S. Boston, *passim*.
12 In my view, the masquerader is a performer; he requires only a plot-based role to become a character-in-drama.
13 Koestler, pp. 308–9.
14 Clark, *op. cit.*
15 Cornelius Loew, *Myth, Sacred History and Philosophy: The Pre-Christian Religious Heritage of the West*, New York, 1967, pp. 239–40.
16 Ibid., pp. 33–4.
17 The re-enactment of the coming of the god, *Ulu*, in Achebe's *Arrow of God* would be drama, in any sense of the word.
18 As one Ebenezer Ozo, an Aku student formerly at Ahmadu Bello University, says of that matter, there is a proclivity to become drunk. Women and children are no longer hindered from drinking wine. This freedom, together with many other shelved restrictions, augurs well for a happier celebration.
19 Another fertility festival is the *Alu* (or *Ani*) festival which is held in the 'third month', within the period of the *Odo* ceremonies.
20 In recent years, this practice has been held responsible for the unusually high incidence of prostitution among some of Ojiyi's wives who can thrive, as one source put it, 'without molestation or discrimination' because they are sacred to the god and are 'unable to secure alternative husbands'.

2 Myth, ritual and drama in Igboland

Ossie Enekwe

There is a serious effort among Igbo scholars to define the relationship between Igbo myth, ritual and drama. M. J. C. Echeruo who expresses the view that myth is the main substance of drama, argues that Igbo drama cannot evolve until this myth is freed from the ritual in which it is buried.[1] Echeruo's article has generated much controversy, especially at the University of Nigeria in Nsukka where the article was first presented at a seminar on Igbo language and Literature in November, 1971. A battle line seems to have been drawn:

> So far, two schools of thought seem to crystallize around the question deriving from attitudes which one could reasonably call evolutionary and relativistic. The evolutionist theory is well represented in an article by Professor M. J. C. Echeruo called 'The Dramatic Limits of Igbo Rituals'. Professor Echeruo uses the *Odo* Festival to illustrate his thesis. His central proposition is that the *Odo* Festival, like the Greek Dionysian and Apollonian festivals contains dramatic elements capable of future development into full-bodied drama. Ritual and myth, in his view, would first of all be shorn of their coagulating sacredness and rendered sufficiently mobile for use in a secular drama built on the destiny of differentiated, individual characters.
>
> The relativistic view flatly contradicts the evolutionary one and insists that the ritual festivals in Africa represent full and authenticated drama that should be recognized as such; that they are communal dramas which differ from secular, individuated modern drama with its precise separation of its stage from the auditorium, of actors from the audience and stage time from the duration of the experience enacted on the stage.[2]

While Obiechina thinks that the evolutionists are right in comparing the *Odo* and *Omabe* festivals in Nsukka to the Greek Dionysiac and Apollonian festivals, he rejects their position that modern Igbo drama must follow 'identical linear development of the classical Greek drama from the Dionysian and Apollonian festival'.[3] Obiechina insists that African drama cannot develop like the classical Greek drama, because Africa has a history and a culture that are different from those of the Greek. As one goes deeper into Obiechina's paper, one cannot help concluding that he is in the relativist camp, for he argues that the *Omabe* and *Odo* communal performances though different from modern, individualistic and literacy-mediated dramas, are drama all the same. He thinks that 'the evolution-ists have been misled by their too great reliance on writing and the facilities it provides and too little confidence in an oral tradition'.[4] Obiechina points out that the Greek situation is not paradigmatic of every dramatic development, and argues that there is no incontrovertible reason why the Greek example must be repeated everywhere else.[5] He then wonders:

> Is there any particular reason, except that of meeting the specifically practical pressures of the present age, why an enactment should last only two or three hours instead of six months? Is the sense of organic unity which we assume in the modern theatre and its conventions not possible on an extended scale among a people whose sensibilities are trained to absorb more diffused ritual and symbolic significance of action? Is a broad communal canvas not more suitable for painting more inclusive social and emotional action than the mere mouse-tongue platform called the modern stage?[6]

The preceding query from Obiechina has been motivated by Echeruo's view that myth is an indispensable element that develops into drama through selective elaboration, re-enactment and reinterpretation.[7] Against this view, Meki Nzewi has noted that there is no reason why ritual should be forced to yield its story, except to serve audiences that are strangers to the latent nuances and symbolisms of Igbo rituals.[8]

Elsewhere, I argued against Echeruo's opinion that myth is the soul of drama, pointing out that drama does not have to evolve from myth, and that if it contains elements of myth, the myth is not used for itself, but, rather, for social restructuring. In other words, 'myth is important in terms of an ideological position, that is, the ideology of the moment'.[9] In this paper, I intend to advance my argument by considering the relationship between myth, ritual and drama with particular reference to Igboland.

Since Echeruo bases his view on the classical Greek tradition, it is necessary for us to turn to that tradition, and to others, for comparison. Greek mythologies were not presented in their pristine form by Homer who was mainly occupied in entertaining an essentially patriarchal and military audience. About much of the nocturnal, and funeral side of Greek religion and mythology, Homer says very little. About Dionysus, the Greek god of wine and vegetation whose worship is said – perhaps, erroneously – to have brought about tragic drama, Homer makes only an allusion to an incident in his childhood.[10] In Greece and elsewhere, myth remains a malleable material in the hands of artists. In the making of literature, myth in its broadest sense, provides material and, perhaps, structure, but it plays a very subordinate role in the theatre where impersonation and interactive activity are of the essence. As for the origin of Greek tragedy, there is no convincing proof that it evolved from myth extracted from ritual.[11]

Myth as infrastructure (myth=plot?)

Echeruo attaches much importance to myth or story partly because it gives form and meaning to experience. Myth, he argues, gives clear outlines to dramatic action whose sequence of events is 'invariably of a deliberate kind'.[12] From his talk of 'a pattern of ordered events', it is obvious that he is concerned with the Aristotelian unified plot-structure, with logical cause-and-effect progression in time. However, the implied syllogism has nothing to do with dramatic experience. There is ample evidence in theatre history to show that linear plot is not essential to good drama, and that function determines the form of drama in every culture.

Lack of space restricts me to mentioning names of very few movements and traditions in the theatre. There was, for instance, the Doric mime which together with its later counterpart – the Italian *Commedia dell'arte* – was characterized by improvisation. In mime, whether European, Asian or African, literature always takes a subordinate place.[13] What is the significance of dance in the theatre? Dance, which is organic to the life of the Balinese, is also the foundation of the Balinese theatre in which stories are suggested tenuously. The Balinese *Legong* drama is so far removed from the narrative that it is almost pure dance. Generally, Balinese theatre does not present ideas in a clear, predigested form, nor is the audience expected to derive an intellectual pleasure from a working out of the subtle meanings of the drama.[14] In the Indian Sanskrit drama, oldest of the major theatre forms in Asia, the main purpose is the portrayal of emotional states of *bhava*, not the narration of human action as in Greek drama. Similarly, the Japanese Noh drama 'is not a story-teller's art; it does not often present the unfolding of a human action. Rather, through recollections of the past, it evokes a mood, an emotion, a religious state'.[15] The knowledgeable spectator perceives the performance, 'not as emotionally bound human actions but as elegantly formed patterns of sound and colour that impinge on his emotions peripherally if at all'.[16] The Elizabethan theatre of Shakespeare was not what it was because of the clear outlines of its stories. Because the Elizabethan playwright concentrated a great deal more on the effects of action on his characters than on the causes of the action, he substituted a rhythmic framework for dramatic causation.[17] He selected scenes which would contrast with, or echo, others or which would illustrate various facets of a single experience.[18] This accounted for the looseness of Elizabethan plays. The scenes of an Elizabethan drama often appear to be hanging from a thread of narrative, instead of being lineally connected to other scenes.

We have pointed out that function determines the nature of drama in every culture. In 5th century B.C. Greece, for instance, poetry was central to drama because for the Greeks it was the most desirable and perfect art form. In Asia and Africa, on the other hand, dance, mime and music are of the essence in the theatre. While the mainstream European theatre is syllogistic in form, the Asian and African theatres are ritualistic. In Greek tragedy where moral rhetoric is emphasized, the moral order must be reflected by the order of events – 'the right of the story'.[19]

Nigeria has numerous examples of drama that are structured on dance. Robin Horton writes that the real core of the Kalabari *Ekine* masquerade drama is dance and that 'by and large other elements are only considered important in so far as they contribute to it.'[20] The sketchiness and brevity of Kalabari *Ekine* plays are explained by Horton:

... the masquerade is not intended as the enactment of verbal narrative. Its dominant symbols are those of rhythmic gesture, dictated by the drum; and in so far as its verbal commentaries have a use, it is one of directing attention to the broad area in which the meaning of the dance gesture lies. Words here provide no more than a bare, crude outline of meaning, and it is left to the language of the dance to fill in the detail which makes the masquerade rich and satisfying to its audience.[21]

For those who have been nurtured in the tastes of European theatre, the *Ekine* performance is not drama, because it lacks linear structure and has little linguistic content. Thus, Ruth Finnegan says that 'drama in Africa is not typically a wide-spread or a developed form, and that what Africans have are "certain dramatic and quasi-dramatic phenomena" ', for example, the celebrated masquerades of Southern Nigeria.[22] Finnegan is in search of African performances that are analogous to what she is familiar with in Europe, Echeruo appears to be doing the same thing when he calls on the Igbo to force their ritual to yield its story,[23] and seeks for a European meaning in the *Odo* Festival.

The *Odo* Festival is essentially a communion between the Igbo and their ancestors who 'shed their munificence among the living, and then depart to reappear during the next cycle of ritual celebration'.[24] It is the living who really need the communion, for the *Odo* ensure good harvest and wealth, increase in birth rate, and decrease in death rate. But, because of his interest in myth-criticism, which seeks for 'universal' or 'archetypal' patterns behind particular events or phenomena, Echeruo describes the *Odo* in Apollonian terms: 'The *Odo* Festival celebrates the return of a lost or wandering hero, god or kinsman.'[25] Echeruo (and Kalu Uka who shares his view, more or less) agree with Finnegan that absence of 'linguistic contents, plot, represented interaction of several characters, specialized scenery, etc.' in African traditional performances is a limitation.[26]

What these scholars fail to realize is that Africans are not interested in portraying an Aristotelian action that is whole and complete, with a beginning, a middle and an end, or in working out the subtle meaning of a play. While the Asian and African traditional theatres are not averse to intellectual activity, they are not interested in syllogistic action. Moreover, they are more presentational than their European counterpart. By presentational, I mean that there is considerable interest in activities that are designed to astonish and delight the audience – dancing, acrobatics, etc. Also, traditional African and Asian dramas are stylized. This means that the actors are not interested in exact or elaborate imitation of reality. Stylization means simply 'approaching reality through a different perspective, choosing what is more significant, meaningful, pleasing, or dramatically effective'.[27] Moreover, because of its importance in Africa, ritual is an integral part of the African theatre. Consequently, African traditional dramas are participative and celebrative.[28] It is also total, because it combines many art forms, music, poetry, dance, acting, miming, mask, painting, singing, dialogue, etc., hence, speech is not dominant as in the mainstream European theatre. This combination of various art forms is also an attribute of the Asian theatre. So also are ritualization and stylization. African theatre is closer to Asian theatre than to the European theatre. Critics of traditional African theatre should, therefore, not ignore the Orient as is the case right now.

It is surprising that most of our writers and critics are still enchanted by the European theatre that is considered by many Westerners themselves as effete, dull and mechanical. Some of these Europeans have even gone on to imitate the forms of Asian and African traditional dramas so as to bring their theatre back to life. Leonard C. Pronko, a European who is very familiar with both European and Asian theatres, has even gone as far as to question the validity of the former:

> The traveler who has feasted on the theatres of Japan, China, and Bali cannot repress the feeling, when he returns to the West, that the actors are exceedingly loquacious and singularly incapable of doing anything other than talking. Our hypertrophied rational faculties have led us in the past three hundred years, and particularly since the industrial revolution and the late nineteenth-century age of science, to a theatre that is most often as small as life itself, a theatre that requires careful listening and intelligent under-standing. We sit in plush seats, fatigued after two or three hours of dialogue interspersed with a bit of movement, then disperse to discuss the 'issues' of the play, if it was a drama of any 'significance'. Our serious theatre is so sociology–psychology–philosophy centred that it begins to acquire (as Lonesco claims Brecht might wish) all the charm of a night-school course. Instead of a feast for all the senses and for the mind as well, we are given the intellectual scraps from the top of the table of theatrical history.[29]

When Echeruo talks of interpreting and reinterpreting 'that serious view of life which is now only so dimly manifested in our festivals',[30] he is operating within the European theatrical tradition that is psychological, peripheral, ametaphysical and intellectual, against the traditional African one that, like the Asian theatre, is religious, integral, metaphysical and sensuous. The object of theatre is not the discovery and reinterpretation of meaning. Theatre is first and foremost an experience.

Ritual–theatre relationship

There is also a suggestion by Echeruo that ritual and theatre are mutually exclusive. How far is this true? Doubtless, ritual and theatre are, by strict definition, different as water and air. But, judged from their relationship, they are not antipodal. They are reciprocal in function and similar in structure. Richard Schechner argues convincingly that context, not fundamental structure, disting-uishes ritual, entertainment and ordinary life from one another.[31] Hence, ritual can easily be transformed into theatre and vice versa – in a number of ways. A ritual becomes entertainment once it is outside its original context or when the belief that sustains it has lost its potency. There are many instances of the transformation of ritual into theatre, instances which disprove Echeruo's claim that ritual 'is, and has always been a dead end', that it cannot grow.[32]

One example is the *Nwaotam* or *Nwatam* play that is performed during the new year at Opobo and Bonny. For most participants in *Nwaotam* at Opobo, the performance has no story or dogma. For them, *Nwaotam* is a pure aesthetic experience now, though it was a ritual in Ndoki from where the Opobo people took it. If *Nwaotam* has no story, what is its source of appeal? It's main appeal is abstract – its pageantry, its powerful music, its movements and groupings of more than three hundred participants and its change from apparent chaos to order. The movement, grouping and coordination of the several age groups – including males and women – are fascinating to the eyes. The age groups, differently costumed and each singing its own song with its peculiar music, move above the performance area. But, when *Nwaotam* masquerade enters with its own orchestra, all the other groups stop playing their instruments, as *Nwaotam* drums take over. At this point all the groups, except that immediately assisting *Nwaotam*, become part of the audience. The culmination or climax of the performance occurs when *Nwaotam* suddenly appears on the roof of a house, and after long duel-like manoeuvres and gestures, jumps into the outstretched arms of the men in the age group sponsoring him.

Many of the participants in *Nwaotam* performance at Opobo work in distant parts of Nigeria. Most of those I interviewed in 1978 could not tell me the meaning of *Nwaotam*. People participate in it because it provides physical, emotional and psychological release. Many others enjoy it because it offers them opportunity to socialize, and meet or see people they have not seen for a long time. Some participants are merely perpetuating the tradition of their people. From the preceding, it is clear that *Nwaotam's* theatrical impact does not derive from its story or myth.

There is, however, a story behind *Nwaotam*, but it is not an elaborate one. *Nwaotam* is on the roof in order to bring blessings to the people. There, he is confronted by evil forces. The activities of *Nwaotam* on the roof symbolize and actualize for Opobo a struggle against the forces of Evil. When *Nwaotam* leaps into the outstretched arms of his followers, the mission is deemed to have been accomplished. Once this happens, the play is over.[33] Apart from demonstrating the phenomenon of ritual transforming to theatre, I have used this description of *Nwaotam* to further show that theatre is an experience, and does not have to be explained.

What makes *Nwaotam* a drama (without its mythical content)? I think one can reasonably say that it has the essential elements of theatre: an actor, and an audience conscious of itself as such. The individual in the mask is an actor, an impersonator recreating an experience or creating something new. Although knowing the story increases our appreciation and enjoyment of *Nwaotam*, the story is not indispensable, for theatre is more than stories and words. It is essentially a sensuous medium:

> …. long after typographic man is supposed to have been thinking by linear reasoning, that of words spaced syntactically upon a printed page the theatre persists in communicating by a simultaneity of sensory impressions. Now as then, it demands that its audience perceive its configuration, its Gestalt, of impressions.[34]

Let us return again to the call for the recovery of myth buried in Igbo ritual, a myth like one I have just come across in Akpugo, Uzo-Uwani Local Government area, Nsukka. Sometime ago in the distant past, in the ninth month of the year, a certain widow called Urunye, with her baby boy on her back, was going to collect firewood in the forest, when suddenly, she was confronted by a strange creature covered with young palm leaves. The creature ordered her to call his name, but Urunye could not do so. She was terrified. Thrice the creature demanded that she call his name, but she still failed. Urunye started to run home, but was obstructed by the creature who then asked her baby boy Ugwunyeke to call his name. Without delay, the boy called out 'U-ii'. Immediately, the creature disappeared. In fear, Urunye ran home and told her people of the strange apparition. After a month, the creature appeared again to the small boy, gave him *oji, opi, mbuba*,[35] and asked him to call him again. The boy called him 'Akawo'. Again, the creature asked the boy 'What is my name?' Thereupon, Ugwuyeke called him *Odo*.

Odo began to appear to Ugwuyeke and the entire village from time to time for seven months. Two years after, the creature appeared in the early morning of *Afor* day, and began chasing people about. Ugwuyeke was asked to appease him. The little boy took a lump of *odo* ('glorizza' powder), alligator pepper and fresh palm wine in a calabash which had never touched the ground from the day such wine was put in it, and offered them to the *Odo*. From that day, the *Odo* ceased chasing people. Eventually, the *Odo* disclosed that he came from Nri, Igbo-Ukwu, the 'real' and mythical home of the Igbo.

How important is this story or myth to the development of drama? Certainly, it offers a story which can be elaborated, reinterpreted and re-enacted. But any other story or piece of experience can go through the same process. History, ritual or any form of activity can be used as material and structure for drama. Moreover, drama is more than story-telling. Drama is imagined act involving impersonation and the presence of a conscious audience. From the point of view of the European drama which is concerned with the portrayal of action and revelation of character, there must be dramatic choices and motivation.[36] From the point of view of African theatre which has ritual concerns, drama recreates or affirms models of familial and communal life. So, African drama is both mythic and ritualistic.

Of what significance is the *Odo* Festival? It is both a re-enactment of a primordial event and an actuality. During the festival, 'the protagonists of the myth are made present', and we become their contemporary.[37] When the *Odo* arrives, chronological time is displaced by primordial time.

What should we call the *Odo* Festival, ritual or drama? I think one could say that it is a ritual drama. It is efficacious, bringing children, good harvest and wealth to the living who are united in a ritual communion. However, it also provides a great deal of entertainment.

The *Odo* Festival contains many dramatic moments which will increasingly lose their efficacy as belief in *Odo* ritual declines. When this happens, the performances will become drama with or without some ritual associations. The *Odo* ritual can therefore become theatre without the aid of elaborate mythology.

But, we must distinguish between a ritual such as the *Odo* Festival and the dramas it contains. As a festival, the *Odo* is essentially a ritual of communion between the living and their ancestors. But, as part of this reunion, and in keeping with the *Odo's* objective of teaching the people and ensuring social solidarity, drama is introduced as a model for meaningful and ethical life. An example of this drama is the *Odo* masquerade performance portraying a family in Abu-Ugwu Festival at Okpatu in Udi Local Government Area. Through mime and songs, the *Odo* masquerade performers show the Okpatu people models of social behaviour.[38]

The play provides a good model for family life. It features Ezembo, the father of the family; *Ogolimaluihe* (or Ogoli for short) the mother; Akawo, two teenage sons, and Ada Odo, the daughter. They are all appropriately costumed to reflect their social roles. The father (Ezembo), beautifully costumed in colourful clothes and stripes of cloth with ribbons and ornaments hung around his head, appears like an elder and leader. He looks calm and noble, with his walking stick and a big fan. Ogoli's mask is delicately cut to reflect the beauty of womanhood. On her chest are two projections that represent breasts. Her costume is made up of very expensive materials. She wears expensive beads, and bangles, and carries a fan decorated with tiny mirrors. In the modern time, she may wear a wig. As her name suggests, *Ogolimaluihe* – literally meaning a sensible woman, she is a model housewife.

Akawo's costume is rough and unkempt, because he represents a troublesome youth. He carries a knife, canes, and other things with which he scares or attacks people. The Ada's costume, on the other hand, reflects the delicate and ethereal Igbo ideal of feminine beauty. This masquerade is the type generally referred to as *Agboho Mmuo* (Maiden Spirit).

The performance takes place, not in the *Eke Ugwu*, the ritual ground where the *Odo* reside, but in the central square called *Obom Oshaka*. Sheds for the audience are built around the arena. For the *Odo* family, there are about two huts at one end of the square. This serves both as a home and a dressing room. The *Odo* performance is accompanied with dance, music and songs. While Ogoli sings, the audience responds. Through song, she instructs the people and praises her husband.

Because of scarcity of space, let us go straight to the performance. A flutist blows his flute in praise of Ezembo, who, together with the rest of his family, is in the hut at the rear of the playing area. Ezembo steps out from the hut and moves round the arena slowly and majestically, surveying the ground to ensure that the environment is safe for his family. He returns to the hut, and comes out with his shy and beautiful wife whom he fans. As they take their seats, Akawo the rough son, dashes out of the hut and charges at the spectators who run back in fear. Ezembo chases his son, catches him, and drags him to a seat. There is an interlude of music during which Ezembo persuades his wife, Ogoli, to dance. She dances with slow steps, shaking her body and waving her hands sideways. Next, Ezembo asks her to sing for his guests (the spectators), but she declines, feigning headache. But, after a while, she gets up, kneels before her husband, who wipes her face with a cloth. She then stands up and sings in praise of him. As the audience sings the chorus, she starts dancing, and Ezembo, impressed and thrilled, pastes coins on her face, according to custom. The *Odo* escorts and the audience follow his example. Afterwards, Ezembo and Ogoli embrace each other, and the music stops. This scene shows how a father should control his family and how couples should live and love one another.

Another episode dramatizes the need for self-control in young people. Seeing a beautiful maid, a masquerade, Akawo begins to chase her about. Ezembo asks some of his aides to catch Akawo and drag the rough youth to him. This done, Ezembo pushes Akawo away – an expression of disfavour. Grumbling and pointing at his father, Akawo runs off to the family hut at the rear. Ashamed of what her son has done, Ogoli covers her face. Then, she goes to Ezembo (with his hand on his chin), kneels before him, and enquires what she should do to mollify him. But, he ignores her. Thereupon, she hurries to the hut and brings Akawo – who now is repentant – along to his father before whom they kneel as a sign of respect and Akawo's repentance. Ezembo signals that he has forgiven the son. Thereupon, Ogoli jumps and dances for joy.

Soon after, another female masquerade appears, passing along slowly, deliberately seductive. Although she is more beautiful than the one that Akawo chased, she is ignored by him. The audience cheers because the rough youth has at last improved.

The whole drama shows how the head of a family should lead and direct his wife and children. Ogoli illustrates the right behaviours of women, superlative loyalty to their husbands, and concern for the moral upbringing of their children. As a demonstration of the ideal unity that should exist in families, the *Odo* family move back to their hut, holding one another by the hand with Ezembo in the centre.

There is an interlude of flute. The father returns in a celebrative and triumphant mood. Amidst the rejoicing of his aides and the audience, he dances and moves in a dignified manner, miming heroic acts he had done when he was living on earth. The spectators paste money on him. The performance ends with Ogoli telling women to respect and obey their husbands through a song called '*Ogolimaluihe*' (wise women).

From the foregoing, it is clear that the *Odo* Festival or ritual is not a dead end. It contains drama, though this drama occurs within a ritual context. This drama is not structured on myth, even though it is enacted by masquerades representing mythical figures, and reinforcing a certain ideology in a mythic atmosphere. We also see that there is no linear plot, although it is clear that Akawo improves his character as a result of his father's chastisement of him.

There are many examples of the dramatization of family life all over Igboland. There is, for instance, the '*Omelu Nne Na Nwa*' masquerade at Oba, Idemili Local Government Area. It comprises a father, mother, daughter, and a police sergeant who appears first. After clearing the way, and surveying the playing space, the latter salutes the rest and beckons to them to come into the space. The father's mask and costume show him to be very old. The father has an ancestral crown, adorned with a red cloth tied round it and white feathers that symbolize rank and age. The mother has a beautiful mark, the epitome of stylized beauty. She is dressed to kill – with lace wrappers, blouse, earrings and necklace. The little daughter has an *agbogho mmuo* mask, with stylized features, as usual. The daughter has a baby doll strapped to her back, and dances very fast and nimbly. The mother's dance is lively and seductive. On the other hand, the father seems to be weighed down by age. He shows little interest in things going on around him, until he is struck by the beauty of his dancing wife. He pulls out his penis (made of cloth) and mimes a urinating act. Then, his wife comes to him and wipes his face with a handkerchief. He follows her closely as she dances – so as to show that he cares. In the process, he is slowly seized by the power of music, and he begins to dance rather energetically. This is the climax of the drama. In their loving relationship, age and gravity are conquered by beauty. In their dancing, they seem to say that the members of a family should inspire and encourage one another. This is quite clear, and needs no commentary. Again, it has no elaborate story or plot. It is an image of human life, presented by means of music and dance. The music is supplied by six followers, all dressed in raffia, beating drums and blowing flutes.

We have seen, in the preceding passages, that myth is not the essence of drama, that the structure of drama is determined by the function that theatre serves in a particular culture, and that, far from being a dead end, ritual can easily be transformed into drama. Because Igbo theatre has a different function and a dissimilar method from that of the Greek theatre, for example, it is wrong to demand that the Igbo should develop a form similar to the Greek's. What the Igbo need they have developed, based on their own tastes, outlook, and the resources available to them. There is no need for us to keep talking of evolving Igbo drama when it is already flourishing all over Igboland.

Notes

1 Michael J. C. Echeruo, 'The Dramatic Limits of Igbo Ritual', *Research in African Literatures*, vol. 4, No. 1, spring, 1973, pp. 29–30.
2 Emmanuel Obiechina, 'Literature – Traditional and Modern – in the Nsukka Environment', *The Nsukka Environment*, ed. G. E. K. Ofomata, Fourth Dimension Publishers, 1978, pp. 28–9.
3 Ibid., p. 30.
4 Ibid., p. 30.
5 Ibid., p. 31.
6 Ibid., p. 32.
7 Echeruo, pp. 23–4.
8 Meki Nzewi, 'Traditional Theatre Practice', *Nigeria Magazine*, Nos. 128–129, 1979, p. 22.
9 Ossie Onuora Enekwe, 'The Modern Nigerian Theatre: Which Tradition?' *Nsukka Studies in African Literature*, vol. 1, No. 1, March 1978, p. 33.
10 Mircea Eliade, *Myth and Reality*, trans. from the French by William R. Trask, Harper & Row, 1963, p. 150.
11 Gerald Else, *The Origin and Early Form of Greek Tragedy*, W. W. Norton, 1972, pp. 9–31.
12 Echeruo, p. 21.
13 Allardyce Nicoll, *Masks, Mimes and Miracles*, Copper Square Publishers, New York, 1963, p. 50.
14 Leonard C. Pronko, *Theater East and West: Perspectives Toward a Total Theatre*, University of California Press, 1974, p. 28.

15 James R. Brandon, *Theatre in Southeast Asia*, Harvard University Press, 1974, pp. 176–7.
16 Ibid., p. 177.
17 Bernard Beckerman, *Dynamics of Drama: Theory and Methods of Analysis*, New York: Alfred A. Knopf, 1970, p. 33.
18 Ibid., p. 33.
19 Richmond Lattimore, *Story Patterns in Greek Tragedy*, University of Michigan, 1969, p. 7.
20 Robin Horton, 'The Kalabari *Ekine* Society: A Borderland of Religion and Art', *Africa*, XXXIII, April, 1963, p. 100.
21 Ibid., p. 98.
22 Ruth Finnegan, *Oral Literature in Africa*, Oxford University Press, 1970, p. 500.
23 Echeruo, p. 30.
24 Obiechina, p. 14.
25 Echeruo, p. 28.
26 Finnegan, p. 501. See Kalu Uka's 'Drama in Nigerian Society', *Hoe*, vol. 1, No. 1, pp. 24–5. Lack of space does not permit me to comment particularly on his paper. However, my 'Modern Nigeria Theatre: What Tradition?', *NSAL*, Vol. 1, No. 1, 1978, pp. 26–43, gives considerable attention to Uka's view that we have no drama (but elements of drama) in Igboland. In any case, my comments on this paper touch on much of his points.
27 Pronko, p. 188.
28 J. N. Amankulor's 'Festival Theatre: An Aesthetic Concept in Traditional and Modern Nigerian Dramatic Art', an unpublished paper, stresses the element of festivity in traditional theatre.
29 Pronko, p. 1.
30 Echeruo, p. 30
31 Richard Schechner, 'From Self-contained, Self-sustaining Performance as Part of Ecosystems to Becoming Trading Partners with other Professional Theatres', *Bulletin*, 7, June 1975, p. 30. Published by the International Association of Theatre Critics.
32 Echeruo, p. 31.
33 From interview with Professor S. J. Cookey at Opobo on January 2, 1978.
34 J. L. Styan, *Drama, Stage and Audience*, Cambridge University Press, 1975, pp. 3–4.
35 *Oji* – a metal rod that rattles when struck into the ground; *opi* – horn; *mbuba* – a wooden object used in weaving.
36 Lattimore, p. 14.
37 Eliade, p. 19.
38 This description is based on a B.A. thesis by Christiana Unoma Eneh, 'Drama in the Religious and Secular Ceremonies of the Aba-Ugwu Festival of Okpatu', University of Nigeria, 1979.

3 What's in a mask*

John Picton

Introduction

When Charles Jedrej suggested that '... to describe some institution as a "mask" is as likely to be misleading as informative' (1980: 229), it was at the end of a paper written to demonstrate and to resolve some of the confusion in our use of this word. It is not that people who use masks are necessarily confused about what they are doing, though they might be, given the complexities of human motivation: this confusion is all 'ours' for having taken it upon ourselves to explain what other people are doing. Earlier, in the same paragraph, Jedrej noted that it is '... the product of a point of view located in the observer's European tradition. Only by concentrating on the evidence of what actually happens, rather than on what we think is going on, can we hope for any comprehension.' I am assuming, of course, that the people who wear masks are, by and large, not the same as the people who write about people wearing masks. I realise that some people would have us believe that all social life is about masks, but this dramaturgical view seems excessive, if not obsessive: I relay some comments to this end in due course.

This paper is about the relationship between a person, a mask, and that person's masked identity; or about the rôle of the mask in mediating the relationship between the performer and his identity in performance: or, simply, about what happens when someone puts a mask on. One can put it in various ways, but I must be careful that I am not advancing the proposition that someone is more or less categorically different in virtue of the mask he had put on, for this is a proposition that cannot be taken for granted. Apart from anything else, it would ignore questions of local, culturally specific categories of thought, language, practice, e.g., the fact that 'masks' and 'masquerades' do not necessarily take visible form, e.g., that the re-definition of a performer's identity, when it does happen, may be prior to, and therefore not dependent upon the wearing of a mask, as in the Ebira feast of ekueci.[1] I must not even assume that masks are necessarily dramatic things.

---

* I offer this paper in memory of my close friend iKarimu Ihiovi (see Picton 1988) who died in 1988.

As soon as one begins to talk about masks, there seems to be an infinite variety of questions all competing for attention, themselves like all those performers in a masked celebration intent upon some reward for their display. I refer, of course, to questions of mediation, reversal, representation, re-definition, power, secrecy, iconography ...; and about motivation, possession, performance, creativity ...; but this paper is certainly not an attempt to produce a comprehensive account of the phenomenon of masquerade: my concern is with the questions: what is a mask, and what is supposed to happen when someone puts one on? The answers are fundamental, but they represent only a very small part of all those things that masks and masquerades are, and are about.[2]

However, a word of warning: the discussion also suggests part of a history of the practice of masquerading that was so popular and obvious a part of the culture of Ebira people; and it is impossible to avoid matters some of which would be considered by Ebira men as not appropriate for open discussion in the presence of women. The 'history' follows from the discussion of the relationship between performers and masks, but in Ebira terms this makes for a problem with moral and metaphysical dimensions. It could be a problem for me if the women who choose to read further are 'strong', for the energy we call witchcraft is directed, predictably, against those who flout the moral consensus, as well as unpredictably against anyone they choose: and it could perhaps be a problem for a woman herself if she is without that strength, for inappropriate knowledge itself can harm.[3]

Theory and practice in Ebira masquerade

As I lived with the experiences of Ebira masquerade, two things became clear: (i) as eku, a man was changed, for though still himself, yet he was not himself; (ii) Ebira ethnic identity was defined, in part, in the performances, the festivals, at which eku appeared; all of which might seem as one should expect in a sub-Saharan community still retaining an interest in its pre-colonial traditions.

Masked performers, *eku*, appearing in the day-time, will enter the houses of men belonging to the lineage of the owner of the mask. Food and drink for the performer and his gang of musicians and young men will be provided. Although the performer will remove the mask, once inside the house and out of sight of women, in order to eat and drink, his followers will continue to call him by the name of the mask. There is no sense of a dislocated personality: he is not possessed; but he is no longer himself. The removal of the mask is merely a temporary strategy, and it will soon be replaced as they prepare to move on. In any case, the performance is not interrupted by the removal of the mask. The relationship between performer and entourage is still in place and remains a source of energy and entertainment, and women of the household will still call through the door of the room where the performer rests to consult him as an oracle. I later discovered that, in such circumstances, the use of the performer's everyday name would incur a fine and perhaps even sacrificial reparation; but this was not just a way of talking reinforced by negative sanctions: many performers were possessed of oracular and healing powers they did not, apparently, ordinarily possess. The proof of this statement rests in the as often as not successful result of a consultation.

There are two major festivals at which masked performers appear: a mid-year festival, some time between May and July, depending on the district, in the day-time; and a night play that closes the new year period in late November or early December. The night festival is called *ekueci* 'eku comes down'. The verb *ci* 'to descend' is also used of visitors coming to your house and receiving hospitality; the feast can thus be interpreted as a time when the living entertain the dead. However, women shut themselves away for the night, which perhaps explains why the mid-year day-time feast is called *ec'anẹ* 'feast of/for/with women'. These celebrations, and especially the night-time ekueci, more than any other pheno-menon of Ebira cultural practice, define Ebira identity and difference. Singing eku appear in the course of the night, as well as other masquerade performers, but no-one wears a mask in the sense of a disguise hiding its wearer's face. Some of the performers, otherwise appearing in the day-time, and whose masked identity is defined in terms of the day-time performances, will wear elements of their costume (but not the mask), some will have an alternative costume specific-ally for the night-time appearances, and some will just wear their ordinary clothes. They will each carry a thick stick and run and chase and gesture in the expected manner, as if in the day-time costume. Once again, none of these performers could be said to be himself: each is *eku*; but there is no mask, for the women have shut themselves away. The event re-defines, or, to be more exact, common knowledge about events and performers re-defines the identity of the performer. The mask is needed only in the presence of women.

The finest night *eku* draw large crowds (of men only, of course). Their singing provides for discussion through the year that follows. The young man repairing your motor-car tyre near the market in Okene will sing some of the songs of his favourite performer; likewise young men at farm. People remember the songs from year to year, and would soon jeer any performer who repeated himself from one performance to another. That would be the end of his singing career. Ebira men will come home from wherever they are for the occasion; and we are no longer talking of a rural community of peasant farmers, but one that includes farmers, of course, and senior civil servants, indeed senior men of all walks of life in modern Nigeria.

The night festival clearly has an antiquity within Ebira tradition that is impossible to determine; and the night singers are the focus of attention, or at any rate they are nowadays. However, it was generally acknowledged that the first person to gather people together and sing during this festival was someone by the name of Itemirege. He did not invent the festival, but he did invent the rôle of singing *eku* as part of it, a form of performance that has become so popular that a town like Okene has to have three night plays to accommodate all the performers! Then, to my surprise, I found that some old men remembered the performances of Itemirege, and how they differed in style from those of today. That put the invention of this kind of entertainment to within the past hundred years, but I gave up testing this discovery on people – its logic was always flatly denied: they had always done it; it was what they came to meet their fathers doing, and so forth.

In other words, Ebira people have a theory of mask use, but it does not exactly fit with the practice of mask use. Then, Ebira masquerade exhibits a profound sense of tradition in which practices of established efficacy, justified by ancestral precedent, are carefully replicated; but Ebira masquerade also appears to embody a history: once again, the one proposition does not fit the other.

There is, of course, no reason to be surprised by an apparent disjunction between theory and practice, nor by the fact of a legitimation of novel practices by a sense of tradition that effectively denies the novelty; but what are we to make of the mask as an afterthought, necessary for those women of little faith and/or too much power in order to maintain a re-definition of identity that is already and otherwise achieved? Is the Ebira case the exception that proves the rule, or have we got the rules wrong? Jedrej (1980) reminds us that at the very least we have taken the mask as an artifact of African cultures too much for granted, and the very notion of its wearer's re-defined identity likewise.

Translating 'mask/masquerade'

The mask is, for me as for anyone writing in the English language, a word, of course, and an idea and a metaphor, as well as an artifact, of European culture; and yet, as Jedrej (1980) has reminded us, even so obvious a thing as the 'mask' embodies taken-for-granted ideas about Africa and its arts that are informed by presuppositions hidden within the history of ideas in Europe: the 'mask' is, indeed, another of the problems of understanding and explanation that arise as a function of translation.

'Mask' is a word

The words 'mask', 'masquerade', 'mascara' come into the languages of Europe from Arabic. This is a relatively well-known fact which can easily be confirmed with the aid of an appropriate dictionary, and which is confirmed by the following note from Shelagh Weir, curator of Middle Eastern ethnography at the British Museum, to John Mack: 'JP is right about the Arabic source for masquerade. There is in fact an Arabic word for the same thing: maskharah, from the root skhr. The Arabic verb (perf. sakhira) from which the noun is derived means "to laugh, scoff, jeer, sneer, ridicule, mock, deride, make fun".'

Ebira masquerade is certainly a parody: performance style invariably exaggerates ordinary behaviour, providing entertainment thereby. It is also a deceit, for as I never tire of relating, although men would tell me that God had made *eku* for men, witchcraft for women, almost in the next breath, having said that, someone might say *eku* is a trick to get money out of women.

In my grandfather's copy of Webster (1932: 602) I read as follows:

> mask, n. (F. *masque*] 1. A cover for the face, for disguise, protection, etc. 2. An artificial figure of a face or head, worn by ancient Greek and Roman actors. 3. A sculpted face, or a copy of a face molded in plaster, wax, etc.; as, a death *mask*. 4. That which disguises or conceals; as, the *mask* of night. 5. One

wearing a mask; a masker. 6. A masquerade; hence a revel. 7. An old form of dramatic performance in which the actors wore masks; also, a dramatic composition for such a performance ...

masquerade, n. ... 1. An assembly of persons wearing masks, for dancing, etc. 2. A costume for wear at such an assembly. 3. Acting or living under false pretenses; disguise ...

There is no entry in that edition for 'mascara', though one can find it easily in other dictionaries. I grew up to know this as the black paste women put round their eyes. It is probably called something else now.

Whatever the common derivation and significance of these words, however, most of us would wish to separate mask/masker/masking and masquerade/-er/-ing in some such manner as John Boston proposed in his 1960 discussion of northern Igbo masquerades. He used the first set of terms to refer to an 'internal' view, from the performer's end of things, and the latter to refer to an 'external' view, from the audiences' end. This, of course, is yet one more example of that very familiar problem of translation.

In Ebira, the word *eku* refers primarily to the domain of the dead, in contrast to the world we inhabit, and only thence to those liminal extensions of that domain, whether masked by material forms or by the night. This point needs to be emphasised, for if I use the word 'masquerade' of Ebira cultural practice, this is a translation that covers one part of a category of far wider significance, referring, of course, to the conceptual grounding of performance and healing and, indeed, existence.

The artifacts relevant to that performance, however, have quite other names: *ọpọ* 'wooden mask', *omurumuru* 'fabric mask', *ṇmọmọ* 'the full costume, including mask'. Moreover, it will be clear that other things act as masks, even though we would not call them masks in the ordinary sense of the word in English. I have already mentioned the door of a room, for example, that effectively masks the identity of the masker within (resting without the mask on) from the women outside waiting to consult him. At night performances, the relative locations are reversed, for now women are indoors and the performers are outside. In this case, there is a further dramatic irony in that 'night' is a euphemism for the destructive energies of women (Picton 1989); but on that one night of the year, 'witchcraft' has been chased out of the community at the same time as women know they must go indoors and stay there. There are other circumstances in which *eku* might be heard at night, or from within the *irẹba*, a ritually protected place of significance in the theory and practice of masquerade (Picton *op. cit.*) that is located just beyond the village community. The night and, in the case of the *irẹba*, the rocks and/or uncut woodland in the latter, are the 'masks'. These things would not be called 'masks' in Ebira, for, as I have just said, the word *ọpọ* refers only to the wooden artifact carved to fit over a man's face, and I have no recollection of its use in a metaphorical or ironic sense. If I refer to all these things as 'masks', it is only because I can categorise them as serving to establish distance between certain people and certain other people; but, as I have already said, common knowledge in appropriate circumstances achieves the same end. If anyone in Ebira were to refer to an unembodied mask, *ọpọ*, as *eku*, it would be taken for granted that he had in mind the recollection or expectation of that mask in performance and the magical energies it had acquired over time. Distinct Ebira concepts are conflated in the etymology of a single English word, but the fact that I can refer to all of these things as 'masks' illuminates at the same time as it confuses.

Having raised the matter of 'distance', it is worth noting that my relationship with Ebira people has lasted many years,[4] long enough for my presence to become commonplace; but to begin with, I was inevitably surrounded by people of both sexes curious to know exactly what I was. The discussion would turn to certain matters, and someone (male) would shout, '*Eku* is coming out'. Any females within earshot would scatter, leaving us in peace to talk about the serious things of life. Evidently, whatever else *eku* might be, it is a word with the power to move people.

'Mask' is an idea

Arabic provides us with the words 'mask' and 'masquerade', and with some of our ideas about masks in Europe; but, as Webster reminds us, we are obliged to consider another source of ideas in the theatres of ancient Rome and Greece, and the use of the *persona*, the mask worn by an actor in a play. Hollis (1985: 219) tells us that 'the route is from masks to privileges of those with a right to the masks, to *patres* who represent their ancestors, to anyone with ancestors, a cognomen and family property. Hence we arrive at a notion of a person as a possessor of rights ...' The history of ideas about evolving notions of person, self and rôle is complex; and in regard to rôle Hollis (1985: 221) continues:

> Even if the notion arises with masks worn in sacred dramas, it is not so simply divorced from that of self as the image of the mask suggests in our secular age. Today, it has, I suppose, two main uses. One is in analysing social institutions and practices ... The other is in analysing more intimate reaches of social life, where it borrows from the theatre, making a dramaturgical analogy with *dramatis personae* or characters in a play.

However, Giddens (1984: 125) writes as follows:

> If agents are only players on a stage, hiding their true selves behind the masks they assume for the occasion, the social world would indeed be largely empty of substance ... Those who do feel this way characteristically display modes of anxiety of an extreme kind.

For better or for worse, the dramaturgical analogy is more widespread than one might realise. For example, quite by chance I came across what I presume to be a secondary school textbook (Kaye-Besley and Byles 1979) written, according to its preface, 'to meet the needs of young people who are about to make the transition from school to the "world outside".' In a chapter called 'Coming to grips with self', the student is asked, 'which mask are you wearing today?'

Other cultures may have other ideas about self, person and rôle, and other ideas about masks. The fact that the artifacts we call masks tend to be of a certain shape and size, and the fact that the placing of a mask over one's face makes for a certain distance between wearer and viewer, cannot be taken as presupposing anything more about the significance of any given mask, or about masks in general. The assumption that a mask in Africa effaces its wearer's identity, therein and thereby re-defining it as something other, might now seem to be derived less from the uses of masks in Africa than from the dramaturgical implications of the evolution of 'person' from *persona* in Europe. This is not to insist that masks in Africa were never intended to serve such purposes, but rather that we cannot presume that they must inevitably do so.

I have already referred to the status of the Ebira masked performer as still himself yet not himself, and how this being no longer himself will perhaps be manifest in oracular and healing powers. This transformation is effected in virtue of the liminal status of masquerade, a status made clear in the very category eku. As a performer, one is occupying a space that belongs to that other domain of existence, to which one otherwise passes at death; and yet, that space can by common consent exist without the physical necessity of the costume. Moreover, it is that space, whether conceptual, material or dramatic, that gives the performer his power: it is not something already within him that the mask simply brings to the fore. Even when he employs magical medicine to enhance his performance, it is none the less a source of energy that is external to the performer. In any case, the intention is to protect him, as a medium of ancestral authority, from witches and jealous rivals.

'Mask' is a metaphor

The metaphorical utility of 'mask' draws upon all of this: the distancing capacity of the artifact; the properties of parody and pastiche; the 'mask' as revealing, proclaiming, hiding, denying, etc., personality, truth, etc.; for example, 'War of nuclear words masks a way to victory' (*Sunday Times*, 19 June, 1988); or 'Private lives unmasked as pictures tell a potent story' (*Sunday Times*, 23 October, 1988), the headline for a review of paintings by Eric Fischl; or the review on the women's page of *The Guardian* of 22 November, 1988, of a biography of Anthony Blunt, *The Mask of Treachery*, subtitled 'The Surveyor of the Queen's Pictures' mask hardly ever slipped. When it did, he confided in women'. Was treachery the mask, or was treachery masked? At any rate, the reviewer notes, 'Clearly he was able to present different faces to his different friends.' Then, more recently, there was a review of Terry Eagleton's play *Saint Oscar* in *The Guardian* of 12 March, 1990, headed 'The man in the ironic mask', and it refers to a suggestion 'that wearing masks was Wilde's personal adjustment to modern life as it was Nietzsche's; and, in essence, Mr. Eagleton's play consists of a series of confrontations in which chameleon Oscar strenuously and wittily avoids being categorised.' One further example will suffice, from *The Independent on Sunday*, 23 September, 1990: a piece about Cambodia headed 'Prince Sihanouk searches for the mask that suits the moment', in which we read that 'there is a Khmer saying that to be a politician in Cambodia you need two masks – one to wear in front of your supporters and another for your opponents. The problem with Prince Sihanouk is that you never know which mask he is wearing.' This does rather seem to drain the metaphor of any useful significance, and it might be that the answer to the reporter's problem is the rather obvious one that the Prince is not actually wearing a mask at all. However, whether or not Blunt, Wilde or Sihanouk could be said to have manifested the extreme anxiety to which Giddens refers, these uses of 'mask' can be taken as representing a way of talking about people that most obviously demonstrates the mask still hidden in the idea of the person; and they all imply a concealing.

'Mask' is an artifact

Part of the dramatic irony of Verdi's *Un ballo in maschera* is, surely, that it is the mask worn by Gustavus that enables his recognition and assassination. Its distinctiveness is, of course, revealed by his page in an act of treachery that takes for granted the mask as a disguise. When we consider the artifacts in which we might have thought the metaphor 'mask' was founded, we also find wearers protected at least as often as disguised (the mask worn by Gustavus was allowed to give him neither protection nor disguise.)

For the past couple of years I have been cutting out illustrations of masks from newspapers we receive at home. The collection includes a cartoon of Reagan slipping on a George Bush mask, a Palestinian with a sling and some stones, a young woman whose face was disfigured when a jilted boyfriend threw acid in her face (she is now obliged to wear a surgical mask), veiled Afghan women, IRA terrorists, clowns, Venetian carnival goers, and so forth: these are, indeed, all about disguise.[5] The cuttings also include oxygen masks, welding masks, anti-nuclear masks; and in the past few weeks, the Iraq–Kuwait crisis has ensured that the papers are full of masked people, whether American soldiers testing their gas masks, or Arab refugees wrapped up against wind and sand. Among these various artifacts are some, which though lexically and etymologically disparate, are nevertheless conceptually and functionally related, e.g., visor, veil, camouflage – and sometimes the word 'mask' is interchangeable and sometimes not.[6]

One day, when iKarimu (see Picton 1988) was at my house, I placed some lavatory paper against my comb and began to sing through it. At once, iKarimu jumped up and rushed to the window, shouting at me, 'Don't do that! There might be a woman about.' There are two forms of kazoo in Ebira, each providing the voice of particular species of eku, one used by akatapa (see Picton 1992), the other by *ekuọba* (see below), to mask the voice of the human agent.

Another day, I saw a woman tying strips of cloth to a stick a few inches in length. She said she was making (an) *eku* for her child. Boys chase one another holding one of these in one hand, with a longer stick in the other to beat anyone within reach. (For her daughter, a woman might clean up a bone of some six inches in length to carry about in her wrap-around skirt as a doll.)

Still within the same cultural rubric, is the son *aj' o, aj' ov' eku ni*. The appearance of *ni* at the end of a sentence in this way indicates a transposition of word order: i.e., object–verb–subject (rather than subject–verb–object). This gives us a translation, '*eku* is a nightjar (*a ja*)'. The breeding plumes of the standard-winged nightjar are worn by ancestral impersonators and by lineage title-holders. The rite of introducing a newly-made ancestral mask into the community, and the rite of handing a title on to its new incumbent, are analogous and are recognised as such; and each is provided with a crown of nightjar breeding plumes, an artifact essential to their status. The bird itself wears them during that autumn period when two years meet, and this together with the fact that the nightjar is, in any case, always seen at dusk suggests a piling up of one sign of the liminality to which I referred above, upon another.

What's in a mask?

Masked performers, words that make people run away, the night, a door, common knowledge (about local events), a rag doll, kazoos, feathers ... they all have to do with the category and concept of *eku*, and I have written about all of them in some sense as 'masks'.

Jedrej draws attention to the differing relationships between performer, mask and identity in performance. He suggests '... three possibilities. Firstly, that in which ... maximum significance attaches to what is concealed ... Secondly, ... attention is focused on a materially and symbolically elaborate mask ... Thirdly, there is the interesting possibility of both mask and what is being masked being accorded equal significance' (1980: 221). In the first case, the masker is changed but the mask is necessary to hide this: the emphasis is on what is hidden. In the second, the masker is merely the animator of whatever it is that is somehow embodied as the mask: the emphasis is on what is revealed.

In my re-working of this, I note that there are also very great differences in the amount of iconographical matter presented by particular masks. In some cases this is minimal to the extent that 'meaning' derives entirely from the context of performance with little added by the mask and its accoutrements beyond the fact that it is a mask. Secondly, I have to avoid the assumption that masked figures are 'spirits' of some kind. This merely begs the question in regard to the identity of masked performers. I must also remember that other possibility, as in Ebira, that the 'mask' may be a conceptual reality rather than, or prior to its being a material reality: for even if re-definition does take place, we must still ask when? and how? and not take it for granted that this is achieved in the putting on of the mask.

The typology that follows, and which is summarised in Figure 3.1, is a typology of polarities, of end points on a four-part continuum, and it is only concerned with questions of the identity that may or may not be created when someone puts on a mask within one of the essentially pre-colonial traditions of sub-Saharan Africa. It is not some kind of all-embracing, all-explaining paradigm of masks and masquerade performances. For example, all the masks to which I refer throughout the rest of this paper have dramatic purpose, but a welder's mask, or

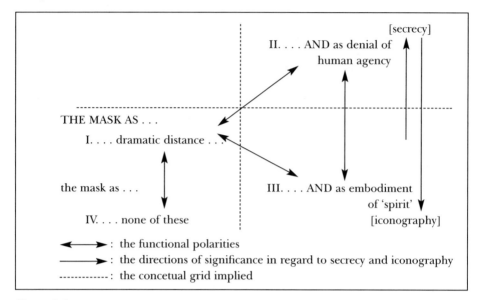

Figure 3.1

military camouflage, can only be considered as dramatic in a metaphorical sense, unless one really is a thoroughly dramaturgical interpreter of human behaviour, for that would not seem to be their immediate purpose.

I

In this context, then, masks enable a dramatic intention (but see IV below for some exceptions) by effecting distance between performer and audience, perhaps by creating an identity in performance that is, in turn, distanced from that everyday self as known otherwise than in performance. This does not mean of necessity that a metaphysical transformation has to take place; for the performer wearing a mask can be nothing more than a performer wearing a mask. The presentation is accepted as nothing more than what it is in itself, representing no other reality. The distance, in whichever dimension, is for dramatic effect alone. If other things are intended, these will not be about metaphysical transformation, let alone secrecy, at least not as far as the performer is concerned.

Among the most obvious examples here would be the south-western Yoruba *ẹfẹ-gẹlẹdẹ* festivities (Asiwaju 1975; Drewal 1974a, 1974b; Drewal and Drewal 1975, 1983; Harper 1970). While the sacred mother masks described by Drewal and Drewal (1983: 65–82) may well belong under III. below,[7] the identity of the *ẹfẹ* singers is no secret, and neither is the *ẹfẹ* masked performer anything but a man performing with a mask on. Indeed, Asiwaju and the Drewals suggest that for many people in a south-western Yoruba community, the *ẹfẹ* mask, while it effects that distance necessary to a dramatic event, at the same time also serves to establish his everyday place within that community. Moreover, Drewal and Drewal

(1983: 17–18) quote an *ẹsẹ ifa* verse in which Orunmila has to strike a bargain with the witches in their forest grove, and to protect himself he is told to wear, among other things, the mask. It is also evident (Asiwaju *op. cit.*; Harper *op. cit.*) that the performances so entrance 'our mothers' that the performers enjoy their protection, and not just in performance, but throughout the year and from one year to another. In other words, the mask signifies the performer's protection by witchcraft as well as his protection from witchcraft. It shares something of the capacities of the oxygen mask and the welding mask in the material culture of Europe: and none of these signifies a metaphysically re-defined state of being within the mask itself.

II

However, there are masks that effect dramatic distance and at the same time deny human agency. For the masker the separation between everyday self and performed identity is extreme. He is, at the very least, metaphysically re-identified, and in the most extreme cases the mask, in effect, effaces his very existence. The mask, with its costume and accoutrements, is the acceptable face, so to speak, of something, a power, an energy, a metaphysical presence, otherwise too dangerous to see. Secrecy will be an essential in a way in which it is not in other cases, for the human agent in performance is no mere animator of a mask, nor is he just an actor in a play. He has entered a space that belongs to and is held to be, in itself, something other. As Jedrej (1980: 223) points out, this procedure is dangerous and is likely to be preceded and succeeded, when the performance is done, by rites of purification, sacrifice, or whatever; and the masker in some sense becomes whatever it is that the mask hides, sometimes in a state of possession by that metaphysical presence, sometimes not, though invariably with the authority to speak as its oracle.

Those Yoruba egungun that manifest an ancestral embodiment hidden within their clothing would be case in point; and so likewise are the *eku/egwu/ekwu* ancestral masking institutions of many Benue valley and Niger–Benue confluence cultures, including Ebira. In such cases, however, the use of masks may constitute something of an intellectual puzzle in that it must seem as if power, i.e., metaphysical energy, is mediated (as indeed it is, however one chooses to explain it) by a deceit. This must be particularly so when, as in Ebira, there is neither the theory nor the practice of possession, whereas senior Yoruba egungun are, or are presumed to be, 'clothed' by possession in addition to their overt costuming.

Questions of re-identification and secrecy need careful investigation. Is it really possible to keep things secret? What do people do about knowledge they find themselves having when they should not have it? Certainly, in my experience, in Lagos (e.g., the identity of the leading adimu-oriṣa performer in the early 1960s), and in Ebira, 'secrecy' was much less a matter of the lack of knowledge, than of the time and place of discourse: i.e., of what could one speak to whom, and when?[8] We do need to be clear about why secrecy, whether in practice or in theory, matters; just as it is important to know the extent to which any ritual before, during and after the performance contributes to the status of the performer in these circumstances. One might also assume that performance in masks intended publicly to deny the performers' identity would pose interesting questions about the psychology of masquerading.

III

In contrast to the previous examples, there are masks that create dramatic distance in the context of performance, but which at the same time are the literal embodiments of metaphysical energy, or presence, or 'spirit'. What matters in this case is the visible, tangible, material reality of the artifact rather than what it causes to remain hidden: the mask reveals rather than conceals. Jedrej (1980: 225) suggests that performance will not present the kind of dangers to the performer characteristic of the previous type, for the artifact is itself the metaphysical presence; and in consequence there is nothing in the space enclosed by the mask for the performer to become, or to displace, or to be displaced by. The question of secrecy in regard to the identity of the performer may not arise, for the intellectual problem here is of quite a different order. Secrecy is, indeed, likely to be an irrelevance in terms of the essential nature of the mask: for if the thing itself is the source of energy, what is there to be hidden? If secrecy and magical protection are relevant to the performance of masks of this type, then we must be careful to understand why, for one might predict other reasons, about the nature and context of performance in a given community, rather than about a local theory of masks. Sometimes 'secrecy' turns out to be little more than a matter of talking, with little by way of negative sanctions to reinforce the expectation. Here 'secrecy' can be construed as part of the apparatus of dramatic distance, rather than as a means of protecting the energy source.

As to the temporal status of the embodiment as mask, one might expect it to be permanent, but it can also be temporary. Among the obvious examples of permanent embodiment are Dan forest spirits in Liberia, and the Sande association masks, the unique example of women as masked performers, of Mende, Vai, Sherbro and Gola communities in Liberia and Sierra Leone (d'Azevedo 1973; Jedrej 1976, 1986; Phillips 1978). The masks used in the Kalabari ekine association (Horton 1963, 1965) provide an example of temporary embodiment, and also an example of secrecy maintained as a matter of not talking about what everyone knows for dramatic rather than ritual purposes. To judge by descriptions published by Carroll (1967) and Ojo (1978), supported by my own field research in 1964–5, it would seem that the helmet masks of eastern Yoruba, sometimes generically labelled in the published literature as *epa*, are also embodiments of energy, though their temporal status in this regard remains unclear.

Given that these masks are visible embodiments, this is as good a place as any to consider the iconographical capacities of masks, and their costumes and accoutrements, particularly in the light of this typology. One might expect, for example, that with the suggested contrast between revealing and concealing in mind, those masks which exhibit the more elaborated iconographies are also those for which a concern with secrecy is minimal, or perhaps, even absent. The idea of an inverse relationship between a ritually sanctioned concern with secrecy and the elaboration of an iconography is, undoubtedly, oversimplistic: human culture is never that simple; but the idea is worth playing around with for the moment, provided one remembers that it is all a matter of balance and emphasis. The proposition can easily be discarded if the exceptions are too many.

There is, however, another iconographical possibility that must be mentioned even though it takes us well beyond the scope of this paper: the mask as part of a visual system that is independent of, perhaps alternative to, the purposes of the masked performance. Such, at any rate, would be my interpretation of the sculpted imagery of *gelede* masks and, perhaps Afikpo *okumkpa* masks likewise (Drewal 1974b; Ottenberg 1975).[9] There is, after all, no obvious reason why an artwork must articulate only one system of communication, and only to one end.

IV

The fourth part of this typology provides for masks which seem to be none of the things discussed above. They are 'masks' in virtue of their size, shape, etc., but their place in dramatic performance is of a very different order: for example, the Lega *lukungu* 'skull', the ivory or bone masks which are '... never worn on the face or elsewhere on the body' (Biebuyck 1973: 213), though wooden masks can be worn '... on the face, on the skull, on the back of the head, on the temples, near the shoulder on the upper arm, and on the knee ... The mask that A now calls "skull of my father" was called "skull of my father" by B and C, and so on ...' (Ibid., 211). The context is, of course, initiation into the various grades of *bwami* in which things of all sorts have mnemonic value. Other examples that seem to fit this end of the typology would include the ivory masks, such as those now in the British Museum, London, and the Metropolitan Museum, New York, that once were among the regalia of the Kings of Benin, Nigeria, and were worn at his waist (see illustrations in Ben Amos 1980; and Dark 1973).

Figure 3.1 summarises the argument and, I hope, clarifies the proposition that we are not dealing with self-contained categories, but with functional polarities distributed along a four-part continuum. Thus, while some can be located under one heading or another, others occupy points along one continuum or another: the Lega 'skull', for example, would lie well on the way from I to IV.

The figure suggests another kind of question, this time about the ritual status of particular masks. Masking is, of course, a ritual, whatever else it might be, but there is a contrast to be made between masks primarily intended only to ensure dramatic distance (I and perhaps IV>) and those which either conceal or embody some metaphysical agency (II and III). Are the latter, i.e., masks which one might locate towards or along the righthand side of the figure, the more likely to be set apart from other artifacts by ritual sanctions?

Towards a history of Ebira masquerade

Ebira masquerade is evidently of that second category in which human agency is denied. Some men present this as a trick, and indeed the stories men tell are full of anecdotes about famous performers outwitting women intent upon discovering how their deceased husbands or fathers would be manifested as masquerade. These stories reinforce the idea of trickery while at the same time also presenting the theory of masquerade as ancestral presence: the problem is that women are not to be trusted with the knowledge of how this is achieved. For the most part, men seem convinced of that presence even though one cannot see it. The whole enterprise is riddled with puzzle and paradox: it works yet it is a deceit; women should not know, yet if they are 'strong' they do; the powers of women are set against male interests, including the powers mediated by masquerade, and yet women enable and ultimately guarantee the system (Picton 1988), and yet again women can be harmed by masquerade if they do not observe the rules; and so it goes on. Faith and deceit are disconcertingly combined.

However, Ebira culture, though conceptually rooted in tradition, is not static; and the discussion that follows is about masquerade history. Three distinct categories of masquerade are considered: *ekuǫba, eku'rahụ,* and *ekuęcici.*

Ekuǫba – 'the eku that stretches up'

This name describes the variable height of the costume in performance. These were made to commemorate individual deceased male elders returning to greet their wives and children at some time after their burial. The costume, *ụmǫmǫ* is a long tube of cloth pinned together at the top. Also at the top is fixed a strip of cloth into which are sewn relics cut from the corpse of the deceased, except that if for some reason they were not removed they could be faked by sewing in a kola nut instead to give a lump of the appropriate size. The relics, whether fake or genuine, provide an additional form of ancestral presence, and a focus for sacrificial offerings, all of which enhances the authority of the performer as the oracle of the particular deceased elder. The costume takes the form of a shrouded corpse: there is neither face nor limbs; and one *ekuǫba* looks very like another.

Masked performance is a specialist business: if you become involved in one species, you do not then take up another. In the 1960s, in any community there were likely to be no more than one or two men with the expertise needed for *ekuǫba*. This involved not just experience in the wearing of and dancing in the *ụmǫmǫ*, but also distinctive poetic skills: knowledge of the invocations, the praises, the stories ... These skills were displayed at the installation of lineage title-holders, and during the month before the popular night festival that closes the period in which one year overlaps with the next. At this time, one *ekuǫba* will be chosen as representative of the deceased of the community to initiate the celebration of a new year with an extended poetic and invocatory recitation followed by daily visits to every household. It follows that the performer would assume the identity as *eku* of whichever deceased elder whose oracle he was supposed to be at any given performance. In other words, while the identity of a particular *ekuǫba* with a particular ancestor was specific, both the form of the costume and the manner of performance were generic.

The *ekuọba* was the basis, historically and conceptually, of the masquerade tradition in Ebira, and its performers were evidently highly esteemed within the closed circle of Ebira male culture. Nevertheless, at some time in the recent past, the making of new *ekuọba* ceased for reasons I am none too sure of, and various strategies have had to be devised in order to maintain the annual rites and title installations, given that the costumes themselves are destroyed by the practice of burying the *ụmọmọ* with the last surviving son of the deceased whom it commemorated. It is hardly surprising that by the 1960s this was a style and manner of performance that had come to be regarded as very definitely on the decline, although I did meet a couple of younger men who had taken it up.

Eku'rahụ – 'the eku of the night'

These provide the main focus of interest in the course of that night when all the dead return to visit the living, when women are shut indoors and their energies constrained. *Eku* of the night are said to be sons that have predeceased their mothers, but there is no direct connection: rather, if someone seems to have the making of a singer (and boys practise at farm out of the way of women), an identity will be invented. The popularity of these performances is amazing: the most enormous crowds of men gather to listen to the best singers, and, as I have said, these masquerades have proliferated to the extent that in Okene, and in some other communities, there are performances on three separate nights. That way all the available performers get to have their turn.[10] However, as I have already suggested, there is evidence that this kind of performance was invented within the past hundred years – not the festival, but this form of *eku* as the focus of its entertainment. I do not have an exact date, of course, but one gets a rough idea from the fact of elderly men in the 1960s, themselves born around or no later than the turn of the century, remembering the performances of Intemirege in the days of their youth. This suggests a time in the latter half of the nineteenth century, well before the advent of colonial rule.

In contrast to *ekuọba*, therefore, the creation of an *eku* of the night begins with the performer, and his identity as *eku* is unique to him. When he dies the *eku* will die with him (whereas an *ekuọba* 'dies' with a son of the deceased elder it represents), for it has no existence but for the performer. As might be expected, the *ụmọmọ* is also highly individualistic, for example in its use of flashy textiles, and there is no attempt to shroud the human figure; indeed, as these *eku* only appear in the absence of women, no covering of the face is needed. Women prepare food for the dead of the community, before they go indoors for the night. During the night, men tuck in to the food with that same sense of deceit and faith: for some, the dead are there but you do not see them; for others, it is a joke against women.

Ekụẹcịcị – 'the eku of rubbish'

These are the servants of the domain of the dead. When a deceased elder was re-introduced to the community embodied as *ekuọba*, in the context of his obituary celebrations, an *ekuẹcịcị* was invented as its servant with the duty of keeping people at a distance from the ancestor, in case they should step on the costume and cause him to fall over, and to clear the way of sticks, stones and other detritus, *ẹcịcị*. There are other ways of inventing *ekuẹcịcị*, around the emerging skills of a young man likely to prove a good performer: again, young men practise masking at farm in the absence of women. Nevertheless, the obituary celebration provides the theoretical model, within Ebira culture, for the status of all *ekuẹcịcị*. In any case, having been invented, these *eku* have an existence independent of the circumstances of their invention, especially at the mid-year festival. Here they parade about the community in a style that parodies the Ebira young male: tough, volatile, unpredictable; and some also mediate a healing presence.

As with the *eku* of the night, identity in *eku* is essentially a fiction, and in this case entirely generic in that no-one in *eku* is represented thereby. On the other hand, an *ekuẹcịcị* has obvious human shape, each with a mask together with a costume that is recognisably different from any other, and worn by its own individual masker. Indeed, this individuality can be enhanced by changing the colours and textures of the costume from year to year (see Picton 1990). By the 1960s, many performers did not bother with a wooden mask, preferring a cloth mask as it facilitated movement and display. Some had both, changing from one to the other as the performance proceeded. Others just had the wooden face. As with the *eku* of the night, there was evident proliferation of masked performers linked with the athletic abilities of those men who chose to take up the style appropriate to this class of eku. Neither the *eku* of the night, nor the *eku* of rubbish showed any signs of cultural obsolescence. Indeed, they had proved to be vehicles of an Ebira identity that for men was not replicated by any other form of cultural practice.

These developments are summarised in Figure 3.2.

Some *ekuẹcịcị* do, however, exist beyond the lifetime of the individual performer. This is invariably when the mask itself acquires a reputation for healing power. In these cases, there is always a wooden mask. All masked performers have the potential for mediating healing power and some gain a particular reputation for this. The mask itself becomes the recipient of blood and other sacrifice as a means of promoting and preserving that demonstrated efficacy of which the performer is the medium. Magical medicines will be attached for much the same reasons, i.e., to preserve and promote the healing energies of the mask. The assemblage that results begins to take on a life of its own, no longer just a representation and a mediation of ancestral power, but as a vehicle in its own right. The term *ekuẹcịcị* is no longer used; they have become *ekuobanyi* 'big *eku*'. In other words, such masks have become embodiments of power, even though they remain at the same time denials of human agency.

My purpose in writing this paper was to think about some of our ideas and perceptions of masquerade, and, following Jedrej (1980), to explore the manner in which a mask structures the relationship between the masker and masquerader. The functional model that has emerged seems, in addition, to have a further utility in providing a historical model; for it is possible to

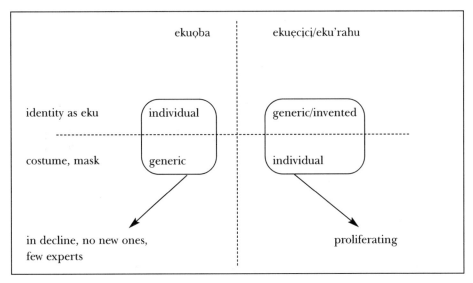

Figure 3.2

understand the recent history of masquerade in Ebira culture in terms of two movements each from one category towards another. The very proliferation of *eku'rahu* and *ekuẹcịcị*, when taken together with the declining interest in *ekuọba*, the ancestral mask *par excellence*, can be understood as a movement away from II, i.e., ancestral presence and the denial of human agency, towards I, the mask simply as enabling dramatic distance. The very proliferation is itself an emphasis on display and entertainment at the expense of ancestral presence.

In contrast, those *ekuẹcịcị* that survive the declining abilities of their performers do so in virtue of a healing capacity embodied and developed in the particular mask by means of medicine and sacrifice, and the consequent development of that mask as a metaphysical entity in its own right: the movement is from II towards III. This is, of course, always a possibility in the life history of an individual mask; whereas the developmental programme outlined in the previous paragraph is about an overall pattern in the recent history of Ebira masquerade. This in turn suggests, further, that in practice the closer an *ekuẹcịcị* is to I, in terms of the circumstances and intentions surrounding its invention, the less likely it is to acquire its own inherent magical potential.

How do we explain this? It would, of course, be tempting to do so in terms of developing ideas of self and person as a result of, or as a response to, colonialism, education, etc., but this would be yet one more oversimplification, and, in any case, as yet this is not an area in which I feel secure. It will have to do for the present merely to note the question.

These developments are summarised in Figure 3.3:

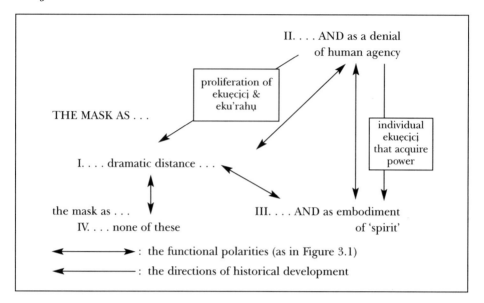

Figure 3.3

References

Asiwaju, I. 1975. Gelede songs as sources of Yoruba history. In *Yoruba Oral Tradition*, ed. by W. Abimbola, pp. 199–66. Ife: Department of African Languages and Literatures, University of Ife.

d'Azevedo, W. 1973. Mask makers and myth in western Liberia. In *Primitive Art and Society*, ed. by A. Forge, pp. 126–150. London: Oxford University Press.

Ben Amos, P. 1980. *The Art of Benin*. London: Thames & Hudson.

Biebuyck, D. 1973. *Lega Culture*. Berkeley and Los Angeles: University of California Press.

Boston, J. S. 1960. Some northern Ibo masquerades. *Journal of the Royal Anthropological Institute* 90: 54–65.

Carroll, K. 1967. *Yoruba Religious Carving*. London: Geoffrey Chapman.

Dark, P. 1973. *An Introduction to Benin Art and Technology*. Oxford: Clarendon Press.

Drewal, H. J. 1974a. Lefę, voiced power and pageantry. *African Arts* 7, 2: 26–9; 58–66; 82–3.

—— 1974b. Gelede masquerade, imagery and motif. *African Arts* 7, 4: 8–19; 95–6; 162–3.

Drewal, H. J. and M. T. Drewal. 1975. Gelede dance of the western Yoruba. *African Arts* 8, 2: 36–45; 78–9.

—— 1983. *Gelede*. Bloomington: Indiana University Press.

Giddens, A. 1984. *The Constitution of Society*. Cambridge: Polity Press.

Harper, P. 1970. The role of dance in the Gelede ceremonies of the Yoruba village of Ijio. *Odu*, n.s. 4: 67–94.

Hollis, M. 1985. Of masks and men. In *The Category of the Person*, ed. by M. Carrithers, S. Collins, S. Lukes, pp. 217–233. Cambridge: Cambridge University Press.

Horton, R. 1963. The Kalabari *ekine* society. *Africa* 33: 94–113.

—— 1965. *Kalabari Sculpture*. Lagos: Nigerian Museum.

Jedrej, M. C. 1974. An analytical note on the land and spirits of the Sewa Mende. *Africa* 44: 38–45.

—— 1976. Medicine, fetish and secret society in a West African culture. *Africa* 46: 247–257.

—— 1980. A comparison of masks from North America, Africa and Melanesia. *Journal of Anthropological Research* 36, 2: 220–230.

—— 1986. Dan and Mende masks: a structural comparison. *Africa* 56, 1: 71–80.

Kasfir, S. (ed.) 1989. *West African Masks and Cultural Systems*. Tervuren: Musée Royal de l'Afrique Centrale.

Kaye-Besley, L. and D. Byles. 1979. *Skills for life*. Cheltenham: Stanley Thornes.

Ojo, J. R. O. 1978. The symbolism and significance of Epa-type masquerade headpieces. *Man*, n.s. 12.3: 455–470.

Ottenberg, S. 1975. *Masked Rituals of Africa*. Seattle: University of Washington.

Phillips, R. 1978. Masking in Mende Sande society initiation masks. *Africa* 48: 265–276.

Picton, J. 1988. Some Ebira reflexions on the energies of women. *African Languages and Cultures* 1.1: 61–76.

—— 1989. On placing masquerades in Ebira culture. *African Languages and Cultures* 2, 1: 73–92.

—— 1990. Transformations of the artifact: John Wayne, plastic bags, and the Eye-That-Surpasses-All-Other-Eyes. In *Lotte, the Transformation of the Object*, ed. by C. Deliss. Graz: Grazer Kunstverein.

—— 1991. On artifact and identity at the Niger-Benue confluence. *African Arts*, 24, 3: 34–49.

—— 1992. Masks and identities in Ebira culture. In *Concepts of the Body/Self in Africa*, ed. by Joan Maw, Beiträge zur Afrikanistik, Band 43, Vienna; JP essay, pp. 67–86.

Picton, J. and J. Mack. 1989. (2nd edn.) *African Textiles*. London: British Museum.

—— 1996. The masque of words, in K. Arnaut and E. Dell (eds), *Bedu is my Lover*, Brighton Museum, pp. 5–8.

—— 1997. On (Men?) Placing Women in Ebira, in F. E. S. Kaplan (ed.) *Queens, Queen Mothers, Priestesses and Power: Case Studies in African Gender*, New York, the New York Academy of Sciences, 1997, pp. 337–69.

Webster's Collegiate Dictionary. 1932. (4th edn. of the largest abridgment of *Webster's New International Dictionary of the English Language*.) London: Bell; and Springfield: Merriam.

Notes

1 See Picton 1988, 1989, 1990, 1992, and Picton and Mack 1989: 4, 72–3, 76. Ebira is a language, spoken by people calling themselves an' ebira 'inhabitants/people of Ebira', living/originating in an area they call et'ebira 'Ebira land', who manifest ebira, a character generally presumed, because of its very origins, to be good. In geographical terms, it is the area immediately south-west of the confluence of the Niger and Benue rivers in Nigeria. In May 1990, I found that masquerades in Ebira had been proscribed two years before with justification due to escalating levels of violence, although there was a movement towards the re-institution.

2 In 1980, after the publication of the first edition of *African Textiles*, John Mack and I conceived of the possibility of a book on masquerade. After a time, I concluded, rightly or wrongly, that the attempt was premature, and it remains a project still to be realised. This paper is an attempt, also, to rethink some of the inherent conceptual problems that we began to discuss at that time.

3 This paper has been given several times, in Los Angeles, Glasgow, Leeds, Norwich, and finally at the Eighth Triennial Symposium on African Art, Washington DC, 15–17 June 1989. There was a certain irony in that at the symposium panel at which this paper was given, the three paper givers were male (Herbert Cole, Christopher Roy, and myself), whereas the three discussants were female (Sidney Kasfir, Mary Jo Arnoldi, and Margaret Drewal): the overt pretence of male authority countered/constrained/ enabled by the covert reality of female power perhaps, as described in Picton 1988!

4 The time spent with Ebira people at various times from 1965 to 1969 was made possible by the Nigerian Federal Department of Antiquities, in which I was employed from 1961 to 1970. For subsequent visits in 1971, 1981, 1982, and 1990, I must thank, in addition to the Federal Government of Nigeria, the British Museum, the School of Oriental and African Studies, and the British Academy.

5 My first encounter with a masked man was on the streets of the Brazilian quarter of Lagos Island, soon after I first arrived in Nigeria in 1961. At the time, I did not see him as masked as his appearance was nothing like the things I had seen in the British Museum! He was dressed literally from head to toe in close-fitting khaki clothing, with a hood that provided the complete disguise. On his head was a large cylindrical container into which he emptied the contents of Lagos Island thunder boxes. The mask was a function of what was regarded as a shameful occupation, and very few among those forced by their circumstances to engage in it wanted to be recognised.

6 Moreover, there are all those artifacts that distance without covering the face: the vestments of kings, priests, judges ... the list is endless. Another criterion becomes relevant, i.e., the extent to which rôles, titles and offices such as these provide for dominant and more-or-less permanent *personae*.

7 I am grateful to Sidney Kasfir for reminding me of this.

8 The dressing and undressing of an ekueçiçi (see page 64) in Ebira is an entertainment in itself, the performer posturing, screaming, full of energy; and sometimes chasing his entourage out even as he is half clothed. On one occasion, while all this was going on in the house, Andrew, my field assistant, and I were outside (we had seen it all before) chatting to the performer's elder sister. Suddenly, there was her brother at the window having chased everyone out, wearing nothing but some magical medicines around his neck and trousers made of the particular indigo and white cloth used only for shrouds and masquerades. The sister averted her gaze, and I, thinking to seize the chance for some cross-gender discussion, said (in English, which she did not speak) to Andrew, 'Let's ask her what she saw', but he replied, 'No! You cannot ask her that: she will say she saw nothing.'

9 Drewal (1974b) attempts to systematise the extraordinary prolific collection of representations carved on the tops of gelede masks. I would argue that a concern with display overrides any concern with 'information' (even assuming I thought art was about 'information' anyway). Some of the masks do certainly present well-known stereotypes, but there is no reason why they must all fit an iconographical scheme, quite apart from the proposition that the perceptions of carvers and their patrons in one place cannot be reckoned identical with those in another.

10 In Adavi district and at Okene, there are preliminary night festivals coinciding with the ekueci of Okehi and Eika districts, respectively. Then there are the ekueci celebrations proper in Adavi and Okene. Finally, some time later, there is the feat of ebe, and although it is theoretically quite separate, in practice it serves as a third opportunity for the performance of eku'rahu. Each night singer chooses one of the three nights at the time of his initiation as the time of his major annual performance.

4   Acting Africa

Loren Kruger

I begin with two images of African actors. The first, from *Asinamali* by the South African playwright Mbongeni Ngema (1985), shows a group pose drawn directly from protest theatre – angry men in prison khaki, with fists clenched, bodies tensed in readiness and, one can assume, voices raised against the invisible but all too palpable forces of apartheid. The second, from the centenary celebrations of the American Board Mission in South Africa (1935), portrays the 'smelling-out of a fraudulent *umthakathi*' (which can be translated as diviner or trickster), which were followed, on this occasion, by other scenes portraying the civilizing influence of European settlers. While the first offers an image of African agency and modernity in the face of oppression, the second, with its apparently unmediated reconstruction of pre-colonial ritual and, in its teleological juxtaposition of 'tribal' and 'civilized' custom, seems to respond to the quite different terms set by a long history of displays, along the lines of the Savage South Africa Show (1900), in which the authenticity of the Africans on stage was derived not from their agency but by their incorporation into the representation of colonial authority.

Histories of South African theatre have typically shored up the authority of protest theatre by highlighting the differences, marked by these two images, between the neo-colonial objectification of 'savage Africa' and the portrayal of vigorous resistance to its legacy. In this account, which generally endorses the narrative of national non-racial liberation promulgated by the ANC, the political and aesthetic value of protest theatre is seen to lie in its absolute opposition to neo-colonial spectacle. Resistance theatre may be distinguished from protest theatre by its stress on the representation or, at least, assertion of defiance over and above the portrayal of suffering.[1] In the long view, however, they share a thematic emphasis on bearing witness to the brutality of apartheid and the effects of state violence not only on the social and political aspirations but also on the bodies, voices, and dreams of the majority of South Africans.[2] Its distinguishing features have been the dramatization of racial and class conflict generally involving African workers, usually men, a repertory of performance techniques derived in varying measure from agit-prop, Brechtian distanciation, Grotowskian poor theatre, the improvisation and testimony of the workshop format and the practices of popular township theatre, a mixture of the musical and the domestic melodrama, often including comic skits and dance numbers not immediately connected to the plot or political point of the drama. It has generally shunned the idea of 'traditional' performances, in large part because these have been historically associated with the enforced tribalism that was the cornerstone of apartheid cultural policy. The best of South African theatre, according to this model, has been characterized by the vivid representation of the political struggle against apartheid and tribalism and for liberation and modernity.

This – perhaps necessary – dichotomy has led to the neglect of an engagement, critical, affirmative, or otherwise, with repertoires and practices that draw attention to African or specific ethnic identity. There is a significant, if unevenly recorded, history of performance that engaged critically with the question of a pre-colonial inheritance and with colonial stereotypes of rural and urban Africans as well as those in between. Especially in the decades of accelerated African urbanization, c.1920–50, as white experts sought to divorce African culture from urban influence while nonetheless rationalizing the exploitation of African labour, educated Africans in the cities created performances that confounded segregationist ideology. Drawing on the legacy of English, European and American theatre imparted by the mission schools, on American minstrelsy and on reinterpretations and reinventions of local folk memory, these African entertainers (their phrase) criss-crossed the boundaries between Western and African, modern and traditional, invented and authentic culture in search of what they called a New African way. Marginalized in a general South African public sphere defined in racially exclusive terms, New African performance articulated what might be called a *virtual public sphere*, a discursive and social field within which alternative representations of South Africa could be entertained without direct exposure to the wrath of the state.[3] As a virtual public sphere, performance operates in the subjunctive rather than indicative mood. It skirts the dangerous field of immediate political action in order to gain a testing ground for competing representations of the nation or the folk.

The reconstruction of a legitimate (rather than verifiably authentic) folk culture in this period relies heavily on the invention of tradition 'out of the disparate remnants of a shattered rural order', by modern agents.[4] In the creation of African entertainments, finding a usable past was not so much an act of pure discovery as a process of collection, recollection, and invention. Favouring the elastic forms of variety rather than the strict dramaturgy of the well-made play, New Africans sought to reinvent a hybrid African legacy that might be more resilient than any single one of its parents. Acting Africa, as it were, in different idioms at once, they defied attempts – by traditionalists and civilizers alike – to push African development in any single direction. The strict correspondence between individual actor and his or her embodied character as well as the naturalist convention that legitimates the actor's portrayal of interior states by placing it in a set designed to replicate an exterior or interior space, both defining characteristics of most metropolitan modern drama, had little in common with the more fluid and more overtly rhetorical relationship between performer, character and location in the praise-songs, folk tales, and community dancing characteristic of pre-colonial performance.[5] The variety format or the revue, on the other hand, allowed for more flexible modes of impersonation, representation and recognition, including the incorporation of traditional motifs. What is at stake in these variety shows and especially in the 'tribal sketches' at their centre, is not so much a neo-traditional return to origins deemed intact and timeless as a strategic *re-traditionalization*, the recovery and reinvention of 'folk' elements in the interests not of a return to a lost past but of an alternative modernity that, unlike colonial modernization, would respect African agency.[6]

The syncretic character of these shows resides not only in their simultaneous deployment of different forms but also in the tension between the form and occasion of performance. To plot these points of tension in a preliminary way, we might begin by looking at the ways in which a particular item in the repertoire of the tribal sketch, such as smelling-out the *umthakathi*, is modified by the conventions of different occasions. Occasion here implies not only place and time, but what I would call the *genre of the event*. The conventions governing the first recorded version of the *umthakathi* sketch, presented as part of an 'exhibition of Native Zulu Kafirs', mounted by the Natal colonist A. T. Caldecott and documented by his son in London in 1853 for the purpose of attracting further English settlement, are likely to be those of the metropolitan exhibition of colonial possessions, already established by the mid-nineteenth century, which frame the performance with condemnations of 'savagery' and the 'vile imposture' of pre-colonial custom.[7] In contrast, the conventions of the occasion framing the sketch staged in 1935 in various Natal locations and in Johannesburg by the Lucky Stars, Zulu graduates from Adams College, sponsored by the American Board Mission, are likely to combine those of a celebration of Zulu heritage with a demonstration of African agency – embodied in the impresario as well as the performers.

Although fostered by the missions, alongside performances of Shakespeare and bible stories, New African interest in tribal sketches is not to be explained away as the mere consequence of mission dressage. The shows of the Lucky Stars testify to the appeal of re-traditionalization but they also illuminate the modernity of the re-traditionalizing gesture. Founded in 1929 by Esau and Isaac Mthethwa, the Lucky Stars performed traditional dances and enacted sketches in reconstructed Zulu custom and in the Zulu language, portraying such subjects as *Umthakathi*. Unlike the Caldecott or the American Board Mission sketches, however, this one framed the condemnation of this particular imposter with a sympathetic recreation of Zulu traditional society more generally.

The several parts of the show – sketches, dancing, and often choral singing of African Nationalist hymns in Zulu – as well as quite varied places of performance from mission stations to the Durban City Hall, suggest a more complex mesh of occasion and meaning than a transparent reconstruction of pre-colonial practices. A white observer's account of a performance in rural Natal is illuminating:

> This new departure among the black races is valuable in presenting to the public scenes of native domestic life with a realism which would be otherwise unobtainable. Such education of the white man is a necessary preliminary to his understanding of Bantu problems. [...]
>
> These plays are presented with a naiveté which would be impossible for the white man to imitate. The style of acting is much more free than we have

been accustomed to see on the more civilized stage. The producer is an educated Zulu [Isaac Mthethwa] but the players have only a rudimentary knowledge of reading and writing. Consequently, the parts are learned by word of mouth and no strict adherence to the original wording is insisted on. [...] This induces a freshness and vigor of presentation which is a welcome relief from the too conscious presentation of our own stage.[8]

This account rehearses the familiar colonial opposition between jaded metropolitan culture (whether the 'public' clamouring for performances 'at the hotels and socials in Durban' or the 'too conscious' artifice of the 'civilized' actor) and the fresh naiveté of the 'black races'. At the same time, it concedes the artifice of this native naiveté, in the shape of Mthethwa's guiding hand and the fact that the lines were learnt. This acknowledgement of acting skill also allows for the possibility that the 'education of the white man' might be the object and not merely the incidental result of this performance. Even the natural setting, 'the lush sub-tropical bush of the Natal coast', is framed by the thoroughly modern contrivance of the illusionist set: 'The scene was set by ... a canvas sheet with a painting of a Zulu hut'. If the content of the sketch harks back to 'scenes of native domestic life', this canvas backdrop points to the economy of naturalist illusion and theatre-going habits shaped by mission education and the dichotomy between work and leisure in the city. The self-reflexive, indeed modern, character of the show as a whole, over and above the content of the sketches, is confirmed by the 'historical songs' that concluded the show, which would have included such numbers as Reuben Caluza's 'iLand Act', precursor to the ANC anthem, 'Nkosi Sikelel' iAfrika'.

Although shaped in large part by places and occasions dominated by educated Africans, the sketches of the Lucky Stars were well received by black workers and those marginalized by the formal economy, especially in less industrialized Natal where audiences found in these 'idealized images of a rural past' an escape from their alienation in racial and class terms, from 'civilization'.[9] Nevertheless, claims that the Lucky Stars offered an unmistakable instance of black political theatre and should therefore be seen as forerunners of the anti-apartheid protest theatre of the 1970s,[10] ought to be treated with caution. The origins of the sketches in the folkloric recuperation of the missions did not prevent them from being appropriated by a diverse popular audience, but the ethnic emphasis, even exclusiveness, of the sketches reflected the Zulu pride of the performers more than a desire to challenge the social and economic discrimination against all Africans. Performed in the Zulu language and in historically reconstructed Zulu costume (rather than the mixed attire actually worn in Zululand at the time), the critical edge in the sketches would have been only partially accessible to speakers of other Bantu languages who saw the shows, whose response may have been affected as much by the tangible presence and implied agency of African actors, as by the authentic details of their appearance.

The implied agency of these actors, however attractive in performance, must be qualified. Groups such as the African Own Entertainers (founded, like the Lucky Stars, in 1929) and the Darktown Strutters (active by 1931) took their variety shows of music, comedy and sketches on the road in the Union and beyond, but made a living by other means, such as teaching. Restricted from owning property and capital, financial or cultural, in the cities, even relatively well-educated Africans found it difficult to escape dependence on well-meaning whites. 'Discovered' at the Bantu Social Centre in Durban, the Lucky Stars were managed in Johannesburg by a white impresario and talent scout, who saw herself as a successful impersonator of Zulu dance.[11] The social and economic dependence of Africans reinforced the appeal of primitivist nostalgia in the metropolis as well as in the Commonwealth and encouraged impresarios like Bertha Slosberg to claim ownership of these shows even while emphasizing their exotic otherness. In this context, the spectacular fuses with the folkloric and the thrilling dancing becomes the reason 'to salvage from European influence, ... the native simplicity, the splendid savage grandeur of a dying pagan land'.[12] The authenticity of the spectacle is derived from its visible difference from the self-proclaimed modernity of the white spectators. From their perspective, a clear distinction between 'native simplicity' and the 'progress of the Union' is the *sine qua non* that confirms their affinity with Europe and thus with modernity.

Yet the form of modernity desired by the spectators of the 'Union's progress' was not the only kind on offer. While the Lucky Stars appeared willing or at least resigned to accommodate metropolitan expectations of 'native simplicity', other variety troupes were not. The practice of perhaps the most influential and certainly the longest surviving group, the Darktown Strutters, and their leader Griffiths Motsieloa, suggest the critical potential of hybridization for modern African agency. Their longevity was due in large part to the management of Motsieloa, but also to the patronage of Gallophone Records, who employed Mosieloa as a talent scout from the mid-1930s on and thus gave the group a rare measure of economic independence. Like many New Africans, Motsieloa qualified as a teacher at Lovedale College and went on to study elocution at Trinity College of Music in London, where he earned the reputation of 'London's Favourite Bantu Actor'.[13] From the mid-1920s, he ran a series of variety groups, from the African Darkies in the 1920s to the Darktown Strutters in the 1930s and as the Pitch Black Follies in the 1940s, who in turn influenced the work of younger impresarios Wilfred Sentso and Gibson Kente, who developed what came to be known as the township musical.

The entertainments of the Darktown Strutters and their imitators were remarkable for their deployment of diverse traditions severally and simultaneously. Although dismissed as 'elite' entertainment by some critics,[14] they regularly performed at venues other than the respectable Bantu Men's Social Centre in places as far away from their Johannesburg base as Queenstown in the Eastern Cape, Serowe in the Bechuanaland Protectorate (Botswana) and Lourenço Marques (now Maputo) in the Portuguese colony of Mozambique,[15] and so had to offer a broadly appealing programme that crossed class lines and the ethnic boundaries maintained, for instance, by the Lucky Stars. As their name suggests, they drew on the repertory and the ideological ambiguity of minstrelsy, but also paid attention to an American and especially African American species of 'uplift melodrama'. Their repertoires combined the genteel *amakwaya* (choir) music of the mission schools with the *marabi* dance music favoured in the townships,[16] as well as minstrel gags with more sustained dramatic representation of the modern African (and African-American) condition, using Sotho and Zulu as well as English.

Unlike the Lucky Stars, who drew continual attention to their Zulu identity but played down the individual identities of the performers, the Darktown Strutters borrowed the conventions of Western variety that foregrounded the star in performance and in publicity. A typical programme included:

1 The Xhosa prophet Ntshikana: Ntshikana's vision, tribal dance, Ntshikana the prophet sees the coming of the white man (led by Victor Mbiza)
2 Jim Utakata Kanje [Jim the Trickster] (Petrus Qwabe)
3 Die Oorlams Mense [the streetwise people] van Vrededorp
4 'The Recruiter', a two-act play by J. Mathews [sic] 'written by a Negro during the early days of the USA's entry into the Great War'.[17]

In this 1938 performance, the *umthakathi* motif functions more as a vehicle for the star, the 'Zulu king of laughter and mirth', than as a weapon for the defence of traditional culture. Despite the association of this kind of skit with Jim Crow minstrelsy, its coupling with more serious representation of African and African-American history, from the pre-colonial to the industrial, lends Petrus Qwabe's rendering of this gag a certain irony.

Reviews of the Darktown Strutters in the African press suggest a willingness on the part of performers and audience alike to celebrate the African, European, and African-American aspects of the show without regarding them as separate elements. Thus a reviewer of the show praises Qwabe as the 'Zulu king of laughter and mirth' and his companion, the tap-dancer and the choreographer, Johannes Masoleng as 'South Africa's Stephen [sic] Fetchit'.[18] While the allusion to Stephin Fetchit might alarm present-day readers familiar with critiques of this Jim Crow stereotype, its appearance in this review is likely to be entirely complimentary. In so far as Stephin Fetchit was the image of a 'successful and self-conscious urban black', he represented a positive role model.[19] At the very least, the virtuoso *impersonation* was worthy of emulation.

The play accompanying the variety show, *The Recruiter* (or *'Cruiter*), by the African-American folklorist, John Matheus, is particularly interesting for several reasons. The first was its topical subject: the recruiting of rural blacks, not for the army as the brief description implies but for the factories of the Northern cities, pointed to the acceleration of what came to be known as the Great Migration and the mass urbanization of African Americans:

> At that time the negroes on the plantations were bound on contract to the cotton plantation owners, and the recruitment of labour for the factories was in consequence illegal. Led by promises of emancipation and riches, scores of negro youth left their homes where their forebears lived as 'Squatters' for many generations.
>
> This play serves to illustrate the antagonisms of the negro youth to the superstitions and willing subjection of their parents.
>
> (SAIRR, AD843/Kb28.2.2)

The references to squatters is an oblique but telling reference to the consequences of the Land Act in South Africa, while the final sentence of the outline
equates the urbanization of the youth with their emancipation from superstition.
These were clearly issues of great interest to New Africans at a time when the
Union government was placing ever greater constraints on African mobility and
employment in the cities. Equally important, however, was the institutional status
of this text. Written by an African-American intellectual and published in
Opportunity, the organ of the National Urban League (USA) and much quoted in
African newspapers in South Africa, the play not only addressed the pressing
question of the links between modernity, urban life and economic self-sufficiency
for Africans, but also demonstrated that this modern theme could be legitimately
addressed in folk idiom.[20] In the South African performance, a black performer
would have played the white recruiter, which would have allowed for further
levels of irony. The recruiter offers escape, but could also be a trickster and,
impersonated by an African, would have drawn attention to the fact that, in
contrast to the American case, Africans were being driven away from South
African cities.

This combination in the African variety repertoire of drama and comic skits,
uplift and self-mocking exaggeration, relied for critical as well as entertaining
effect on a knowledgeable (urban, African, and relatively educated) audience that
could interpret this syncretic show as a pageant of a nation in the making. I have
focused on this occasion on the evolution of one particular persona – that of the
trickster – so as to pinpoint traces of this evolution in different kinds of
performers, performances and occasions and to at least point to ways in which
colonial stereotypes may be appropriated through what might be called a critical
embodiment. Acting Africa by way of the embodiment, New African entertainers
sketched out a mode of performing their agency that escaped, however sub-
junctively, the disabling dichotomy between 'European' civilization and its
colonial other.

The creation of Isaac Mthethwa, Griffiths Motsieloa and their contemporaries – an urban African hybrid performance culture – lives on in the work
of writer-impresarios like Gibson Kente (active since the 1960s, creator of *How
Long?* and *Too Late*, 1974) to Mbongeni Ngema, creator of *Asinamali* and
Sarafina – 1987 – but active since the 1970s) and John Ledwaba (acting since
the 1970s but most recently creator of *Jozi, Jozi* (1994), which deals with the
precarious life of local and migrant Africans in Johannesburg, now the world's
fourth fastest growing city). Their legacy is not yet well-known or much
documented, however. Despite recent scholarship on writers and composers
who were active in the rapidly urbanizing and relatively fluid 1930s and
1940s,[21] the contribution of those working in the more ephemeral media of
performing, directing and producing African variety to South African theatre is
only gradually emerging from under the neglect of the apartheid era and from
behind the more militant protest and resistance culture. A full understanding
of the present and recent past of South African theatre will depend on the full
investigation of this complex inheritance.

Notes

1 Ian Steadman, 'Theatre Beyond Apartheid', *Research in African Literatures*, 22: 3 (1991), p. 84.
2 Robert Kavanagh's pioneering but idiosyncratic *Theatre and Cultural Struggle*, London, 1985, emphasizes the paradigm of theatre as a cultural weapon, as does Martin Orkin's more recent and more comprehensive *Drama and the South African State* (Johannesburg: Witwatersrand University Press, 1991). Ian Steadman's work traces this trajectory, from the focus on protest theatre in 'Black South African Theatre after Nationalism', *English Academy Review* 2 (1984), pp. 9–18 and in 'Towards a Popular Theatre in South Africa', *Journal of Southern African Studies*, 16: 2 (1990), pp. 208–28, but critiques it in 'Theatre beyond Apartheid', ibid. See also Loren Kruger, 'The Uses of Nostalgia: Drama, History and Liminal Moments in South Africa', *Modern Drama*, 38: 1 (1995), pp. 60–71.
3 As Negt and Kluge have argued in response to Habermas's classic conceptualization, *Öffentlichkeit* ('publicity', usually translated as 'public sphere') includes not only physical space for public activity but also the civic and cultural mobilization necessary if the popular majority is to emerge as the public. It also acknowledges the experience of exclusion from public action which might precede such mobilization. See Oskar Negt and Alexander Kluge, *Public Sphere and Experience*, trans. Peter Labanyi, Jamie Owen Daniel and Assenka Oksiloff, Minneapolis, 1993. For a more thorough-going theory of theatre as virtual public sphere, see Loren Kruger, *The National Stage. Theatre and Cultural Legitimation in England, France, and America*, Chicago, 1992, pp. 3–29.
4 The concept of 'invented tradition' is that of Eric Hobsbawm and Terence Ranger, *The Invention of Tradition*, Cambridge, 1983, p. 3. Veit Erlmann uses this concept to illuminate the construction of a folk tradition by New Africans who drew on urban and rural, modern and pre-colonial practices; see Erlmann, *African Stars: Studies in Black South African Performance*. Chicago, 1991, p. 150.
5 Herbert Dhlomo, playwright and essayist of Zulu parentage, argued in the 1930s for the dramatic elements in *izibongo* (praises), but notes that each was delivered by a single speaker; Dhlomo, 'Nature and Variety of Tribal Drama' (1939), reprinted in *Literary Criticism and Theory of H. I. E. Dhlomo*, ed. Nicholas Visser, special issue of *English in Africa* 4: 2 (1977), pp. 23–36. Ruth Finnegan, in her classic account, *Oral Literature in Africa*. Oxford, 1970, notes that South Bantu conventions favour the sequential impersonation of several characters by the storyteller or praise poet, rather than the dramatic imitation of individual characters, each by a designated actor (p. 501).
6 I am drawing here on V. I. Mudimbe's reflections on re-traditionalization as an alternative to rather than repudiation of Western modernization; see Mudimbe, *The Invention of Africa*, Bloomington, 1988, p. 169, and, for further commentary on the ambiguity of re-traditionalization as an alternative road to modernity in the New African context, Loren Kruger, 'Placing the "New Africans" in the "Old" South Africa: Drama, Modernity and Racial Identities in Johannesburg, circa 1935', *Modernism/ Modernity*, 1: 2 (1994), pp. 117–19.
7 C. H. Caldecott (son of the impresario, A. T.) *Descriptive History of the Zulu Kafirs*. London, 1853, p. 26. For detailed comments, see Elizabeth Dell, 'Museums and the Re-presentation of "Savage South Africa" to 1910'. Ph.D Dissertation, School of Oriental and African Studies, University of London, 1993.
8 T. C. Lloyd, 'The Bantu Tread the Footlights'. *South African Opinion* (8 March 1935), pp. 3–5.
9 David Coplan, *In Township Tonight!*, London, 1985, p. 127.
10 Albert Gérard, *Four African Literatures*, Berkeley, 1971, p. 197; Kavanagh, p. 45.
11 Bertha Slosberg, *Pagan Tapestry*, London, 1939, p. 194.
12 Slosberg, p. 192.
13 T. D. Mweli Skota, ed. and comp. *The African Yearly Register. Being an Illustrated National Biographical Dictionary (Who's Who) of Black Folks in Africa*, Johannesburg, 1931, p. 215.

14 See, for example, Coplan, pp. 113–42.
15 *Bantu World* (hereafter BW), 7 May 1932, p. 17; 28 September 1935, p. 4; 14 March 1936.
16 Christopher Ballantine's book and accompanying tape, *Marabi Nights: Early South African Jazz and Vaudeville*, Johannesburg, 1993, definitively demonstrates the diversity of the repertoire.
17 South African Institute of Race Relations: AD843/Kb28.2.2; Historical Papers, Witwatersrand University Libraries.
18 William Mbali, 'The Darktown Strutters and Merry Blackbirds play in Queenstown', BW 24 April 1937, p. 17.
19 Erlmann, p. 63.
20 John Matheus (1887–1983) published *The 'Cruiter*, in 1926, after the first wave of the Great Migration had brought close to a million African-Americans to the Northern cities. The play portrays, in two brief but vivid scenes, an encounter between a share-cropping family and an unnamed white recruiter, distinguished by his formal wear (hat and gloves) as well as formal speech, as opposed to the sharecroppers' dialect. It is not known whether Motsieloa and his company attempted to imitate this folkloristic rendering of African-American speech or whether they followed the example of the Bantu Peoples' Players, who substituted local African English for the American dialects of *The Hairy Ape* in a 1935 production on Johannesburg; see Loren Kruger, 'New Africans and Neo-Colonial Theatre', *South African Theatre Journal* 9: 1 (1995), pp. 29–51.
21 Tim Couzen's study of the playwright and essayist Herbert Dhlomo, *The New African: The Life and Work of H. I. E. Dhlomo*, Johannesburg, 1985, and Veit Erlmann's essay on the composer, Reuben Caluza, Dhlomo's cousin (Erlmann 112–55) are exemplary.

5 National erotica

The politics of 'traditional' dance in Tanzania

Laura Edmondson

The stubborn persistence of the 'primitive' and 'erotic' African stereotype provides rich terrain for ongoing explorations and interrogations. '[T]he stereotype', Homi K. Bhabha declares, 'is a form of knowledge and identification that vacillates between what is always 'in place', already known, and something that must be anxiously repeated' (1994: 66). Bhabha's concept has proven immensely useful as a means of excavating the anxiety that underlies the perpetuation of the 'duplicity of the Asiatic or the bestial sexual license of the African' (66). This postcolonial framework, however, does not account for the proliferation of cultural stereotypes in the domain of African popular culture, where the colonial gaze presumably does not need to be affirmed. In my first encounter with Tanzanian 'traditional' dance in 1996, I was immediately faced with such stereotypes, even though I was exploring urban popular culture in Dar es Salaam instead of tourist performance 'on safari' in the Serengeti plains. Despite my own anxiety to question and deconstruct these initial images, the stereotypes seemed at first impervious to theoretical tools.

This encounter occurred in a bar called Vijana Social Hall located in Dar es Salaam, the commercial centre of this East African country (5 October 1996). Like countless other bars throughout this city of approximately three million people, Vijana Social Hall doubles as a performance venue for local theatre groups and bands. Mandela Cultural Troupe, which was the group performing that particular night, adhered to the usual vaudeville format that characterizes Tanzanian popular theatre, intermingling a dizzying variety of dances, music, place, and acrobatics in the course of the four-hour performance. This night, Mandela opened with a version of *sindimba*, the most famous – and notorious – 'traditional' dance (*ngoma*) in Tanzania.[1]

As a newly arrived researcher on constructions of gender and national identity in popular theatre, I tried to suppress my unease as I watched the women of Mandela Cultural Troupe dance in a circle, swaying their hips in a sexually inviting way. Meanwhile, the men of the troupe approached them from behind and 'tried out' each in turn. A male dancer with an especially youthful appearance approached one of the older female dancers and ground his hips into hers, eliciting shouts of laughter from the audience: 'She can be your mother! Mind your manners!' The women steadfastly danced in their circle, smiling all the while. I dutifully watched as Western stereotypes of the 'bestial sexual license of the African' and the passive African woman were gleefully played out before my discomfited gaze.

In the course of my fieldwork. I saw *sindimba* performed time and time again, in addition to several other *ngoma* that accentuated the women's erotic movement of the hips and pelvis. In contrast, the male dancers vigorously stamped their feet, turned cartwheels, and improvised comic routines around their pursuit of the ever-smiling, hip-swaying women. I learned that this hip-swaying movement, called *kukata kiuno* (to cut the waist), had become virtually synonymous with the concept of *ngoma* in the cultural imagination. The ubiquity of this image could be explained as an inevitable result of urban commodification in which African traditional dances are appropriated and 'depopularized'. Gaurav Desai describes this process as a means of 'entertain[ing] the urban elite and reassur[ing] the developing nation that it has not ignored its national culture' (1990: 68). It could be argued that a similar process enshrined Tanzanian *ngoma* as a cultural stereotype of African 'tradition'; concomitantly, the female body was appropriated and contained by this repetitive, rotating motion.

This containment, however, occurred through a complex process of inventing, counterinventing, and reinventing tradition. In the course of this article, I examine the state's appropriation of *ngoma* as a national symbol, the transformation of this symbol in the domain of popular culture, and its recent incarnation as a tourist attraction. Through an interrogation of the smiling, hip-swaying women in *sindimba*, the following analysis pays tribute to the multiple interactions among performers, audiences, and the state, as well as introduces the global factor of cultural tourism. The contextualization of *ngoma* in this network of forces foregrounds the underlying anxiety that sustains this cultural image of the sexualized, passive Tanzanian woman.

Of course, a blanket categorization of *ngoma* as commodified would dismiss the agency of performers and spectators in the moment of performance. The final section of this article investigates a provocative example of how women seize the ' "right" to signify from the periphery of authorized power and privilege' (Bhabha 1994: 2) in *ngoma* through the employment of 'tradition' as a resource. The 'otherness' of *ngoma* within urban society clears a space for certain marginalized ethnic groups in which difference is *recognized* instead of denigrated and suppressed. These examples are scant in comparison to the numerous performances in which the stereotypes of 'tradition' and 'woman' hold firm, but the vividness of these exceptions complicates the effort to fix Tanzanian dance as a static fact of female oppression and as a tool of national homogenization.

Inventing tradition

In his inaugural speech in 1962, the late Julius K. Nyerere, the first president of Tanzania (then Tanganyika)[2] spoke eloquently of the need to reclaim African culture from the clutches of the former colonial powers: 'Of all the crimes of colonialism there is none worse than the attempt to make us believe we had no indigenous culture of our own; or that what we did have was worthless' (1967:

186). The newly created Ministry of Culture, he explained, would promote the traditional arts as a reminder of the vitality of this precolonial era and thus rekindle 'our pride in our own culture' (187). With these words, Nyerere trod the usual path of Third World nationalisms in his nostalgic construction of a glorious precolonial past. Moreover, in his formation of a socialist Tanzanian society, Nyerere asserted that socialism heralded a return to this past since African society was 'traditionally' communal and harmonious (1968: 12). With these statements, Nyerere smoothly swept the diverse cultures of 120 ethnic groups under the carpet of harmonious village life.

In the attempt to reclaim 'tradition', the newly independent administration proved to be as repressive of certain indigenous structures as the former German and British colonizers had been (Forster 1995: 109). Long-established villages were uprooted in the name of building socialist societies, and secondary school students, teachers, and government officials were frequently transferred to distant regions in order to suppress ethnic ties. A crucial step was the designation of the Swahili language as the national language – a policy that sharply contributed to the decline of ethnic 'traditional' languages. In the realm of *ngoma*, the Ministry of Culture took careful steps to contain dynamic and ephemeral performance traditions through an intricate network of bureaucratic procedures, which required an often bewildering series of permits for performances and travel (Askew 1997: 288). In the interests of nationalism, the state resolutely marched down an authoritative path toward a homogenous society.

In the process of homogenization, *ngoma* legislation and rhetoric consistently revolved around issues of female sexuality and rural, 'primitivist' Tanzania. In a discussion of English nationalism, Bhabha draws attention to 'how the demand for a holistic, representative vision of society could only be represented in a discourse that was [...] obsessively fixed upon, and uncertain of, the boundaries of society and the margins of the text' (1994: 144). This concept suggests that the rural and the female body, both located on the margins of the Tanzanian state, serve as objects of obsession and uncertainty. As such, these bodies are subjected to state control in an effort to maintain a holistic vision of the unified nation. Although this particular article focuses on the politics of gender, an oscillating tension between ethnicity and gender emerges in an examination of contemporary *ngoma* performance.[3]

The rural and the female body, both located on the margins of the Tanzanian state, serve as objects of obsession and uncertainty. As such, these bodies are subjected to state control in the effort to maintain a holistic vision of the unified nation.

This framework helps to illuminate the restricted choreography that currently defines female movement in the ngoma. In the early 1980s, the Ministry of Culture founded the College of Arts in the coastal town of Bagamoyo in order to uphold the preservation of officially sanctioned culture. The college, which accepts 10 to 15 students each year, offers a three-year course of study in drama, music, acrobatics, and ngoma. For the most part, the inventiveness and creativity of the students and faculty prevents the college from becoming a cultural museum, which, as Eric Hobsbawm points out, is a common result of cultural nationalist agendas (1983: 2–4).[4] In the case of *ngoma*, however, this creativity is replaced by conformity to official guidelines that dictate the form's codification and the subjugation of female dancers.

In accordance with the official policy of nationalization, the college teaches its multi-ethnic student body a variety of *ngoma* from across the country which supposedly reflect the diversity of Tanzania's 120 ethnic groups. A closer examination reveals that this apparent diversity can be distilled into a group of eight *ngoma*, all of which have been taught to successive generations of students for years.[5] Like a canon of literature, these dances have been distilled into a representative group of Tanzanian ngoma sanctioned by the authority of the state. The *ngoma* canon is disseminated throughout the country in ways similar to those of literary canons, which are locked into a cycle of self-perpetuation through their repetitive use in education. Students usually graduate knowing only this canon of *ngoma*, which they subsequently use in their own work as teachers in various far-flung regions of the country.

As a representative sample of the 'traditional arts', these *ngoma* reveal an especially troubling politics of gender. At the college, the erotic movement of *kukata kiuno* is markedly subdued in the canonized *ngoma*, in keeping with the state's directives to desexualize the dances (these directives as discussed in more detail below). Even so, the women are marked as subordinate through their restrained movements, which contrast sharply with the male students' expressions of vigor and strength. Moreover, the women almost always exit before the men, leaving the men to dominate the stage in the final moments of the ngoma.

The popular *ukala*, a hunting dance of the coastal Zigua people, is an especially vivid example of female subservience. The men mime the use of a bow and arrow in the course of the hunt, stamping their feet in a vigorous rhythm. Once the men have mimed the successful kill, the women enter for a brief interlude as 'window dressing', during which they gather the meat and celebrate the men's bravery through song.

Even when the *ngoma* is inclusive of a greater variety of female movements, the narrative of restraint intrudes. In a vigorous harvest dance called *bugobugobo*, for example, both men and women twirl hoes over their heads and around their bodies at a dizzying speed. The teachers saw fit to add an introductory skit in which the female dancers greet the men in true 'traditional' fashion by kneeling before them. Of the many versions of *bugobugobo* I observed, only the college adopted this particular introduction, which situated the women's energetic and powerful movements within a framework of submission.

Students invariably responded to my questions about this pattern with the invocation of 'tradition'. They insisted that men were permitted greater freedom of movement because it was 'true' to the way *ngoma* is danced 'in the villages' (*kijijini*) – the usual barometer of a dance's authenticity. In an ironic example of the vast difference between the codified 'invention of tradition' (Hobsbawm 1983) at the college and its fluid existence at the local level, Stumaii Halili, a faculty member, conducted research on *ukala* among the Zigua people. She found that one of the lines in the song, in which the men order the female dancers to prepare the meat, was removed because it was disrespectful to women.[6] The faculty subsequently resolved to discard the offending line in order to conform to the 'authentic' tradition. The teachers and students had become so accustomed to singing this line, however, that they usually neglected to exclude it. Although this forgetfulness is more indicative of the force of a codified habit than a reactionary agenda, the commensurability of this particular habit with the pattern of female oppression in the *ngoma* canon at the college is strikingly coincidental.

In the concluding section of this article I address an example of *ngoma* in which the students challenge this narrative of subjugation. For the most part, however, the creativity and imagination that the students and faculty display in numerous performance traditions at the college become abruptly curtailed in *ngoma*. Representations of ethnicity and gender are thoroughly tamed and controlled, which indicates that a potential source of anxiety for the state has been successfully subdued. Even so, popular culture has managed to subvert the postcolonial government's cultural agenda. In the counterinvention of tradition, the rhetoric of cultural nationalism is playfully defied.

Counterinventing tradition

On the surface, the urban popular troupes in Dar es Salaam mirror the College of Arts in their seeming embrace of nationalist rhetoric, marked by numerous ngoma songs in praise of Tanzanian culture. A closer examination of the popular troupes' *ngoma*, however, reveals that the incessant praise serves as a pretext for the troupe's own particular version of national culture – a 'counter-canon' of *ngoma*. In an intriguing theorization of nationalism, anthropologist Michael Herzfeld suggests the 'possibility of the subtle recastings of official discourses that we might call *counter*inventions of tradition, in which local and minority groups variously (and often discordantly) propose a host of alternative pasts' (1997: 12; emphasis added). The official version of the precolonial past, as adopted by the College of Arts, excludes the erotic dances of the south such as the *sindimba* described above. In contrast, the popular troupes propose an alternative past through their 'subtle recastings' of the *ngoma* canon in which the sexuality of southern *ngoma* prevails.

These recastings can be discerned in the suggestive choreography. Although the popular troupes avoid criticism of the government and the ruling party in their lyrics, their physical movements directly refuse the directives of the state that call for subdued sexuality. The seemingly un-ironic praises can be explained as an 'erotics of politics' (Sommer 1990: 76), in which sexual movements are danced to the tune of official praise. Theatre scholars at the University of Dar es Salaam react uneasily to these spectacles, as demonstrated in Elias Songoyi's study of the commercialization of *ngoma*. After relating his experience of watching a cultural troupe perform the erotic *lizombe* while singing: 'The chairman of Tanzania, Nyerere/Live forever', he rails:

[A]s one watched he [*sic*] could clearly see that there was no correspondence between the vigorous [...] waist wriggling and stamping on the one hand and the song on the other hand. What was all the violent waist wriggling [...] expressing? Happiness? Not at all.

(1983: 34)

Leaving it to the reader to answer the question of what the dance *was* expressing, Songoyi proceeds to lament that in urban versions of ngoma, 'movement is all that matters', as opposed to rural versions in which the lyrics provide a vehicle for responding to immediate local concerns. The movement 'that matters' was, and continues to be, *kukata kiuno*. *Lizombe*, a *ngoma* of the southern Ngoni ethnic group, is second only to *sindimba* in notoriety for its overt simulations of sexual intercourse within its choreography.

Although the popular troupes are commonly blamed for the 'degradation' of *ngoma*, this particular recasting of tradition predated the formation of the popular urban troupes in the 1970s. In the early 1960s, shortly after independence, the government banned sindimba in public performances (Lange 1995: 56), indicating that authorities were already trying to establish a suitably tasteful 'canon' of *ngoma*. These attempts apparently failed; in 1974, Luis A. Mbughuni and Gabriel Ruhumbika referred to *sindimba*'s enduring popularity in their critique of Tanzania's cultural policy:

> If you ask a primary school boy what *utamaduni*, culture, means the answer will most certainly be: *Sindimba* – a traditional dance which apparently is the favourite of school-masters, even though when performed out of context, as it is at the schools, it borders on obscenity.

(276)

Schools were encouraged to teach 'traditional' dance in the interest of fostering national culture. As this passage indicates, however, schools also cast 'tradition' as they saw fit and participated in the widespread eroticization of official rhetoric.

The conflation of *sindimba* with 'culture' endures, despite the Ministry of Culture's efforts to separate the two. Theatre scholar Amandina Lihamba cites a Ministry directive from the 1980s that reiterates its stand on sexually explicit performances: 'It is clearly understood that the guidelines for Tanzania emphasize national integrity and respect. Therefore, the nation forbids all acts which are hooliganistic in nature and corrupt values for the good upbringing of children' (in Lihamba 1985: 480). The directive then mentions nudity, vigorous hip movements 'without cause', and fornication as examples of actions that were unsuitable for the stage. The positioning of *kukata kiuno* in the same category as the sexual act itself implies the magnitude of the officials' distress. More recently, in a 1997 article in the English-language newspaper *The Guardian*, Michael Eneza bemoans 'the continuing waist wriggling culture', calling it the 'African version [...] of the worldwide provocative music [referring to singers such as Madonna and Michael Jackson] which has for years been accepted as the hallmark of Western decadence'. Instead of nation formation, *ngoma* serves as a symbol of nation decay.

A contextualization of *kukata kiuno* clarifies this ongoing controversy. This movement is supposedly taught to girls of certain southern and coastal ethnic groups during initiation rites (*unyago*) as part of learning sexual techniques with a male partner. Although these rites are shrouded in secrecy, they have assumed an apocryphal, titillating status among urban Tanzanians. Men especially delight in sharing stories of what 'really happens' during *unyago*, particularly in the rites of the southern Makonde, whose women are considered to possess special sexual skills in comparison to women of other ethnic groups. Concealed from the public eye, *kukata kiuno* is symbolic of the private space: the 'inside' identified by Partha Chatterjee as the domain of the female and spiritual in postcolonial cultural nationalism (1993: 119–21). The transformation of *kukata kiuno* into public spectacle reverses the usual hegemonic flow of nationalist discourse from center to periphery. Herzfeld notes that: 'In the intimacy of a nation's secret spaces lie at least some of the original models of official practice' (1997: 4). In this instance, the nation's secret space – the female initiation – *is* a model of official practice. Official directives changed in response to audiences' tastes and thus disrupted the hegemonic flow.

This counterinvention, however, largely caters to male spectators. Herzfeld points out that intimate aspects of cultural identity that 'provide insiders with their assurance of common sociality' are transformed into a source of embarrassment when externally placed (1997: 3). As a result of the external placement of *kukata kiuno* – a source of 'common sociality' within the confines of female initiation – female spectators now shun ngoma out of embarrassment and shame. In all of the performances I watched, male spectators occasionally participated in dancing *ngoma*, but only once did I see a woman do so (17 August 1997). Her participation immediately prompted comments from other spectators that she must be intoxicated, with the subtext that only chemical influence could have loosened her supposedly embedded sense of propriety. The postcolonial vogue of *kukata kiuno* has resulted in women's rejection of *ngoma* – a form that has historically served as a uniquely female means of artistic and political expression.[7] In other words, while the cultural troupes have rejected the state's invention of tradition, the female spectators are in turn rejecting the counterinvention. They do not hesitate to participate in other segments of the performance, such as during the plays and musical acts; *ngoma* alone proves too 'embarrassing' for these urban women.

Issues of ethnicity and sexuality overlap in this point of contention, for the intermingling of primitivism and sexuality in the southern erotic female body flaunts the cultural mission that the college supposedly upholds.

Students and faculty at the College of Arts also seem 'embarrassed' over the blatant sexuality of the popular troupes' *ngoma*, and they often expressed concern that I would interpret those versions as 'authentic' examples. Although the college's *ngoma* canon includes various sensual movements for female dancers, such as slow shoulder rotations and a gentle swaying of the hips, the absence of explicit *kukata kiuno* marks the college's alignment with official cultural rhetoric. Students and faculty also disparage the troupes' *ngoma* with the assertion that the eroticism makes the entertainment unsuitable for children, who make up a sizable percentage of urban audiences. In turn, the troupes claim that the college's dances are uninteresting and dull. Issues of ethnicity and sexuality overlap in this point of contention, for the intermingling of primitivism and sexuality in the erotic southern female body flaunts the cultural mission that the college supposedly upholds.

In terms of praxis, however, the college's mission is becoming increasingly rhetorical. Despite the professed distaste for the troupes' erotic choreography, the college increasingly participates in this counterinventing move. Although *lizombe* is excluded from the canon, the 1997 dance majors sought to learn it on their own in response to the dance's popularity with local Bagamoyo audiences. The college's version was more 'tame' than that of the popular troupes; however, it remained undeniably sexual. Instead of male and female couples simulating intercourse, a female dancer performed a solo in which she would slowly rotate her hips as the audience shrieked with delight. *Lizombe* was often the high point of the college's public performances, marking the victory of popular taste even at this bastion of national culture.

Economic factors are highly influential in the college's contradictory attitude toward *kukata kiuno*. The faculty of the college has formed a group called Bagamoyo Players, which, in addition to working on theatre for social change and various development projects, also provides entertainment for expatriate or business functions. Disparagement of the popular troupes' counterinvention aside, the Bagamoyo Players are quick to participate in erotic performances to suit their audience's expectations. When the Bagamoyo Players performed for the National Cashew Association in the elite Kilimanjaro hotel in Dar es Salaam (20 February 1997), the women performed a dance that depicted female initiation, in which the older women are teaching *kukata kiuno* to the young initiate. Before the dance began, the women pretended to chase away the men in the group, scolding them for peeking at a 'woman-only' dance. This tactic called even more attention to the numerous European, African, and Asian men in the audience, who watched as the initiate gradually learned the movement until she closed her eyes in ecstasy, gyrating slowly to the cheers of the other women. Granted, this version of *unyago* was enacted in the (private) confines of one of the most expensive hotels in the city and thus does not signify the public sphere to the same extent as the college's auditorium or Vijana Social Hall. Even so, it pushes officially acceptable limits to the same extent as the performances of the maligned 'immoral' popular troupes.

The force of the counter-canon threatens the country's bastion of cultural nationalism as popular pressures increasingly take precedence over decades of nationalist rhetoric. In recent years, however, the tourist economy has entered to reshape the dominance of southern *ngoma*. In the section that follows, I theorize the emerging patterns of *ngoma* in tourist performance as a *re*invention of tradition. Tourism is linked to nationalism as a hegemonic force that reworks popular conceptions of *ngoma* to suit new audiences and shifting political needs.

Reinventing tradition

An examination of Tanzanian *ngoma* would not be complete without a discussion of tourism, given that the tourist economy is threatening to take up the hegemonic slack left dangling in the wake of socialism's demise.[8] As anthropologist Siri Lange points out, 'Tanzania's cultural bureaucrats have realized that the idea of building a national culture on the many ethnic dances did not work out, but they can still use dance as a symbol to the outside world' (1995: 66). The need for such a symbol has markedly increased since the state has prioritized tourism as a means of economic survival in an attempt to compete with neighbouring Kenya. During 1997, three *ngoma* troupes formed with the express purpose of playing for tourists; their names – Simba, Serengeti, and Kilimanjaro – correspond to three major tourist attractions: lions (*simba*), Serengeti National Park (a favored safari destination), and Mount Kilimanjaro. As implied by their choice of names, they are carefully marketing themselves for a growing tourist audience. In the course of my fieldwork, each troupe approached me with the boast that their work was more 'traditional' than Muungano, Tanzania One Theatre (TOT), or Mandela – the three popular troupes that were the focus of my study. Aware of foreigners' liking for 'authentic' dances, they assumed that these claims would pique my interest.

In general, however, these troupes are more likely to challenge the tourist gaze than satisfy it. The 'invasion' of mass tourism is still relatively new to Tanzania, and local producers of tourist art have yet to become familiar with typical Western expectations of the 'performative primitive' (MacCannell 1992). Furthermore, the legacy of Tanzania's historical emphasis on nationalism pervades even tourist art. The combination of these factors has resulted in tourist performances that do not fit the description of 'savage male' and 'erotic female' typically found in descriptions of tourist performance (Desmond 1997; Balme 1998). Seldom did I see stereotypes of the 'primitive savage' played out; instead, the restrained, subdued quality of the tourist performances seemed more appropriate for an audience of cultural officials than for tourists. Because of this subdued, desexualized quality, I have categorized tourist *ngoma* as a reinvention of tradition, since it has led to a *return* to the 'invention of tradition' seen at the College of Arts discussed above.

This discursive bleeding of nationalist discourse into the domain of tourism is not surprising, considering that the performance of nationalism also demands 'staged authenticity'.

For example, Lange tells of a troupe's performance at a tourist hotel, in which the announcer boasted that none of the dancers were from the places where the various *ngoma* had originated. Lange notes:

> [H]e had internalized the governmental policy of nation-building and de-tribalizing, happily ignorant of the fact that the tourists probably would have been more excited to hear that what they were about to see was the such and such tribe performing their authentic esoteric dances.
>
> (1995: 18)

Although troupes have become more savvy about tourists' preferences since the period of Lange's research in the early 1990s, disruptions of these expectations still proliferate. As revealed in a Swahili newspaper article (Komba 1997), for example, the tourist group Serengeti also participates in the rhetoric of nation-building. The leader of Serengeti, after boasting to the reporter about the number of times his troupe had performed in tourist hotels, proceeds to criticize the popular troupes TOT and Muungano for perpetuating European culture (*uzunguni*). His own troupe, he claims, preserves 'traditional' culture (*utamaduni*). His investment in participating in anticolonial discourse demonstrates that the troupe's alignment with cultural nationalism, even though fellow Tanzanians are hardly the targeted audience.

This discursive bleeding of nationalist discourse into the domain of tourism is not surprising, considering that the performance of nationalism also demands 'staged authenticity'. Dean MacCannell writes that 'tourism is not just an aggregate of merely commercial activities; it is also an ideological framing of history, nature, and tradition; a framing that has the power to reshape culture and nature to its own needs' (1992: 1). This same definition could easily be applied to nationalism, given Nyerere's revision of the African past to conform to socialist ideals and the legislation of 'tradition' enacted by the Ministry of Culture. The 'ideological framing' of both nationalism and tourism require the containment of tradition into a realm of purity, supposedly uncontaminated by modernization and Westernization. Christopher B. Balme identifies the peculiar irony in the 'aporia of the tourist gaze, which on the one hand appears to demand authenticity and on the other works to deauthenticate anything which comes into its field of vision' (1998: 64–5). This irony can be likened to Hobsbawm's 'invention of tradition', a phrase which itself encapsulates the underlying contradiction of cultural nationalism.

This intermingling of tourism and nationalism is most clearly discerned in the performances of gender in tourist ngoma. Since Western notions of African authenticity include stereotypes of the eroticized, passive 'African woman', the tourist economy seems unlikely to disrupt the sexual stereotypes performed in the counterinvention of ngoma discussed above. The rendition of the female initiation ceremony performed by the Bagamoyo Players for the Cashew Association, which was staged for foreign visitors as well as local elites, provides one such example of this eroticization of the female body. This exception aside, however, I did not find stereotypes of either the 'savage male' or 'erotic female' played out. Instead, the tourist choreography often reverted to the 'appropriately' desexualized movements preferred by the state. For example, the troupe Simba performed a version of *sindimba* that was far more restrained than anything I had seen performed by the popular troupes. Although the characteristic *kukata kiuno* remained the defining movement of the female dancers, it was greatly subdued, and the usual segment in which the male dancers 'try out' the females was discarded. Furthermore, the female dancers do not conform to conventional standards of attractive female bodies as defined by the West. In each of the tourist groups mentioned above – Bagamoyo Players, Simba, Serengeti, and Kilimanjaro – the female dancers embody a variety of physical shapes and ages. While this variety apparently pleases the Tanzanian male gaze, it once again confounds the tourist's objectification of the African woman.

In an attempt to 'cash in' on tourist dollars, the popular theatre troupe Muungano created a striking example of 'nationalized' tourist performance. In December 1996, Muungano tried to secure a contract at Nyumba ya Sanaa (House of Arts), an arts-and-crafts shop catering to tourists located next to the Sheraton Hotel. They managed to produce one performance on the evening of 3 December; the admission fee was 3,000 shillings (U.S.$5), three times the cost of their usual performances in neighborhood bars. For this occasion, they eliminated plays from the program, realizing that tourists would be unable to follow the Swahili dialogue. Despite these attempts to conform to a tourist aesthetic, however, they (inadvertently) managed to defy the expectant tourist gaze at every turn. Muungano retained the boisterous and unwieldy quality of its popular performances, with the sound system turned up to top volume despite the intimacy of the performance space. As a result, pained *wazungu* (foreigners, usually with connotations of whiteness) clapped their hands over their ears throughout the show. The Sheraton building looming overhead was unable to dampen Muungano's exuberance; as a result, Muungano failed to secure the coveted contract.

The intermingling of popular culture and the reinvention of tradition meant that Muungano's representations of gender defied tourist expectations at every turn. For example, an abrupt desexualization of *ngoma* signified the discursive meshing of tourism and nationalism described above. Muungano went a step further than the group Simba and dropped *sindimba* from the performance altogether; indeed, the ubiquitous *kukata kiuno* did not make a single appearance throughout the evening. They did, however, include their vigorous and eye-catching version of *bugobugobo*, the harvesting dance often performed at the College of Arts, described above. In addition to the use of twirling hoes, Muungano added a segment in which the male and female dancers marched with wooden guns, followed by a 'gender war' between the men and women enacted through hand-to-hand combat. Instead of the eroticized African woman, Muungano served up images of female soldiers insisting upon their rights. They finished the evening with a round of *taarab*, a genre of musical performance in which Islamic women sing dramatic tales of love and betrayal, which typically cause a stampede of female fans onto the stage to dance and tip the singer. Instead, my fellow *wazungu* seemed more amused by the singer's elaborate sequined gown than impressed by her powerful stage presence.

The Muungano performance provides a reminder of the ways in which *ngoma* exceeds the limits of commodification. Michael Denning has argued that in late capitalism very little cultural production survives other than in the forms of commodities (1990: 9), an argument that seems applicable in the age of the 'new' market-driven Tanzania and the commodification of *ngoma* throughout official, tourist, and popular spheres. Even within this framework, however, moments that invite identification rather than alterity counteract these stereotypes.

Narrative disruptions

The following examples of narrative disruptions fall into two categories – those *ngoma* performances in which ethnic identities are celebrated rather than commodified, and those in which the subjugation of 'woman' is challenged. This division echoes Bhabha's point that marginal communities are focal points of anxiety in the construction of a homogenized nation, as discussed above. The 'either-or' pattern of these examples – either ethnicity is celebrated *or* female subjugation is challenged – serves as a reminder of the systemic control in which *ngoma* is embedded, for I never found the two disruptions integrated into a single performance. Those moments of ethnic celebration were often performed through the objectification of the female body; in turn, those moments of female agency excluded marginalized ethnicities.

The 'either-or' pattern of these examples – either ethnicity is celebrated or female subjugation is challenged – serves as a reminder of the systemic control in which ngoma is embedded, for I never found the two disruptions integrated into a single performance.

Yet the unique role that *ngoma* plays for marginalized ethnic groups in popular theatre cannot be overlooked. Often, in the creative hands of groups such as TOT and Muungano, southern *ngoma* such as *lizombe* and *sindimba* became affirmations of ethnic identity instead of portrayals of the primitivist other. For example, at a performance on 29 June 1997, TOT announced a special 'dance contest' between the Ngoni, represented by *lizombe*, and the Makonde, represented by *sindimba*. It quickly became difficult to see the dancers due to the crowds of spectators swarming onto the stage to tip or dance alongside them; occasionally, some spectators would mock the movements, signifying their allegiance to the rival ethnic group. None of this mockery contained hostility; indeed, the sense of celebration and enthusiasm that pervaded the bar during this contest was unparalleled.

On the other hand, TOT's dance contest could be interpreted as an attempt to channel ethnic identities into carefully contained modes of expression. Once both dances had been performed, the emcee promised that the winner would be announced at the performance the following week. Not surprisingly, no winner was ever declared. The designation of a victorious ethnic group would have contained connotations of tribalism, thus disrupting TOT's rhetorical support of national unity. Also, this celebration could have been allowed precisely *because* of the marginalized status of the Ngoni and Makonde; T.L. Maliyamkono dryly notes that groups such as the Makonde are expected to speak their languages in public 'but it only takes one Chagga or Haya [economically advantaged ethnic groups] to do so for others to conclude that "this is tribalism"' (1995: 45). Southern ethnic groups are considered to be especially impoverished and therefore bear no threat to the nation-state. Even with these considerations in mind, however, the intensity of audience participation suggests that spectators seized the potential of performance to reclaim ethnic identities and refuse the homogeneity of nationalism.

Muungano went a step further and staged a contest between races instead of ethnic groups. During a performance at the College of Arts in Bagamoyo (11 February 1997), Muungano incorporated a 'dancing contest' into *masewe*, a storytelling dance in which the narrative is intermingled with singing and dancing. In this story, a male traveller returning to his home village came across a dancing contest between white and African women. A white woman, signified as a tourist by her brief shorts, was coaxed onto the stage and instructed to follow the lead of the Muungano dancer, who enacted the movement of *kukata kiuno* to the shrieks of the audience. The bewildered tourist awkwardly wiggled her hips, fulfilling her role as 'other' next to the smoothly erotic moves of her African rival. Through an affirmation of racial stereotypes of the 'natural' superior musical and dancing ability of Africans, the contest invited Tanzanians to identify with the Muungano woman, who was loudly cheered. Muungano cleverly reversed the tourist gaze by transforming the typical tourist watching an African dance into a spectacle for the consumption of the Bagamoyo audience.

Through staging a contest, both TOT and Muungano clearly intended to invoke a sense of identification – with either the Ngoni or Makonde, with either the awkward tourist or skilled African. These examples gesture to the potential of *ngoma* as a means of exploring and celebrating ethnic difference.

In each of these examples, however, *gender* difference remained binarized, with the women positioned as subordinate to the men. In the dance contest between the Ngoni and the Makonde staged by TOT, the dancers of *sindimba* enacted a short comic skit in which two male dancers attempted to seduce a woman through their skill. The woman was played by a cross-dressed male, precluding the participation of a female performer in a moment when she could have displayed her own comic skills. Moreover, the racial challenge posed in Muungano's version of the dance contest was enacted on the site of the eroticized female body – dancing, as usual, *kukata kiuno*.

Aside from the startling exception of Muungano's *bugobugobo*, described above in the section on tourism, the passivity of female dancers is a trope repeatedly affirmed in the *ngoma* of the urban popular stage. From a feminist perspective, the outlook for *ngoma* seems rather bleak, since this recourse to sexual stereotyping sharply delimits women's subjectivity. Anne McClintock believes that '[a]ll too often, the doors of tradition are slammed in women's faces' (1995: 385). In the case of *ngoma*, the door seems quite thoroughly slammed in the faces of the women performers, and the female spectators have simply retreated to other segments of the popular performance such as *taarab* music as a more fluid and accessible form of female expression.

Still, a dismissal of urban *ngoma* as yet another example of appropriation and capitalist commodification does not account for the potential for agency in the moment of live performance. Amidst the sexual stereotypes, I witnessed some striking – albeit few – examples of the potential of using tradition to carve out agency which challenge a categorical condemnation of urban *ngoma* as a mode of female oppression.

Once such challenge occurred at the College of Arts during *masewe*, the storytelling dance described above in which Muungano staged a dancing contest between white and African women. At the College of Arts, the third-year dance majors (Robert Ajwang', Deograsias Ndunguru, and Aloyce Makonde) worked with their teachers Basil Mbatta and Luiza Maganga to create a unique expanded version of the dance, which premiered at the end of the term (27 May 1997). In the process of transformation, it became a vehicle of power for Ndunguru, the only woman among the three dance majors.

As explained by Mbatta (1997), women of the southern Yao ethnic group typically used *masewe* as a means to educate young girls during initiation.[9] Reflecting its historical role in female initiation, Ndunguru took the role of storyteller, and a humorous storyline often used to teach the initiates about childcare was adapted. In search of a cure for infertility, the female protagonist of the story travels through Tanzania toward the southern region of Mtwara, where she is told she will find a Makonde *mganga* (healer) equipped with the medicine she needs. She experiences a loosely connected series of adventures along the way, many of which are connected with motherhood. Eventually, the woman finds the Makonde healer who provides her with the needed medicine, coupled with a stern warning that she must never let rain strike the child. She readily agrees and immediately gives birth to a son, Katope. Tragedy strikes when rain abruptly begins to fall, and the woman frantically tries to dodge the raindrops to protect him. At this point, the story usually comes to an abrupt end.

In the course of telling the story, Ndunguru spoke of the woman in the third person, but she frequently assumed the woman's character through her actions. For example, she held the new baby out with pride to the audience and other dancers, and she searched desperately for refuge from the rain at the story's conclusion. Her easy movement through a range of characters and her command of the story meant that Makonde and Ajwang' were continually responding to her lead throughout the dance. Ndunguru, herself a charismatic performer with a strong voice, embodied her role as storyteller with authority and presence.

Although three other students were incorporated into the dance when *masewe* was selected for inclusion in the 1997 National Arts Festival, Ndunguru remained the undisputed leader. For the festival performance (25 September 1996), Mbatta expanded the ending: after the mother loses Katope to the rain, she returns to her husband, who scolds her and drives her into the streets. The new ending was meant to warn parents about the dangers of arranged marriages (Mbatta 1997). Apparently, the new version demonstrated that arranged marriages would result in the unhappy end of *masewe*, in which the courageous woman who had traveled throughout the country is transformed into a forlorn abandoned wife.

Ndunguru, however, had other ideas. When the husband, played by Omari Mwarape, began scolding Ndunguru for losing their son, she responded by pushing him to the floor, startling even Mwarape since Ndunguru had told no one of her plan. As the audience cheered with delight, Ndunguru then pulled a child from the audience onto the stage and admonished Mwarape, mocking him for acting no older than this child. The *ngoma* thus ended with a female dancer seizing the moment and proving her improvisational skill. In a showcase of Tanzanian culture, Ndunguru refused to be contained.

Although these moments caution against a categorical dismissal of ngoma, they also recall the vexing issues that make *ngoma* a site of unease. At the College of Arts, female performers manage to challenge gender norms; meanwhile, on the urban popular stage, spectators work to reclaim ethnic identity in a challenge to nationalist homogenization. This distinction between performers challenging gender norms in Bagamoyo and spectators challenging nationalist norms in Dar es Salaam recalls the oscillating tension between gender and ethnicity, serving as a reminder of the threat that 'tribalism' and female identity pose to the nation. It seems that one cultural 'sore zone' (Herzfeld 1997: 27) can be safely challenged without censure, but never the two shall meet through the performance of *ngoma*.

Given the limited range of choreography for women dancing *ngoma*, it is difficult not to conclude this article on a pessimistic note. Studies of rural *ngoma* are filled with references to the potential of *ngoma* as a means of female empowerment (Mwakalinga 1994; Swantz 1995); however, with the exception of the isolated examples discussed above, the economy of the stereotypical smiling, hip-swaying woman has effectively contained the female dancers in nationalist and urban popular culture. Bhabha, on his part, cautions against using the stereotype as 'the scapegoat of discriminatory practices', describing it as 'a much more ambivalent text of projection and introjection, metaphoric and metonymic strategies, displacement, overdetermination, guilt, [and] aggressivity' (1994: 81–2). The anxiety and desire that circulates around female initiation throughout these various inventions, counterinventions, and reinventions serves as a powerful reminder of the potential of ngoma; however, it is a potential that has been successfully subdued. As a result, the 'African Woman' almost disappears from view, overshadowed by her leaping, aggressive, and/or comic male counterpart. The nation defines her in terms of her ability to 'cut the waist' – smiling all the while.

Notes

1 *Ngoma* is a broad term that includes the drums and music as well as the actual dances themselves. In the context of this article, however, it refers mainly to the movements and the song lyrics. This article is based on fieldwork conducted on the coast of Tanzania from August 1996 to December 1997.

2 Tanganyika was the name of the mainland given by the German colonizers in the 19th century. In 1964, Tanganyika and the island of Zanzibar formed an uneasy union and the name 'Tanzania' was coined.

3 See Edmondson (1999a) for a fuller exploration of the play of ethnicity within ngoma discourse in Tanzania.

4 See Edmondson (1999b) for a more comprehensive discussion of the College of Arts.

5 These eight ngoma include *ukala* of the coastal Zigua, *bugobugobo* of the Sukuma, *mganda wa kikutu* from the Morogoro region, *mawindi* of the Nyaturu (Singida region), *lipango* of the Nyakyusa, and three that are of Makonde/Yao origin *masewe*, *ngokwa*, and *malivata*.

6 The 'offending line' is *mbili mbili kidenyama*, 'You have to prepare it'. Words and translation provided by Stumaii Halili (Halili 1997).

7 See Geiger (1997) for a fascinating description of how ngoma groups provided a means for women to participate in the independence movement.

8 As the result of a sustained economic crisis, Tanzania began a slow transition from a socialist, one-party state to a capitalist economy and a multi-party state in the 1980s.

9 The Yao are related to the Makonde ethnic group: the two groups are occasionally referred to as the 'Yao/Makonde'.

References

Askew, Kelly Michelle. 1997 'Performing the Nation: Swahili Musical Performance and the Production of Tanzanian National Culture'. PhD diss., Harvard University.

Balme, Christopher B. 1998 'Staging the Pacific: Framing Authenticity in Performances for Tourists at the Polynesian Cultural Center'. *Theatre Journal* 50, 1: 53–70.

Bhabha, Homi K. 1994 *The Location of Culture*. London: Routledge.

Chatterjee, Partha. 1993 *The Nation and Its Fragments: Colonial and Postcolonial Histories*. Princeton, NJ: Princeton University Press.

Denning, Michael. 1990 'The End of Mass Culture'. *International Labor and Working-Class History* 37 (Spring): 4–18.

Desai, Gaurav. 1990 'Theater as Praxis: Discursive Strategies in African Popular Theatre'. *African Studies Review* 33, 1: 65–92.

Desmond, Jane. 1997 'Invoking "The Native": Body Politics in Contemporary Hawaiian Tourist Shows'. *TDR* 41, 4(T156): 83–109.

Edmondson, Laura. 1999a 'Popular Theatre in Tanzania: Locating Tradition, Woman, Nation'. PhD diss., University of Texas at Austin.

—— 1999b 'Saving Whiteface' in Tanzania: Intercultural Discomforts'. *Theatre Topics* 9, 1: 31–50.

Eneza, Michael. 1997 'National Dancing Style and Obscenities'. *The Guardian*, 15 November: 6.

Forster, Peter G. 1995 'Anthropological Studies of Kinship in Tanzania'. In *Gender, Family, and Household in Tanzania*, edited by Colin Creighton and C.K. Omari, 70–117. Aldershot, England: Avebury.

Geiger, Susan. 1997 *TANU Women: Gender and Culture in the Making of Tanganyikan Nationalism 1955–1965*. Portsmouth, NH: Heinemann.

Halili, Stumaii 1997 Interview with author. Bagamoyo, Tanzania, 4 April.

Herzfeld, Michael 1997 *Cultural Intimacy: Social Poetics in the Nation-State*. New York: Routledge.

Hobsbawm, Eric. 1983 'Introduction: Inventing Traditions'. In *The Invention of Tradition*, edited by Eric Hobsbawm and Terence Ranger, 1–14. Cambridge: Cambridge University Press.

Komba, Robert. 1997 'Serengeti Yabeza Mipasho ya TOT na Muungano'. *Nipashe*, 25 July: 9.

Lange, Siri 1995 *From Nation-Building to Popular Culture: The Modernization of Performance in Tanzania*. Bergen, Norway: Charles Michelsen Institute.

Lihamba, Amandina 1985 'Politics and Theatre in Tanzania after the Arusha Declaration, 1967–1984'. PhD diss., University of Leeds.

MacCannell, Dean 1992 *Empty Meeting Grounds: The Tourist Papers*. New York: Routledge.

Maliyamkono, T.L. 1995 *The Race for the Presidency: The First Multiparty Democracy in Tanzania*. Dar es Salaam: Tanzania Publishing House.

Mbatta, Basil 1997 Interview with author. Bagamoyo, Tanzania, 24 September.

Mbughuni, Louis A., and Gabriel Ruhumbika. 1974 'TANU and National Culture'. In *Towards Ujamaa: Twenty Years of TANU Leadership*, edited by Gabriel Ruhumbika, 275–87. Nairobi: East African Literature Bureau.

McClintock, Anne 1995 *Imperial Leather: Race, Gender and Sexuality in the Colonial Contest.* New York: Routledge.

Mwakalinga, Mona N. 1994 'How Women Use Dance as a Means of Conscientization: Nsimba Dance as a Case Study'. BA thesis, University of Dar es Salaam.

Nyerere, Julius K. 1967 *Freedom and Unity: A Selection from Writings and Speeches 1952–1965.* Dar es Salaam: Oxford University Press.

—— 1968 *Ujamaa: Essays on Socialism.* Dar es Salaam: Oxford University Press.

Sommer, Doris 1990 'Irresistible Romance: The Foundational Fictions of Latin America'. In *Nation and Narration*, edited by Homi K. Bhabha, 71–98. London: Routledge.

Songoyi, Elias 1983 'Commercialization and Its Impact on Traditional Dances'. BA thesis, University of Dar es Salaam.

Swantz, Marja-Liisa 1995 *Blood, Milk, and Death: Body Symbols and the Power of Regeneration among the Zaramo of Tanzania.* Westport, CT: Bergin and Garvey.

Part II

Performers and performing

6 Individualism and community in the theatre of Serumaga

Andrew Horn

After several well-received international tours of his plays by his own Theatre Limited – Abafumi Company,[1] Robert Serumaga has probably become the best-known East African dramatist to audiences outside the region. This is a result not only of his dedication to the theatre but of his extraordinary entrepreneurial ability, a commercial and publicity sense at least comparable to his acting, directorial and writing talents.[2] But while his skills as a theatre craftsman have been generously acknowledged, and his ambitions as a political figure have been widely noted, Serumaga has often been bitterly criticized for an apparent lack of social commitment and political concern in his plays,[3] quite contrary to most of his contemporaries in East African theatre. This apartness is the inevitable consequence of a radical individualism, tending distinctly towards solipsism, which characterizes all his central characters. It is not that the social and political are absent, for they form the necessary back-drop to each of his five plays and his novel. But however social and political issues may precipitate crises in Serumaga's work, they are never closely examined, receding quickly into the middle distance. For Serumaga's Olympian protagonists are always men apart, what Herman Melville called *isolatoes*,[4] cut off not only from nation and community but from friends, family and in the final exigency of alienation, from self, by madness, hallucination and self-deception.

However self-indulgent they may be, these artists and intellectuals live in a terrifying loneliness. The sensitive individual of heightened, if distorted, perception must face alone the horrors of failure, public exposure and painful self-knowledge. He inevitably bears, in the pattern of romantic individualism, a deep wound, a secret sin, an unrevealed weakness which he tries to conceal behind an elaborate performance. For Serumaga's main protagonist is always an actor: a player, a compulsive raconteur with a slick music-hall patter, whose extravagant rationalizations are woven out of ironic quips and baroque fictions. In the end, however, this central figure – essentially the same character throughout Serumaga's work despite variations of circumstance – is forced to acknowledge that beneath his histrionics, cynicism and cavalier postures of self-confidence, he is a failure.

Serumaga is concerned with both the agony of self-discovery and the tragic collapse of the gifted deceiver. But it is never the character's failure alone. Society is always shown to have betrayed him and forced him into compromise, deceit and degradation: it is, therefore, civil community and its directive polities which Serumaga most condemns. It is this particular attack, not on specific social structures but on human community itself, which goes so abrasively against the grain of East African writing and theatre. For while John Ruganda may call for a moral renewal in *Black Mamba*,[5] Ngugi wa Thiong'o for economic and political reconstruction in *The Trial of Dedan Kimathi*[6] and *Ngaahika Ndeena*,[7] Elvania Zirimu for the revision of traditional social codes in *Family Spear*,[8] Byron Kawadwa for the humanization of administrative authority in *Oluyimba Iwa Wankoko*,[9] Chris Mukiimbi for a reassessment of Buganda's feudal past in *Kikwambaga*,[10] and Nuwa Sentongo for the revaluation of perception and inter-personal obligations in *The Invisible Bond*,[11] only Serumaga rejects the very possibility of progress in confederation. In Serumaga, Hell is not only within oneself but, as for the closeted travellers in Sartre's *Huis clos*, 'other people'.[12]

Serumaga's formative theatre experiences were, unlike most of his East African contemporaries, in Europe where as an undergraduate in Dublin and later as a radio producer in London,[13] he not only saw a good deal of professional theatre but acted on stage and television. Perhaps of greater significance, however, to his development both as actor and playwright (and an influence neglected by other critics) was Serumaga's work in variety and revue as a 'stand-up' comedian. No one in the theatre is more isolated and exposed than the solitary 'stand-up comic', precariously negotiating the shifting moods and disparate interests of an often vocally critical audience, without the support of elaborate staging and, above all, without other actors.[14] This unique loneliness seems to have been for Serumaga emblematic of the isolation of the artist-intellectual. For each of his main characters is a solo showman and each of the plots pivots on this single self-dramatizing figure – one deeply defined introspective Consciousness – around whom other, flatter characters are used merely as foils.

Nihilism and foreclosure: *A Play* (1967)

Serumaga's first staged play was Elizabeth Keeble's Theatre Limited production at Kampala's National Theatre of *A Play*, in October 1967.[15] Performed, like several of his subsequent pieces, without act, scene or interval divisions, *A Play* was written for a conventional box set, proscenium arch and an essentially naturalistic *mise en scène*, although overlaid by an expressionist dream-play. He was later to move farther and farther away from these conservative stage conventions: towards the spareness of absurdist theatre in *Majangwa* (1971); the explosive staging of Grotowski and African ritual in *Renga Moi* (1972); and *Amanyakiriti* (1977).

On the anniversary of his wife's mysterious death, Mutimukulu, the main protagonist of *A Play*, is haunted by an unfocused sense of guilt, precipitating the long central dream sequence in which several vaguely threatening characters remind Mutimukulu of his moral culpability and his human vulnerability. These figures include a distinctly Beckettian pair called John and Peter who, strongly reminiscent of Vladimir and Estragon in *Waiting for Godot*,[16] spend most of their stage time at 'play' (hence the title): 'Let's play a game about death' (p. 93). The action is largely made up of these games: the game of the wife's re-murder (pp. 80–2); the game of 'Heavensgate' (pp. 93–4); and the game of the hanging (p. 95).

In what is the most direct statement of the play's theme, the Head of Mukasa, the Kiganda[17] thunder god,[18] speaks of a guilt that must eventually reveal itself, of lies that must return to harry the liar like a horned leopard:

> Mutimukulu, what have you done? ....
> I am Mukasa, God of thunder and lightning.
> I am crime-is-dry-meat-that-never-rots.
> I am poison, which once eaten will show up sometime.
> Death holds no secrets for me, and I dig guilt out of the darkness of men's souls....
> There is an anthill where I am sitting,
> And you and the truth have parted, and gone your different ways.
> When you meet on the other side of the raised ground,
> The truth will have become a leopard with horns on its head.
> Will you let it eat you, or will you speak out in its face?
>
> (p. 57)

It is significant that this moral foreclosure is pronounced by Mukasa, whom John Roscoe identifies as 'the god of plenty', 'a benign god ... sought to heal the bodies and minds of men',[19] and whom Sir Apolo Kagwa describes as:

> ... very good and kind ... consider(ing) everybody his child, never killing anyone. Whenever he came around all the prisoners on his estates were set free. Whenever a priest committed an offence for which he was to be killed Mukasa offered a bull in his stead ...[20]

Here even the forces of increase and renewal are turned against the *isolato* and become the agents of reduction, slaughter and dissolution.

But if Mutimukulu's torment is guilt, Serumaga never clarifies the reason for it. The wife, Rose, seems to have been shot accidentally by her lovers – perhaps John and Peter (p. 80, p. 100) – who meant to kill Mutimukulu in a chieftaincy struggle (p. 79). Her adultery makes suggestions of her husband's complicity in her death even more obscure.

Also unresolved are the ideological contradictions suggested in Mutimukulu's philosophical exchanges with the Old Man. At first Mutimukulu, once a 'man of principles and convictions' (p. 59), seems to be arguing for social co-operation and communality:

Mutimukulu: Egoism, greed, self-perpetuation, dominance, that's what competition is about.

Old Man: On the contrary: there is no better way of fostering human co-operation and self-improvement.

(p. 75)

But later he turns passionately on the democratic institution of voting in an assertion of autocratic individualism:

Mutimukulu: Vote? The vote! That's what's wrong with this whole place. Every cretin, every putrifying mass of human refuse thinks they can settle all manner of issues by the simplest act of their hands being counted. What makes you think that your two miserable votes can cancel out or even balance my vote.

(p. 77)

The play seems to hover between an exposition of nihilism – life as pointless 'play' between birth and death[21] – and an assertion of a para-human fate which inexorably pursues every misdeed and its perpetrator. Distinctly Roman Catholic references abound[22] – 'Jesus, Mary, Joseph, I will kill you' (p. 90) – and even the judgement of Mukasa has more the texture of Christian damnation than of Kiganda traditional cosmology. Indeed, Serumaga's only published poem, 'End of the Road', is a statement of religious doubt in orthodox trinitarian terms:

> That egg will split into a bird;
> The rainbow is drops of rain
> Seen against the sun.
>
> White hens egg-bound for the market
> The bearded kid is a goat
> A shilling a pound.
> Caterpillar into butter-fly.
> Sperm into man
> No dust, no doubt
> Mystery has left the baobab tree.
>
> My facts are straight now
> But where is the meaning?
>
> I need a symbol
> Fused with a fact
> Or I'll act
> As if
> There were three in one
> Only two remain
> The third is dead.[23]

All here is change – transmutation, division and reconstruction – but without any apparent unifying motive force. The dead limb upon which the trinity is seen to hobble is presumably God. In the end, one wonders whether the 'play' we see in Serumaga's first stage piece is not less that of Beckett's clowns in the *néant* than that of T.S. Eliot's Auto-Catholic Furies in *The Family Reunion*. As these comments suggest, *A Play* is not particularly 'African' in the most parochial sense: its theme is universal, its dramaturgy wholly European and its language (except for Mukasa's few lines) nowhere coloured by the unique locutions and rhythms of Ugandan English. At times the 'Britishness' of the English is quite discordant, cutting across characterization: Mutimukulu calls the Maid 'love' (p. 55), and man's nature 'a ruddy crocodile' (p. 58). This stands in contrast to the conscious use of Ugandan English in the plays of, for example, Ruganda, Zirimu and Sentongo.

It should also be noted that the language of *A Play*, as well as lacking a local texture, often works against Serumaga's superb sense of the theatrical.[24] In, for example, the exchanges between Mutimukulu and the Old Man, a self-consciously gnomic manner, a derivative writing style, and the use of undramatic images more suited to print than to the stage reduce the dialogue to a disjointed series of flatly abstract statements of the 'life is…' variety:

Old Man: Escaping from the prison of your own folly. Life has a substance and a shadow. And more often than not, we chase the shadow and miss the substance. The fault lies with us, not with nature.

(p. 59)

The play is also fractured by the grave discontinuities of structure. When, just after mid-point the focus shifts from Mutimukulu to the extended asides of Peter and John, a wholly different play begins to grow in the belly of the text, as catalysts overshadow the reagents. This digression is all the more distracting for being theatrically far more effective than the main body of the action. Later, the use of a single actor to play both the Old Man and the Doctor (p. 100) serves only to diminish the quality of indeterminate reality which Serumaga has laboured so hard to establish, suggesting that the play's action has been only a lunatic hallucination, a *rêve à clef*, reducing Mutimukulu's existential anguish to a clinical curiosity.

In sum, *A Play* is challenging, if gravely flawed, and clearly demonstrates the thematic dramaturgic concerns, which were to preoccupy Serumaga for several years. It is perhaps best read as an *incunabulum*, pointing towards the playwright's more mature and ambitious work in the 1970s.

Concealments and disclosures: *The Elephants* (1969)

Mutimukulu was played by Serumaga in the 1967 Kampala production[25] and is a prototype of the character recurrent throughout Serumaga's writing: the tortured, isolated individualist. Such a figure is David, in *The Elephants*.[26] A research fellow in an African university not unlike Uganda's Makerere, David has become attached to Maurice Diop, a refugee painter from an adjacent Franco-phone country. David, whose own parents were shot during some past political disturbance (pp. 24–6, pp. 38–9), has hidden from Maurice the fact that his family also have been killed by soldiers (pp. 47–8) and has regularly written letters, posted covertly across the border, purporting to be from Maurice's father:

Yes, I've built a life for Maurice through the written word. It's a web of existence: father, mother, brother and two sisters. Real to him. In here! (*Shows letters.*) I have written it all!

(p. 49)

Into this delicately constructed relationship is thrust Jenny, a white American Peace Corps volunteer who, unknown to David, has been planning with Maurice to be married. (There is no strong dramatic reason for either Jenny or her admirer Richard to be expatriates, except to give the play a cosmopolitan patina and to allow a few tangential swipes at stereotypically depicted white liberalism.) In the final scene the various fictions and obsessions are revealed and the revelations, in turn, destroy Maurice, David and Jenny.

The background to these elaborate concealments and disclosures suggests Uganda, with its vast lake and troubled Francophone neighbours.[27] The civil disruptions in which David's family have died recall Dr Milton Obote's 1966 republican *coup d'état*, the setting for Serumaga's earlier novel *Return to the Shadows*,[28] and the description of David's home – hilly, overlooking a river, amongst coffee and banana shambas (p. 38) – is similar to the West Bugandan settings of *Majangwa* and the novel. But Serumaga has consciously distanced the action from any specific social context: unlike Makerere, his university abuts directly onto the lake shore; the political circumstances of the slaughter of David's parents are never mentioned: and Maurice Diop's surname is distinctively West African (Senegalese). [29] For *The Elephants* is not intended as a social or political statement.[30] It is, rather, an exploration of individual psyches in the process of dissolution and of the 'self-destructive pretence[s]' (p. 48) upon which human egos rely. 'Art,' says David, 'no longer deals with revelation but concealment' (p. 7), as he proceeds, like Mutimukulu, to discover the vital cost of such concealments.

The play's central metaphor, that of the pygmy and the elephant, concretizes the notion first articulated by Mukasa in *A Play*, of the lies which destroy every man from within:

David:	… Do you know the pygmies? Well, they have a most sophisticated way of eating elephants. Poisoned darts and all that are figments of tourist imagination. When a pygmy decides to eat an elephant, he does not kill it. What he does is he gets inside it, and starts eating away. The elephant experiences only slight discomfort, until the pygmy strikes some vital part. It could be lunch time or dinner time. That's when the elephant falls. Do you know that?
Jenny:	No.
David:	Well, when you see a herd of elephants eating grass and thorns, there is probably a pygmy inside every one of them. So I told Richard he was a big elephant, with a little man inside him eating away. He will weaken. In fact, elephants do weaken considerably. In the end they are no better than just big mice.

(p. 32)

As Serumaga explained, when asked by a *Uganda Argus* interviewer why he had earlier intended to call the play 'The Fishnet':

> We all have these holes, and if someone comes along and blocks up these psychological holes then we suffocate. The play is about a man who creates a certain kind of world around himself with the help of his friends. He is not aware of having created this world until the holes in its artificiality are blocked up by someone else. I am interested in a man living in an artificial environment which he has created, unknowingly perhaps. We might see all sorts of weaknesses in this life form, but do we stop to contemplate that if we destroy it, we might destroy the man?[31]

If *The Elephants* shares the thematic concerns of *A Play*, the Beckett/Pinter music-hall qualities of John and Peter also reappear in David, whose patter of philosophical wise-cracks probably owes a great deal to the 'stand-up comic' routines of Serumaga's student days. But now the showmen have moved to centre-stage and been consolidated into a single character: in his story of the pet-food purchaser in Westbourne Grove, David acts out both the grocer and the West Indian (pp. 16–8); in the report of his mother's murder, he is both narrator and little boy (pp. 24–6).

Mutimukulu's assertion that 'life is no more than a communal dream' (p. 9) is further elaborated in *The Elephants* in enactments and concealments, although within a plot as flawed by centrifugal distractions as that of *A Play*.[32] Indeed, in both these early stage pieces, as in *Return to the Shadows*, one has the sense of a striving for a tone of significance which is never quite achieved, of plots which have been only sketchily worked out and must be patched together and swept along by the power of the featured performer for whom the play was conceived, Serumaga himself.

The Olympian in retreat: *Return to the Shadows* (1967–9)

Having examined these two early plays it might be useful to look back at the work which preceded and presaged them, Serumaga's only major non-dramatic piece,[33] his novel *Return to the Shadows*. Written while Serumaga was still living in London,[34] it strikes themes and rehearses narrative forms which deeply inform the two subsequent plays. Here, in Joe Musizi, the 'lawyer, economist and rich businessman'[35] who is the novel's narrator-protagonist, is the prototype of Serumaga's isolated egoist. A man of 'intellectual rationalizations and cynical explanations' (p. 5), Joe has begun as an idealist, full of what his friend Moses calls 'high falutin ideas about African Socialism, African Democracy and African you-name-it-we've-got-it' (p. 139), storing up arms and funds against the opportunity to mount a 'revolution' (p. 45). But he is disillusioned when the childhood friends who are his co-conspirators prove to be as venal and unprincipled as the incumbent politicians they oppose.

As the novel opens, Joe finds himself in flight from the violence of a *coup d'état*. The narrative then charts his arduous journey upcountry to his mother's home, where he finds his family raped and slaughtered and back again to the capital, all his intellectualizations now rendered barren: 'as they went, Joe's hand went to his thigh to take a note but he found that he had nothing to say' (p. 171). Joe's journey is set in a thinly disguised Uganda – the inverted 'Adnagu' (p. 1) – against events very similar to those of 1966, when the then prime minister Milton Obote abrogated the constitution, suspended the president Sir Edward Mutesa (who was also the hereditary Kabaka of Buganda), declared a state of emergency, and ordered the army under Colonel Idi Amin Dada to storm the Kabaka's palace at Mengo.[36] Serumaga, a staunch loyalist and royalist,[37] had reacted deeply, if idiosyncratically, to these events, especially as he had been in Uganda at the time and had undergone indignities at the hands of the military. Obote's radical action had seemed to many conservatives, monarchists and Buganda supremacists to be, in the Kabaka's phrase, 'a desecration', eclipsing traditional feudal personalism with a resolutely populist republicanism.

Yet much of this deeply felt political background remains background, displaced by the novelist's preoccupation with Joe's individual psyche. Joe's credo – Olympian, individualist and detached – is articulated early on:

> ... let fate run its course, get a small area of safety for yourself and hold on to it. The world beyond, its sufferings and its glories, are only the macabre orchestrations of a band of inherently imperfect men. One's duty was to seek a little comfort and not be sacrificed on the altar of an idealism pursued by creatures so obviously unworthy of such providence.
>
> (p. 7)

As later in *Majangwa*, it is society – human community – which is identified as the ultimate source of evil. The individual's achievement is only attained despite society, but his crime is always imposed by and is the direct responsibility of society: 'Then you find when the killing has been done and the destruction complete, a soldier stands, dazed, before the society which forced his hand and warped his consciousness' (p. 22). Here, as elsewhere in his work, Serumaga seems to box himself into a self-contradictory position. Excluding both behaviourism and indeterminism, his preoccupation with the individual moves towards a romantic anarchism. As Moses says of Joe: 'Some of you African Socialists make Adam Smith look flaming red by comparison' (p. 140). Even the dashed revolutionary plans of Joe and his colleagues seem to be without any specific programme. They are to be implemented against a stolid and corrupt mediocracy of 'intellectual mercenaries' and 'assembly line civil servants' (p. 133). But there is no vision offered of what would constitute the new order.

Some years earlier, before he had begun to write seriously, Serumaga had demonstrated a profound discomfort with the options apparently presenting themselves to the newly self-governing nations of Africa:

> Which way are we going to achieve economic development faster? Can we say that with socialist methods we may achieve economic development faster than by capitalistic methods? That is one choice, but the other is whether we

are going to preserve the communalistic elements in the old society and bring them into the new society. Is this a good thing or shall we split our society and become individualistic? This is an ethical choice.[38]

But it was a choice Serumaga was not then prepared to make, as the preponderance of interrogatives in his statement suggests. Even in this early novel, intimations are introduced of the impossibility of consolidation and re-integration, of resolving these tensions between the individual and the community. As his work progresses, Serumaga's voice becomes increasingly that of disillusion and disintegration, of informed and jaded despair.

In style and form, *Return to the Shadows* often seems to be a narrative pressing forcefully towards theatre. Dialogue exchanges have the rhythm and pattern of spoken conversation and could easily have been written for the state. It is hardly surprising, therefore, that Serumaga turned next to drama. In *A Play* may be found distinct echoes of the novel: Joe's 'shadows' – the accusing dead enthroned upon lavatory seats (pp. 91–4) – become Mutimukulu's ghostly visitors; the violent role-playing of the *kondo* (criminal) 'Yakobo' Katende and his wife Rozalia (pp. 102–5) develops into the 'games' of John and Peter, and later of Majangwa and Nakirijja. Even the structure of *A Play* is similar to that of the novel, with its digressive chapters (chapters 5 and 6) which shift focus onto the catalytic characters 'Yakobo' Katende and Jeronimo, as they play-act like John and Peter, around the margins of Joe's nightmare.

The artist compromised: *Majangwa* (1971)

In *Majangwa: A Promise of Rains*,[39] a far more adventurous work than its predecessors, the personal illusions of Joe Musizi, Mutimukulu, and David are more purposefully shaped and the eponymous central character more richly realized. Majangwa was a real person: a travelling entertainer who worked the markets of towns and villages in Buganda some decades ago, achieving early honour as a royal drummer and ending as a cheap and extravagantly degraded buffoon. But this is no historical reconstruction and Serumaga's Majangwa is far more than a mere figure of popular scandal and contemporary folklore.[40] He confronts, more explicitly and vividly than anywhere else in Serumaga, the realities of the artist's role in society.

The first act opens, like so many Ugandan plays, on a stretch of rural road.[41] Majangwa, now in ravaged middle age, and his wife Nakirijja, once an inspired dancer, are preparing to rest for the night. Majangwa begins to recollect his past – selecting, embellishing, revising and inflating himself like '[t]he old frog. One day he puffed himself beyond his size, and he burst' (p. 11). It is Nakirijja, her vitality eroded by years of enervating degradation, who punctures his self-delusions by recalling bitterly what has really happened in their lives. To satisfy his audiences' limitless demands for novelty, she reminds him that he was compelled at first to vary, then to compromise, and finally to debase his performances until his art had turned into an obscene public display of the sex act:

And I told you: don't give in to the crowds. Don't pander to their whims. Stick to the drum I said, and I to the dance. But no. You had to start. Plays you call them, funny words and actions. In between the songs, you talked and played with me. It was all right in the beginning, but the crowds taunted us and asked for one more inch. Then your embraces became kisses, in public, till even these could not satisfy the devil in the audiences. Your speech was gone, together with the drum and song. After that it was only a matter of time before I had my back to the pavement.

(p. 30)

What this erotic spectacle offers the squalid market audiences is more than just passing titillation. It is 'a promise of rains' (p. 20), a tonic for renewal and regeneration, a ritualistic act of sympathetic healing:[42]

Did you think we were cheap entertainers? No, woman. I see it all now. We were the gods' go-betweens, putting bones back into broken limbs. Yes, five shillings and they watched us, and waited and hoped that a whiff of passion would rub off on them and arouse them. The chance of a cure, woman, that's what we were to them.

(p. 21)

But by transferring their own vitality to their audiences in this ceremony of carnal theatre, they themselves have been left barren,[43] impotent. In the first moments of the play Majangwa establishes his concern with the 'mysteries of the womb' (p. 7) in a rapturous panegyric to the mythical mother of Buganda's twin rivers, Mayanja Kato and Mayanja Wasswa (pp. 7–8). Later the couple discuss their failure to produce children:

Nakirijja:	Do you think we will ever have a child?
	(*Silence*)
Majangwa:	(*very sadly*) I don't know.
Nakirijja:	My womb has been silent for too long.
Majangwa:	It may not be your fault.
Nakirijja:	… I wanted a child so much …
Majangwa:	Oh, I don't know, woman. I have drunk from the earthen bowl many times, taken to the root and examined the cock's entrails, but nothing seems to add any edge to my approach. What else can I do but wait?

Like the warrior Renga Moi in Serumaga's next play, they have sacrificed the life of their flesh to preserve and regenerate the flesh of others in the community. Yet, as in *Renga Moi*, the community does not appreciate this sacrifice and even turns upon the sacrificer, destroying not only his house but the very emblem of his art, the drum:

The house. They burnt our house. How can you forget? The flames, the smoke, the ashes. They burnt our house and all our belongings. (*Heavily, after a pause*) They burnt our drum too. (*Silence*) Why did they burn our drum?

(*Silence*) Well, after that we had no strength against the audience. We had to beg. Do as asked. What else? Five shillings is a lot of money when all you ever possessed is a heap of ashes and no drum. Only our ingenuity saved us from becoming eternal beggars.

(pp. 31–2)

Majangwa is thus seen to be only partially accountable for his personal failure. It is society, Serumaga argues, that exploits, exhausts, degrades and eventually discards the artist. In this essentially romantic notion, the artist, like the traditional spirit-medium, purges society's ills by his own suffering and is rewarded only with indifference or hostility:

Majangwa:	I can look back at my life all right …. What I can't look back at without puking my guts out is the society which paid to watch us …. What pleasure did they get out of seeing and not doing? Little men with ten-cent coins in their palms and their hands in their pockets watching the sun and hoping for rain!
Nakirijja:	(*pensively*) Yes we were the pus of a very diseased society.
Majangwa:	On the contrary, we were the wound; the opening through which society got rid of its excess pus. The cure for a diseased people which has to hide behind closed doors, drawn curtains and five blankets just to sleep with their wives.

(p. 15)

In this indictment, the play's own theatre audience are themselves implicated:

Nakirijja:	Where are the crowds now and their five shillings?
Majangwa:	Audiences are fickle, you know that.
Nakirijja:	Where are they?
Majangwa:	Out there.

(p. 13)

In the hope of reinvigorating himself and Nakirijja, Majangwa devises a scheme for turning the tables on his parasitic voyeurs by watching them make love in the back seats of parked cars: 'Tonight, they'll be the performers and we the owners of the five shillings' (p. 23). But, during the brief second act, even this desperate plan to secure compensation from society is frustrated. The apparently arbitrary spot they have chosen on the Kampala–Mityana road is discovered to be the village of Tanda (p. 46) where, according to the Kiganda creation myth, Death descended into the earth and from which he emerges to claim the living.[44] In a terrifying mime (the Theatre Limited production used back-lighting and strobes), Death appears and shatters Majangwa's 'promise of rains', not by killing him but by frightening away the lovers (p. 51). For Majangwa, life remains, to adapt Hobbes's phrase, nasty, brutish and long – a succession of tomorrows without hope: 'It's been a long time. It'll be a long time tomorrow, too. A long way from both the beginning and the end' (p. 44). If Beckett's seminal *Waiting for Godot* posits an endlessly recurring 'now', *Majangwa*, like Athol Fugard's *Boesman and Lena*, presents life as a prolonged attenuation, a slow and painful dismantling.

Majangwa is Serumaga's first explicitly drawn artist[45] and as a theatrical performer he develops the role-playing games of Jeronimo in *Return to the Shadows*, John and Peter in *A Play*, and David in *The Elephants*. He involves Nakirijja[46] in his animated playlet of the anthill razed by a Stirling Astaldi tractor (pp. 32–4), then diverts her with the one-man routines of the 'bunch of bananas' (pp. 42–3) and the tale of Kayikuuzi and Death at Tanda (pp. 47–9). Indeed the whole play is a *tour de force* vehicle for a single actor,[47] an extended virtuoso monologue by Majangwa as he compulsively permutates his memories until he can no longer discern those which are real from those he has fabricated. This close focus on the solo performer represents a formal distillation of Serumaga's notion of the isolated individualist – the *vox clamantis in deserto* – whose spiritual gifts are perverted by a Philistine society and turn destructively inward. In form, *Majangwa* bears an arresting resemblance to Fugard's South African 'road' play *Boesman and Lena*,[48] (although without Fugard's political resonances) in its presentation of dispossessed wanderers yoked by marriage and common humanity, yet threatening each other's delicate tricks of survival. But while Serumaga sees society as a demonic assailant, Fugard sees community as the only salvation, one denied by the cynical divisiveness of an oppressive state.

When *Majangwa* was performed at the Third World Theatre Conference in Manila in December 1971, it was interestingly, Serumaga's acting rather than the play itself which brought the accolades.[49] *Majangwa* seemed too westernized for the Philippine press, which clearly entertained a rather more narrow and unadventurous idea of what African theatre should be than does Serumaga. To this line of criticism Serumaga responds convincingly:

> The traditions of the past can only inspire the present. They cannot satisfy the creative urge of our generation. Between the theatrical technique of the foreign play, the symbolism of tradition and the controversy of contemporary issues, a synthesis of body and spirit must be achieved.[50]

This insoluble and often nebulous dispute over Africanness aside, the play does present substantial problems. The dialogue, thickly aphoristic and metaphorical, sometimes demands the leisure of the book reader rather than the fixed time of a theatre listener. Structurally, Majangwa's brush with Death is less well prepared for than it seems to be in performance. Above all, the play's argument has been criticized by some in East Africa as fundamentally reactionary and suggestive of an unwelcome elitism.

The hero betrayed: *Renga Moi* (1972)

Serumaga's next project with his now renamed Abafumi Theatre Company was *Renga Moi* ('Red Warrior').[51] With dialogue in four Ugandan languages and the music and dances of several regions, it represents an attempt to broaden the ethnic base of *Majangwa*[52] and to reach into the non-verbal expressionism of

African ritual, as perhaps filtered through the theatre techniques of Stanislavski, Grotowski, and The Living Theatre.

Renga Moi is based on an Acoli legend, from northern Uganda, in which the warrior-chief of the Village of the Seven Hills must choose between defending his people from armed attack and completing the ceremonies which will preserve the lives of his newly born twins, during which he is expressly prohibited from shedding blood.[53] Selflessly he decides for the common weal and leads the villagers into battle. But during his absence, grave privation stikes the village and, to propitiate the misfortune-bearing spirits, the powerful priest-diviner[54] (who frames the action with an English commentary and was played by Serumaga), decrees that Renga Moi's twins be sacrificially impaled. Upon return-ing home after successfully staving off the attackers, Renga Moi finds that the villagers decline all responsibility for the deaths of his twins. The warrior turns on the diviner and kills him, but this resolves nothing as the infants are already dead and their twin spirits will surely seek revenge on the father who abandoned them.

Renga Moi is Serumaga's clearest statement of the problem which has been his central concern from the beginning of his writing career. As he said in an interview during the play's London run, 'we are posing a universal question about the choices an individual has to make, between himself and his social commitment'.[55] Renga Moi's choice is to act for the community, but, like Majangwa, he discovers that the community not only undervalues his giving of himself, it ravenously demands more. Like the mob which drained Majangwa's life force and then burned his drum, the villagers of the Seven Hills accepted the warrior's self-abnegatory heroism and then destroyed his very flesh.[56] Social commitment, Serumaga seems to be arguing, is an illusory ideal. The self-sacrificer is betrayed; the brave warrior, like the intellectual and the artist, is savaged by society and remains always an *isolato* – a man alone.

The story of Renga Moi and his village is dramatized through gestural acting,[57] music and the interweaving of local languages, all orchestrated by the participant-narrator, the Diviner. In his figure Serumaga consolidates the theatricality of *Return to the Shadows* and the fictionalizing of the plays (the fabulists John, Peter, David, and Majangwa), by resolving these generic tensions in a return to the local tradition of the story-teller's enactments. As Serumaga observed some years earlier: '... the practice of people getting together to watch the story-teller act out his story, or to hear a musician like the famous Sekinnoomu of Uganda relate a tale of trenchant social criticism, dramatized in voice, movement and the music of his *ndingidi*,[58] has been with us for centuries. And this is the true theatre of East Africa.[59] It was therefore appropriate that with this production Serumaga's troupe changed its name to *Abafumi* – the story-tellers.

Although the play's array of tongues, use of total theatre and open staging techniques, inclusion of spectacular dances like *larakaraka* and *otole* and adapt-ation of wrenching communal rituals elicits a greater visceral than intellectual response, it is wrong to conclude, as have some, that it lacks either design or programmatic purpose. Serumaga seems to be working towards the development of a non-verbal, theatrical objective correlative. As he argued in his own controversial review of *Renga Moi*, 'The Critical Silence':

> Theatre is first and foremost a visible medium, well placed to trigger off emotions in its victims, through the presentation of concrete images. Where the novel describes, theatre exhibits the real. So that although to the critic more versed in the literary theatre, the Script (capital S please) seemed lacking, the total impact of the play drew its power from its ability to avoid the straight line story, clarify its images by its anti-naturalism and weave its pattern through a juxtaposition of images which aimed at a direct mental association rather than perception by intellectual analysis.[60]

Lewis Nkosi has presented the interesting suggestion that: 'Serumaga's stratagem of staying clear of literal language ... may have been partly self-serving. Given the political situation in that country [Uganda], dialogue in the theatre could have been too dangerously explicit and implicating.'[61] Certainly, while *Majangwa* was written and produced during the first, relatively liberal, year of Amin's rule, by 1972 repression had begun to be far more deeply felt. The official murder in March 1977 of Luganda playwright Byron Kawadwa, whose revival of his early religious folk-opera *St Charles Lwanga* fortuitously coincided with the killing of Uganda's Archbishop Janani Luwum,[62] confirmed apprehensions about the risks attendant on spoken theatre in Uganda. On the other hand, it should be realized that most of what is spoken in *Renga Moi* is in local languages, always considered by uneasy governments to be potentially a more effective medium than the colonial tongue, as theatre is usually acknowledged to be more persuasive than the printed word. Indeed, the arrest by the Kenya Police of Ngugi wa Thiong'o in December 1977, was precipitated not by his revolutionary English novel *Petals of Blood*[63] but by the performance of his Kikuyu play *Ngaahika Ndeenda*, which propounds the same political argument.[64] And yet, if there had been anyone in Amin's State Research Bureau astute enough to contemplate on *Renga Moi* he would quickly have identified the play's thesis – that the man of special qualities should retire from society rather than be involved in and consumed by it – as one which should be comforting to an unstable autocracy.

In Serumaga's most recent work he has continued to move away from the intellectualism of his earlier plays towards extra-verbal expressive forms. A Kenyan review of the 1978 Abafumi production *Amanyakiriti* (*The Flame Tree*) comments that the 'cast became living sculptures' and that the play 'appealed to the deepest emotions through mime, dance and song, leaving the audience awestruck and in some cases in tears'.[65]

Although he is often clearly derivative and prone at times to neglect both idea and form for style, and his polished and startling surfaces may sometimes conceal confused or pedestrian thought, Serumaga does remain unique in East African theatre; a man whose achievement is, admirably, more theatrical than literary and whose work shows a clear and logical development. He is, above all, sensitive to the gallops, lurches, and hiatuses of human speech, to the thrusts and hesitations of human action. The rhythms of his plays are always meticulously calibrated.

But, like his protagonists, Serumaga remains an *isolato* both professionally and ideologically.[66] While so much of contemporary East African writing has been concerned with both a perception of community and a community of perception, Serumaga has persistently argued that community can only be destructive of the individual. Each of his embattled individualists – intellectual, politician, scholar, theatrical performer, and heroic warrior – is crushed by society, turning inwards in an implosive, nihilistic solipsism. Each becomes a strafed consciousness scrutinizing itself, its thoughts centripetal and distorted. This notion of unique-ness – Georg Simmel's *Einzigheit*[67] – is romantic and fundamentally conservative, consistent with training in eighteenth-century liberal economics. But such an aggressive individualism and the solipsism consequent on its frustration have led to the rejection of Serumaga by many in East Africa who, like Peter Nazareth, feel that his 'apparent non-political approach' reveals a 'lack of sensitivity to what is going on'.[68] Be that as it may, Serumaga, unlike his vanquished protagonists, seems to thrive in his chosen isolation.

Postscript

Since his flight into exile in 1977, Serumaga has been the subject of far more attention as a political figure than as a dramatist. In March 1979, when armed opposition to the Amin regime was gaining strength, Serumaga was briefly bruited as a 'strong candidate' for the leadership of a new Ugandan republic.[69] Some weeks earlier, he had been arrested and detained by the Kenya police at Kisumu, near the Uganda border, presumably for anti-Amin activities.[70] But, having only recently suffered the international embarrassment caused by the year-long detention without trial of Ngugi wa Thiong'o, the Kenyan government clearly wished to avoid another *cause célèbre* and released Serumaga within days.[71]

During the short tenure of Yusufu Lule as President of Uganda (11 April–20 June 1979), Serumaga was first named an assistant minister,[72] and was then reshuffled upwards to become Minister of Commerce, only to retreat again into exile and opposition when Uganda's Consultative Council replaced Lule with Godfrey Benaisa.[73] Serumaga's identification with conservative, regionalist Baganda royalists had been thus publicly confirmed. His subsequent emergence as a leader of the 'right-wing Uganda Nationalist Organization (UNO)' and his alleged control of a 'missing arms supply', led correspondent Victoria Brittain to observe that, in the future, 'Mr Serumaga and friends could cause difficulties in Uganda'.[74] There is, therefore, a profound discrepancy between the doctrine of disengagement elaborated in Serumaga's writing and the political activism into which he has thrust himself. But through it all – in both plays and politics – one may discern the figure of the Olympian romantic, the self-dramatizing individualist, the playhouse solipsist, besieged.

Robert Serumaga's death in Nairobi in 1980 was announced after this article had been edited.

Notes

1 Theatre Limited was formed as a professional acting company in 1968, jointly by Serumaga and several other Uganda and expatriate theatre people. See Janet Johnson, 'Theatre Limited', in Serumaga and Johnson, 'Uganda Experimental Theatre', *African Arts*, III, 3, Spring 1970, pp. 54–5. By 1971, the group had become exclusively Serumaga's project, for the production of his plays and the training of young performers. By the time of its participation in London's World Theatre Season of 1975, the troupe had changed its name to the Abafumi ('Story-tellers') Company. In 1977, it transferred its activities from Kampala to Nairobi.

2 Johnson comments that Serumaga's 'knowledge and love of the theatre and his business instincts give the company a sound basis', (op. cit., p. 54). Serumaga also helped to establish Kiyingi Productions Limited, in Kampala, for the marketing of advertising, music, and theatre and spent several years as the Sales Manager (Motor Division) of the powerful Uganda Company. He received an MA in Economics from Trinity College, Dublin, in 1965.

3 See, for example, Peter Nazareth, 'East African Literary Supplement', *Joliso*, II, 1, Nairobi, 1974, p. 13; and Chris Wanjala, 'East and Central Africa', in 'Annual Bibliography of Commonwealth Literature', *Journal of Commonwealth Literature*, VIII, 2, December 1973, p. 14.

4 'They were nearly all Islanders on the Pequod, *isolatoes* too, I call such, not acknowledging the common continent of men, but each *isolato* living on a separate continent of his own.' *Moby Dick*, New York, Rinehart, 1948, p. 118.

5 John Ruganda, *Black Mamba*, Nairobi, East African Publishing House, 1973.

6 Ngugi wa Thiong'o and Micere Githae Mugo, *The Trial of Dedan Kimathi*, London, Heinemann (AWS 191); Exeter, NH, Heinemann Inc., 1977.

7 Ngugi wa Thiong'o and Ngugi wa Mirii, *Ngaahika Ndeenda (I Shall Marry When I Choose)*, Heinemann East Africa, 1980 and Heinemann AWS 1982. It was the production of this play, as part of the community education programme of the Kamiriithu Cultural Centre in rural Limuru, which led to Ngugi's arrest and detention without trial, from 31 December 1977 to Jamhuri Day (12 December) 1978. See Karugu Gitau, 'The Play That Got Banned', *Weekly Review*, Nairobi, 9 January 1978, p. 13; Chris Wanjala, 'Where is Ngugi?' *Black Phoenix*, 2, London, Summer 1978, pp. 23–4; Margaretta wa Gacheru, 'Ngugi wa Thiong'o Still Bitter Over His Detention', *Weekly Review*, Nairobi, 5 January 1979, pp. 30–2. See also Andrew Horn, 'Theatre in Africa: Docility and Dissent', *Index on Censorship*, IX, 1, London, January–February 1980.

8 Elvania Namukwaya Zirimu, *Family Spear*, in Gwyneth Henderson (ed.), *African Theatre*, London, Heinemann (AWS 134): Exeter, NH, Heinemann Inc., 1973, pp. 109–29.

9 Byron Kawadwa and Wassanyi Serukenya, *Oluyimba lwa Wankoko*, unpublished, first performed at the Uganda National Theatre, 6 November 1971, and later presented at the Festival of Black and African Arts and Culture at Lagos, Nigeria, February 1977.

10 Chris Mukiimbi, *Kikwambaga*, unpublished, first performed Kampala, 1972.

11 Nuwa Sentongo, *The Invisible Bond*, in Michael Etherton (ed.), *African Plays for Playing 1*, London, Heinemann (AWS 165); Exeter, NH, Heinemann Inc., 1975, pp. 13–44.

12 '[L]'enfer, c'est les autres', *Huis clos*, 1944, in Sartre, *Théâtre 1* Paris, Gallimard, 1947, p. 182.

13 After completing his studies in Dublin, Serumaga worked as editorial consultant to the Transcription Centre in London and produced the BBC's programme 'Africa Abroad'. See *Transition*, 24, Kampala, January 1966, p. 2; *Transition*, 26, Kampala, 1966, p. 2; and Donald E. Herdeck, *African Authors*, Washington, D.C., Black Orpheus Press, 1973, p. 404.

14 For a particularly harrowing account of one such performer's life, see Albert Goldman, *Ladies and Gentleman, Lenny Bruce*, London, Picador, 1976, New York, Random House, 1974.

15 *A Play*, Kampala, Uganda Publishing House, 1968; republished with *Majangwa*, Nairobi, East African Publishing House, 1974. All parenthetic page references are to the Nairobi edition. A portion of *A Play* was broadcast on the BBC's Radio 3, in April 1971.

16 See Samuel Beckett, *Waiting for Godot*, London, Faber, 1956 New York, Grove. Like Beckett's ravaged clowns, John and Peter are called 'jesters' (p. 65) and 'tramps' (p. 65, p. 66, p. 67, p. 97); their language, larded with theatrical phrases – 'a good line' (p. 65), 'his bit slightly overplayed' (p. 66), 'this is a death cell, not a theatre' (p. 92); and their interactions often in the form of music-hall turns (e.g. the story of the dog and the flag, p. 92). John's 'We must pass the time somehow, before we die ... tomorrow' (p. 92), recalls: Vladimir: That passed the time. Estragon: It would have passed in any case (*Godot*, p. 48); and Estragon: That wasn't such a bad little canter. Vladimir: Yes, but now we'll have to find something else (*Godot*, p. 65).

17 The people of Buganda are the 'Baganda' (singular 'Muganda'), who speak 'Luganda'. The adjectival form is 'Kiganda'.

18 John Roscoe talks of Mukasa as the 'god of the Lake' (Victoria) who 'controlled the storms', *The Baganda* (1911), second edition, reprinted Totowa, Biblio Distributors, London, Cass, 1965, p. 300. But Sir Apolo Kagwa claims that the 'god of the thunderbolt and the lightning' is Kiwanuka, in *Ekitabo Kye Mpisa za Baganda*, Kampala, Uganda Printing and Publishing, 1918, translated as *The Customs of the Baganda*, translator Ernest B. Kalibala, ed. May Mandelbaum Edel, New York, Columbia, 1934, p. 122.

19 Ibid., John Roscoe, p. 290.

20 Ibid., Kagwa, p. 116. This notion of Mukasa's benignity is, however, somewhat tempered by Kagwa's report that when prisoners were killed as sacrifice, the 'head captain ... announced to all of them: "It is not I whom am killing you, or is giving you away to death, but Kibuka and Mukasa are killing you"' (p. 81).

21 Samuel Beckett, op.cit., see Pozzo's 'They give birth astride of a grave, the light gleams an instant, then it's night once more', (p. 89); and Vladimir's 'Astride a grave and a difficult birth. Down in the hole, lingeringly, the grave-digger puts on the forceps. We have time to grow old. The air is full of our cries', pp. 90–1.

22 Similar Catholic influences are discernible in Zirimu, *When the Hunchback Made Rain* and *Snoring Strangers*', Nairobi, East African Publishing House, 1975, and Sentongo, *The Invisible Bond*, op. cit.

23 *Transition*, 26, VI, (1) 1966, p. 44.

24 Adrian Roscoe speaks of 'occasional linguistic ineptness' in *A Play*, 'when the wrong register is used', *Uhuru's Fire*, Cambridge, CUP, New York, CUP, 1977, p. 262.

25 The original Kampala cast of *A Play* also included Rose Mbowa as Rose and the Malawi-born Ugandan poet David Rubadiri as the Mask of Mukasa. (See *A Play*, p. 53).

26 *The Elephants*, Nairobi, OUP, 1971. All parenthetical page references are to this edition.

27 Uganda has for years hosted thousands of refugees from Rwanda, Zaïre and Anglophone Sudan. See United Nations statistics reported in *Transition*, 39, VIII, (2) 1971, p. 56.

28 See pp. 29–32.

29 One should note, however, that specific mention is made of 'Swahili' (p. 31), 'Kiganda poetry' (p. 15), the 'heroic poetry of the Bahima' (p. 31) and a 'Kisoga flute' (p. 37).

30 Bahadur Tejani misses the point when he over stresses the prominence in the play of 'criticism of the attitudes of university academicians, of the greed and narrow vision of westerners who come to East Africa for research, of the romantic vision of Africanists, of the dynamic existence of racial tensions', in 'Robert Serumaga', *African Arts*, III, 4, Summer 1970, p. 78.

31 *Uganda Argus*, 19 September 1969, and excerpted in *Cultural Events in Africa*, 61, London, 1969, p. 3. Even earlier, Serumaga seems to have provisionally entitled the play 'People Who Eat Dead People'; see the programme notes for Theatre Limited's National Theatre production of Edward Albee's *Who's Afraid of Virginia Woolf*, in which Serumaga played George, 28 March 1968; and *Cultural Events in Africa*, 41, 1968, p. 2.

32 In his cursory survey, *African Theatre Today*, London, Pitman, 1976, Martin Banham comments on *The Elephants*: 'Though some of Robert Serumaga's prose is a little forced, the overall impact of his play is very successful', p. 88. Adrian Roscoe (op. cit.) is rather less accommodating: '*The Elephants* ... is a useful example of a play with a measure of psychological power, but which, stylistically, is rather vapid. Except in isolated cases, and despite Serumaga's claim in the introduction that "every word matters", there is neither rhythmic energy nor pungency of statement ... But *The Elephants*' warm reception in Nairobi and elsewhere suggests how skilfully Serumaga has exploited those areas of his craft where he knows his strengths lie', pp. 263–4.

33 A second novel, 'A Whippcot Butterfly', remains unpublished. It is mentioned in the programme notes for the Theatre Limited production of *Who's Afraid of Virginia Woolf*. See also *Cultural Events in Africa*, 41, 1968, p. 2, and 50, 1969, p. 3.

34 See W. Stephen Gilbert's interview with Serumaga in 'Around the World in Thirty Days', *Plays and Players*, XXII, 7, London, April 1975, p. 11.

35 Robert Serumaga, *Return to the Shadows*, London, Heinemann (AWS 54), 1969; Exeter NH, Heinemann Inc., p. 4. All parenthetical page references are to this edition.

36 See, *inter alia*, Ali A. Mazrui and G. F. Engholm, 'Violent Constitutionalism in Uganda', in Mazrui, *Violence and Thought*, London, Longman, 1969; N.J., Humanities Press, pp. 147–62; Mazrui, *Soldiers and Kinsmen in Uganda*, Beverly Hills and London, Sage, 1975, pp. 14–18; Mahmood Mamdani, *Politics and Class Formation in Uganda*, London, Heinemann, 1976; New York Monthly Review, pp. 228–46. Obote's apologia appears as 'The Footsteps of Uganda's Revolution', *East Africa Journal*, V. 10, October 1968. The Kabaka presented his version of these events in his autobiography, *Desecration of My Kingdom*, London, Constable, 1967, pp. 9–26, 181–94, et passim.

37 After the 1971 *coup d'état*, Serumaga produced a film documenting the return from Britain of the Kabaka's body for reburial at Mengo and lauding Amin's overthrow of Obote's government. The film, premiered at Kampala's Neeta Cinema in September 1971, was broadcast several times by Uganda Television.

38 'Talking Aloud on African Socialism', *Transition*, 24, V, January 1966, p. 47, the transcript of a discussion between Serumaga, Anthony Crossland, Ernest Gellner and Paul Mbayi, chaired by Margaret Roberts (Legum).

39 *Majangwa: A Promise of Rains*, Nairobi, East African Publishing House, 1972. All parenthetical page references are to this edition.

40 Serumaga has said of *Majangwa* that it is 'in many ways a synthesis of several strands of my theatrical development ... such, for example, as its use of fact and legend, reality and myth and its exploration of the subconscious fears within a basically conscious level'. See *The Sunday Post*, Nairobi, 1 September 1971; and *Cultural Events in Africa*, 77, 1971, p. 2.

41 See John Ruganda, *Covenant with Death*, 1973, in *Black Mamba*, pp. 71–120; Zirimu, *When the Hunchback Made Rain*, 1970 and *Snoring Strangers*, 1973; Sentongo, *The Invisible Bond*, 1972. One might usefully compare these with Beckett's *Waiting for Godot*, 1955; and Athol Fugard's *Boesman and Lena*, 1969, in Fugard, *Three Port Elizabeth Plays*, London, OUP, 1974, pp. 165–221. For a discussion of this last, see below.

42 For a discussion of theatrical performances as sympathetic magic, see Andrew Horn, 'Ritual, Drama, and the Theatrical: The Case of *Bori* Spirit Mediumship', a paper delivered to the seminar on the Interrelationship of the Arts, Lagos, Nigeria, February 1978.

43 Cf. Lena's childlessness in *Boesman and Lena*: 'One, Outa, that lived. For six months. The others were born dead', p. 193.

44 Majangwa's account of the creation myth (pp. 47–9) – of the first Man, Kintu, his wife Nambi and her brother Death (Walumbe) – is quite orthodox. The myth is presented in full by John Roscoe as 'The Legend of Kintu', pp. 460–4. Roscoe's principal informant was Sir Apolo Kagwa, the Katikiro (Prime Minister) and Regent of Buganda, whose own brief comments on 'Mister Death at Tanda' appear in Kagwa, p. 113.

45 Maurice, in *The Elephants*, is said to have 'taken to painting' (p. 2), but his art is not central to the concerns of the play.

46 A similar device is used in the powerful central scene of John Ruganda's *The Burdens*, Nairobi, East African Publishing House, 1972, pp. 51–64.

47 Serumaga played Majangwa in his own 1971 Theatre Limited production. The only other speaking role was played by a talented young actress, Gladys Nakazibwe, whose performance, although somewhat overshadowed by Serumaga's, was well received by the press. See, for example, 'Insight into Real African Culture', *The Sunday Nation*, Nairobi, 5 March 1972, p. 25.

48 Serumaga saw Fugard's August 1971 production of *Boesman and Lena* at London's Young Vic theatre. But although Serumaga admits that *Majangwa's* final scene was composed only hours before the first performance (see Bill White, 'Uganda's Olivier', *The Sunday Nation*, Nairobi, 30 January 1972, p. 28), most of the play had already been written well before Serumaga's London visit. *Majangwa* also opened in August 1971.

49 See *The Manila Chronicle*, 5 December 1971, and the *Manila Bulletin*, 5 December 1971; both quoted in *Cultural Events in Africa*, 77, 1971, p. 3.

50 Serumaga and Johnson, op. cit., p. 53.

51 *Renga Moi*, 1972, unpublished. The title has been variously translated from the Acoli: as 'A Brave Warrior' by Excalibur, in 'Robert Serumaga Shows You War-torn Village', *Uganda Argus*, Kampala, 12 July 1972, p. 2; as 'The Red Warrior' in the 1975 World Theatre Season (Aldwych Theatre, London) programme and in most articles based upon it. A. C. A. Wright, in 'Some Notes on Acoli Religious Ceremonies', *Uganda Journal*, III, 3, January 1936, explains that the '*moi* name, which is very highly prized, can be gained by killing any person, male or female, full-grown or a child' (p. 187), that the title is adopted at the '*Kwer Merok*', or 'Ceremony for the Killing of an Enemy' (p. 186), and that the new name adopted, ending in '*moi*', is 'usually of untranslatable meaning' (p. 187). In his discussion of Acoli 'warrior titles', in *The Horn of My Love*, London, Heinemann (AWS 147); Exeter, NH, Heinemann Inc., 1974, Okot p'Bitek renders '*Arengo-Moi* … one who kills an enemy after hunting him out of the main body', p. 177.

52 Serumaga has been attacked as a Buganda regionalist. See, for example, Wanjala, op.cit., p. 14.

53 T.T. Steiger Hayley writes, in 'The Power Concept in Lango Religion', *Uganda Journal*, VII, 3 January 1940, that the: 'birth of twins is a happy event in so far as two individuals arrive to strengthen the Clan. But … the presence of *Jok* power thus manifested necessitates magical control by those affected. The twin ceremonies serve to exercise this control', p. 100. Sidney Higgins observes, in 'Acoli Birth Customs', *Uganda Journal*, XXX, 2, 1966, that the Acoli: 'recognize two distinct types of birth, the normal birth and *jok anywala*, the godly birth', p. 175, and that twins are the most common type of *jok anywala*, p. 178. In his 'Songs and Dances of the Acoli', in Denis Hills, *The White Pumpkin*, London, Allen and Unwin, 1975, Okuma Pa'lukobo notes that: 'of all *Jok* (spirit) dances, the *Rut* (twin) is the most important. *Rudi* (twins) are believed to be the special gift of *Jok anyodo* (the spirit of birth), and the wish of the ancestors. *Jok Rut* is performed before the ancestral shine' and is 'intended to persuade *Anyodo* not to call away one or both of the twins. For twins are more vulnerable, more likely to die, than normal infants', pp. 275–6. For discussions of the meaning and nature of *Jok*, over which there is great scholarly controversy, see Okot p'Bitek, 'The Concept of Jok Among the Acoli and Langi', *Uganda Journal*, XXVII, 1, March 1963, pp. 15–29; J.H. Driberg, *The Lango*, London, 1923, pp. 216–68; Renato Boccassino, 'The Nature and Characteristics of the Supreme Being Worshipped Among the Acoli of Uganda', *Uganda Journal*, VI, 4, April 1939, pp. 195–201; Hayley, op. cit.; A.C.A. Wright, 'The Supreme Being Among the Acoli of Uganda – Another Viewpoint', *Uganda Journal*, VII, 3, January 1940, pp. 130–7; N. Akena, 'Lango Religion', *Uganda Journal*, XXIII, 2, September 1959, pp. 188–90.

54 Okot p'Bitek says of the Acoli-Langi *ajwaka* (diviner) that he 'was a consultant psychiatrist, chemist and priest combined', Okot p'Bitek, 1963, op. cit., p. 17.

55 Serumaga quoted in Gilbert, op. cit., p. 14.

56 In another of Serumaga's Christian images, the sacrificial martyrdom of Jesus was suggested by the massive wooden cross, centre stage, before which the Diviner stood. See photographs in Gilbert, op. cit., pp. 11 and 13.

57 In this, Serumaga has been influenced strongly not only by African performances modes and contemporary *avant-garde* western theatre, but by the theatres of the East, particularly Japanese Kabuki and Nō, after the Philippine tour of *Majangwa*. See Barbara Kimenye, *Daily Nation*, Nairobi, 24 November 1972, and White, op. cit.

58 The *ndingidi* is a one-stringed bowed viol.

59 Serumaga and Johnson, op. cit., p. 52.

60 'The Critical Silence', *Uganda Argus*, Kampala, 3 August 1972, p. 4.

61 Lewis Nkosi, 'The British Theatre and Africa', *Africa*, London, March 1976, p. 63.

62 Information based on a report from Nairobi by Victoria Brittain, 'Arts and Africa', BBC Africa Service, 13 March 1977. See also Andrew Horn, *'Uhuru* to Amin: The Golden Decade of Theatre in Uganda', *The Literary Half-Yearly*, ('Africa Number'), XIX, 1, January 1978, pp. 22–49; 'Retreat from Collision', *Time*, 14 March 1977, p. 7; 'The Curtain Closes on Uganda's Theatre', *Viva*, Nairobi, March 1978, p. 93. It was later reported by Charles Harrison on 'Arts and Africa', BBC Africa Service, 12 October 1977, that Kawadwa's successor as Director of the National Theatre, Dan Kintu, had also been killed by the military, as had playwright John Male and John Sebuliba, of the Ministry of Culture. See also Andrew Horn, 'Uganda's Theatre: The Exiled and the Dead', *Index on Censorship*, VIII, 5, September–October 1979, pp. 12–15; Amnesty International, *Human Rights in Uganda*, London, Amnesty International, 1978, pp. 9–10. For further material on Ugandan theatre during the Amin years, see Andrew Horn, 'African Theatre: Docility and Dissent', *Index on Censorship*, IX, 3, May–June 1980.

63 *Petals of Blood*, London, Heinemann (AWS 188) 1977. New York, Dutton, 1978.

64 For a discussion both of the general problem of official censorship in African theatre and of Ngugi's particular case, see Horn, 'Theatre in Africa: Docility and Dissent', 1980, op. cit.

65 'Lively Kenyan Scene', *Viva*, Nairobi, March 1978, New York, Dutton, p. 94.

66 See, for example, the bitter comments on Zirimu, Sentongo, Ruganda, and Bob Leshoai, in 'The Critical Silence'.

67 See Simmel, *Die Probleme der Geschictsphilosophie*. Leipzig, Duncker und Humboldt, 1892, passim.

68 Nazareth, p. 13.

69 Victoria Brittain, 'Uganda Battle Leaves Amin Still Clinging to Power', *Guardian*, London, 19 March 1979, p. 5.

70 Report by Charles Harrison from Nairobi, 'Focus on Africa', BBC Africa Service, 19 February 1979.

71 For a further discussion of this episode, see Andrew Horn, 'Arts Worldwide', BBC Radio 3, 20 February 1979; and Andrew Horn, 'Arts and Africa', no. 269, BBC Africa Service, 22 February 1979, BBC Script Service, p. 5. This latter transcript also includes a general survey of Serumaga's theatre career.

72 Victoria Brittain, 'Uganda Scratches for a Start', *Guardian*, London, 7 May 1979, p. 13.

73 Victoria Brittain, 'Lule Held Under Armed Escort', *Guardian*, London, 7 July 1979, p. 6, and other similar reports.

74 Victoria Brittain, 'Lule Denounces Nyerere's Role in New Uganda', *Guardian*, London, 18 July 1979, p. 6.

7   The gods as guests

An aspect of Kalabari religious life

Robin Horton

The Kalabari people live in some thirty villages in the tidal zone of the eastern Niger Delta. Linguistically they are part of the great block of Ijo-speaking peoples, but they form a distinct sub-group both in dialect and in culture.

So far as the evidence goes, the majority of these villages have always lived by fishing. One or two communities with a fortunate geographical position near the mouth of the New Calabar estuary abandoned this occupation about four hundred years ago for trade with Europe in slaves and oil – whence the great city-state of New Calabar or Owome. But although the switch in economy had some marked effect on the scale and political organization of the groups concerned, they still retain a culture which is basically the same as that of the villages whose inhabitants remained fishermen.

The Kalabari village settlement commonly appears as a mass of mangrove-pole or wattle houses jostling each other in wall-to-wall confusion on a cramped patch of raised mud – though migration inland beginning about seventy years ago brought some villages into tracts of more truly dry land and enabled them to spread out a little. Each village, however cramped, has nevertheless a large central square used for sessions of the village assembly and for religious festivals. Each is made up of a number of descent-groups, whose founding ancestors are generally seen as unrelated to each other, and are often thought to have converged on the present site from very diverse directions. Instead of looking to descent from a common ancestor as the basis of its identity, the Kalabari village looks to a culture common to all its members and distinctive set of laws. Government was traditionally carried on by an assembly of the entire adult male population of the village, which sat in three age-grades and had both legislative and judicial functions. The assembly was presided over by the *Amanyanabo* or village head, who also led the community in war – at least whilst he was young. The *Amanyanabo* was generally chosen from a single descent group, though changes of dynasty were not unknown.

Of the villages who went into trade with Europe, the first and foremost was Owome or New Calabar. The most marked consequence of this change of livelihood was a great increase of population through the buying of slaves for integration into the community as well as for resale, a development probably facilitated by the stress on learnable culture rather than descent as the criterion of membership of any Kalabari community. There was also a concentration of power in the hands of the great traders and their successors. Each of these built up a team of slaves to operate his trading canoes, and when he died his successor assumed authority over these slaves and their descendants. If the trader himself had no sons of adequate ability, an outstanding man of slave birth might succeed him. In the internal affairs of such a trading corporation or 'house', its head had a high degree both of authority and of responsibility for collective welfare. As the house's representative to the state at large, its head also sat in the assembly under the presidency of the *Amanyanabo*. It is a significant pointer to the concentration of power that took place with the change in economy that this assembly consisted no longer of the total adult male population, but of the *Amanyanabo* and house heads only.

But although the City State of Owome was a very different kind of political organization from the fishing village, much else in the culture defied change. The general picture of the world and its working remained essentially the same, and so therefore did ideas about the world of the gods and their relations with men. Although the hectic competition for power and wealth which followed the economic revolution in Owome brought an element of ostentation into those religious practices which were carried out on a house-by-house basis, nothing in Owome religion would be unfamiliar to a fishing villager. Indeed, in fishing village and city state alike the festivals which are the subject of this monograph were once among the culminating events of the year, prepared for and looked forward to for months ahead, remembered and gossiped about for months afterwards. In this intensely pushful, virile culture where the skills of ruthless political struggle, war and head-hunting once engaged every normal man's attention, it may seem strange that so much enthusiasm could be spared for religious activities, and so much admiration spared for those who excelled in the dancing and other skills involved in them. I hope I can convey in the ensuing pages enough of the quality of these occasions to dispel this mystery.

An understanding of the Kalabari world-view, and of the gods' place in it, is essential if sense is to be made of the great festivals of Kalabari religion.

Kalabari divide their universe into two great orders of existence: that of *oju* – the bodily or material, and that of *teme* – the spiritual or immaterial. Things that have *oju* can be seen and touched by anyone suitably positioned to do so, and they are thought of as having definite locations in space. Things existing in *teme* only can be seen by ordinary people when they are very young, but after the first few years of life the accumulated pollution of the material world spoils their senses and they are no longer clairvoyant. To regain this lost faculty, one must submit to a special herbal treatment known as 'clearing the eyes and ears'. (A number of people do this in order to become diviners, since it enables them to carry on conversations with *teme* and to ascertain their will.) Though one can talk about *teme* coming to a certain place and staying there, in other contexts they are spoken of as if they were anywhere and everywhere at once. In this respect, they are 'like the breeze'.

Many *teme* exist without any bodily counterpart – for instance those of the dead and of the village hero-gods. Such *teme* are sometimes referred to as 'the people we do not see'. On the other hand, all things having *oju* also have a counterpart in *teme*; and if they lose this they die (if living) or disintegrate (if non-living). This is true for all objects of the everyday world, and even for certain of the gods, i.e. the Water people. In these cases, it is the *teme* that controls the behaviour of the *oju*, and in this Kalabari compare it with the helmsman of a boat.

Any *teme* can in principle be given prayer and offerings by way of worship or placation. This is one point of the Kalabari saying that if one cuts a stick and pours wine before it, the stick has become a god. In practice, only a limited selection of *teme* are powerful enough to warrant such attentions, though different people will draw different lines between those which are negligible and those which are not. Thus some men will make prayer and offerings to the *teme* of the various parts of their house: whereas the more tough-minded will consider these of too little power to be worth troubling about. It is often stressed, however, that the extent of human attentions can itself influence the power of the god: as Kalabari say, 'It is men who make the gods great'. Fervent worship will add to a god's capacity to help the worshipers; and just as surely the cutting-off of worship will render the god impotent or at the very least cause it to break off contact with its erstwhile worshippers. This fact has more than once been used to put an end to the influence of a god which has started to act maliciously towards its congregation. In one case during the last century, the Owome city-state practised regular cult of a Water Man known as *Owu Akpana* who materialized from time to time in the form of a great shark. After an unusually large number of people had been eaten by sharks in a small space of time, diviners laid the blame on *Owu Akpana* and the council of chiefs decided they must put a stop to his unwelcome attentions. To do this, they had a shark caught and its blood poured into the village well. Everyone was then ordered to drink of the water and this symbolic act of communal rejection was allegedly sufficient to destroy the god's power either for good or for ill.

Kalabari explain the effect of worship on the god by analogy with human beings, whose *teme* become strong and forceful or ineffectual and apathetic in proportion to the approbation they receive from their fellows.

In general, correctly worded invocation and correctly chosen offerings are believed to have an automatic effect in securing what benefits have been asked of the gods. Where prayer and offering fail, a diviner may be blamed for directing suppliants to a god who is not in fact concerned in the situation, or blame may be put upon the incorrect performance of the ritual. 'Man proposes, God disposes' is not a proverb that would make much sense to a Kalabari priest.

Despite individual differences as to what merits worship and what does not, there are two distinct systems of gods whose influence on man and nature is so great that no one disputes the need to take heed to them at every turn.

The first of these systems comprises those gods whom we may call the Arbiters of Form and Process. In giving a broad explanation of the origin and course of the world, Kalabari attribute its creation of the female principle *Tamuno*, and the control of its subsequent course to the male principle *So*. Both of these are thought to be closely associated with the sky: *So*, indeed, seems to be the sky personified. In other contexts, *Tamuno* and *So* are treated as many. Thus everything in the material world has its particular *Tamuno* and *So*. This applies, for example, to each level of social group, where *Ama Tamuno* and *Ama Teme So* (i.e., *Ama* making *So*) respectively control the creation and life course of the *Ama* or village, *Polo Tamuno* and *Polo Temeso* the creation and life course of the *Polo* or compound. *Mbo Tamuno* and *MoSo* the creation and life course of the individual. In the latter case, a person's *teme* is supposed to go before birth to his *Tamuno*, telling the latter what course of life it chooses. *Tamuno* keeps its words in her care: personified, they are the *So* of the individual whose *teme* came before her to speak them. The *teme* itself she sends to combine with a body which she had created in a mother's womb. This is why an individual's destiny or *So* is also referred to as *o fiee boye* – lit. 'What he speaks before he came'.

Kalabari often say that all the various *Tamuno* are yet one great *Tamuno*, and that all the various *So* are similarly one *So*. The paradox in this statement is resolved when we see that what is postulated here is a system in which both *Tamuno* and *So* act in a distinct (and distinctly-named) role towards each entity in the material world. And just as in everyday life we tend to treat the several roles played by a single person as if each were a distinct personality in its own right – think of one's friend who is also a policeman! – so too the several roles of *Tamuno* and *So* are treated in some contexts as if each were a distinct person.

What has been said above should make it clear that the state of everything in the material world can in principle be explained in terms of the system comprised by *Tamuno* and *So* acting in their various roles. In this respect, the system is virtually self-contained. The style of thought behind it is also quite distinct from that which sustains the other great system of gods. Thus *Tamuno* and *So* are defined in terms of functions of an austere and abstract kind – i.e., creation and the control of process. These functions apart, their lives and characters remain blank. No passions, no prejudices, no human quirks. In austerity, they come near to the sort of gods approved of by modern atomic physicists.

The second system of gods is made up of the Village Heroes, the Water People and the Ancestors. Each of these groups is concerned with its own particular range of human and natural situations; but in this each is complementary to the others, and together they too can provide an explanation of everything that goes on in the Kalabari world. Let us look at each group in a little more detail.

ORU – the Village Heroes

Although *oru* exist today in *teme* only, at the times of founding of the various Kalabari villages they lived among men in the material world; and a rich mythology tells of their lives and characters during their bodily existence. According to this mythology, most of the *oru* of any village came to live there after leaving some distinct and frequently unspecified community. Each of the more important *oru* excelled in some particular activity which he or she proceeded to teach their new neighbours. Thus in the city-state of Owome, *Owamekaso* brought and taught the skills of trade, *Ekine ba* the skills of dancing and drumming for the masquerade, *Okpolodo* and *Siriopubo* the skills of various types of war and hand-hunting, *Amakarasa* and *Kugboso* various types of curative and cleansing rite. Sooner or later all the *oru* became tired of life in the village, often because the villagers refused to keep certain taboos which they had laid down as essential to the skills in which they specialized. After warning their people several times without effect, the *oru* vanished one by one, sometimes just disappearing and at others flying off as birds into the sky. Before going, however, each of them laid down instructions that prayer and offering should always be made to them, in return for which they would continue to look after the community from the plane of *teme*. Although they often entrusted responsibility for their cult to the descendants of certain individuals whom they had befriended during their bodily existence, this cult was to be carried on for the benefit of the community as a whole.

OWU – the Water People

Whereas *oru* are closely concerned with the invention and maintenance of human skills, *owu* are concerned with the control of Nature, and especially with those of its fluctuations which human skills are seen as powerless to command. Thus they control the water level and the waves in the creeks, and the movements and depths of the fish shoals. Every *owu* is associated with a particular tract of creek, generally one with clearly-marked geographical boundaries, and people who fish in this area must pay special attention to it if they are to be successful.

Like the *oru*, the more important *owu* are described in a rich mythology. This recounts their life in the town of the Water People below the creeks, and the circumstances in which they first met their worshippers. Unlike the *oru*, however, these gods never lived with men in their villages. Their contacts with men were loose and transitory. Whereas the Village Heroes are concerned exclusively with the collective welfare of their particular human communities, the Water People are not strongly committed to the welfare of particular groups. They can in fact be approached by anyone of any provenance; and they will sell their favours to the highest bidder. This makes them particularly useful in satisfying individualistic aspirations, for which neither the Village Heroes, nor the Dead cater.

DUEN – The Dead

These are the *teme* of human beings which escaped from their bodies at death and continued existence on the immaterial plane. They are believed to retain the character and values they held when alive, and to participate in a society not unlike those of living Kalabari. Like Village Heroes and Water People, the Dead too are portrayed in a detailed mythology describing their life-time in the world of men. The Dead concern themselves with neither villages nor individuals, but with the collective welfare of the descent-groups to which they gave birth; all questions of the rise and fall of the various descent-groups in a community are generally explained by reference to the Dead.

It will be clear from these summaries that Village Heroes, Water People and the Dead are neatly complementary in respect of the social contexts to which their powers are relevant. Village Heroes and Water People are also complementary in their respective influence over human skills and environmental variation. Together, then, these three groups offer means of explanation and control of every situation in the material world. As a system of explanation, they are as self-contained as the system made up of the Arbiters of Form and Process. Indeed, they form a complete alternative to it. Even more remarkable, however, is the utterly contrasting style of thought which lies behind them. In place of the faceless austerity of *Tamuno* and *So* in their various roles, we find a system permeated by a full blooded sense of personality.

Why, we may well ask, this duality of explanatory systems? And why the contrast in the styles of thought underpinning them?

An answer to the first question comes readily enough to mind. In the Kalabari view of the world, certain techniques of invocation and offering correctly carried out are thought to bring automatic response from the gods. Clearly enough, the prospect of such automatic response is a mainstay of men's peace of mind in a difficult and threatening universe: and the inevitable failure of invocation and offering are a nasty threat which presses for some solution, however wishful. One way round this is to lay the blame for failure on mistakes in a very complicated sequence of ritual: room for hope can then be held out in the form of a corrected performance. Such reasoning is very characteristic of the Navaho Indian religion of the New World, whose rituals are by and large of such intricate complexity that possibilities of error are endless. In Kalabari and many other West African religions, the complexity of detail in the procedures of invocation and offering is not great enough to give much scope for this line of thought. Instead, by acknowledging that more than one system of gods is potentially concerned in any given situation, Kalabari are enabled to face and explain failure of worship by the knowledge that they may have been addressing themselves to the wrong person. Who is in fact the right person, in any case, can only be discovered by consulting a diviner. Now any diviner can always be mistaken or fraudulent in his diagnosis; so after a failure one can always hope that another expert will 'see more clearly' and so put one in contact with the god really concerned.

Although this makes the duality of explanatory systems in Kalabari religious thought more understandable, it does not tell us why the two self-contained systems we have outlined above should differ so much in the style of thought that lies behind them. Here, perhaps, we should remember the truism that the gods of any community are caught up in the pressure of a great diversity of human desires and interests; for different interests may press the gods into incompatible moulds.

Both of the two systems of Kalabari gods are activated in people's thoughts by the desire for explanation of some situation as a prelude to its control. But in Kalabari communities as elsewhere, some people at least have an interest in explaining the world which is quite independent of their concern with controlling it. Anyone who has lived in an African village knows that it has as many wiseacres as an English village. Now what interests such people is neatness, simplicity and economy in explanation – everything that happens in the world should be deducible from a few clear cut postulates of great generality. The system of Arbiters of Form and Process – the faceless gods of Kalabari religion – is a perfect answer to their needs.

On the other hand, pressure of a very different kind comes from the desire to participate in a wider-than-human society. This is something weak in some cultures and strong in others, weak in some members of some cultures and strong in others. Witness a culture like that of Nupe where the gods are uniformly treated as pure instruments of environmental control, and never as persons in any fuller sense of the word. In Kalabari, where the reverse is true, there is a great pressure for the elaboration of gods as persons in their full panoply of passions and prejudices, as tangible characters.

The desire to develop the gods as full people must conflict with the desire for neatness and simplicity of explanation. However, by accepting the co-existence of two systems of gods moulded in utterly contrasting styles, Kalabari are enabled to give full vein to both types of interest.

This basic cleavage in the tenor of Kalabari religious thought makes intelligible the difference in approach to the gods of the two great systems. More especially it makes clear why the kind of ritual dramatizations which are the main theme of this essay are developed only for the second of these systems.

On the one hand, with *Tamuno* and *So*, the faceless gods, we find intercourse of a restricted and somewhat arid kind. An invocation is made, an offering given, and the matter is closed but for the awaiting of results. But with the Village Heroes, the Water People and the Dead, approach to them becomes a more elaborate affair, altogether richer in the sentiments it draws upon. As the time of the rituals draws near, a chorus of singers (generally women) chants the praises of the gods in songs which allude constantly to their characters and achievements. Then, after the invocation and offerings, there follows the most notable part of Kalabari religious practice. This involves the dramatization of the gods' presence by human actors who go through sequences of behaviour which in some way or other typify their characters and attributes – a procedure seen by Kalabari as bringing the gods as guests into the village. During such a dramatization, they react as if the gods were human guests of an exalted kind whom it was their business to greet and entertain: and on such occasions Kalabari often talk of people 'playing with their gods'.

It is not difficult to see why such ritual dramas are limited to one of the two systems of gods: of the Arbiters of Form and Process, *Tamuno* and *So*, are not defined by the sort of attributes that could be acted out in any of the ways which we shall shortly describe. On the other hand, the tangible personalities of Village Heroes, Water People, and the Dead cry out for dramatic presentation.

There are three different ways in which human actors are thought to 'bring the gods into the village'. First of all there is the simple mime, in which a man or woman runs through behaviour that exemplifies the character of a god or illustrates an episode in the god's life. This is perhaps the least widely used technique, and is usually subsidiary to the other two. Then there is the masquerade. In this, a man once more mimes the character and attributes of the god; only now he is covered in clothing and a mask, which also symbolize the god. Finally, there is possession, in which the god is alleged to 'come into the man's head' and displace the *teme* in control of his body.

All three kinds of behaviour are closely related in Kalabari thought; for all alike serve to bring the gods into contact with their people. How this can be so is not at once evident to the outsider: for although it is clear in what sense inducing possession brings the god to the community, we need to know more about Kalabari premises before seeing how mime and masquerade can be thought to have the same effect.

The key idea here is summarized in the maxim 'It is with their names that the gods stay and come'. By 'name' in this context is implied any word, object, or act which can be taken to symbolize the god – either its name in the literal sense, the sculpture, the masquerade and its carved head-dress, or the sequence of action by means of which a human being represents it. For all of these, the fact of their presence or occurrence in a given place is enough to secure the presence of the god they refer to. Whether one utters the name of a god three times, drums it three times, makes a new sculpture, purifies an old one, dons a masquerade or acts out behaviour attributes to the god, one is doing something which brings him automatically close because it is his symbol. This is why the mime and masquerade are just as effective means of bringing the gods into the community where they are performed as is the induction of possession. By 'playing' with his impersonator, the villagers are playing with the god himself no less surely than when they confront a possessed medium.

Given their close similarity of meaning for Kalabari, it is not surprising to find that these three means of compelling the presence of the gods are apparent cultural equivalents. Thus ritual for the head of the Village Heroes may involve induced possession in one village and mime or masquerade in the next. Again, someone performing a mime or masquerade may suddenly taken leave of his senses and become possessed by the god he has just been impersonating. In this system of thought it is but a small distance from the close presence of a god brought about by mime or masquerade to actual possession by him.

The various models of dramatization of the gods must now be described in greater detail.

The mime

This, the simplest of the three modes of dramatizing the gods, is generally found as a subsidiary device in rituals where the principal god is brought to life by masquerade or possession. Nevertheless, there are various occasions when it is used alone to great effect.

Most striking is the ceremony of the coming of the 'Dead without Houses', something which formerly took place in several Kalabari communities, either before or after rites for the founders of the various descent groups of the village. Prestige and contentment in the world of the dead depend on the size of one's descent group in the land of the living: the 'Dead without Houses', forgotten and neglected in this world because they have no descendants, are therefore assumed to be the most despised and embittered denizens of the other world. Hence they too must be collectively entertained, lest in their bitterness they upset the feasts of their better-favoured companions. Impersonation of the Dead without Houses is laid on by members of the *Ekine* society, an association I shall mention at greater length in connection with the masquerade.

After the coming of the Dead has been announced by a village crier at sundown, women cook the evening meal and shut themselves and their children into their houses for the night. Then *Ekine* members assemble quietly in the dancing square. A senior member allots the rest to various parts of the village, where one by one they start to call and answer in the weird nasal voice of the dead. Tapping their throats and holding their noses, they give vent first of all to harsh, querulous staccato cries. Gradually they become more coherent, falling into the refrain 'We who cry with tearful voices, we are hungry.' After a while the actors emerge from their various corners and troop around from house to house demanding food and drink from the inmates. Women answer sleepily and crawl off their mats to get out a dish of soup or a bottle of gin put by for this contingency. As they come to the door with their offerings, *Ekine* members scuttle out of sight until they have gone back to bed again, then seize gleefully upon the things put out for them. They wish a loud nasal blessing upon the housewife for health, children and a powerfully amorous husband. Their tour of the village complete, they take its fruits to the house of one of their members and eat them with a good deal of joking about the reluctance of women to get out of bed for them, and some heated discussion about how to proceed against the odd women or child who defied their curfew.

In all this the victims of the mime are as much in on its secret as are the performers. No woman and few children of talking age are under any illusion that their callers are other than human – nor are they supposed to be. Yet when they are ordered to get off their mats and bring out food, they do so with an acquiescence which they never show on other occasions when they consider themselves genuinely imposed upon by the menfolk. Their attitude makes sense only when one remembers the doctrine that 'the gods stay and come with their names'. For the mime here is one form of 'name' for the Dead without Houses and its performance compels their presence. In the sense that the dead are 'with' the human actors, giving food to the latter who are known to be merely greedy is giving food to the spirits, who may be helpful. This too is why the women must keep themselves from confronting the human actors; for in a sense they would also be confronting the gods, and the contact would be one of great danger where such potentially malicious personalities are involved.

The masquerade

Village Heroes, Water People and the Dead are all on occasion represented by means of the masquerade; but those most frequently treated in this way are the Water People. The reason for this is lost in unrecorded history, so we need not waste time in speculating about it. However, we shall take the Water Peoples' masquerade as representative of this technique generally.

In every Kalabari village, responsibility for these masquerades is vested in *Ekine*, an association containing most of the adult members of the community and named after the hero-goddess who is supposed to have been shown the secret of their dancing by the Water People themselves. Entry to this association is secured by finding oneself a member who has been impressed with one's dancing abilities, and who will sponsor one before his associates. A small payment and seven bottles of palm gin must then be given. One of these bottles will be taken to the priest of *Ekine Ba*, who invokes her on the new member's behalf. He asks her to protect her child and to give him strength to 'play her game'. Then he pours a glass of gin to her and smears kaolin on the candidate's forehead. This symbol of association with the gods signifies entry into the association. Finally, the other members escort the novice to his house, where he must entertain them.

In the small fishing villages, *Ekine* is generally concerned with the masquerades of thirty or fifty Water People, whilst in the city-state of Owome the number is probably a little higher. Today, the list of Water People masquerades varies only a little from village to village, though in most cases a single village is cited as the point of origin for a given play. The reason for this seems to be that prominent players in every village have always scoured other communities for new performances with which they could outshine their rivals: after a player has purchased the cult-rights of such a new *owu* from its previous masqueraders, his community can add it to the list of Water People tended by its own *Ekine*.

Each of the Water People tended by the *Ekine* has his own festivals at which he is entertained by the members. The whole cycle of festivals unfolds in a fixed order, which must be rigidly kept. It is generally opened after the periodic festivals in honour of the Village Heroes and Dead have been completed; and the character of the Water People as lords of the creek rather than of the village is dramatically illustrated by the nature of the opening rites. When the time is ripe, *Ekine* members take out a large canoe and go with it to a spot some way away in the open creeks known as the Beach of the Water People. Here they offer a goat to the Water people, begging them to come in from their various creeks as their entertainment is about to start. Getting into the boat again, they return to the village singing *Ekine* songs; the Water People are thought to return in *teme* with them. A day or two later, a dog is given to their patron goddess *Ekine Ba* by her priest. Then in the night the great *Ikiriko* drum which is her special instrument is lowered on to its side; and on the next day the first of the cycle of masquerades comes out to dance to its beat.

Every one of the Water People tended by the *Ekine* is masqueraded and entertained in turn (the lapse of time between one festival and the next may be anything from four days to some months). Then when the whole cycle is complete, a crier comes out one morning and calls upon all the Water People who have been entertained to gather in the dancing place, as their season has come to an end. Soon after this a player of every masquerade comes out into the central square; and now all the masquerades are danced together instead of one at a time as before. This ceremony is known as *Owu Aro Sun* – 'filling the canoe of the Water People'. Finally the whole body of maskers goes down to the special beach known as *Owusera* – 'the resting-place of the Water People'. Screened from the eyes of women they take off their masks. Then they dip themselves in the water – a symbolic gesture designed to speed the *owu* back to their homes in the creeks. *Owu Aro Sun* has been completed and the dancers go home. That evening the *Ikiriko* drum is put down into the village well and the season of the Water People is at an end until the next round of festivals for the Village Heroes and Dead has finished.

In most Kalabari communities the cycle opens with festivals for three or four of the Water People whose masquerades are the property of the community and are produced by the *Ekine* as a whole. These are followed by a succession of festivals for those whose masquerades are the property of a particular descent group; the latter's ancestor either was the first to encounter the god in question or else purchased the rights to his play from a neighbouring community in the distant past. In such cases, though the whole village takes part in the festivals, members of the owning group actually make the offerings and don the masquerades. (Although the cults of these *owu* are organized either on a communal or on a descent group basis, such cults can be transferred from group to group in a way that is never seen in the case of the Dead and the Village Heroes. The most rigid social attachments implied in the definitions of these two categories of god rule out any sort of transfer from one group to another.) The final festival of the cycle is generally a communally-owned masquerade – often that of the most powerful *owu* known to the village. Before the Pax Britannica it seems that the whole cycle seldom took up a whole year, though now for various reasons it may be many years in completion.

The festival of any particular *owu* comes in with a great deal of activity for those who have to sew together the cloths and decorate the wooden head-dresses which cover the dancer as symbols of the god. On the evening before the masquerader comes out to dance, those responsible for the cult come together in the shrine where the head-dresses are painted ready for the performance. A cock, or sometimes a goat, is killed for the *owu* in front of its head-dress, with a prayer which asks that the pollution from those who have handled it should be taken away by the blood of the animal, that the *owu* should spare the dancer any accidents, and that peace, prosperity and issue should come to the owners of the cult. Often a long procession, mostly of women, files in and out of the shrine. Each brings a few pennies to drop before the head-dress with a request that the *owu* take sickness away from her children or protect an unborn child still in the womb. The men of the group concerned bring out their palm gin and as the spirit warms them they start to chant the praise songs of the *owu*. Even if the cult is the property of a single descent group, members of the *Ekine* will nevertheless come round to visit the shrine and swell the noise. Sometimes the whole congregation will sing through till morning, carried along on a mounting tide of euphoria, welcoming in the Water People.

A little after dawn, the *Ekine* drummer calls the maskers to the dancing field. Male helpers crowd into the shrine, sewing and strapping the dancers into the many cloths they must be burdened with. As each vanishes slowly into his cloths, he falls into a nervous silence at the gruelling prospect ahead, and a thoughtful helper gives him a glass of gin for his courage. Where the *owu* is known to be a powerful one, there is added to the prospect of physical exhaustion that of the close presence of the spirit, readily angered at any mistake made. Even if the dancer avoids all error, he may become possessed by the spirit as a consequence of his virtuosity, and this too is a little fearful. Dancing an important masquerade is work for a man of strong *teme* and dancing it successfully one of the most admired achievements in the community.

At last the cloths are sewn and the head-dress secured, and with praise shouts of '*Owu* has come out! *Owu* has come out!' his people take the dancer to the square. As the procession leaves the shrine, an old man of the dancer's family will pour a small libation to the ancestor who first introduced the cult, telling him, 'This your child is going out to the field in your name; give him a quick ear, a smart leg, and let no ill thing harm him in the dance'.

Before he takes to the field, the masker must first go to the tree where stands the shrine of *Ekine Ba*, patroness of the masquerade. Beside the tree waits her priest to whom he gives a small bottle of palm gin. With this the priest invokes the goddess: '*Ekine Ba, Ekine Ba, Ekine Ba!* This is what you have said, that at any time the dancing people are going to bring out *owu*, every one of them who is going to play the *owu* should come before you to give you drink in case he has been polluted by women or some other things. This is *Karibo*: please open his ears to understand the meaning of drums; open his eyes to see everything that may come before him; give him strength to dance the *owu*; let his legs and hands be nimble.'

After the invocation the priest pours a libation of gin before the shrine. The masker cautiously opens his face and the priest tips a glass of gin down his dry throat. Then he bends down, dips his fingers in the earth moistened by the libation and smears it on the forehead and chest of the masker. As he puts on the mud, he soothes the dancer, telling him that with this he is receiving strength and has nothing more to fear. Now, with all pollution gone from him, the masker steps out into the field as the drummer calls the god's name. Out in the middle, with the eyes of all the village on him, the dancer's heart grows big. As he starts into his step, joyful shouts of 'The Water People have come' greet him from all sides. Though in cold blood he acknowledges the distinction between himself and the god of the mask, it is his every movement that compels the presence of the god with him in the dancing arena. It is not hard for elation to blur the boundary of his identity a little, and not far to go before his everyday conscious-ness gives place altogether to something quite alien to it.

The variety of performances carried out by maskers dancing to represent the Water-People makes a summary of their characteristics very difficult. At one extreme we have graphic portrayals of character. There is *Igbo*, a lascivious good-time 'bluffer' who can never resist using up all the family funds in buying the favours of a woman when his father sends him up-river to buy yams; in masquerade, he continuously falters in the serious business of dancing and rushes off for a lecherous advance upon some pretty girl in the audience. There is *Ngbula*, the ugly, deaf and paranoic water-doctor, whose masquerade stares at people as if to read their lips, then rushes savagely at them because he thinks they must have been insulting him in his infirmity. There is *Igoni*, the self-pitying old woman whose own troubles are insufficient and who therefore takes up everyone else's sorrows to slake her thirst for misery: in masquerade, she wanders mournfully about alternately dirging her own misfortunes and those of members of the audience.

Another common content of masquerade is not so much character summary as straight episode from the life of the *owu*. Thus in part of *Ngbula's* play as performed as Teinma there are a series of sketches of dramatic events in his history. Among these are the conflict between *Ngbula* and the fisherwomen of *Degema*, who mistakenly set out their fishing fences in *Ngbula's* private domain; then there is the mounting of King *Amakoro's* boat by *Ngbula* as the King was crossing the New Calabar river. In the *Agiri* play in the village of Bile, there is a conflict between *Agiri* and *Sabo*, the brother of *Agiri's* girl-friend *Data* who unsuccessfully tries to prevent her marriage because of *Agiri's* ruthless nature. In such episodes, the tone is comic as often as it is serious. Sometimes as with *Agiri* the *owu* being entertained is the hero of the fun, sometimes as with *Igoni* the butt of it. Although it is generally the lesser *owu* who are portrayed in a ridiculous light, even the more powerful do not escape a few shafts. But these are occasions of joy for both god and audience, and the god seems to tolerate the laughter of his hosts.

Yet another element, often the one that supplies the heights of climax in these visits of the Water People, is a game of risk played with the young men of the village. A common form of this is where the masker slashes at the audience with a matchet, whilst the young men compete in creeping as close to the menacing figure as possible. It is brought to its most exciting pitch in the *Agiri* play at Bile, where the masker alternately slashes with a matchet and hurls heavy staves in long, well-directed volleys – the supply being kept up to him by a retinue of attendants carrying bundles of these staves.

A typical Kalabari masquerade festival tends to alternate such high-tension bouts in which the Water People show themselves as powerful and ruthless with lighter-hearted sequences involving character sketch and comic episode. Often, as indeed in the *Agiri* play, the principal *owu* dominates the high-tension phases, whilst his followers and minions among the Water People come on for the interludes. This setting-off of successive climaxes of tension with a series of relaxed interludes is a favourite pattern in Kalabari ritual.

Perhaps the most striking development of the masquerade is one which makes use of the custom of which any god or its human representative must always salute other gods when their names are called in the drum. He must do this by pointing either to the appropriate shrine or in the direction of the god's abode. In a few masquerades this has been developed into a competition in the correct answering of drum calls – notably, as one might expect, in the city-state of *Owome*. In this type of performance, several descent-groups of houses bring out their maskers at once, and these are put through their paces one at a time. The central square of the community is generally surrounded by thirty or more shrines of the Village Heroes, whilst yet others lie out of sight; and when each dancer comes out, the drummer dodges about those shrines with his calls until he has run through the lot. Tension mounts as the dancer successfully calls shrine after shrine. When the last one is called there is a wild commotion and the dancer's own housepeople rush on to the field, hoist him on to their shoulders and rush him back to his house to strip the cloths from him before he suffers heat stroke. But whatever his prestige as a result of this performance, his disgrace had he failed would have been far greater. The reason for this is that the masquerade is not only the representation of the particular *owu*, it is also a symbol of the ancestor who introduced it; a symbol, indeed, of all the dancers' ancestors who performed it before him. This association with the ancestors is vividly illustrated by the memorial screens made for the chiefly dead in *Owome*. In these, the human figure is individuated and identified not by portraiture but by a miniature replica of the masquerade head-dress which the ancestor in question introduced or danced outstandingly. In a culture where such store is set by virtuosity in the masquerade, and where a man's prowess with a particular *owu* is one of his most important attributes, this secondary significance is hardly surprising. For the dancer it means that a serious mistake will amount to 'spoiling the name of his ancestors'.

Not only does this imply public shaming of the dancer's whole descent-group. Worse, it puts this group in danger of ancestral anger. Little wonder, then, that a mistake in these performances is so disgraceful. But the very extent of the risk creates just the sort of high-tension ordeal that appeals to Kalabari and undoubtedly adds to their fascination with these drum-answering competitions.

In much of the ritual drama in this culture, religion and recreation are inextricably blended. Men play with gods. In some of these developments of the *owu* masquerade, however, recreation seems to have broken loose from religion. The motives of dancers and audience in the drum-answering competitions are no longer focused on concern for the gods; even less so were the motives of nineteenth century *Owome* chiefs who combed the Eastern Delta for new plays to devastate their rivals. True, most of the performances involved are preceded by prayer and offerings to the gods represented. But in some cases these seem to have become little more than precautionary measures to ensure that no accidents mar the play. Although this applies only to some *Owu* masquerades and chiefly to the *Owome* community, there is little doubt that a secular dramatic form was beginning to emerge from the religious practice. How far this development would have gone had the culture received no violent jolts, we shall, alas, never know.

Although by sheer weight of numbers masquerades for the Water People tend to eclipse those for other gods, some of the latter are of great importance. Perhaps the most striking example here is one that unfortunately died out two or three decades ago. However, as I have cross-checking accounts from two or three old men who attended it in their youth, the outline of the performance seems worth giving.

The festival in question was held for *Ópu So*, head of the Village Heroes in the large village of Ke. The nature of the proceedings is expressed in its name – the Creek Swimming festival. When it fell due, the whole community cooperated in preparing a large canoe. At its completion, a day was decided, and, on the evening before, an offering was made to *Opu So*, begging him to help them in what was to come. Next morning the canoe was dragged into the water, and mounted by a masker representing *Opu So*. At once a dozen young men dived into the water, caught hold of long ropes which had been tied to the canoe and started to tow it across the creek. As the canoe got under way, all the younger age-grades of the village who could swim jumped in after it. The canoe was first of all towed across the creek, then down along the opposite bank; all the while

Opu So as represented by the masker on top poured libations of gin to the Water People of the area. At last, on reaching the mouth of a smaller creek, the canoe came to a halt. The towers simulated inability to pull it any further. Great excitement ran through the audience, for this was the spot commanded by the most powerful of the local Water People – a deaf man who had heard no news of the festival and so refused to let the canoe pass. For some time, *Opu So* continued to invoke him and pour libations; but in vain. Finally, several of the young men swam back to the village, secured new stocks of gin and returned with it to the canoe. Now at last the invocations had their effect on the *Owu*, and there was a wild shout of joy from the entire village as the canoe slowly got under way again and returned to the waterside. That evening the priest of *Opu So* made a further thanksgiving offering to the head of the Village Heroes, and the festival closed with three days' dancing.

This dramatic sequence, however bare the outline now available to us, is a particularly fascinating one; for it gives a vivid, almost diagrammatic statement of the complementary parts played by Village Heroes and Water People in man's struggle with his environment. Man, guided by the Heroes, strives to impose his skills upon the waters, whilst the controllers of the creeks continually oppose him until both he and his village gods recognize their dependence on them and pay respect accordingly. But this is not the whole story. It is clear from my informants that this, like the other dramatic representations of the gods, secured their presence in person. *Opu So* himself was in the canoe; and the safe passage and return of canoe and swimmers despite the opposition of the Water People was an example of his willingness to support the people in their life on the creeks during the coming year. If there were an accident to the canoe or, as indeed happened from time to time, a swimmer failed to return, the god had failed to exert his power over the forces opposed to him, and this was a sign of his anger. In such a case diviners would have to be consulted as to the human errors which were responsible for this, and steps would have to be taken to set them right before the villagers could count on further help from *Opu So*.

Here, then, we see yet another angle to the ritual drama – its use as a device to make the gods show their hands to men. This oracular element is even more important in possession, the last of the three modes of dramatization.

Possession

Where mime and masquerade produced very close association between the dancer and the god represented, inducing possession means compelling a god to take over control of a man's body from his own *teme*. A new personality temporarily guides his behaviour; and when his own *teme* returns to control, it naturally enough knows nothing of what happened in its absence.

Possession is induced in rites for Village Heroes, Water People and more rarely for the Dead. For most of these rites, there is a medium who has been appointed by the cult group after divination to ascertain the god's choice, and who holds this office until death. The man (or woman) must present himself at the beginning of each festival for his god and submit to certain techniques of 'calling the god to enter his head'. Such techniques make use once more of the Kalabari doctrine and 'the gods stay and come with their names'. First of all, as the rite approaches the time appointed for the god's appearance, the medium is dressed in clothes which symbolize the world of spirits – the red woollen cap, the fishing eagle's feathers, the *Ekaki* cloth about the waist. He is taken and made to stand before the shrine of the god where often he is given to hold one of the latter's material symbols. Thus Water People's media are often made to hold paddles bearing reliefs of the python – the usual materialization of this group of gods. Finally, the drummer starts to call over and over again the drum-names of the god; and after a few minutes the god comes. For the outsider, Kalabari possession is often difficult to identify: the gods manifest themselves as more or less coherent actors, and often only a knowledge of the normal personality of the medium shows the way in which the possession is taking place. This difference in personality, however, is often very striking, especially where a normally placid medium changes into a dominating and aggressive god. Unlike the Yoruba, who stress, at least as an ideal, a harmony between the personality of the medium and that of the god, Kalabari stress the fact that a god may select anyone for his medium, even a person of the most improbable character. Indeed, it is those cases where a placid, temperate human being is transformed into an intransigent and aggressive god which Kalabari seem to find the most thrilling of the possession rituals, and which they stress most in reminiscing about such things.

The variety of themes coming up in possession sequences is similar to that encountered in the masquerade. As in the latter, behaviour summarizing the character and attributes of the god bulks large. Thus in the case of the Water People, their connexion with a particular stretch of creek is emphasised in rituals where the medium not only becomes possessed when the canoe carrying him enters his god's domain, but also tries to throw himself overboard into the water beneath which the god is thought to live. Again, the ability of all Water People to materialize as pythons is emphasized in possession dances where the god turns from acting like a man to writhing on the ground and even slithering about in the rafters of houses as the great snakes do. Often there is a demonstration of the relationship between several gods – as in the rituals for the Waterman *Duminea* of the village of Soku, where the god's wife also possesses a medium, and acts as would a human wife preparing her husband for a day's headhunting. Thus she carries a platter down to the waterside where her husband is waiting to depart in his canoe, and in the act of giving it to him as a vehicle for the meat he will kill, she tries frantically but successfully to get into the boat with him. Attendants drag her off, since this is a man's work; and *Duminea* and his helpers paddle off into the creeks alone. Once in *Duminea's* domain, they kill a goat for the god; and the remains of its meat are taken home in the platter brought down to the canoe by his wife. As they return to the home waterside, she is there waiting for *Duminea* like any good wife. She rushes to the canoe to embrace him, and receives on her platter the goat's head – the traditional wife's share of the head-hunter's prey. With this she tears through the village excitedly showing it off, then finally goes back into *Duminea's* shrine.

An element of comedy is not uncommon, especially in the rites of individual Water People's cults started by self-styled media. As the rites connected with these are not under public control, the opportunity for innovation during possession is much greater, and comic elaboration of these performances is probably one of the more effective forms of propaganda for the building up of a clientele. As festivals for the *Owu Ojoye Adamu*, the subject of one of the most important and successful private cults, the medium's body is invaded by a rapid succession of minor Water People – generally a different collection of them at each festival. These minor gods show all sorts of bawdy traits and infirmities such as uncontrollable lechery and elephantiasis of the scrotum; and their antics keep the audience in a storm of laughter between the greater tensions of the festival patron's appearances. They are the clowns which the patron brings with him as his foil.

As in the masquerade, the game of risk is an important feature of possession behaviour, especially where the gods concerned are patrons of headhunting or some other aggressive activity. Typical of such games is the spectacular *Iju Ti* which *Feni Be So*, the patron of headhunting, plays with the young men of Soku village. On the day after an offering has been made to the god, he is called to the head of his medium on a trio of special drums. The young men, dressed in their best clothes and each equipped with a matchet, line out around the cult house clashing their weapons once upon the other to 'shake the god up'. The medium stands impassively at the door of the culthouse, waiting for the drums to take effect. As the drumming and clashing goes on, the whole village streams expectantly into the square. Many take care to station themselves suitably close to half-open doorways or side-lines in case the game becomes 'too hot'. After some minutes of waiting, tremors start to pass down the medium's body; the young men redouble their clashing and the drummer his beat. Suddenly an enormous shudder racks the man, and he rushes out into the square with *Feni Be So* on his head. Whirling an old and villainous sword about him, he nearly decapitates one of the young men, plunges his weapon deep into a house-post, then tears at the drummers and chases them off their pitch. The inflammatory beat silenced, he becomes calmer. Then begins *Feni Be So's* game. As the god approaches each of the young men participating, the latter must hold out the blade of his matchet towards him. If the youth has the nerve to stand his ground, the god may bring down his sword on the matchet with a bone-jarring vertical blow that sends a ring through the village and is answered by a roar of approval – a point of honour. On the other hand, the god may make a sudden horizontal swipe aimed at reaching the body, and the youth must be ready for instant flight if he sees this coming. A variety of nasty wounds awaits the slow and unalert; and several of the older dancers can show a scar from *Iju Ti*. This hectic sport goes on morning and evening for three days; then on the last evening there is a dance of all the players, whose sweethearts and other admirers vie in throwing them coins in token of their admiration. The art of *Iju* playing is to score as many points as possible with the maximum of impudent clowning at the god. The more impudent the player the more pleased *Feni Be So*; for this is a sign of prowess in the pursuits of violence which he patronizes.

And although these pursuits are a thing of the past, an outstanding *Iju* dancer is still a noteable in the village.

As we mentioned before, the oracular element in ritual drama is best developed in possession sequences. Every one of these gods must be in good humour for him to enter a man's head at all, so his very arrival is a sign that nothing major is wrong between himself and his worshippers. The god who refused to come to the medium's head when called would be a portent of major trouble requiring immediate divination and diagnosis. Each such sequence, then, is a way of forcing a god to show his hand; and his reception when he arrives owes to this an intensity of feeling seldom paralleled by the other two modes of dramatization.

Mention has already been made of the possibility of both mime and masquerade passing into possession behaviour. In the case of the masquerade, not only may this happen during an actual performance; the closeness of association established between a really accomplished masker and the *owu* he generally represents is sometimes such that he becomes possessed from time to time even away from his mask. Singing a snatch of the *owu's* songs or even dancing one or two of his steps may be enough to bring the god into his head.

In some masquerades, the performer is expected to await possession before dancing, the god being called to his head by a drummer as in a simple possession rite. This happens in those more violent types of masquerade involving duels of matchet and spear with the young men of the village. In such cases, the idea that the masker is also possessed would seem to enhance the effect created by the masquerade pure and simple; for the implication is usually that the god will be restrained by none of the scruples which might deter a more human impersonator from injuring his fellow villagers or even his close relatives during the course of the play.

These possessed maskers give rise to some curious instances of double-thinking. Thus despite the official dogma about them, they are often treated by individuals as though the masker was in his everyday senses. In one case, a prominent villager who wanted to show off gave a masker money just before a big festival at which the latter was to dance the principal *owu*. The idea was that this would secure him immunity from pursuit during the matchet play, so that he could pose as a figure of nerveless calm whilst all about him dashed hither and thither. The festival came, and the man was all-too-obviously exempt from chasing by the god. Afterwards the village elders, who were angered by this, showed just the same attitude to the masker as had the giver of the money. Instead of regarding the whole thing as coincidence it must have been had the possession been genuine, they gave both briber and dancer a furious reprimand for spoiling the play.

This may sound like an exhibition of cynicism about the whole religious basis of such masquerades; but on Kalabari premises the enactment of the *owu's* representation nonetheless implied his presence. So the action of the elders is more accurately looked at as stemming from a concern from the dramatic impact and vigour of the play and not from a desire to keep up a religious pretence over something they knew to be secular.

In other cases, where the notion that a mimer or masker is possessed does not play such an important part in maintaining the full impact of the proceedings, people are apt to be little concerned as to whether he is or is not dissociated. Some people may judge from the fervour of the play that he is. Others may disagree. Anyway, since for Kalabari mime, masquerade and possession are three ways of accomplishing the same thing, the matter is often of little consequence to anyone but the performer.

All three modes of the ritual drama – Mime, Masquerade and Possession – use much the same range of themes in presenting the gods to their audience. Individual gods are referred to by character summary, biographical incident or allusion to important attributes. Often several gods are referred to by a vivid presentation of the relationship they bear to each other and to the world of men – as where the respective roles of Village Heroes and Water People in the battle of human skill versus environmental forces are given illustration in the Creek Swimming festival at Ke. In all these themes there is a close correlation with doctrinal portrayal of the god's characters and place in the world.

Except where secularization has started in some of the masquerades, the most remarkable feature of these dramas is the intimate blend of religion and recreation to which they so often give rise. It is no coincidence that when they are used to bring the gods to the village as guests, there is generally an important part of the performance of which the word *ti* is used. For the concept *ti* has exactly the same range of application as the English concept of play. It is used in opposition to the idea of work, of games, and sometimes of frivolous treatment of things that should be taken seriously. Thus an angry person may say: *E na ti ma* – 'Do not play with me!'

But it should not be thought because of this that Kalabari religion is a light-hearted one. Not a few of these dramas, as we have seen, conceal the taking of omens about matters of vital importance to the community's very existence. The grim moods of the religion are all too apparent in another type of rite known as *agba*, whose intention is to beg a god to take away some misfortune for which he had been diagnosed responsible. In making *agba*, people go to an appointed place with an offering which they tie up for the god to take away. They make a brief demand that with this he should 'take his hand from them'. Then they disperse without thought of cooking and sharing the meat. The *agba* are not entertainments of the gods: they are more like the grudging payment of blackmail.

By contrast, the *alali* (festivals) which are the theme of this essay are naturally called *ti* because they are occasions of joy for the congregations giving them. Often they are held in thanks for some benefit already received. At other times the joy is in a confident assurance that the gods will continue to see that things prosper as they have done to date. On such occasions, the appropriate way to receive the gods is a light-hearted one, in which the respect due to them is tempered with gaiety and even teasing – as when the young men taunt a matchet-twirling masker. Since the gods are greater in every way than men, the scale of entertainment due to them is correspondingly greater than anything due to one's fellow human beings; and so it is that many religious rites are at the same time the most elaborate and flamboyant recreation periods of the Kalabari year.

During *alali*, one sees the particular style of Kalabari living intensified almost to the point of caricature. Notable in all of them is the predilection for building up every situation into a series of climaxes of increasing tension set off with periods of relaxed calm. At festival times this pattern is magnified tenfold, people go about like sensitive guns ready to be triggered by the slightest vibration; and the living of four months seems compressed into the four days of the ritual week.

One salient feature of Kalabari ritual drama is the relatively poor development of straight acting as compared with masquerade and induced possession. The reason for this may be that such acting lacks characteristics which serve to maintain the distinction between the actor's everyday person and his dramatic role.

In the European theatre, it is possible to maintain this distinction using straight acting alone (a) because the actor is in general not personally known to most of the audience, and (b) because it is possible to use the apparatus of stage and stage-set to emphasize the discontinuity between the performer at work and off-duty. In Kalabari religious dramas the performer is always personally known to his audience; and the value set upon audience participation precludes the use of any device like the stage. Some additional contrivance must therefore be used to preserve the distinction between the actor's role in the drama and his role outside it. One very simple way is to carry out the acting at night – as is done for the Dead Without Houses, and for the night parades of some of the masking Water People. It is much easier for an actor to emphasize the break with his everyday self when his audience merely hears him without seeing him as well; and this perhaps is why most instances of pure acting in Kalabari drama are in fact nocturnal. Presentation of the gods in daytime requires something extra – either the total extinction of one's everyday appearance and style of behaviour imposed by the masquerade; or the striking discontinuity in behaviour which marks the personality dissociation of a genuine possession episode.

It is not for nothing that the mask is often associated in the European mind with so-called 'primitive peoples'. For if they have nothing else in common, people labelled 'primitive' are always dwellers in small-scale societies. Now this smallness of scale creates a grave problem of social organization: it means that one man must often be required to take up several very different roles toward the same set of people, and that these people in turn are required to accept the differences and behave accordingly. Religious drama is by no means the only context in which this problem arises. It is just as urgent where an ordinary villager has intermittently to act as executive of the village body politic, and where people who have known him as a friend suddenly have to accept him as a public disciplinary agent. In such a situation the masquerade is as valuable an aid as it is in the religious drama; and it is not surprising to find a great many small-scale societies in all parts of the world, where the maskers who represent gods in ritual drama also act as executives of the communal authority. Examples near at hand are the maskers of the *Odu*, *Omada*, and *Mmo* cults in Iboland, those of the *Ekpe* cult at Old Calabar, and those of the *Poro* cult in Mendeland. In West Africa, indeed, Kalabari and other Ijo maskers are somewhat exceptional in their lack of political function.

In the large-scale societies of Europe such extreme devices as these are unnecessary. The theatrical actor is scarcely ever a personal friend of his audience members; and the executives of the state have very limited outside acquaintance with members of the public whom they control, discipline and direct. By and large, a change of clothing suffices to do here what masquerade and induced possession are called upon to do in a small-scale African community.

The picture of the world that makes sense of Kalabari ritual dramas is still a very live one. As a system of explanation and control of the universe it is constantly drawn upon even by many of those who have had contact at secondary school with a very different world-view. Nevertheless, in all Kalabari communities today one sees a steady stripping-down of traditional religious practice to its bare essentials. The various techniques of making the gods manifest in person at the time of their rituals are among the first items to be dispensed with; and the peculiar intensity of feeling which they bring to religious occasions may soon be a forgotten experience.

This decline is a consequence as much of the Pax Britannica as of the spread of Christianity. Formerly, relations between one village and another were often so hostile that people venture no further than necessary from their home creeks for fishing trips. Now, with violence outlawed, people are free to follow the logic of their production methods: when the fish shoals move unpredictably from one estuary to the next, so now do the fishermen – even if it means moving into quarters where they breathe down the necks of traditional enemies bent on the same quest. The relentless pursuit of constantly and capriciously migrating fish now keeps many people as much as thirty miles of creeks and estuaries from their home village for much of the year. The festivals that previously demanded nothing more than four days' holiday from fishing excursions based on the home community, now require tedious journeys back and forth from the fishing camps plus equally tedious packing and unpacking of possessions; so a growing reluctance to attend festivals is inevitable. Its result is that the personnel required for proper performance of a ritual is seldom available nowadays. People content themselves with contributing money which priests or their substitutes in the home town can use to make offerings to the gods whilst they themselves remain out at the camps.

The truncation of religious practice resulting from all this has left a big gap in Kalabari culture. As to what will fill it, or as to whether it will be filled at all, at the moment there are few clues.

8   Masking in Mende Sande society initiation rituals

Ruth B. Phillips

Public masquerades constitute extremely important symbolic forms among the Mende of Sierra Leone.[1] Masquerades are a means of mediating between the secret Societies which dominate Mende social life and the general community. Through masking performances the public is kept informed of important events which occur in the secret domain and is allowed carefully limited participation in the experience of Society members. The masquerades make visible the powerful 'medicines' (*haleisia*) of the secret Societies without revealing their essential mystery. Maskers personify and dramatize the powers of the 'medicines' and exact respect and tribute from the spectators. At the same time, participants and audience are drawn into a common experience, which is aesthetically heightened by techniques of theatre, dance, music, and the plastic arts. The resultant feeling of unity and harmony helps to overcome the threat of disunity implicit in the division of the community into separate secret factions.

The masquerade of the women's Society, the Sande, is of special ritual and artistic interest. The Sande masker, the *sowei* (pl. *Soweisia*, commonly referred to by the Sherbro term, *bundu*) is the most artistically elaborated of the Mende mask types. It is also the only documented mask in Africa worn by women. Although the cultural role and general features of the Sande Society have been described, precise information about the ritual context of its public masking performances has not yet been made available.[2] An examination of the ritual context of Sande masking provides essential background for the understanding of the *sowei* mask as an art form and illustrates the role of masquerades in Mende life.

The Sande Society is one of a number of associations which regulate conduct and perform special services in Mende life and whose activities are kept secret from non-members. Sande, one of the most important, is a women's Society entrusted with the education of young girls. Traditionally this included all the ritual knowledge and many of the practical skills women needed throughout life and paralleled the training given to young men by the Poro Society. Proper attitudes towards their future husbands, sexual behaviour, childbearing, and rearing were all expounded to young girls during Sande initiation. For non-urban Mende membership in the Society remains an essential precondition to marriage and acceptance as a responsible adult woman.[3] At puberty, or in past years sometimes earlier, girls are taken from their families to the Society enclosure or 'bush', built especially for each new session just outside the village.

There, segregated from the rest of the village, they are instructed by officials of the Society, and traditionally circumcision – excision of the clitoris – is performed. Formerly the girls remained initiates for several years, interrupting formal Sande sessions with periods of normal activity amongst their families. During the whole period, however, sexual relations were forbidden and severe penalities were exacted from those who broke this rule. Initiates were instructed to avoid men they encountered outside the village by passing quickly by without speech or contact. Thus one important function of Sande was to protect the virginity of girls until the completion of their training as responsible adults, and the close of the initiation period was traditionally followed by marriage. Now the initiation period is usually shortened to a period of months or even weeks, often timed so that the major ceremonies take place during school vacations.

After the initial period of seclusion following clitoridectomy is over, Sande initiates return to the village during the day to perform chores for their families and for the Sande leaders. As in Poro initiation the girls have been given new names by which they are addressed for the rest of their lives. On request groups of initiates may come out from time to time to perform the special dances they have been taught in the bush. In the past this was one of the finest entertainments a chief could provide for important visitors. Instruction in singing is also an important part of Sande training and provides women with a repertoire of songs which are used on special occasions throughout their lives. Professor Little also points out that Sande training, which includes the performance of many chores for the older women, is designed to inculcate values of modesty, diligence, and respect for one's seniors.

The importance of Sande membership does not stop with the instruction of the young. Membership in both Sande and Poro continues to be a strong bond among adults, enabling these Societies to act as central institutions exerting considerable economic and political power in Mende life. Little has stressed the parallel ritual functions of Poro and Sande. These are indeed striking, yet the structural implications of initiation into the two Societies cannot coincide exactly because the position of women in a predominantly patrilineal and virilocal society is fundamentally different from that of men. Girls are initiated into the Sande Society in the town of their birth and early childhood, although they may later leave to marry men from other villages. Furthermore, girls are usually entrusted to a Sande group attached to the patrilineal lineage group. The strong bonds which are formed with other initiates and the older women who have been their preceptresses thus reinforce loyalty to the descent group and to the childhood community. These bonds offset the ties which are formed through marriage and increase, in a sense, the options available to a woman. Throughout her life a woman remains a member of the Sande group into which she was initiated. Those who marry out of the village may return to it in old age as respected elders of the Society.

The higher offices of the Sande Society are titles inherited through the patrilineal descent groups, preferably from mother to eldest daughter or younger sister. Since the normal Mende custom of marrying out of the descent group would thus result in control over Sande leaving the family, descent groups controlling the Society discard the usual prohibition against marriage between paternal first cousins in order to retain possession of Sande titles and medicines. When necessary the family may also appoint a woman who is related by marriage rather than blood to high Sande rank, or they may recall a blood relative who has married out and gone to another town.[4] Each Sande group is led by one or more Soweisia who have custody of the *sande* 'medicine' and the *sowei* masks. Though a woman of lesser rank may own a *sowei* mask, it must be kept for her by the Society head in a special enclosure called the *kunde* together with the *sande* 'medicine' and other masks. In a large town there are usually several Sande groups which will join forces to initiate new members, although each girl is attached to a particular group and pays fees to its officials. One amongst the Soweisia in a town will be chosen as the supreme head and has the title of Sande Wa Jowei (big Sande Sowei) or Sowo Kindei (keeper of the *kunde*). She is assisted by the Nyande Jowei (the beautiful Sowei) who can act for her and by one or more Ndogbo Jowei (bush Sowei), responsible for 'begging' the bush from the chief for Sande sessions. Other administrative and financial duties, such as collecting fees from the initiates' families and preparing food and water for them, are carried out by the Ligbeisia, (sing. Ligba), the next rank of Sande officials. These are in turn subdivided into Ligba Wa (big Ligba) and Ligba Wulo (small Ligba). To dance with the *sowei* mask or to act as its attendant, a woman must be of Ligba rank. The ordinary members of the Society are known as *sande nyahei* (Sande wife), the initiates as *gbomogboi*, and non-members as *kpowa*.

Mende terminology provides useful clues to the identity of the Sande masker. The Mende do not have a separate word for 'mask' itself, for to distinguish the costume from the human being who wears it, or the headpiece from the rest of the costume, would contradict the notion that a masked figure is an *ngafa*, a spirit. The Mende recognize different types of *ngafa*. There is the *ngafa* in each person which survives after death and goes to join the ancestral spirits. There are spirits which live in the bush and in rivers and which can appear to human beings in different guises. These spirits must be treated with great cleverness lest their trickery bring disaster, but they can also be made to bestow riches and knowledge on their human correspondents. A third category of spirits, those connected with the secret Societies, reveal to the leaders of the Societies through dreams the locations and uses of special herbs or other substances imbued with supernatural power. Each chapter of a secret Society must possess such 'medicine' or *hale*, which legitimizes its activities and gives it power. The Society as a whole is known by the name of its *hale*: thus the *hale* of the Sande Society is *sande*, of the Njayei Society, *njayei*, and so on. The *sande* is collected in rivers where the Society *ngafa* is found, and a woman who dreams of *sande* or of the *ngafa* must be initiated as a Society official if she does not already hold office.

The Sande masker, as we have seen, bears the same title as the highest rank in the Society, Sowei. This title gives an extra dimension to the masker's identity. Like the other secret society masquerades, she is both *hale* and *ngafa*, a personification of the Society medicine and an embodiment of its particular spirit. But unlike the other Mende masquerades the Sande masker is also given the same title as the human leaders of the Society. This title can be translated as 'expert', indicating that she is expert in the secret knowledge and wisdom of Sande.[5] To distinguish the *sowei* masker from the other Soweisia and also to characterize her particular role in the Society the masker is usually referred to as *ndoli jowei*, the dancing Sowei. The choice of this term is significant, for dancing is a key part of the masquerade. Thus, though the Mende say that it is theoretically possible to hold Sande initiation without a *sowei* masker, since the possession of *sande* is the only essential for the efficacy of the session, in practice it is felt that the masking performance adds so much to the ceremonies that the rare village Society which has no *sowei* masker of its own will go to great lengths to borrow one or more from neighboring villages. Dancing, if not essential in ritual terms, is necessary to provide the festive mood appropriate to the completion of the several stages if initiation, and it is *ndoli jowei* who provides the focus for the celebration. Without dancing, in the words of one Mende man, 'the town will not be lively,' for dancing 'demonstrates its well-being.'

During Sande initiation *ndoli jowei* is seen in public at three key moments in the initiation period.[6] Her appearances serve to announce to the families of the initiates and to the public that certain stages of initiation have been successfully accomplished and that preparations and donations of food and money must be made by the village. The first of these appearances occurs two or three days after the girls have been taken to the bush and circumcised and is known as *yaya gbɛ gbi* or simply *yaya* (they hunt *yaya*).[7] The *ndoli jowei* comes into town with a group of Sande women while the new initiates remain secluded in the bush. This is a time of danger, for the initiates are still recovering from circumcision and the families of the girls have not previously had news of them. The women 'come out to tell men they've initiated people into Sande,' it is explained, and 'they rush around the town waving leaves and taking food and things they need which don't belong to them.' The *ndoli jowei* does not dance on this occasion, as it is not yet time for celebration, but her presence is a visible reminder of the powerful medicine which has been invoked by the Sande session and which legitimizes the lawless behaviour of the women on this occasion.

In some villages of the central (Sewa) Mende the *ndoli jowei* also comes out at a minor feast which occurs a week or so later called *kpɛtɛ gbula yombo le* (to make the mud of the swamp mushy) or *sowo mba yili gbi* (the cooking of the Sowei's rice).[8] On this occasion the Soweisia collect supplies for a special dish to be eaten by them and by the girls in the bush. In most towns where the *ndoli jowei* appears at this time she does not dance, and the occasion may be used to announce the date for the imminent *gani* celebration.

One evening, about two weeks after *yaya*, *ndoli jowei* comes out again. The Soweisia announce that the new initiates will be brought to town for the first time the next day, and to celebrate the event *ndoli jowei* dances through the night. Contributions of rice, oil, fish, and money are collected from the initiates' families and the Soweisia prepare *gani*, a special dish containing 'medicinal' herbs which they take into the Sande bush for the initiates. Portions are also distributed to the girls' relatives, as it is held to be beneficial to partake of the food. After eating the *gani* the initiates come into town wearing headcloths tied in a special way around their waists and a necklace (*gbali*) on which is strung an animal horn or bell, cowrie shells, and a leopard's tooth, the ancient symbol of the well-born. White clay (*wuji*) is rubbed on their faces and they wear ropes of beads around their waists. The girls dress in this way until the end of the initiation period as a visible reminder of their special status – and a warning to men to keep their distance. The reappearance of the initiates in town is known either as *gani* or as *ndahiti* (they are ready.) 'They come to deliver greetings to their families,' one informant explained, and from this time on they spend their days in the village and return to the Sande bush to sleep at night. Despite the joyous atmosphere of the *gani* celebration, the demeanor of the initiates is solemn and they are led forth in an orderly row under the supervision of the Soweis. *Ndoli jowei* accompanies them and dances are performed both by the maskers and the initiates.

The final release of the girls from the initiation session is known as *ti sande gbua* (they pull *sande*) which, these days, usually occurs one or two months after *gani*. The night before the 'pulling' begins the Soweisia cut branches of leaves (*ta tifei lo gbia*) and the initiates are collected from the houses of their families and brought together in a special round enclosure built near the house of the Sande Wa Jowei called the *gumi*.[9] The girls are dressed all in white – white clay is rubbed on their upper torsos and faces and they wear white wrappers and headties. The Soweisia, too, wear white headties on this as on other ritual occasions the significance of which is explained as 'unity'. The initiates remain in the *gumi* for three days, while final preparations are made for their release, and each night there is dancing by the *ndoli joweisia* known as the *ja wa* (big *ja*, or Sande dance.) New clothes and finery are collected for the initiates during this time and the final payments are made to the Society.[10] When arrangements have been completed the Sowei march around the village carrying the *kunde*, the *sande* medicine contained in a rectangular box draped in white cloth. This is one of the rare occasions on which the *kunde* is seen in public. The *ndoli jowei* is not present since the *sande* and the masker do not appear together as their combined powers would be too powerful to control. On the following morning the initiates are led by the *ndoli jowei* to be ritually washed at the river, dwelling place of the Sande *ngafa*. The special protection extended to them by the *sande* is removed or 'pulled' and they are released from the prohibitions of the period of initiation. The white clay is washed from their faces and, according to traditional practice, their skin is rubbed with oil to make it gleam attractively.[11] They are dressed in the finest clothes their parents are able to buy or borrow and, in the past, they were decked with heavy silver jewelry. Today European clothes and make-up are often worn and umbrellas may replace the traditional canopy of country cloths under which the new Sande members are escorted to the town.

During the washing ceremony the *ndoli jowei* again disappears because she may not be present together with the Sande *ngafa* who is being invoked at the riverside. The masker comes back, however, to lead the procession of richly dressed initiates, Sande officials dressed in white robes and headties, and older women carrying branches of leaves back to the town meeting place, the *bari*. There the Sande graduates are seated in state and are feasted and made much of for several days. At the close of the celebration they either go to their appointed bridegrooms or, these days, return to school. *Ndoli jowei*, having presented the girls to their parents, disappears until the next Sande session. 'She will almost cry,' it is said, 'at being dismissed from her post, and appears angry as she goes away.'

The *gani* and *ti sande gbua* ceremonies are the highpoints of Sande initiation and they are conducted in much the same way all over Mendeland. There is considerable variation, however, in the occasions on which *ndoli jowei* appears between the start of the initiation session and the initiates' first appearance in town.[12] In Kailahun District among the eastern Mende, *ndoli jowei* parades around town on the day the girls first enter the Sande bush, but the *yaya* rite is not observed. The ceremony is called *sande wa gbii* (they all go to Sande) or *kpowa gowi* (non-initiate path). The attendants of *ndoli jowei* announce what has taken place but there is no dancing. In the Gola/Mende area, the *ndoli jowei* comes out on the evening before the start of initiation to celebrate the 'buying of the bush' (*ndogbo wu ma wo le*) and a small dance is held. Instead of the *yaya* or *kpɛtɛ gbula yombo le* appearances of the Sewa Mende, here the *ndoli jowei* comes out again seven days after initiation to announce that the girls are 'under the water' and demands contributions of money for the buying of fire and rice. There is no dance for, as at *yaya*, the time has not yet come to celebrate. This occasion is known as *ngombu yeya le* (buying the fire). In the Vai/Mende area the first appearance of *ndoli jowei* occurs about two weeks after the start of initiation to celebrate the completion of the first stage of initiation and to beg food from the initiates' families. This is known in Vai as *bo maɛ* (we have done it) and the Mende translation is given as *kpɛtɛ gbula yombo lɛ*, although the event is observed differently in the Vai/Mende area than among the Sewa Mende since a small dance is held.

Ndoli jowei is often referred to as the 'tutelary spirit' of the Sande Society since her public appearances occur primarily during Sande initiation and because, as we have said, she bears the title of a Society leader. During Sande initiation her appearances tell the community that specific stages of initiation have been successfully completed, and they act as the focus for public celebration. *Ndoli jowei* also appears, however, on certain other occasions when her presence is a means of impressing on the community the unity and strength of the female corporate body. Thus the Sande Society expresses its respect for the chieftaincy by causing *ndoli jowei* to dance with the other masked *haleisia* at the crowning of a Paramount Chief or the funeral of a prominent man. She may also dance if another chief or high government official visits the town. That the participation of *ndoli jowei* on such occasions has specifically political significance is made evident by the fact that on purely festive occasions, such as Christmas and the end of Ramadan, when many masked *haleisia* come out to dance, *ndoli jowei* does not appear.

In past years *ndoli jowei* also came out to bring to justice an offender against Sande laws, such as a man who has spied on the Sande bush or had sexual relations with an initiate. In such cases the offender is pointed out by the Sande masker and led to the chief, who imposes the punishment demanded by the Society. Depending on the offense this might involve initiation into the Society at great expense or a substantial fine and ritual 'washing'.

The Sande masker must also come out if a Sowei or an important Ligba dies. On such an occasion it is the *ndoli jowei* rather than members of the family who 'pulls the cry' for the deceased, walking around the house of the dead woman with her attendant Ligbeisia in attitudes of mourning and announcing the death. Since men may not see the body of a dead Sowei they first prepare the grave and then retire, allowing the Sande women to conduct the burial. The *ndoli jowei*, hands on her head, leads the procession to the grave. If a three or seven-day ceremony is held for the dead woman, the *ndoli jowei* will again appear and dance.

Lastly, a small dance may be held when a new *sowei* mask is 'initiated' into the Society, for, since the *ndoli jowei* is a leader of the Sande group, she too must undergo the ceremonies a woman would go through. Masks are frequently acquired by women who at first lack the status and money to have them initiated. Such a mask is known as *kpowa jowei* (uninitiated mask) and although it may be danced with at Sande celebrations it lacks the supernatural power of a true *sowei* mask. The ceremony of initiation may be held at any time and is called *ti kpia ngiti ya* (they bring it outside). The other *ndoli joweisia* in the town bring the new masker outside and present her after the owners of the new mask have paid a fee of money, rice, oil, fish, and a goat to the owners of the old masks. A gun is shot off and the new *ndoli jowei* is taken to call on the chief and important men of the town. Feasting and dancing follow.

The dancing performances of the *ndoli jowei* follow the same general pattern as the other secret Society masquerades. The *ndoli jowei* emerges from the Society enclosure or from a house, depending on the occasion, and she is accompanied by a Ligba who carries a straw mat which is draped over the masker's lap when she is seated and which may also be used to screen her if she wishes to rearrange her costume. Her attendant calls out the masker's personal name in a short wailing chant to introduce her to the crowd and warn of her presence as they approach. The *ndoli jowei* wears, in addition to the black helmet mask, one or more capes of blackened palm fiber around her neck and waist and under this a shirt, pair of trousers, and shoes which cover the masker's skin completely. Traditionally these clothes should be black as well, but today garments of other dark colors are occasionally worn and tennis shoes are not uncommon. She carries a switch in one hand with which she gestures, and bells are tied to her costume which jingle when she moves. The costume, like those of other maskers, includes various traditional herbal charms encased in *fritambo* or sheep's horns, as well as Moslem amulets folded into leather or cloth packets. These are intended to increase the masker's powers and afford protection from witchcraft.

A group of Sande women accompanies the dancing, singing and rhythmically shaking *segbura* (gourds filled with seeds encased in a netting sewn with more seeds), and they are joined by men beating the *sangbei* and slit *kili* drums. If there are a number of *ndoli joweisia* each dances in turn for short periods of time. The dancer faces the drummers and does not move far in the course of the dance. The Mende characterize the dancing of *ndoli jowei* as 'tight' and 'awkward' (*komo loongo*), and value the quickness and intricacy of the footwork. The dancer moves her feet in a rapid series of steps capable of much individual variation. The raffia capes flare out and swirl in wide circles with the dipping and turning of the dancer. As at other dancing performances the audience forms a wide circle around the dancer and shows its appreciation at the end of each performance by means of gifts of money. There is humor, too, as *ndoli jowei* assumes playful, spirited, or restless attitudes which her attendants must control, often by presenting her with more money.

The use of dramatic mime is an important part of the *ndoli jowei*'s performance and her behavior, as we have seen, varies according to the occasion which calls her forth. At *yaya* while the new initiates are still in a precarious state, her wild rush around the town with the Sande women demonstrates the power which has been released by the opening of the Sande session and the care with which it must be controlled. At the death of a Sowei her behavior dramatizes the grief of the Society. On occasions of rejoicing, such as *gani*, 'pulling', the crowning of a Paramount Chief, or the visit of an important personage, *ndoli jowei* dances because dancing creates an atmosphere of infectious happiness and harmony. As one man expressed it 'dancing is what [we] do to forget about death.' And the dancing of the Society masker is felt to be both the spark necessary to set off general rejoicing and also the highlight of the celebration.

In addition to the *ndoli jowei* there are two other minor women's masquerades which add greatly to the texture and enjoyment of Sande entertainments. These are the *gonde* masker described as *ngengema jowei*, the 'funny Sowei', and the satirical masker *samawa*. They often appear on the periphery of the performances of *ndoli jowei*; and the humor of *gonde* in particular is heightened by her juxtaposition with the object of her parody. Like the male *gongoli*, *gonde* is not a real *hale* but a clown-like figure which overturns all the conventions and decorum proper to *ndoli jowei*. Her costume is a pastiche of rags and tatters, and she is hung about with all sorts of junk – rusty old tin cans, shells, and other discarded fragments. Like *gongoli* too, she represents the anti-aesthetic, purposely reversing the normal criteria of beauty. Because *ndoli jowei* is always in black, *gonde* wears any color; because the *ndoli jowei*'s headpiece is always beautifully blackened, polished and intact, and surrounded by a full raffia cape, *gonde*'s mask is weathered, broken, daubed with paint, and possessed of only the wispiest raffia. The headpiece of the *gonde* is, in fact, often an old *sowei* mask discarded because of insect damage or breakage. When the headpiece is carved specifically to be *gonde* the workmanship is crude and the features made to look grotesque. Most upsetting of all to the approved behavior of a masked *hale*, *gonde*'s face and body are often left half-uncovered by her disarray. One song about *gonde* goes, '*gonde* is shameless, she's not ashamed to show her face,' and she may actually push her mask up as she dances to reveal even more of her head. *Gonde* is also shameless in going right up to people and asking for money despite her utter unworthiness, rather than waiting in a dignified manner for people to present whatever gifts they might want to give her. This angers *ndoli jowei* (who, people explain, wants all the money for herself) and, to the amusement of the crowd she will try to chase the *gonde* away.

The *samawa* masquerade makes use not only of parody but of satire, and the masker's costume changes depending on her object. *Samawa* wears no headpiece but face paint, exaggerated clothing, and the appropriate appended objects. In one version the *samawa*'s face was painted with black and white spots to represent leprosy, a strip of fur was tied around her chin as a beard, and she was dressed in dirty rags. A big bulge under the front of her costume represented a swelling of the scrotum, and she hobbled about leaning on a stick like a cripple. All these deformities, she sang, would afflict any man who disobeys Sande rules, and she interrupted her song with bursts of loud raucous laughter.[13] Another interpretation of *samawa* in a nearby village satirized Moslem 'learned men'. She scribbled away with a crabs claw and 'divined' people's fortunes with a collection of old shells and pieces of broken toys. In her kit she carried many pairs of spectacles for her 'reading' which she constantly put on and off, and she wore a necklace of bones which she kissed and touched to her forehead in imitation of Moslem prayer beads. She also had a collection of horns and bones slung over her back to 'dance with,' satirizing the *wudi* worn by the male *falui* and *goboi* maskers. She wore mismatched shoes and an old battered straw hat, which she proclaimed were her 'badges of office' in the Poro Society.[14] Although the *samawa* masquerade is not nearly so widespread as *gonde* (which is found in nearly every village that has sowei masks), it is probably quite old and may have been borrowed from neighbouring peoples.[15]

Gonde and *samawa* are, in different ways, good examples of Turner's distum that: 'Cognitively, nothing underlines regularity so well as absurdity or paradox. Emotionally nothing satisfies as much as extravagant or temporarily permitted illicit behavior' (1969: 176). *Gonde*, through her absurdity, serves not only to reinforce the dignity and transcendent power of *ndoli jowei*. *Samawa* in her graphic representation of the ills which befall offenders against Sande demonstrates the helplessness of men before the power of *sande*, and her open satire is itself made possible by the position of power she occupies as a member of Sande. The weakness of men, normally more powerful than women, is thus shown up in a temporary assumption of supremacy by women during Sande Society masquerades. Issues fundamental to the very survival of the group are at stake, for the Mende believe that male impotence results from transgressions against Sande, just as female barrenness is caused by the breaking of Poro laws. In laughing at these 'comic' maskers, then, one is also laughing at the folly of ignoring the principles of right conduct. Thus, through comic and serious masquerades the Sande Society provides the public with periodic reminders of its teachings and powers. And equally importantly, its masking performances afford occasions for community-wide celebrations of the successful application of these powers and teachings as each new group of young women enters into Sande.

Notes

1 This article is part of an art historical study of *sowei* masks dealing with questions of iconography, provenance, style change, regional variation and ritual context. The fieldwork on which it is based was carried out in Sierra Leone and Liberia over a period of seven months between March and November of 1972, as part of my doctoral research. I wish to thank the Canada Council and the University of London Central Research Fund for their generous support.

2 Kenneth Little's publications on Mende ethnography are fundamental to this study and, indeed, to all work on the Mende. For this reason I have not felt it necessary to provide detailed citations. For the Sande Society his account is less satisfactory than for the Poro and this is where the present study, it is hoped, can make a contribution.

3 My findings contradict Richards' statement that membership in Sande has become less important in recent years (1974: 279). In fact, the sporadic challenge of reformist and iconoclastic Islamic groups in this century has been met by the formation of Mori Jande, or Moslem Sande chapters. Although modified by the loss of masking traditions and other pagan features these reformed Sande groups thrive, often side by side with traditional Sande chapters.

4 This flexibility is illustrated by the history of a typical Sande chapter, one of three in the village of Mende Kema, Jaiiama-Bongor chiefdom, Bo district: 'At about the time the white man came [1890s] Bundu Ka paid a certain sum to the head of Sande in order for his elder wife Lawobu to begin her own Sande Society [after she had found *sande* 'medicine' in the river as the result of a dream]. When she died Kuji took over; she was no relation to Lawobu but was elected by the elders of the family and Society officials. Then Gombε took over, wife of a nephew of Bundu Ka named Foreka. Then Yende became head, wife of a nephew of Foreka.' Although women informants almost always state that *sande* is inherited through the female line in uninterrupted fashion the actual practice appears closer to the example quoted above, through women connected affinally to the patrilineal descent group.

5 The etymology of the term Sowei can be understood from the related words in Vai (Zo ba) and Gola (Zogbe). D'Azevedo defines those who bear the title of Zo as 'masters of crucial knowledge and skills that have benefited the entire community' (1973: 133) Caine gives a similar definition for the Vai (1959: 60). *Wa* in Mende, like *ba* and *gbe* in these languages means 'big'.

6 The summary below is based on a systematic study of the villages of Jaiiama-Bongor chiefdom, Bo district, and on discussions, in particular, with Paramount Chief B.A. Foday-Kai, OBE.

7 The term *yaya* appears to derive from the chorus of the song sung by the Sande women on this occasion: *O ya ya go yo…*'

8 The phrase 'to make the mud of the swamp mushy' is usually explained as referring to the swamp as the source of the ingredients used in the dish.

9 'Pulling' is also commonly referred to as *tifei* (leaves).

10 Alldridge in his early account of Sande 'pulling' and Hoffer, sixty years later, both emphasize the hard bargaining which goes on at this stage (Alldridge 1910: 224; Hoffer 1972: 160). In Alldridge's account the offerings were placed in front of the seated *ndoli joweisia*.

11 Alldridge also describes (1910: 226) the ritual application and washing off of a cap of black mud called *soboro* for those girls already betrothed. My informants did not mention this.

12 The following brief discussion is not meant to be comprehensive, but rather suggestive of the degree of variation to be found. Customs may differ not only between districts but also within the same chiefdom.

13 Kpakuma, Jaiiama-Bongor, Sept. 29, 1972.

14 Buma, Jaiiama-Bongor, Oct. 3, 1972.

15 Alldridge describes a Gbandi comic female masquerade called 'Santelule' which sounds very similar to the *samawa* (1901: 223).

References

Alldridge, T. J. 1901 *The Sherbro and its Hinterland*. London: Macmillan.

—— 1910 *A Transformed Colony*. London: Seeley.

Caine, Augustus Feweh 1959 *A Study and Comparison of the West African Bush School and the Southern Sotho Circumcision School*. Northwestern University, M.A. Thesis.

D'Azevedo, Warren 1973 'Mask makers and myth in western Liberia', in *Primitive Art and Society*, ed. Anthony Forge. London: Oxford University Press.

Hoffer, Carol P. 1972 'Mende and Sherbro Women in High Office', *Canadian Journal of African Studies*, 6 (2): 151–64.

Little, Kenneth 1949 'The role of the secret society in cultural specialization', *American Anthropologist* 51: 199–212.

—— 1951 *The Mende of sierra Leone*. London: Routledge and Kegan Paul.

Richards, J. V. O. 1974 'The Sande: a socio-cultural organization in the Mende community in Sierra Leone'. *Baessler-Archiv* 22 (2): 265–81.

Turner, Victor 1969 *The Ritual Process, Structure and Anti-Structure*. London: Routledge and Kegan Paul.

9 Gyinna-Gyinna

Making the *djinn* manifest

René A. Bravmann

Throughout the Islamic world, among both the clerical elite and the mass of believers, the concept of *djinn* is an ever-present feature. From Morocco through Islamized portions of black Africa, the Middle East, and as far afield as Southeast Asia, the mysteries and workings of the *djinn* form a central part of the scriptural, magical, and popular dimensions of the faith. Theologians and jurists have pondered over the definition of *djinn*, and they have served as a leitmotif in the great classics of Islamic literature, such as *The Thousand and One Nights*, and as constant characters in the everyday language and folklore of the faithful; verbal descriptions of the *djinn* are easily collected, and they are vividly engaging accounts. The Islamized Zara of Bobo-Dyula of southwestern Upper Volta, however, approach the ambiguous world of the *djinn* in a totally unique way. Through the agency of the mask and its surrounding artistry and ritual, the Zara give form and body to this ephemeral spirit, thereby enabling members of their society to comprehend and relate more fully to this important element within Islam. It is hardly surprising that it is within an Islamized African culture that the mask would be employed in making the *djinn* manifest. How and why it is done, however, are important questions, and their answers can help us to gain a further appreciation of the creative contributions made by West African Muslims to the religious and cultural dimensions of Islam as a whole.[1]

As a background to a look at the masquerade known as the *Lo Gue*, the dance of the white masks, and the central most important masked figure *Gyinna-Gyinna*, a brief look at the concept of the *djinn* in both official and popular Islamic circles would be in order. The *djinn* are as old as the faith itself, for the earliest mention of them appears in the Koran, where they are described as supra-human beings composed of fire and flames, not perceivable by man, and capable of emerging in a variety of forms. Many regard them as the nature spirits of the pre-Islamic Arabian world, forces that were beyond the control of man and at odds with his desires. These spirits were gradually brought under the control of Allah, the majority of them being converted to Islam and serving as his companions. Those that were not converted formed part of the unbelieving world and were viewed as opposed to the rule and power of Allah. But Islamic religious literature, and the official view of the faith, is generally accepting of the *djinn*. Even the legal literature of Islam seriously discusses the position of the *djinn*, particularly with respect to questions of marriage, death, property, and inheritance. Opinions on their nature and legality have certainly varied over the centuries, but the prominence and strength of this aspect of Islam have never been denied.[2]

If official Islam has at times wavered before the notion of the *djinn* and its relationship to the faith as a whole, this has not been the case with the popular imagination and writings on the subject. The concept of *djinn* has always occupied a prominent place among Muslims, and its use within the magical arsenal of the faith well assured. Muslim literature is replete with reference to fairies, *djinn*, and spiritual forces that are either inimical to mankind or that may serve individuals through positive and enlightened guidance. *Djinn* in particular are described as capricious, taunting and confusing one moment, then mysteriously altering their characters to help, guide, and teach. A *djinn* may even come under the control of an individual, in which case it becomes his or her guiding principle, enabling the person to achieve new heights of success in both his secular and religious lives. Among the descendants of African slaves in Turkey, P. N. Boratav has noted a number of vivid characteristics of the *djinn* in folklore. Here the *djinn* are portrayed as members of both sexes living together in the world beyond men. They are organized in ways like the living, having their own chief, other leaders, and a variety of associations. The work of the *djinn* takes place only at night and ceases just before the call to morning prayers. They behave in numerous ways, assuming a neutral character with respect to most individuals, and while they may tease or trick people, they are generally neither harmful nor dangerous if they are not annoyed. *Djinn* can also, however, cause great anguish to those who may displease them by punishing and bringing illness. People who have severely twisted limbs, are paralyzed, or are insane, are said to have incurred the wrath of the *djinn*. In contrast, those believed to have been thoughtful and understanding of the *djinn* are the recipients of great rewards in the form of wealth and success. *Djinn* can appear as animals (a black cat or a goat, for example) or as humans. When the appearance is humanoid, the form ranges from dwarf-like stature to extreme height, either form being thin and very white in colour.[3]

Descriptions of the *djinn* and the importance of the concept among West African Islamized societies parallel closely the information available for other parts of the Islamic world. If anything, *djinn* are portrayed even more vividly, making themselves manifest through a variety of disguises that allow them to roam through villages and towns at night. The evil *djinn* among the Songhai of Mali, known as *holy bi*, are said to appear in the guise of dogs and cats.[4] For the Zara of Upper Volta, the descriptive imagination has led to the development of a complete masquerade, giving tangible form and substance to the world of *djinn*.

The Zara of Bobo-Dioulasso are members of Manding civilization, having migrated into this area in the fifteenth or sixteenth century from the trading towns of San and Jenne in Mali.[5] Their settlement at Sya (the indigenous name of Bobo-Dioulasso), at the invitation of the autochthonous Bobo, is vividly recalled in both Zara and Bobo oral traditions.[6] For the Bobo, the arrival of the Zara signaled the development of their primarily agricultural village into a commercial center of future importance and renown. The commercially inclined Zara brought with them the religion of Islam, and as Muslim long-distance traders they were to make of Sya an important way-station along the Manding-dominated trade routes that stretched from the Saharan fringe to the West African forest. Zara traditions assert that they soon gained political dominance over the Bobo, although the latter retained their legal and ritual control over the land. Uncontested Zara control lasted well into the eighteenth century, when the Islamic theocracies of Wahabu and Kong forcibly terminated their hegemony. From this period, until the arrival of the advance columns of the French army at the end of the nineteenth century, the Zara were alternately under the control of the Dafing of Wahabu and the Wattara of Kong.[7] Throughout this time, their commercial instincts and their commitment to Islam not only differentiated the Zara from the Bobo and other indigenous cultures but also enabled them to continue to develop their own group consciousness.

Bobo-Dioulasso and the current Zara community, located primarily in the old quarter of Sya, is still guided by a cadre of Muslim officials. Since the early years of this century, a Zara has served as the Imam for the central mosque. These Imams have long been regarded as the true leaders of the Zara and have effectively directed the spiritual growth of the community. As important as the position of the Imam has been, however, it has been the many teachers, or karamokos, who have effectively directed and regulated the daily religious affairs of Sya. These learned individuals, men who combine a knowledge of the law and teaching and who are interpreters of the precepts and customs of the faith, are the most direct representatives of the religion to the mass of believers. They are leaders of prayers, overseers of the washing of the dead and other funerary procedures, and are present at both naming and marriage ceremonies.

Karamokos also serve as intermediaries between the community and the world of *djinn*, interpreting and helping to control the invisible *djinn* so that individuals may comprehend them and even utilize their powers.[8] Adept in the ways of magic and knowledgeable of the Koran and its techniques, karamokos are able to call the *djinn* through a variety of formulae. The correct and proper prayers, when intoned by the karamoko, can make *djinn* visible. Materials from the natural world in combination with Koranic passages can also help with the controlling process. The power and efficacy of the written word is also recognized, and thus magical formulae that are written on slabs of wood can be washed off and used as a prophylactic against the *djinn* or stored in plastic containers or bottles for such use at a future date. A host of magical manuals, most of them deriving from North African texts, also form part of the arsenal of the karamoko, the most important being *Shams al-Ma ruf* of ibn Abdallah al-Buni.

The majority of Zara come to the karamokos with confidence when they need answers to questions regarding the *djinn*, for only a karamoko can help to mitigate the confrontation between human beings and these spirit-agents. To be troubled by a *djinn* without having consulted a karamoko may well lead to a variety of calamities, and therefore any prudent Zara will seek the advice and direction of the teacher to insure that he is prepared: the karamokos assert that the *djinn* can be controlled if one employs proper precautionary techniques. The *djinn* may even, under ideal circumstances, become allies, helping one to attain such earthly rewards as wealth and prestige. Evidence of the failure of individuals to consult the Muslim teachers with respect to the *djinn* is everywhere obvious.

Zara who are considered failures, either economically or socially, are said to be overcome by them. The mad are felt to be psychologically enslaved by the *djinn*, for they are seen as confused, afraid, and totally disoriented by their spirit-agents.[9] The chatter of the madman, incomprehensible to others, is said to represent the communication between the lunatic and his *djinn*. Cripples, the blind, witches, and others who fall outside the boundaries of normal Zara existence, are other examples of those overcome by a *djinn*.

Discussion of the *djinn* occurs not only among the learned but also among the majority of believers. Zara stories about the workings of the *djinn*, their haunts, their affairs, and their appearance circulate throughout the quarter of Sya. The River Oué, which flows through the quarter, is said to be a favorite hiding place of the *djinn*, who come to enjoy the coolness of the river at night. Zara mothers claim that they are wary of allowing their children to play on the banks of the river at night, for there are many tales of children who have been kidnapped by the *djinn* and returned only after several days. While these legendary children are always returned healthy, well-fed, and often in new clothing, the mothers feel that their offspring have probably been used by the *djinn* for some nefarious purpose.

Some *djinn* may even invade the sexual fantasies of the young, appearing in erotic dreams of adolescent boys as hauntingly beautiful but ephemeral women who disappear when they awaken. A typical dream consists of a young man seated at a movie theatre who is approached by the most beautiful young woman imaginable. Without saying a word she sits next to him, enchants him with her beauty, and follows him out of the theatre when the movie is finished. When invited back to his compound, she gets on the back of his Mobylette or bicycle without hesitation. The young woman still has not spoken, but she has been a willing companion. In all of these dreams, the man does not succeed in arriving home safely: either his Mobylette hits a rock in the road and overturns, or he temporarily loses his way. Embarrassed by this misfortune, he turns to reassure himself of the presence of his companion, but she is no longer there. Her beauty, silence, discretion, and swift disappearance are all indications that she is a *djinn*, for swiftness and elusiveness complete the composite character drawn of the *djinn* from the local descriptions.[10]

Zara society and individuals, however, can flourish and prosper through cautious manipulation and control of the world of *djinn*. As already mentioned, it is the figure of the karamoko and his knowledge and skills that allow for this salutary relationship. Those who are able to withstand the initial confrontation with *djinn* may be able to utilize its powers and insight for personal ends. Worthy and successful people are said to have a strong and viable relationship with a personal *djinn*, their mastery of this spirit having turned it into a personal servant. As the spirit companion of the individual, this *djinn* will guide and protect him throughout life. Only death can separate the two, and it is at the public funeral of a renowned Zara that the masked form of the *djinn* will most often perform.

The mask *Gyinna-Gyinna*, the *djinn* spirit made manifest, is the most important masking agent within the masquerade known as *Lo Gue* (white masks). *Lo Gue* signifies the entire world of the Muslim spirits, consisting of a variety of masqueraders who serve as attendants to the two embodied *Gyinna-Gyinna*. The *Lo Gue* are permitted to perform only at night and generally on the thirteenth or fourteenth evenings of the lunar month when the moon is at its fullest. This two-day period, known as *Yegewulu*, is regarded as the most appropriate time for the appearance of the *Lo Gue*. These nights are considered to be particularly positive for human beings, with children born at these times regarded as being especially lucky and endowed with a heightened dimension of mental clarity. *Yegewulu* is also thought to be particularly appropriate for aesthetic reasons, since dancers can perform more readily in full moonlight when their choreographic excellence can be more completely appreciated by the audience.

Only two occasions in Zara culture call for the appearance of the *Lo Gue*: the annual peformance at *Jombele*, the tenth night of the first month of the Muslim calendar, and the public funerals of Zara notables. Both occasions stress, and implicitly underscore, that nexus between man and the realm of the *djinn*. *Jombele* signifies the annual confirmation of the ongoing ties between all members of this Muslim society and the spiritual realm. The single performance of *Jombele* is critical, for this night is uniformly regarded as the most magical and mystical time of the Islamic year. *Djinn* are said to be particularly alive and brazen at this time, and the Zara must therefore fortify themselves against the spirits through a host of magical, ritual and talismanic elements.[11] *Lo Gue* is performed late in the evening and lasts until daybreak, enabling the world of the living, now in a heightened state of protection, to confront and neutralize the world of the supernatural. Except for this annual appearance, which is devoted to protecting the Zara community as a whole from the capriciousness of the *djinn*, the *Lo Gue* will only be seen again when it appears at a funeral to satisfy the personal *djinn* of a departed Zara. On such an occasion the performance of the *Lo Gue* publicly confirms the human-*djinn* relationship, that vital personal link between a man or a woman and a *djinn*.

The *Lo Gue* masquerade, according to Zara traditions, is a time-honoured manifestation. Zara informants in Bobo-Dioulasso consistently indicate that the origins of the masquerade derive from the northern Zara country and the many small Zara villages and Zara-Bobo communities lying to the north and northwest of the city.[12] They further claim that the *Lo Gue* was introduced into Bobo-Dioulasso and accepted by the Zara community there in the early part of this century. Two independent documents confirm this relatively late date. Sani Sanon's short, unpublished description of a *Lo Gue* performance in 1928 and the diaries of the White Fathers of the church of Tounouma that recall a new and remarkable performance of white cloth maskers in the fall of 1929 suggest the recentness of the performances.[13] Ali Sanu, chief of the Zara community at Bobo-Dioulasso, remarked that the *Lo Gue* was brought to the city at a time when the Zara community was more firmly guided by the leadership of its karamokos, shortly after the Zara community took over control of the central mosque. Its appearance also coincides with the period of Zara independence from Dyula control in the city and when it is said the Zara began to experience a time of heightened economic success.

Beliefs and concerns regarding the *djinn* existed prior to the arrival of the *Lo Gue*, but its acceptance came about due to the advice of several karamokos who saw it as an additional element for their spiritual arsenal. Up until this time, the *Lo Gue* masquerade had been borrowed by the Zara of Bobo-Dioulasso from neighbouring communities, a practice that ended with their acquisition of the masquerade.[14]

Gyinna-Gyinna and their masked companions constitute a panoply of unique mask types in the West Voltaic zone. Their formal appearance is unlike anything else, with costumes consisting of either locally woven white cotton or, more recently, imported white cotton broadcloth. Considered to be expert weavers by neighbouring cultures, the Zara have explored fully the possibilities of cotton cloth in the creation of their masks.

Lo Gue consists of numerous body-type cloth costumes sewn snugly upon the bodies of athletic young dancers in an attempt to impersonate visually the luminous and ephemeral qualities of the *djinn* and their consorts.[15] Two colours dominate the masks: white and black. The male and female masks of *Gyinna-Gyinna*, however, must be all white to accurately portray, on the visual plane, the verbal descriptions of these spirit characters. The consorts' costumes combine black and white in a variety of patterns, *yororo*; these may range from random black and white patches to black vertical and horizontal stripes painted upon a white field with geometric regularity, to cross-like patterns upon the chest and back, either in black upon white or the reverse.

The mask costumes are stark and strongly articulated, allowing the dancing forms to move in an almost ethereal manner. The total form of the *Gyinna-Gyinna* is the most dramatic masked persona. Tall and slender, yet strong and athletically inclined dancers are chosen for this particular character: it is rare to find a man under six feet allowed to dance in such a mask. Height is important, for the *Gyinna-Gyinna* must stand above all other masked forms: the dancer must also be slender, for the *djinn* are described as long, lean and wispish in appearance. Additional height is achieved by a wooden crest with twelve to sixteen vertical dowels that issue above the head. These, along with the cloth face portion of the mask, form the head of the being and are said to represent the hair of the *djinn*, which stands on end and flows toward the sky. The rest of the body is enveloped in white cotton cloth, stretched tight and stitched together in a virtually seamless manner. Fully clothed, *Gyinna-Gyinna* stands nearly eight feet tall, a symbol of spiritual supremacy dominating the other characters of the *Lo Gue*.

The total presence of *Gyinna-Gyinna* needs to conform fully to the official and popular conceptions of the *djinn* held by the Zara, and therefore even the accoutrements of the masked form, its choreographic routines, and the relationship between the musicians and the *Gyinna-Gyinna* must accurately reflect Zara notions of these beings. Fire and heat are regarded as basic aspects of the *djinn*, and these elements are revealed through a further exploration of the character and movements of *Gyinna-Gyinna*. One of the primary duties of the griots in the *Lo Gue* is to 'warm' the bodies of the dancers. This they do by issuing short rapid bursts of the *den den sa*, the lead pressure drum. The pattern is called *Lo gue bi kriho*, literally, 'music that takes the *Lo gue*'. Implied here is the act of the chief griot drumming to a seated *Lo Gue*, which is compelled by the music to rise and dance. This is the only moment when the griots exert their implicit power over the *Lo Gue*. From this point on, any spirit member of *Lo Gue* in the process of dancing is said to be 'fully heated', and his dancing is referred to as 'warm' or 'hot' (*nimi mani töba**).[16] *Gyinna-Gyinna*, however, are inherently 'hot', and thus there is no need for them to be 'taken' by the music in the same way as the other masks.

The *Gyinna-Gyinna* have their own set of gestures, called *yabaro*, which supply their own 'heat' through such actions as vigorous pirouettes and vaulting movements made by jumping with the support of their canes. Only the *Gyinna-Gyinna* exhibit such independence, and the songs devoted to them indicate their powers of fire. Men and women say that one should avoid looking directly at these forms, for to do so would risk injury by the heat that they emit. Nor should one be so foolhardy as to touch the body of a *Gyinna-Gyinna*, for as his primary song, *Malé Gyinna Kouma*, suggests, 'If one touches the body of Gyinna, *'anëwö tögö'* it is like fire'. Choreography, music and song are combined to confirm the essentially fiery nature of the *Gyinna-Gyinna* and its ethereal composition. The drum beats and flute patterns that guide *Gyinna-Gyinna* are unique to the *Lo Gue*, for they are hauntingly slow, consistent in their cadence, and tonally dignified, in keeping with the mask itself. Two balaphones further contribute to the musical dimension by providing a background of muted but eerie riffs. The entire choreography of *Lo Gue* emphasizes the centrally important *Gyinna-Gyinna*, for the other masked spirit characters serve essentially as an introduction to the entrance of these two figures and then as supporting dancers; much of the evening performance will consist of the other *Lo Gue* dancers stirring the laterite floor of the dance circle with their feet and crested manes to create a whirlwind of dust within which the *Gyinna-Gyinna* will dance and leap, creating the effect of ethereal spirits both on the ground and hovering in the air. The light of a full moon only heightens the ephemeral and shimmering effects of the *Gyinna-Gyinna*.

Heated body, independence of power, and the high degree of unpredictability of *Gyinna-Gyinna* are all part of its essential character. Within the context of *Lo Gue*, therefore, it is incumbent upon the directors of this masking organization to control these potentially dangerous elements of its personality. The Zara say that *Lo Gue* can only be successful if the leaders of the masquerade carry out the many ritual procedures that will enable them to direct and guide the ever-capricious *Gyinna-Gyinna* throughout their performance. To this end, a host of talismans will be tucked in the *bamba-da*, the tall, peaked white caps worn by the lead griots who play and dance for *Gyinna-Gyinna*,[17] and tied to the waist of the attendants of these masked figures. Only the *Gyinna-Gyinna* require human guides, two strong young men who hold onto a sturdy rope tied to the waist of the *djinn*. No other *Lo Gue* mask requires such attention, for no other has the independence of mind or the inherent power to lash out at the living who come to observe this honorific performance. All of these precautions need to be strictly followed, for *Gyinna-Gyinna*, within the context of *Lo Gue*, must honor, support, and act as a fitting companion to the deceased spirit.

The essence of *Lo Gue*, this one-night performance lasting from about midnight to daybreak, is described locally as *fougo donbë*, or 'erasing the footprints'. It is the ceremony that honors the death of an important Zara and the nexus between his personal and societal success and his or her guiding *djinn* spirit. *Lo Gue* can occur well after the actual burial and Muslim funerary procedures, but this timing is not important. Since the ritual honors and confirms the prestige and wealth of the individual, it is an occasion that proves costly to the descendants, and time is often needed to collect the goods, services, and funds necessary to pay for the performance. Some Zara suggest that a family should not wait too long to finally free the spirit of the deceased, but for most, time is not a binding element. The majority of Zara say that both the spirit of the deceased and his or her personal *djinn* will wait patiently for the performance of the *Lo Gue*.

The essence of *Lo Gue* is to please both the personal *djinn* and the spirit of the deceased so that they will leave the world of the living together and will continue their positive relationship in the realm beyond. The appearance of the *Gyinna-Gyinna* and their spirit consorts, which includes such masked characters as *Bolofuru*, *Këkërëpogo*, *Boloyororo*, and others, is referred to as *Furu wë*, 'the good is finished'. This phrase, like the performance of *Lo Gue*, acknowledges the existence of a positive relationship between the deceased and the personal *djinn* on earth and implies the hope for the continuation of this bond in the world of the ancestors.

Notes

1 Research among the Zara of Upper Volta was made possible through the generous support of the Social Science Research Council in 1972–73 and the American Philosophical Society in the spring of 1974. I also wish to express my deepest thanks to Chief Ali Sanu of Sya quarter, Bobo-Dioulasso, and to Zouma Sanu, leader of the *Lo Gue*, its most accomplished artist and a former master dancer of the *Gyinna-Gyinna*. Their assistance and understanding have made this article possible.

2 For a detailed exploration of the traditional attitudes toward the *Jinn* see Edward Lane (1836, vol. 1, chpt. 10) and D. B. Macdonald (1965, chpts, 5, 10).

3 P. N. Boratav (1951: 83–8). A more complete discussion by the same author can be found in his 1958 article (pp. 7–23).

4 Jean Rouch's classic study *La Religion et la Magie Songhay* (1960) should be consulted for a thorough examination of the *holy bi, jinn* and magical beliefs among the Songhay of western Niger.

5 Two articles by Guy Le Moal, anthropologist and former director of the C.V.R.S. in Ouagadougou introduced me to the importance of the Zara or Manding element in southwestern Upper Volta: 'Notes sur les populations "Bobo"' (1957: 418–30) and 'Enquête sur l'histoire du peuplement du pays Bobo' (1968: 6–9).

6 Historical traditions of the Zara were collected in the Zara quarters of Sya and Bolomakote in November 1972 and in May 1974. Bobo versions of the Zara arrival were recorded in January and April 1973 and May 1974 at Kounima, Tounouma and Koko quarters, Bobo-Dioulasso.

7 The history and importance of Wahabu is well assessed by Nehemiah Levtzion (1968: 145–52). The most comprehensive account of the impact of the Wattara of Kong on Bobo-Dioulasso can be found in Lucy Quimby's unpublished doctoral dissertation (1972).

8 The position of the karamoko as the chief intermediary between the faithful and the *djinn* is also noted by Quimby (1972, chapt. 2) and was a feature of the teacher-cleric's role, which I observed in 1967–68 among the Manding of the Cercle de Bondoukou, Ivory Coast.

9 The idea that the mad are agents of the *djinn* is certainly not restricted to the Zara. It occurs among the Songhai and Hausa and can be found over and over again in the literature and folklore of Islam. Indeed, this association must be ancient, for as Hunwick (1976: 16) has noted, the very term for 'mad' in Arabic, *majnun*, literally means 'possessed by a jinn'.

10 This composite picture of the *djinn* is drawn from my research and also from the

unpublished sources of Father Montjoie of the Church of Tounouma, discussions with Mr. Sani Sanon of Sya, and Lucy Quimby's observations among the Kong Dyula in her dissertation.

11 For the importance and meaning of *Jombele* within another Manding context, see my comments in *Islam and Tribal Art in West Africa* (1974, chapt. 7).

12 A brief description of the Zara region north of Bobo-Dioulasso is provided by Le Moal (1957: 26–29).

13 Sani Sanon, 'Lo Gué, une fête indigéne de Sya', 1928: and 'L'Histoire de Tounouma', a compilation of the diaries and notes of the White Fathers of Tounouma. I wish to express my thanks to Mr. Sanon and Father Alain for allowing me access to these valuable sources.

14 The tradition of borrowing the *Lo Gue* is still very much alive, and Zara villages around Bobo-Dioulasso without this masquerade regularly ask for the masks and dancers from Sya. This has extended even to Bobo communities who wish to honor one of their prominent members who has converted to Islam.

15 A *Lo Gue* performance will generally include the following mask types: *nyanon tala dungu, bolo-furu, kolingo, bolo-yororo, këkërëpögö, nyanë, të bolo, ligëyara, kikiri dëzugu* and *kubëlu*. Each is regarded as a spirit agent with its own personality, but they are all dominated by the two *Gyinna-Gyinna*.

16 The griots of Bobo-Dioulasso indicate that a *Lo Gue* performer can only dance well (*animi kyë*) if his body and spirit have been fully warmed by the music. This warming process begins in the flexed knees, gradually rises through the upper torso, and finally arrives within the head of the dancer, enabling him to perform impressive turning and twisting head movements that have a life independent from the rest of his body. This dance state, of active and pulsating head in contrast to a composed body, is referred to as *amyo*, 'dancing with one's head'.

17 *Bamba-da*, literally, 'the head of the crocodile', is a peaked cap reserved for male elders and must be worn by the griots when playing before the *Gyinna-Gyinna*.

* For technical reasons it was not possible to employ the open o symbol occurring in certain words in this article. "ö" has been substituted as the nearest equivalent in standard type. For the same reason, ë has been substituted for the *epsilon* symbol.

Bibliography

Boratav, P. N. 1951. 'The Negro in the Turkish Folklore'. *Journal of American Folklore* 64, 251.

—— 1958. 'Les Noirs dans le folklore Turc et le folklore des Noirs de Turquie'. *Journal de la Société des Africanistes* 28.

Bravmann, René A. 1974. *Islam and Tribal Art in West Africa*. London: Cambridge UP.

Hunwick, J. O. 1976. *Islam in Africa: Friend or Foe*. Accra: Ghana Universities Press.

Lane, Edward 1836. *Manners and Customs of the Modern Egyptians*. London: Charles Knight and Co.

Le Moal, Guy 1957. 'Notes sur les populations "Bobo"'. *Bulletin I.F.A.N.* 19, 3–4.

—— 1968. 'Enquette sur l'histoire du peuplement du pays Bobo'. *Notes et Documents Voltaiques* 1, 2.

Levtzion, Nehemiah 1968. *Muslims and Chiefs in West Africa*. Oxford: Clarendon Press.

Macdonald, D.B. 1965. *Religious Attitude and Life in Islam*. 2nd imp. Chicago: University of Chicago Press, 1912.

Quimby, Lucy 1972. 'Transformations of Belief – Islam among the Dyula of Kongbourgou from 1880 to 1970'. Unpublished doctoral thesis.

Rouch, Jean 1960. *La Religion et la Magie Songhay*. 2nd imp. Bruxelles: Université de Bruxelles Inst. de Sociologie, Anthropologie Sociale, 1989.

Sanon, Sani 1928. 'Lo Gué, une fête indigène de Sya'. Unpublished paper.

10 Creativity, participation and change in Theatre for Development practice

Oga S. Abah

Theatre and change

All over the world, whenever Theatre for Development (TfD)[1] is practised, it defines itself as an alternative practice; and the agenda it pursues always is that of change. The notion of other is quite strong in TfD's definition of itself and its role. It is also significant that in its practice 'otherness' is central to TfD's discursive strategy, first in its artistic form and, secondly in the issues and participants involved in it. However, the end point to this exploration of the alternative, and the 'other' as an instrument of alienation and subjugation, is to seek a point of equilibrium or change. It is the conduct of the journey from the point of disjunction to where a resolution, no matter how tenuous, may be achieved that is at the centre of TfD practice.

There is a whole space between these two points, with a myriad of intervening variables, problems and negotiations to navigate. First of all, the alternativeness of TfD is in its movement away from traditional Western and elitist theatre with its separation of audience from actor, its talking *for* and not *with* the community; and in its preoccupation with a finished product meant for consumption rather than allowing a process of creating together. In other words, Theatre for Development is concerned with, and derives its strength from participation. This is in opposition to the emphasis on consumerism of the arts/elite theatre practice.

The reason TfD is always seeking change is to be found in the nature of the environment in which it is practised. It is a situation in which the everyday life of the ordinary person is that of non-availability of basic needs as piped drinking water, health care, access roads, electricity and, in some cases, absence of food and shelter. Therefore, in the marginalized world of the poor, theatre cannot but deal with the daily struggles for survival. Look at this picture:

> You are walking in an easterly direction away from the University of Jos, which is situated in the northern apex of Jos metropolis. This walk will take you between forty-five minutes to one hour. It demands that you make a gentle climb up a knoll that exposes in front of you the beautiful scenery of a range of undulating hills. Below you is a trough of greenery. Inside this valley, some forty-five minutes away lies a village called Mazah with a population of about 1,500. The walk in and out of this village is a tortuous one as you must

weave your way along a narrow and craggy path strewn with rocks and screes. It is not motorable. By the time you have made your descent into this village, you are among a group of farmers who are battling disease and hunger. The farmers here grow grain crops of *acha*, maize and guinea corn (sorghum). Over the years however, the crop yields have been decreasing in the face of soil degradation and lack of financial resources to purchase fertiliser. The supplementary vegetable crops of tomatoes and guava; and the huge and perpetual bundles of firewood which the women take up the hill to sell in Jos are not enough respite.

The caved-in location of Mazah supervised by the overlooking hills describes its neglect and defeat: women deliver their babies at the foot of the hills and very often, mother and child do not survive the ordeal. Here middlemen also stand and wait for the women to climb out of the valley with their load of farm produce. The middlemen buy cheaply and sell at profitable prices in the metropolis. The middlemen's advantage, and the women's calamity, is that there is no motorable road to the village of Mazah.

In places like this the ordinary people are interested in, and are indeed employing various cultural forms to address their predicament. Theatre is one of such media.

Theatre for Development

It is however not the arts/elite theatre conceived in, and resident in the academic institutions that is employed in addressing the everyday lives of these people. The genre of theatre doing this is Theatre for Development (TfD). TfD has come to be widely accepted in Africa and in other parts of the developing world as a theatre of the ordinary people used to address their own problems, in their own terms, from their own perspectives and from within their own art forms. It uses the indigenous performative forms of the people to define the aesthetics of its operation. The people are the protagonists, generating the themes and infusing the drama with conflicts from their daily lives (Abah, 1990; Kidd, 1980; Mda, 1993). It is largely true to say that in this theatre there is no audience in the traditional Western sense of the word. Every one is a participant or a 'spect-actor' (Boal, 1995). Although TfD does admit outside animateurs who function as facilitators to kick-start the process, they often of necessity must, and do yield dominance to the grassroots owners of the problems which the practice interrogates. It is also the ordinary people who have a better semiological grasp of the autochthonous forms which TfD leans towards and always borrows from. Therefore, in its development from indigenous art forms and in its present hybrid existence, TfD has an organic affinity to, and is perhaps to be seen as integral to the sacral life systems of rural Africa. The affinities exist and can be perceived in songs, music and dances. The issue is how these have transmigrated from their original setting, form and functions to service the quest for societal transformation in today's world. They have simply responded to the changing circumstances of the lives of the people who have given shape and meaning to the forms.

In its agenda of change, the progression of Theatre for Development begins with what Paulo Freire (1972: 52) has called 'problem posing' education to raise critical awareness. The development of critical awareness is crucial to the practice of TfD because, for most of the time it is lack of knowledge that the prevailing circumstances of their lives can, and should be, different which keeps the ordinary persons marginalized. It is also, in part, the fatalism of the people which contributes to their state of poverty. To change all this means to alter their ways of thinking, their ways of seeing; for as Paulo Freire (1972: 25), the radical Brazilian educator, argues, 'The central problem is this: How can the oppressed, as divided, unauthentic beings, participate in developing the pedagogy of their liberation? Only as they discover themselves to be "hosts" of the oppressor can they contribute to the midwifery of their liberating pedagogy.' It is in the transformation of people from their passive mode to becoming pro-active beings in shaping their own destinies that TfD implicates itself. Theatre is a powerful instrument in this process as Augusto Boal (1985: 122) notes, 'Theatre is a weapon, and it is the people who should wield it.'

In developing critical awareness a whole range of other knowledges emerge: individuals within the group come to understand that their problems are similar to one another, that their life experiences are common, and that they generally belong in the same category in the society. A sense of collective belonging and cooperative action may consequently result. In the development of individual confidence and group rapport, a cohesive community is discovered. It is indeed a discovery because, the paradox of marginalization and alienation is that, although all the members of a particular community may have the same problems, and may be suffering in the hands of the same subjugator, they live in fear, jealousy and mistrust of each other (Kerr, 1988: 176). So, when this mould is broken TfD can claim success. It can also lay claim to engendering development, not in its statistical listing of physical structures erected in villages, but in the liberation of potential in individuals to understand and be able to change structures in enhancement of the quality of their lives (Abah, 1995: 4). How, therefore, may this happen in practice?

Creativity, participation and change

Within the TfD discourse, theatre functions on several levels and in different dimensions. It provides a forum for a community to discuss the issues and problems of concern in their lives. It is also an occasion in which the village may come together for communal entertainment. It is a medium through which individuals and the community can recreate themselves. In performing these multiple roles, theatre is both agency of change and, is itself a changed entity. The change occurs in a creative environment through participation in which both the participants and the medium emerge differently from the starting point. Let me illustrate this with case studies.

Zimbabwe: performance for change, performance as change

In 1983, three years after independence, Zimbabwe was fighting a different battle than the liberation war it had waged against the Rhodesian army for decades. It was no longer a war with Ian Smith over the transformation of apartheid Rhodesia to become a democratic society. The fight was how to achieve unity and integration in a politically divided country. The two political parties, ZANU-PF led by Robert Mugabe, and ZAPU-PF headed by Joshua Nkomo, were at loggerheads. Demobilised war veterans were complaining of lack of attention and inadequate resettlement arrangements were rife. The entire nation was experiencing the frustration of the reality of the wait before the fulfilment of the promises which the end of the war and the campaign pronouncements of politicians meant for them. Part of the picture and the sense of frustration are captured in the following description of events in a *povo* (meeting) at Karumazondo (Abah, 1995: 3–4):

> The economic problems of the nation are taking their toll on the rural population. In December 1982, the country devalued the dollar by 20 per cent. States tax was consequently raised by 23 per cent to offset the loss to the state from the devaluation. An inflationary rate of 18 per cent resulted. Bus fares were up, fertilisers were more expensive, grinding mill charges were more than before and school fees were on the rise. The problem was compounded by natural disaster: drought. All of these affected the ordinary persons in the villages; and these were the issues the *povo* was addressing.

However, it was apparent that this was not the first time such a meeting was being held; and the frustration of the repeat performance was too much to contain for one old man. He stood up, and trembling all over with anger he exploded: "How many times will you [party officials] ask us these same questions? What have we got, and how long shall we continue to answer your questions?" The old man was shouted down and his protest ignored. It was an important experience for our workshop and it fired several questions in our head. How does theatre/performance operate in a problem-ridden village where party officials intimidate and alienate rather than build. How should TfD negotiate the tensions between government, symbolised by party officials at the *povo* and the people? And how does it mediate the needs of the ordinary people which are in opposition with that of government? It was clear that both government and the people had common interests. The crisis was that of approach. The officials were not listening to the people. They were only trying to pull the wool over their faces through a democracy of declamation! That is, they gave the impression of caring by organising the *povo* only to talk *at* the people. Without any doubt, the government of Zimbabwe was well aware of this crisis when it put money together with UNESCO, the Swedish Development Agency (SIDA), the German Development Agency (DSE) among others, to call theatre to action in order to mobilise Zimbabweans to unite towards the exercise of national reconstruction.

The theatre process in the workshop was not simply endorsing government and its policies. The animateurs were using theatre to examine the nature of the existing relationships and how much room was given to the people to articulate their needs, since the call for reconstruction was a call for participation which must of necessity begin with needs assessment. The *povo* demonstrated that the ordinary persons had no voice. In our discourse therefore, if the old man was shouted down and humiliated by politicians, theatre was to recover his dignity and reclaim his voice, not only for him but for others like him.

Pungwe, the indigenous performance arts of the people (songs, music, drumming, storytelling and children's play) in combination with dialogue drama was the process of reclamation. For example, needs assessment among workshop participants took place in the context of performance, children's play, storytelling and role play: a mother sits her children in a circle and announces to them that she is going to the market, farm or wherever she chooses to go. Before she goes off however, she asks what each child's needs are. The children make their requests and the mother meets them as best she can. This request and fulfilment sequence was executed in performance through song, dialogue and mime action thus:

Mother:	*Chidanga chidanga!*
Children:	*Ya mamai!*
Mother:	Tells the children she is going to the market and asks them to state their needs before she goes away.
Children:	Requests and complaints are made of different needs and problems.
Mother:	Fulfilment of requests in mime. Mother takes no more than two requests at each break in the exercise. She starts the song again and repeats the sequence until every one's needs are met.

The workshop group and village people expanded this exercise to a national level. The woman playing the mother tied a head scarf on which was printed the national colours of Zimbabwe. At the centre of this design was the picture of Robert Mugabe, the president of the country. Mrs Ponde who was playing the mother now symbolised the government; and the children mirrored the people of Karumazondo making requests for improved facilities and social amenities. One of the requests coming from a participant from Karumazondo was for clean drinking water. At this point a Storyteller takes over from the mother and introduces an improvised drama sketch with the age-old prologue of the Shona[2] storytelling tradition:

Storyteller:	*Ngano, ngano, ngano!*
Community:	*Ngano!*

The Storyteller's water story about some girls from the village who play in, and drink from a stagnant pool of water is enacted. The discussion at the end of the improvisation examined the factors which led to Mary's (the girl in the drama) illness with diarrhoea. The debate as to why there was no potable water in the village was a very heated one. Beyond putting the blame at the doorstep of government, the people of Karumazondo also talked about the need to pool resources and how to mobilise the community towards self-help. This discussion was further improvised as a practice of self-help in the community. It was interesting to see that it was the women who were more willing and active in the improvisation. The men were largely reluctant and only entered the drama when the issue of community members' apathy was raised, and the women leading the improvisation decreed that apathetic villagers would be fined!

There are a number of points of interest here. The image of powerlessness witnessed in the *povo* was replaced with brimming energy and vivaciousness. The performance of their stories had given them a chance to reclaim and listen to their own voices on issues politicians and party agents had refused them hearing. They were bonding together through theatre and performance. The people of Karumazondo were also using theatre to test out their own capabilities to tackle the problems described in the performance. Engaging in the analysis and performance of the issues made it clear to the old man and other community members that their allegiance to, and hope for the government to provide immediate action on community problems would have to be re-examined. They were also coming into the awareness that the most coherent agent of change was themselves. This knowledge that they were, collectively, a repository of change was liberating.

All of these were possible because the exercise was participatory, in which Karumazondo 'wrote' and performed itself. In this participatory theatre, culture (*pungwe*) was both a performative as well as a discursive strategy. This is what Paulo Freire would call 'cultural action for freedom'. On the immediate level of change we are talking about re-created individuals in so far as they had developed more confidence in themselves, and come to the agreement that they constituted a community of individuals with common needs. On the larger community level, the change may not be immediately perceptible. However, the building blocks for a larger community impact were being laid.

In the Zimbabwe case therefore, we witness theatre and performance in aid of change. One, it was addressing the need for government and party officials to be more responsive to the cries of the people. Perhaps more significantly, it was attacking despondency and revealing that the people were, in themselves, agents of change. In this exercise *pungwe* was playing new roles, or better put, it was continuing its radical redeployment which had been quite effective in the war years. During the liberation struggle, *pungwe* was used as an instrument of education and mobilisation for national solidarity. In the context of crisis it became a unifying force between combatants in the forests and trenches as they sang songs to boost morale, maintain the night vigil and to plan manoeuvres. In the villages, *pungwe* was enlisted to explain the war, canvass support and to strengthen resolve. Whether in the trenches with soldiers or in the village around log fires, *pungwe* was contributing to nation-building (Abah, 1985: 10; Kidd, 1980: 20). Here also, we could see that in its new format of oral writing and hybridisation, drama was demythologised and reconfigured.

Mazah and Kwanga: gendering the debate[3]

In Mazah it was not the demystification of drama that was the achievement in itself, but the change in the nature of relationship between genders in the discussion of the community issues that was the scoop. Watch this performance:

- Two members of the community, Jenks and Morrison, are walking to a village meeting. They argue quite heatedly and as they get to the centre of the gathering the debate is loud. The fight is about which one of their community's problems is the most pressing. Morrison believes that a motorable road into the village is of utmost priority. Jenks is, on the other hand, convinced that the calamity is lack of fertiliser and that this therefore, is the life and death issue.
- The improvisation freezes and the community is called to arbitrate in the quarrel. The men – not in fiction now – describe Mazah's calamities due to lack of a motorable access into the village. They illustrate by piggy-backing each other to demonstrate how the sick are transported to the hospital in Jos in order to drive home the point about their suffering.
- One elderly woman creeps out of the shadow where she was sitting and 'collapses' in the centre of the gathering. She complains of hunger and as she is helped up to her feet, she declares with a lot of vehemence that what this village must address immediately is the lack of fertiliser.

The stalemate between Morrison and Jenks which took place in fiction is here recreated in reality between the members of Mazah community. The stalemate was, interestingly, not between the men who piggy-backed each other and the woman who collapsed as individual persons. It was a conflict defined along gender lines. The men wanted the road. The women rejected this priority and upscaled fertiliser. In their daily chores of cooking and managing the family, in their role as farmers, the women knew the pain of watching hungry sons and daughters cry. They have also experienced the terror of some husbands demanding food and pummelling their wives, even when such men have made no provisions for food in the house. So, the women maintained their argument and insisted that they were capable of bringing down any amount of loads from the hill top, and that the community did not therefore need a road. In anger at this contradiction of their stand, the men contended that the absence of road serviced the women's economic interest as they shuttled up and down the hill selling their vegetable crops in Jos. The women hit back at the men and described their concern for the village to be economically motivated. The women said the men had a hidden agenda of wanting to open up the village to land speculators!

And twenty-five kilometres south-east of Mazah, in Kwanga, a more subtle debate was going on. The women were using theatre to discuss two related issues in their lives. They improvised their problems of trekking long distances to grind their grains in milling machines some six kilometres away. They lamented poor transportation and the fact that women had died in labour waiting for transport to take them to hospital some twenty kilometres in Jos. Their needs were therefore ranked in priority order of grinding machine to reduce the women's burden, and better road and transportation for the entire community. Unlike Mazah, there was no quarrel about the priorities here. What was in contention here however, was space for women to articulate their own needs as women among themselves and to their own kind without male interference. What they saw as infringement on their own space by men and their resistance was played out in the dramaturgical debate of the issues in the process of improvisation, as against a public performance of conflict which took place in Mazah.

Within the TfD workshop on women's health, we had both men and women facilitators. The bulk of the community participants from Kwanga were women. Therefore, the dramatisation of the community issues were shaped by them. In the process of this exercise, when male facilitators animated discussions the women trumped up the issue of the grinding machine. If, however, women facilitators did the animation, the women discussed intimate women's health issues and the gender problems of the community such as the marginal role of women in community development issues. The practice in operation here was a subterranean performance in which women implemented censorship on men's participation, but at the same time zoning a physical target of achievement, the grinding machine, to them. Yet, this censorship and exclusion of men were in the service of the women's goal of acquiring space for themselves in so far as the machine would reduce the burden of domestic chores on them. At the same time, on the surface, there was a semblance of inclusion of men in the debate in as much as the women had allocated to them the fight for a grinding machine (Abah, 1996).

The power of participation in a dramaturgical process beginning with dialogue which allows for an identification of common group interests can enhance gender perceptions in development action. When at the end of the one-week workshop, the women of Kwanga formed their own organisation with officials duly elected, it was indeed a tribute to enlightenment and the consequent empowerment generated by participatory theatre. The power of performance to reveal hidden tensions plus the power in the possibility of individuals to name their problems, to be capable of acting out one's opinions is a function of a dehierarchialised forum in which participation may cross gender boundaries as in Mazah, or provide space in which gender-sensitive development matters may be articulated as in Kwanga.

The skit 'balloon' featuring Morrison and Jenks created a framework into which the people of Mazah could fit their debates. Although the men held their ground and largely intimidated the women into silence, at the close of the TFD workshop here, both women and men attested that 'Never before have we in this village sat together to discuss our problems as we did in this past one week'.

Onyuwei: theatrical inversion and the agony of the masters of the drama

The 1989 Theatre for Development workshop in Onyuwei encompassed a complex of agendas and occasioned a whole range of discussions, negotiations and reactions. The original intention of the workshop was to examine the agricultural problems of the three villages of Onyuwei, Adankari and Otobi. It emerged during the workshop that agriculture was not in itself a problem in any of these communities, which in their location in the Middle Belt are part of the food basket area of the country. The problems experienced by these villages were the absence of the supporting structures which would make agricultural production viable and to be optimised here. For example, look at this summary of the Iganya scenario (Abah, 1995: 100):

> It is about 5 p.m. You are approaching a village in the late afternoon on a hot September day. A crowd of women are walking towards you. When you meet, it is a group of women, all of whom are traditional birth attendants (TBAs) attending to a woman in labour. Iganya, the pregnant woman, had been delivered of one of the twin babies in the morning around 9.30 a.m. Roughly eight hours on, the second baby had still not been born! The women were therefore walking Iganya for two reasons. One, they were hoping that the walking would help in the delivery of the baby. Secondly, the group was slowly advancing to the motorable road some five kilometres away where they would find transport to take Iganya to the hospital twenty kilometres away in Otukpo. No transport comes into Onyuwei and Adankari in the months of June to October when the rains are at a peak and the villages are isolated from outside contact by flood waters.
>
> Iganya's second baby is born on the other side of the river after the group had been canoed across in their journey to the hospital. They cross back and head for the village. Three months later when I saw Iganya and asked after her twins, they were both dead!

This experience describes the life of calamity of the people of Adankari and Onyuwei live through in their day to day existence. It is a life of absences: no health facilities, no roads, no potable water, *et cetera*. So, what opportunities do people in such marooned villages have to talk about their problems? To whom do they speak? Most of all, do they constitute any force to change things around?

The 1989 Theatre for Development (TfD) workshop, organised by the Nigerian Popular Theatre Alliance (NPTA)[4], was to speak to these issues and to mobilise the communities towards thinking out intervention strategies. Intervention was not just seen in terms of how to build a health clinic in Adankari, or how bridges may be built across the many streams which deny Onyuwei access to the outside world for nearly six months of the year. A critical understanding of the issues was necessary in order for a proper conception of intervention to be grasped. Theatre, as an agency of change, was therefore, in pursuit of an agenda of conscientization.

Performance as intervention

Improvisation, culture and intervention were key elements in the debate and exercise of conscientisation in the workshop. The performance in Onyuwei focused on the problem of access road and absence of bridges across the streams. These problems were discussed in the context of a political campaign in which two sons of the village were contesting with each other for votes in order to win political seats.

The performance began as a festival of masquerades welcoming the home boys and inviting them to put their manifestoes on the table:

- The flute summons the first aspirant, Ejembi, to present his manifesto. The drums begin to pulsate. The mood is that of celebration on one hand, and that of expectation on the other. Ejembi bursts into the arena, with his acolytes all dancing to the drumming which is particular to the *Aringa* and *Ikyahoho* masquerades. With a crisp and authoritative wave of the fly whisk in his hand, Ejembi silences the drums. He is full of political antics and jargons. He cajoles and he bullies. But he also placates. He makes promises to the electorate: he will give them goats, cows, beer and a car each for the farmers! That is not all. He will also give yams and unlimited cash. To top it all, he promises to build the bridge across the stream, *if* the community votes him into office.
- Ejembi calls in his supporters and the team of engineers which he has assembled from Cameroon, Canada, Jamaica and London to build the bridge with immediate effect! Etta, the female singer from Onyuwei who is well known in the district, enters the performance to amplify and embellish this aspirant's speeches in song. She also re-enacts some of the points in the manifesto. Ejembi concludes his solicitations with an expression of his 'largesse' by distributing money to the electorate. He dances out with his team of engineers.
- Ogiri starts fluting again and *Aringa* performs a welcoming signatory of Ejiga, the second aspirant. Ejiga comes forward to defend his decision to contest. He is not as flamboyant as his opponent. He is not as rich as his rival and he makes no elaborate promises. He admits to modesty in his speech, but declares, 'I have good intentions and I know you have been cheated by other politicians many times before'. Ejiga therefore pledges to change things around, with support and cooperation from the people. Before he goes, he reveals that although he does not have money to throw around, he has mobilised a team of engineers from Canada, England, Italy and Japan to build the bridge which has been a constant crisis in the life of the community. He concludes his campaign by leading his team round for a solidarity handshake with the elders.
- At the end of throwing their agendas open, flute and drums summon the two aspirants into the arena to answer questions from the community. Once in the middle of the gathering, the people ask to know what makes them different from all the politicians who had made promises to them in the past without delivering the goods. The aspirants in turn talk political platitudes, they employ theatrics in their bids to convince their listeners. The arena remains sceptical …

The points of interest in the Onyuwei performance were not only about the political manifestoes of the campaigners as presented in performance. The interest was to do with what the community did to the aspirants and their manifestoes and altered the way in which they were performed. Over a period of ten days the animateurs had lived and worked with some members of the community, discussing and analysing the problems and issues of concern to the village. They collectively synthesised these discussions into a community drama.

This exercise holds interest in three dimensions. One is the approach which was participatory. The members of Onyuwei decided on the priority issues to be addressed, they participated in putting the scenario together, and in performing the drama. Two, the drama which was performed to the community on the last day of the workshop was in every sense a community drama. However, the extent to which it conveyed the community's feelings and aspirations was further debated in performance. This occurred through interventions in which various persons who were not part of putting the scenario of the performance together entered into the fiction of the drama to alter the content and narrative direction. For example, when a government official in the drama comes to the village to demand to know why this community is defaulting in its payment, Aladi, one of the women leaders in the village springs up from where she is sitting – outside of the drama – and in a shrill voice declares that they are not going to pay any more taxes in this community. She gives the conditions the government must meet for the village to continue to pay taxes: the government must build a motorable road to Onyuwei so that the farmers can take their farm produce to the market with ease. Aladi, now role-playing, declares that even as she is standing in front of the government official (played by Ghonche Materego from Tanzania), her legs are aching and that she has been having problems with her pregnancy, and there is no clinic to go to. The protest is taken up by everybody, and Agboji, the chief in this village takes a directorial role: 'Move closer to the man from government. Make as if you want to slap him!' The arena is agog with support: '*Ee baa!*' (That's right!), '*Akpabana!*' (Thunder down!). Aladi picks the cue and is energised by the community support. She becomes more belligerent and advances towards the official. Ghonche is becoming uncomfortable and looks round for an escape route, as he is no longer sure if there is any divide between drama and reality. Ndumbe Eyoh, from Cameroon, sends an SOS to Jenkeri Okwori (Nigeria), the group leader, to bring the drama back to the original scenario which they had structured. Jenkeri shoos the messenger off and euphorically declares, 'That is it! The community has taken over, and the people are writing their own drama. Let it go on!'

The intervention which took place showed that popular will was asserting itself over a minority interpretation of the community's problems. What happened here could not have been a better demonstration of Brecht's (1973: 60) dialectical understanding of the popular when he said that:

> Our own conception of 'popular' refers to the people who are not only involved in the process of development but are eventually taking it over, forcing it, deciding it.

In taking over what a representative group had created on their behalf, and changing it in front of everybody in the community, the village arena was not only a site for witnessing performance but a location for negotiation. Indeed as Jeffrey Mason (1996: 307) observes:

If social space itself is a field of contention, then social performance becomes a means of urging that contention, of expressing difference, asserting ownership and displaying relationship.

The negotiation in this contention was between the members of the community and the outside catalysts on one hand, and between the members of the village who were part of creating the drama and those who were not, on the other. On another level, it was between fiction and reality. The catalysts had given an interpretation to both the social and the historical realities of Onyuwei. They had in addition, packaged it for viewing (as opposed to for interrogation). Yet it should have been clear to us that the contractual relationship between the animators and the animated was a mutual agreement to share experiences. Formatted in the context of improvisation which, as Margaret Drewal (1991: 43) notes, 'is transformational, often participatory and competitive, in which case it constitutes a multi-dimensional process of argumentation', set in a social space which 'submits no single individual ..., [which] is produced by the community and becomes the site of constant negotiation', and where 'Authority and access are subject to dispute' (Mason, 1996: 306), the animators ought to have realised that the open framework of the contract of mutuality must allow for revising the terms while the event is in process. Aladi's intervention was part of such a negotiation and revision. Some of the animateurs expected intervention. Others were taken off guard and they howled!

Fiction and reality were also in contest in which the one intermediated the other to decide the course of action. When the government official makes his demand for tax in fiction, and the community applied this fiction to the reality of their lives, both bile and adrenalin rose and Aladi jumped! In concord with her and the community's feelings, the village chief got up from his seat, moved into the performance space and in an ironical twist, this real chief began to explain to the fictional chief in the drama his people's decision not to pay any more taxes to a government which has not recognised their contributions, and indeed their existence. The chief also wants to prove to the official that the payment of tax in the face of government neglect had eroded his respect among his people. At this point also, another twist happens in the dramaturgical procedure. The chief takes on a directorial role again urging the people around the arena to boo him in corroboration. An elderly man gets up, wags his walking stick at the chief and shoos him off. The chief's point is proved, and he concludes, 'You see!'

These interventions reveal a deep closeness to, and the involvement of the people in the matters the improvisation was dealing with. It was alright for the animateurs, in collaboration with some members of the village to construct a drama about Onyuwei. It was fun for every one to watch the performance and enjoy the dances. However, the complexities of the issues and the frustrations of many lifetimes in the evolution of this primal enclave could not be penetrated by ten days of work. So, its members saw the missing articles of the argument in the drama. And the village stood up to re-write the story. Even as this exercise was cast in a playful mould, it was an act of 'revolution' (Van Erven, 1992).

The eurythmics of intervention

All of these twists and turns describe a new aesthetics and a different kind of semiological viewing of theatre practice. It is the aesthetics of un-completion (Etherton, 1988: 3) and of the un-ending play in which oracy plays a significant role (Abah, 1987: 109; Ong, 1982). The aesthetics of un-completion is concerned with process rather than product, it is about participation and action rather than delegation, it emphasises collective creation rather than authorial tyranny. And, the meaning which the whole exercise conveys very often seeks to articulate itself through cultural forms. Participation allows for changes in perspectives occasioning deeper analysis of issues. It also changes the dramatic action. Participation is the road to conscientisation in its dialogic argumentation in both verbal and gestural expressions. Zakes Mda (1993: 164) has also noted this link in his work in Lesotho.

The two most powerful signs of how this aesthetics was explicated in the Onyuwei performance at the 1989 workshop were, firstly, in the way the conflict in the drama was not between the two political aspirants, but was shifted to pit the contestants in the fiction of the drama against the community outside the fiction of the performance. It was the people sitting outside, fringing and defining the performance space who constantly broke the boundary of separation by physically intervening in the action, and by asking questions which required the aspirants to respond. Secondly, the manifestoes in themselves were not the articles of interest but the manner in which they were performed. In performance, Etta, a virtuoso singer from the village, and who is well known all over the district, entered the drama and assigned herself a permanent role. It is significant to note that Etta was not part of the group which put the drama together. She entered the performance to sing the speeches of the political aspirants. In addition to this, she embellished and acted out some points in the manifestoes which she considered important. Etta was, indeed operatising the campaign. However, a closer look at her role revealed that Etta's performance provided a critique of the manifestoes from within the drama. In her operatising of the speeches she commented on the aspirants' agendas, referred listeners to history and threw challenges to both aspirants and the community. Etta was in the process of shaping critical opinion and setting up the politicians for demolition. Her opera was an organised contrapuntal show to subvert the campaign. There were, no doubt, two performances going on at the same time, but in antipodal directions. Etta's subtextual and subliminal performance of subversion and provocation was contributory to sharpening the tension and confrontation which occurred in the arena. Therefore, when the government official from Lagos came to insist that the community must pay tax, enough ground work for challenge had been done by Etta. She had also further contributed to use of cultural forms in the performative process. At this point of a combat between government, symbolised by the Officer, and the people, two powerful masquerades, *Ikyahoho* and *Egede*, were called into action:

> *Kyaa hoho! Kyaa hoho!! Ikyaa ho!!!*
> *Ikyahoho rebe oche!*
> Kyaa hoho! Kyaa hoho!! Ikyaahoho!!!
> Ikyahoho the eater of human flesh!!!

And soon after *Egede* follows:

> *Ola bobo ee, ola bobo!*
> *Ikwu nonm'oche ola bobo!*
> Flaming fire, yes it is flaming fire!
> Death which kills people is flaming fire!

Ikyahoho and *Egede* are masquerades of war which in the internecine period of this community's history performed to celebrate prowess and invincibility in battle. As Abah (1997) observes, 'For these masquerades to be summoned at the high point in the confrontation was an evocation of, and reawakening of the old fighting spirit.' And in identification with this spirit, the community remained resolute in their decision and insisted that the Officer must go back and tell government that tax paying was over here.

Then, the greatest irony of all happened. The people of Onyuwei, and also Adankari, were not only rejecting tax in fiction. They meant to carry the threat through by refusing to pay any more taxes in their real world. And the animateurs began to beg for the *status quo* to be upheld by the villages! I cannot help but recall Julie Salverson (1996: 181) in the way she re-echoes the ethical issues and questions which those of us who are Theatre for Development practitioners in Africa have asked several times, and which we continue to battle with:

> As artists and educators, we must continually ask ourselves: in what context are risky stories told? Within what frameworks did they originate? and what is the cost to the speaker? Taking responsibility should extend beyond an ongoing inventory of who we are as individuals to an understanding that there are stakes for those with whom we work – stakes that exist, but are never more than partially knowable.

In the case of the 1989 workshop in the three villages of Onyuwei, Adankari and Otobi, the animateurs became aware that beyond the euphoria of performance and intervention, that after Etta's opera the dangers of implementing the outcome of conscientisation were too great for both villagers and catalysts. So, we asked for acquiescence and abrogated empowerment and action! We turned round to fight change which we had spent ten days nurturing. Herein lies the contradiction and perhaps the ineffectuality of empowerment/change sponsored by an exogenous group (Epskamp, 1989), even when the process is given an organic veneer of culture. This is an area TfD must continue to interrogate.

Conclusion

In the project of change in Theatre for Development, the procedure encompasses an oral 'writing' of the stakeholders' world in order to create a new vision. The components of this 'writing' which is largely verbal, ephemeral and transient include improvisation, intervention and culture. We should conceive of improvisation here as a series of spontaneous events (songs, dance, drumming, role-play) and actions, at the centre of which lies conflict and negotiation. Consequently, intervention or performative interrogation becomes a way in which improvisation is remixed and reshaped to create new meanings and to change perceptions. Very often, the vehicle is culture – a whole gamut of visceral practices which are integral to the life systems of a particular group of people, through which existence is understood. Culture may indeed be seen as an ontological exposition of both self and community. That is, it is a constant redefinition of community and self, an act of identity in the process of constant formation. The combination of all these in a creative process of shaping vision and engineering change is what I have called perforaltics (Abah, 1997: 34).

It is the improvisatory combination of music, mime and dialogue drama composed orally (as against scripting) from information and facts in the lives of the people, and given life in a cultural framework on the sandy village arena in front of an adjudicating community whose judgement is carried out through entering into the action of the performance to change the narrative and meaning. In this processual practice where consumerism, product and closure are abrogated, the semiology of TfD is defined and decided by an array of occurrences in flux answering to changing perspectives. The *mise-en-scène* is the entire village with forests and singing birds, goats, chicken and crying babies. Costumes are ample in the rags of poverty clinging to people's backs, and bare bodies with scars of labour and suffering tattooed on them. This *mise-en-scène* is the utopian world of sharing and of not knowing much else, and of limited contact that the people have lived in all their lives.

But when the performance is over, they are rustled and agitated. Yet, in this practice it is the community which stays on top of the situation and above the fear which the animateurs feel and out of which they reverse change.

Notes

1 Theatre for Development is also known by a number of other names which include: Popular Theatre, Community Theatre, Theatre for Integrated Development, Theatre for Integrated Rural Development, Peoples Theatre and Political Theatre.
2 Shona is the language spoken by the largest linguistic/ethnic group, the Shona, in Zimbabwe. The second largest is Ndebele.
3 The workshop in Mazah and Kwanga jointly organised by the Nigerian Popular Theatre Alliance and Women in Nigeria, was part of a two-year project on Women's Health issues, 1992–1994, sponsored by the MacArthur Foundation of Chicago. The workshop was in March 1993.
4 The Nigerian Popular Theatre Alliance is a non-governmental organisation using theatre as a means to instigate grass roots development. The organisation came into existence in March 1989. The workshop which NPTA organized in 1989 was sponsored by UNESCO with support from other agencies such as SIDA, DSE, the Commonwealth Foundation and the World Association for Christian Communication.

References

Abah, Oga S. 1985, 'Popular Theatre As a Strategy for Development: The Zimbabwe Example', *Fako: Journal of Literary and Language Studies*, Vol. 1, No. 1, English Department, University of Yaounde, Cameroon.

—— 1987, 'Popular Theatre As a Strategy for Education and Development: The Example of Some African Countries', Ph.D Thesis, University of Leeds, U.K. (Unpublished).

—— 1990, 'Popular Theatre Dissects Community Issues in Rural Africa', *Reflections*, International Fund for the Promotion of Culture (Unesco), Paris.

—— , Ejembi, C. L. and Okwori, J. Z. 1994, *Under Siege: Women's Health Issues*, Report of the MacArthur Foundation-Sponsored workshops in Benue, Kaduna and Plateau States.

—— 1995, 'Perspectives in Popular Theatre: Orality as a Definition of New Realities', in: Eckhard Breitinger (ed.), *Theatre and Society in Africa*, Bayreuth, Bayreuth African Studies.

—— 1996, 'The Dynamics of Intervention in Community Theatre for Development', *Contemporary Theatre Review*.

—— 1997, *Case Studies in the Practice of Theatre for Development*, Zaria, Index Publications.

Boal, Augusto 1979, *Theatre of the Oppressed*, 2nd edn, New York, Theatre Communications Group.

—— 1995, *The Rainbow of Desire: The Boal Method of Theatre and Therapy*, London, Routledge.

Brecht, Bertolt 1973, *Brecht on Theatre: The Development of An Aesthetic*, London, Eyre Methuen.

Drewal, Margaret T. 1991, 'The State of research on Performance in Africa', *African Studies Review*, Vol. 34, No. 3.

Van Erven, Eugene, 1992, *The Playful Revolution: Theatre and Liveration in Asia*, Bloomington, Indiana University Press.

Etherton, Michael 1988, 'Popular Theatre for Change: From Literacy to Oracy', *Media Development*, Popular Theatre Issue, Vol. XXXV, No. 3.

Epskamp, Kees P. 1989, *Theatre in Search of Social Change: The Relative Significance of Different Theatrical Approaches*, The Hague, Centre for the Study of Education in Development Countries (CESO).

Freire, Paulo 1972, *Pedagogy of the Oppressed*, Middlesex, Penguin Books.

Kerr, David 1988, 'Theatre and Social Issues in Malawi: Performers, Audiences, Aesthetics', *New Theatre Quarterly*, Vol. IV, No. 14.

Kidd, Ross, 1980, 'Peoples Theatre, Conscientisation and Struggle', *Media Development*, Vol. 27, No. 3.

Mason, Jeffrey D. 1996, 'Street Fairs: Social Space, Social Performance', *Theatre Journal*, Vol. 48, No. 3.

Mda, Zakes, 1993, *When People Play People*, London, Zed Books.

Ong, Walter J. 1982, *Orality and Literacy: The Technologizing of the World*, New York, Routledge.

Salverson, Julie 1996, 'Performing Emergency: Witnessing Popular Theatre, and the Lie of the Literal', *Theatre Topics*, Vol. 6, No. 2.

11 Playing the puppets

Innovation and rivalry in Bamana youth theatre of Mali

Mary Jo Arnoldi

Theatre – both masked and nonmasked – has a long history in rural Mali. Village communities place a positive value on innovation and rivalry in the theatre, a factor that contributes to its continuing vitality and popularity. In this study I explore one manifestation of this theatre, youth association puppet theatre as it is performed throughout the Segu region and in selected areas of adjoining regions. I focus on one Bamana village's theatrical tradition; on how innovation and rivalry are incorporated into the definition of puppet theatre; how they are articulated in the construction of a performance; and how they shape the participants' reception of the theatre.[1]

Kiranko (Kirango) is a moderate-sized village (upwards of 5,000 residents) approximately 33 kilometers northeast of the city of Segu on the Niger river. The village is multiethnic and comprised of five neighbourhoods: one Bamana, two Somono, one Bozo, and one for strangers. Most of the people in Kiranko are farmers (Bamana) and fishermen (Somono and Bozo), although a number of individuals now work for Malian government services, schools, and hospitals in the area.

In the Bamana quarter the *kamalen ton*, the youth association, performs puppet theatre. Membership in the *ton* is mandatory and includes all young men from the age of 14 to over 40 and young unmarried women over age 14, regardless of lineage affiliation or social status. The association participates as a group in farming activities and local public works projects, as well as in performing puppet theatre.

The puppets are performed twice annually, once prior to the harvest season in October/November and once prior to the planting season in May/June during the New Year festival, *san yelema*. They call the October/November performances *bin sogo bo* (the grass animals come forth). During this season the puppets perform on one afternoon and evening. The May/June performances, *sogo bo* (the animals come forth), occur in the late afternoon and evening on three con-secutive days. Sogo bo is embedded in a larger set of youth association activities which include preparing festival meals for the village, New Year's greetings ceremonies, and so on. The sogo bo performances are relatively recent in the Bamana quarter, dating from only the mid-1950s.

The characters of this theatre include a large number of bush and water animals, mythological and fantastic creatures, stereotyped characters representing conventional social roles such as mothers, farmers, hunters, weavers, musicians, colonial as well as modern-day police, and government officials. The theatre uses both masks and puppets, which the troupe distinguishes according to construction and costume, although not every character falls neatly into one of these categories. There are costumes entirely constructed of grasses or cloth which cover a wooden understructure, as well as dancers who wear only face, crest, or helmet masks. However, the majority of characters consist of rod and rod-and-string puppets. The first category of puppets are large animals heads, known as *sogokun*, operated from below by a wooden rod. They range in height from approximately one to six feet. The puppet heads themselves may also support smaller rod-and-string puppets, generally about a foot tall, which are attached to the crown of the larger head or to its horns.

The puppet head projects from the front of a large costumed construction representing the animal's body which is at least a yard wide and four or five feet high. The understructure of lashed branches covered completely by grasses or cloth houses the dancer/puppeteer. The entire figure including the puppet head and costumed body is known as *sogoba* (the big animal).

A second category of puppet, *sogodenw* (little animals) and *mogoniw* (little people), includes small rod-and-string puppets. Independent of the larger animal head, they emerge from the back of the costumed construction. Several puppeteers hidden under the construction animate the smaller puppets from beneath this mobile stage. These rod and rod-and-string puppets distinguish Segu theatre, setting it apart from other masked youth theatre performed in adjoining Bamana areas.

Bin Sogo Bo: 'The Grass Animals Come Forth' Kiranko, November 1979

Preparations begin in earnest several weeks prior to the performance. Young men harvest the *ko malo* (rice grass) which grows in marshes and canals near the village, weaving it into the skirting characteristic of this season's puppets, *binsogo* (the grass animals). Puppets and masks are brought out of storage to be repainted and refurbished.

The day before the performance the young men retire to compounds scattered throughout the quarter to begin constructing the understructures and costumes. Secrecy must be maintained during all of these preparations so the association declares these compounds off-limits to nonmembers. Ton leaders check the progress of the preparations, settle disputes, and lend their authority to the enterprise – injecting a sense of urgency into the affair. Senior members of the association work on the more complicated constructions, while junior members sew the costumes and prepare the simpler ones. Neophytes run countless errands. Whoever participates in the preparation of a particular character retains the right to escort it during its performance.

The understructures are fashioned from branches lashed together with cords. When they are completed, grass skirting and cloth costumes are sewn onto the structure. Once they are fully assembled, the puppets are danced behind the scenes to test the strength and durability of the construction. Offstage competition among the young men is strong as final decisions are made about who will publicly dance the character. Performers try on the constructions, make adjustments, and practice the appropriate dances.

In the early afternoon the performers move the completed characters to several compounds adjacent to the plaza. Sentries are posted to keep out curiosity seekers, mostly young children. As the audience begins to gather on the plaza, members of the association assigned to crowd control direct the seating and continually chase the young children out of the dance circle. Elder men are seated in a section reserved for important guests; women are seated together on the elders' left; young men not directly involved with the preparations complete this inner circle. Young children sit with their fathers or mothers or sit behind the young men seated around the dance arena. Strangers generally stand behind these reserved sections. During the performance, the young men assigned to crowd-control shout encouragement to the women's chorus, clear a path for the entrance and exit of each puppet, and maintain order.

By about 4.30 when the dance prologue begins, the various drum teams have arrived and the lead female singer and her chorus are seated on the sidelines. Young men and women from the youth association enter the arena and dance as a group, moving counterclockwise. As the dance progresses the drummers gradually increase the tempo until the dancers' unity is broken and they rush to the sidelines. There they quickly re-form and repeat the same pattern several times.

The group dances are followed by a sequence of acrobatic dance competitions among young men in the association. A dance team consisting of two young men in the same age set enters the circle and dances in unison. As the tempo increases the young men punctuate their performances with somersaults, back flips, and leaps. Other young men shout encouragement to their peers, and young women rush into the ring to praise individual dancers, giving them head scarves. The dances gain momentum until several sets of young men from different age groups are competing with one another simultaneously. Suddenly the action shifts and Gon (Baboon) darts into the circle, makes one quick circuit, and exits – cueing the audience that the puppet drama has begun.

Karankaw (the People of Karan) enters. This character, representing an antelope, has a rod-puppet head and a massive body covered with colourful textiles. Out of the back of his body, several smaller rod-and-string puppets appear in the guise of a farmer wielding a hoe, two women pounding grain in a mortar and pestle, a beautiful young woman, and a colonial officer on horseback. As Karankaw enters the circle his male escorts sing his song, which is quickly picked up and carried by the female lead singer and women's chorus. The puppet moves slowly around the circle in a counterclockwise direction. The escorts guide his movements both physically and verbally and keep his cloth costume pulled closely to the ground, effectively obscuring the feet of the puppeteers. Karankaw sways his massive body left and right and then stops and lowers his body to the ground. The tempo of the drumming and singing suddenly quickens and the small puppets on his back begin to dance wildly and dart about. Just as suddenly Karankaw rises, resumes his original gait, and continues slowly around the arena, stopping and repeating the sequence at several points in his circuit. When the puppet makes a full circle, young men seated on the sidelines surge forward to lead him away while singing his praises.

Just as Karankaw exits Gon reappears. He lunges into the crowd scattering the audience. He is forcibly restrained by a rope and pulled back into the circle by his attendant. In contrast to Karankaw, his dance involves quick acrobatic steps. He periodically breaks away from his attendant and darts back into the crowd, again scattering the audience until he can once more be restrained.

A brief musical interlude follows Gon's performance and then Mme. Sarata, two puppets representing beautiful women, enter. The dancers sway gracefully around the circle, flirting with the young men on the sidelines. When they approach a group of young men, they modestly bow and turn their faces slightly away. Emboldened, they then dance, swaying their hips. The young men respond with shouts and gestures of praise and appreciation.

Mme. Sarata is followed by a musical sequence, and then Mali Kono (the Great Bird of Mali) enters the ring. A large and elaborately costumed figure, he is visible from any vantage point on the circle and his arrival draws an enthusiastic response from the spectators. He moves majestically around the arena, slowly flapping his wings and bobbing his head to the ground in imitation of the great fisher bird. Suddenly he stops. The drummers accelerate the tempo, Kono twirls, dips, and brings his wings into full extension as if to fly. Spectators jump to their feet and rush into the ring praising the performance while the crowd shouts enthusiastically.

The final puppet to enter the circle is Taasi Doni (Reflect a Little) in the form of a voluptuous woman. The dancer wears a helmet mask with an elaborately carved coiffure and his chest and buttocks are amply padded. The tempo of the drumming is slow but the clearly punctuated rhythms lend themselves to similarly punctuated and exaggerated hip movements. Taasi Doni's performance elicits laughter and incites a barrage of sexual bantering. Her performance signals the end of the afternoon show and the audience disperses for an evening meal.

Around 8.00 P.M. the audience begins to trickle back onto the plaza for *su fe sogo* (the night animals). The drummers warm up as the children – always first to arrive – dance and mime the various puppets in a general melee. Once the singers are in place and the senior drum team takes its position, the performance begins. In the Bamana quarter, the first character to be played is always Nama (Hyena), a grass full-body mask about six feet tall and four feet wide. He is played in total darkness so that when he enters the circle the moonlight picks up his silhouette. Throughout his performance, Nama continually transforms his shape, sometimes standing boldly upright, then suddenly dropping into a twirling ball of grass brushing up against the crowd. Nama is followed by two other grass full-body masks – a type of bird known as Falakani, and Bala (Porcupine). In the intervals between performances, the women's chorus sings songs on topics ranging from marriage to death.

Following the grass animals' performances, electric lights are turned on, bathing the circle in a soft glow. Two rod puppets, Dage (male and female Roan

Antelopes), enter the ring. Their gait is slow, although they periodically burst into an acrobatic display, twirling and bobbing. As they exit, a large cloth puppet with a gaping mouth, Suruku Malobali (Shameless Hyena), dashes into the circle and quickly exits catching the crowd by surprise. Kononin (Little Bird) then enters the ring giving an extended performance, followed by a second pair of antelope puppets. Suddenly Suruku Malobali re-enters, dashes to and fro, and exits. His brief foray is followed by a musical interlude lasting well over ten minutes during which the chorus sings the legend of Nama of Minjado, a young man who once cured a famous singer. As the song ends, Jolenjo Kono, another species of bird, appears. His movements are quick and alert. Jolenjo Kono flaps his jaw and twirls his head completely around as he dances around the circle.

When he exits the lights are cut and Bilanjan (Tall Beast) enters. This grass full-body mask is well over eight feet high with two winglike extensions at least a yard long. From this stately gait Bilanjan suddenly erupts into a whirling ball of grass, pulling in his wings and completely transforming his shape. This acrobatic display is greeted with great enthusiasm. As he exits the lights are turned on again.

Following a brief musical interlude, Sigi (Bush Buffalo) enters, majestically lumbering into the circle in keeping with his role as Sogo Mansa (King of Animals). His dance is punctuated with brief interludes of energy as he twirls and dips. He is followed by a second musical interlude in which the chorus sings of knowledge and destiny.

The performance is well into its third hour by the time Sogoni Kelen (Little Lone Antelope) enters. In marked contrast to Sigi, he gives an energetic dance display, bringing the audience to its feet. Close on his heels is Suruku Nama, another Hyena. Unlike Nama, the grass version of this character, Suruku is a rod puppet who flaps his jaws and stomps around the circle. His song compares his heavy gait to the lion's light step.

Again the lights are cut and as the audience's eyes adjust to the gloom, Bilisi the three-headed genie enters. He quickly moves about the circle as the chorus sings, 'Who has provoked Bilisi to go on this rampage?' As Bilisi exits, the chorus sings the praises of all the puppets as well as the young men in the association.

The lights go on for the entrance of Waraba Caco – the Great Cat with white markings. His head is a large rod puppet; his body, a massive barrel-like construction. Waraba Caco sways right and left and saunters around the circle, occasionally breaking into an energetic dance. When he exits, Suruku Malobali (Shameless Hyena) again darts into the ring but never one to stay long, he quickly exits. Then two puppets identified as Roan Antelopes enter. Newer versions of the antelopes played previously, their heads shoot up several feet, drop back close into their shoulders, pop up again, and drop at a ninety degree angle perpendicular to their bodies.

The next puppet to appear is an antelope with large silver-colored horns, whose song identifies her as Maisa (a contraction of a woman's name, Umu Isatu), a legendary female beauty who once lived in a neighbouring region beyond the Bani river. As Maisa exits, Misice and Misimuso (Bull and Cow) enter. Their gait is slow and measured and their song speaks of fulfilling the destiny to which one is born. The puppets now follow one another in close succession as the performance moves through its fourth hour.

Saga (Ram), Sine (Gazelle), and Njona (Wildcat) appear one after the other in quick succession. The lights are suddenly cut and Shumusoni (Little Female Sorcerers) enter. All made of grass, these characters swish around the circle, twirling and occasionally brushing up close to the crowd.

The performance is in its fifth hour when Tilen (Giraffe) enters. He extends his neck, bobs, and whirls. Tilen's appearance cues the end of the performance – after he exits, the drumming and singing fade as the audience disperses. The actors gather back in their quarter to replay the event verbally, praise good dancers, suggest improvements for the next season, and enjoy a post-theatre supper.

The aesthetics of performance

By all accounts the village and troupe judged the November 1979 performance as a success. To understand what constitutes a *nyenanje nyana*, a good performance for the Bamana, it is necessary not only to identify formal theatrical rules and strategies, but to examine them as they emerge and are given meaning within a specific socioaesthetic context.

Bamana youth association puppet theatre has a well-articulated social definition. The community characterizes the theatre as *nyenanje*, an entertainment which is part of a larger group of activities defined as *tlon*, play. The puppets and masks are called *tlonke fenw*, playthings.

In Bamana society each age (child, youth, elder) has its own associated activities. Theatre is an activity appropriate to youth, *Kamalen wati*; puppetry is *tonko*, the business of the youth association. Tonko stands in contrast to *ceko*, which includes the activities of elders. In the Bamana men's association, masks controlled by the elders are *boliw* (power objects). Bamana consider ceko to be serious and powerful, while they define tonko as nonserious and powerless. This division of activities as either ceko or tonko is consistent with the everyday roles of elders and youths. Bamana consider elders knowledgeable and responsible, symbols of tradition and order who maintain society. Youths on the other hand are considered ignorant and irresponsible, identified with innovation, unpredictability, and change. Young men not only compete among themselves for reputation, but with their elders and, by extension, their ancestors (see Bird and Kendall 1981). Their ancestors, who were once actors in the theatre, now watch from the audience.

The troupe's ability to create and maintain a tension between the old and the new, between tradition and change, and between order and unpredictability constitutes the basis on which a performance is evaluated. The prologue of group dances followed by more acrobatic competitive ones sets up the creative tension between tradition and change and between old and new. The group dances highlight community and solidarity, hallmarks of tradition associated with elders. The acrobatic dancers foreground individuality and rivalry associated with change, innovation, and youth.

In the puppet theatre itself, these same tensions shape both the repertory and the order of puppet presentations. The afternoon and evening performances are treated as separate by the participants. The order of presentation – from older to newer characters – is maintained in both segments. In Kiranko, Gon (Baboon) opens the afternoon segment, and the three grass masks, Nama (Hyena), Falakani (Bird), and Bala (Porcupine), open the evening segment. According to village historians, these four characters are the original characters borrowed from the theatre of Bozo and Somono fishermen in the first decades of the twentieth century. The troupe always begins the performance with these characters. As the performance unfolds over several hours, the more recent additions to the repertory appear. This order of presentation is consistent throughout the region, constituting a formal performance principle which is given a specific cultural meaning as actors first establish their patrimony through the traditional characters and then compete with it through the introduction of new puppets.

A second principle which shapes the puppet repertory mandates that new characters be continuously added to the drama. In the last 80 years, Kiranko's puppet repertory has changed considerably. Many of the characters in the 1979 performance were said to have been introduced after 1959. New characters often incorporate contemporary themes based on purely local concerns, as well as on regional or national interests. For example, Mali Kono (the Great Bird of Mali), was created around the time of Mali's independence from France in 1962 and people interpret his performance as marking this event. Puppets representing the current head of state, Moussa Troare, and his honour guard were introduced into a number of villages following the 1968 coup d'etat that put him in power. A puppet representing a European woman holding a notepad and pen (not performed in 1979/80) represents that peculiar breed of foreigner, the researcher/ethnographer.

There are several ways to introduce new characters. The ton can commission new puppets such as the bird Jolenjo Kono, presented for the first time in November 1979. Puppets created during a ton's tenure remain associated with it for as long as they are performed. Individual members can also create new characters. A young man can construct the puppet himself or he can commission it from a professional carver and pay for the carving and the costume. He is also responsible for creating the puppet song, often in collaboration with the female singers. Once a puppet has been performed it becomes the property of the association, although the individual retains the right to dance as its attendant whenever it is played. In this way, individual accomplishment as well as group endeavours are recognized and preserved from year to year.

A third way of obtaining new characters is to 'steal' them from other villages. Rivalry among various village troupes is very real. One neighboring troupe said that they would sometimes choose not to play a favorite character if they knew that young men from Kiranko were in the audience. Even if they performed the figure, they would instruct the attendant to steer the performer away from the section of the audience where their rivals were seated.

To alleviate some of the animosity resulting from stealing ideas, and to transform other villages' puppets into their own, troupes will often modify characters by changing their scale, costumes, and accoutrements. They may also create new songs or assign different drum rhythms to 'stolen' characters when performed in a new village. For example, the troupe readily acknowledges that they borrowed Taasi Doni (Reflect a Little) from a neighboring village in the 1970s, retaining the song and drum rhythm but making it their own by changing the image from an antelope to a voluptuous woman.

The community also considers updated versions of older characters as innovations. These revised puppets may replace older versions or be performed together in the same event. Within the last decade, for example, the original Great Bird of Mali, which was first performed at independence, has been replaced by a newer, larger, and more elaborately fabricated version. In the November performance, two versions of Dage (the Roan Antelopes) were performed. The older set of puppets appeared first; the newer set was presented later in the evening.

Before each performance the troupe repaints and refurbishes the puppets, thereby making them 'new.' The troupe's investment of time and resources is an extension of their concern for innovation and competition. The emphasis on newness contrasts sharply with the conceptualization and treatment of masks in this region used in men's association performances like *Komo* and *Kono* (see McNaughton 1979). These masks are power objects rather than playthings, and their transformation over time through the addition of sacrificial materials augments their power.

Innovation also contributes to the creative tension that a troupe accentuates between the expected or normative pattern and the actual performance. This tension is a critical part of the aesthetics of the theatre. When Bamana evaluate artistic form and performance, they use two terms: *nyi* (goodness) and *di* (tastiness). In his research on Bamana aesthetics, James Brink discusses the meanings of these two terms:

> An art form's 'goodness' refers to its basic ordering characteristics, those qualities which give a form of identifiable and appropriate shape in time and space, whereas an art form's 'tastiness' summarizes the qualities which emerge to challenge, develop, embellish, improvise and change this given shape. [...] Those features of form designated as 'goodness' establish the aesthetic order or definition which, then, serves as the condition and ground for the features designated as 'tastiness' to arise and be played against this ground. Managing the interplay between these two dimensions of form, that is, initiating and sustaining resonance between expression which is 'good' and expression which is 'tasty' is, for the Bamana, what imbues form with transforming power, its capacity for creating valued existential states.
>
> (1981: 3–4).

Brink notes that the Bamana use two additional terms: *jayan* (clarity) and *jako* (embellishment). Jayan refers to the cultural identity or 'goodness' of the form and its *cogo*, the means to create specific forms. It is the cogo of a dance, sculpture, or performance which carries the information about the appropriate configuration or patterning of the form. This aspect of form is considered to have been passed down from the ancestors. Jako (embellishments) are those elements which activate the forms, giving them their immediacy. However, for the Bamana, such embellishments must never totally obscure or destroy the basic form (Brink 1981: 9–11).

People's knowledge of the basic ordering of the performance and their expectations in any single performance are drawn from their past theatre experiences. The successful manipulation and embellishment of the tempo and pattern of the drama create the resonance between goodness and tastiness and between clarity and embellishment. This involves the constant interaction between the performers and the audience. The unpredictability, embellishment, and innovation that actors introduce within the performance – short of destroying the basic form – elicits positive evaluations.

The expected pattern is comprised of individual puppet acts of about ten minutes duration followed by shorter musical interludes. In constructing a performance, the troupe plays with this pattern as well as with the tempo of the drama. For example, in the evening segment of the November performance, the Kiranko troupe first established the normative pattern in the first four sequences – puppet act/musical interlude/puppet act. Then they altered this pattern by performing four puppet sequences of varying lengths, one right after the other. The troupe followed these sequences with a long musical interlude lasting well over ten minutes. They then introduced a new puppet character, the bird Jolenjo Kono, and returned to the expected pattern of puppet/musical interlude/puppet for the next four characters. Suddenly, they reintroduced Shameless Hyena who darted in and out of the dance circle. Immediately after his exit the newer versions of the Roan Antelopes performed followed by a musical interlude, then another antelope puppet, a musical interlude, and the cattle puppets. The tempo of the performance picked up as three more puppets performed for about five minutes each, followed by another musical interlude. The lights were again cut and the Little Female Sorcerers entered, performing for a full ten minutes. When they exited Giraffe appeared; the lights were again lit; and after a short performance the drama came to a close.

Besides manipulating the length and order of sequences, actors also juxtapose virtuosic acrobatic displays with the more stately demeanour of some characters. In the Kiranko performance, the first seven characters were energetic while the Bush Buffalo that followed lumbered around the arena. The troupe maintained a slower tempo for the next three characters and then abruptly switched to a fast pace with Shameless Hyena. The pace slowed again for the Roan Antelopes and the silver-horned antelope. The entrance of the cattle further slowed the tempo, which then picked up during the three acrobatic performances by Ram, Gazelle, and Wildcat. The entrance of the Little Female Sorcerers reintroduced a slower pace, and in the final sequence Giraffe gave a relatively sedate performance.

Actors were quite vocal in criticizing their rivals' performances and two examples from performances I attended with young men from Kiranko shed light on the criteria underlying critical evaluations. In one village, midway into the performance, a long interlude of about 20 minutes inadvertently occurred between two puppet sequences. The drummers and chorus successfully held the audience's attention for about 15 minutes. Then both the drum team and the chorus, as well as the audience, began to disengage from the event; there was a real danger of disintegration. In order to save the performance the troupe sent a young actor out into the circle to perform acrobatics on a bicycle, a difficult feat in sand. The audience was at first puzzled, but the novelty of the sequence rekindled their interest and they began laughing, commenting, and encouraging the actor. Shortly thereafter, a puppet arrived in the dance circle. The troupe followed this with a quick succession of puppets, pulling the audience back into the performance. The actors from Kiranko expressed sympathy for their rivals' dilemma, yet they gloated over their theatrical faux pas.

In another village, the young men pointed out a less dramatic example of a timing error involving a puppet staying too long in the arena. Once the puppet had made a complete circuit, the troupe attempted a second circuit. Midway into this extended performance, the audience began to lose interest. The Kiranko actors sensed the problem immediately and were quick to criticize. The troupe suddenly cut the performance short and the puppet exited. They then radically shifted the tempo by bringing out Gon (Baboon) for a second appearance. The audience responded enthusiastically to his short, acrobatic performance. These two examples underscore the importance of tempo in constructing a successful performance and the necessity of continually adjusting to spectator response.

The creative tension between jayan (goodness) and jako (tastiness) also emerges within each individual puppet sequence. As each character enters the circle, drum rhythms establish its appropriate demeanour. Bush Buffalo is stately while Wildcat dashes and stomps around the arena. At various junctures in each of the acts, drummers improvise upon the basic rhythm. This process is known as *cerotike* (cutting the rhythm in the middle), which doubles the tempo and syncopates the beat (Brink 1981: 12). This is the performers' cue to improvise upon the original dance steps and break into an acrobatic display. At these moments spectators rush into the ring to praise exceptional performers. The tempo shifts several times during the character's circuit of the arena, increasing the audience's involvement.

The final criterion for judging a performance is the competence of the dancers. Their understanding of theatrical form is experiential. As young children they regularly attend puppet theatre and are encouraged to recognize the appropriate songs, rhythms, and dances. Informal training in performance skills begins within the household as soon as children can sit up and basic skills are learned through imitation. For example, mothers or older siblings often clap a baby's own hands in basic rhythmic sets. When the child acquires a modicum of dexterity, they place an overturned container in front of her or him and beat out a rhythm, encouraging the child to imitate it. Skills in singing and dancing are also acquired through imitation and games. Marcel Mauss (1979) described this process as 'prestigious imitation' whereby children begin to embody the formal principles that organize skills and allow them to reproduce movements and recognize patterns. In play, the children of Bamana also begin to experiment with embellishing the basic form without destroying it and begin to embody the culturally specific aesthetic framework which underlies artistry in their society.

Regarding puppet theatre, adults encourage children to organize their own mini-performances in imitation of the youth association theatre. Prior to the November performance, groups of five and six-year-olds played at puppetry in the streets outside of their households. On the day of the performance, a large group of children arrived as the drum teams were warming up and staged their own mini-performance of Gon. By the age of 14 when they are incorporated into the kamalen ton, both boys and girls have acquired a working knowledge of the theatrical form and a practical proficiency in the range of expressive behaviour they will need as performers. All children attain at least a basic competency in artistic performance.

The puppet theatre audience bases its evaluation of the performance primarily on how well singers, drummers, and dancers interact. They look for how quickly the performers pick up on each other's cues and the smoothness of the transitions between and within individual acts.

In performance, cueing among the drummers, singers, and dancers is always in flux. In the musical interludes, responsibility for the choice of songs shifts between the chorus and the drummers. In some instances the singer introduces a new song and the drummers follow suit with the appropriate rhythms. At other moments, the drummers introduce a new rhythm and the singers adjust. In the puppet sequences, the young men who accompany the puppet into the circle cue the drummers and singers on the entrance and identity of each character by singing the appropriate song. If the crowd is too large and boisterous and this strategy fails, alternative systems of cueing go into effect. Drummers may quickly reposition themselves within the circle so they can see the puppet's entrance and start the appropriate rhythm. The change in rhythm cues the lead singer to the entrance of a new character and she begins the appropriate song. The singer herself may be informed of a puppet's impending entrance by a member of the association who tells her the name of the character waiting in the wings. Or, depending on her location in the circle, she may see the puppet's entrance. In any case, if the singer identifies the character before the drummers do, she drops the song in progress and begins the correct new one. The drummers switch rhythms and the singer adjusts her tempo to match the drummers. Once the puppet is in the circle, it often becomes an active cueing agent, signalling the drummers and singers to change tempo. In the performance of the Great Bird of Mali, for example, the dancer stops completely and begins an agitated forward and backward movement, fluttering his wings slightly to signal the drummers for a faster tempo. Another method of cueing is to have a small rod-and-string puppet clap its hands in a prearranged pattern as a signal to the drummers that the dancer desires a change in the drum rhythms.

At various points in the performance, individual performers are pulled forward into the limelight. At these moments virtuosity is appropriate and praised by the audience. The musical interludes provide singers and drummers with opportunities to display their skills while the puppet sequences provide them for the dancers. When spectators are moved, they react by entering into the action, showering the performer with verbal and gestural praises. However, when a performer or a performance unit becomes so enamoured of its own virtuosity that it ignores other actors, their self-absorption threatens the unity of the performance and is judged negatively.

I attended one performance in which an inexperienced drum team became so involved in its own playing that it ignored the singers and puppet. An astute lead singer assessed the situation and intervened by abruptly changing songs and leaving the drum team afloat. The drummers quickly got the message and focused their attention on the business of the drama. At another performance, the chorus, tired of repeating the same song, started a new one. For several minutes, there was pandemonium as the lead singer and her chorus competed until the drummers followed the chorus, forcing the lead singer to comply. In both these cases, unchecked competition among the units and the promotion of the individual over the group threatened the performance. Although at different times during an evening's performance one performer or performing unit may hold sway, the ultimate success of the theatre depends upon everyone knowing when to give focus and when to share equal weight.

Bamana value innovation and competition in youth drama not merely for its own sake or for its novelty, but because it is the very core of their definition of youth and the function of art. Theatre is an appropriate activity for young people and, in Kiranko, it is one of the most important formal contexts for displaying artistic competency. In Bamana society, artistic competency is central to the process of socializing young people, leading them into adulthood. Actors come to the performances with a basic understanding of the interplay between tradition and innovation, between unity and rivalry, and between old and new. This interplay orchestrates the dramatic action and shapes the structure of the event as well as the puppet repertory. It is culturally meaningful because it emerges out of, and resonates against, the participants' knowledge and experiences in the everyday world of social relationships. In this wider arena of diverse activities, successfully managing the tension between these forces is the hallmark of a competent social actor. Each performance and each troupe is judged in relation to past performances and past troupes. They act knowing that they will gain their reputations – or be forgotten – not only in light of their predecessors' artistic achievements, but of their successors' as well.

Note

1 Research on the puppet theatre was conducted in Mali between 1978 and 1980 with grants from Fulbright-Hays and the American Council for Learned Societies/Social Science Research Council. My colleague Lynn Forsdale and I became members of the youth association and were given permission to go behind the scenes.

References

Bird, Charles, and Martha Kendall 1981 'The Mande Hero Text and Context.' In *Explorations in African Systems of Thought*, edited by I. Karp and C. Bird, 13–26. Bloomington: Indiana University Press.

Brink, James 1981 'Dialectics of Aesthetic Form in Bamana Art: An Introduction.' Paper presented at the University of Wisconsin, Milwaukee.

Mauss, Marcel 1979 [1950] 'The notion of body techniques.' In *Sociology and Psychology Essays by Marcel Mauss*, translated by Ben Brewster, 97–105. London: Routledge and Kegan Paul.

McNaughton, Patrick 1979 *Secret Sculptures of Komo: Art and Power in Bamana (Bambara) Initiation Associations*. Working Papers in the Traditional Arts, no. 4. Philadelphia: Institute for the Study of Human Issues.

Part III

Voice, language and words in performance

12 Storytelling theatre in Sierra Leone

The example of Lele Gbomba

Julius S. Spencer

Storytelling in Africa has for some time now been recognized as an art form in its own right. And, through the work of scholars such as Ruth Finnegan, Donald Cosentino, and Francis Ngaboh-Smart, storytelling in Sierra Leone has been brought to the attention of anthropologists and literary scholars. However, while it is generally acknowledged that such storytelling is basically a performance art, the emphasis in all the work produced so far has been on the narrative structure of the art form.

But while Ruth Finnegan, one of the earliest writers on storytelling in Africa, sees it as a purely narrative art, Cosentino, whose work is much more recent, recognizes the presence and importance of non-narrative elements of performance in Mende storytelling. As he states, unless a performer can 'effectively objectify the wonders of ... narrative vision with the non-narrative elements of performance', such a performer is not regarded as accomplished (Cosentino, 1982, p. 88). Yet even for him, what he refers to as theatrics (costume, lighting, place) are 'probably the least significant of the elements of performance' (Cosentino, 1982, p. 116).

It can, therefore, be said that storytelling in Africa has generally been regarded by scholars as a narrative art form akin to the novel in western literary traditions, whose orality lends it a certain measure of dramaturgy. I propose in this paper to examine storytelling among the Mende of Sierrra Leone from a theatrical perspective, focusing on the work of Lele Gbomba, one of the most famous Mende storytellers in the country. The aim is primarily to provide a descriptive analysis of what is essentially a traditional form of theatre.

Mende storytelling

Among the Mende of Sierra Leone, there are two major types of narrative. These are the historical narrative called Ngawovɛi and the fictional narrative called Dɔmɛi. As Ngaboh-Smart states,

> the Ngawovɛi is fixed and unique both in form and content. Significantly, whether the Ngawovɛi is narrated, chanted or sung, it reveals elements of

origin and traditional events as remembered through time – the experiences of successive ancestral generations and the prescriptions that have grown out of the experiences. Thus the Ngawovɛi are living spoken documents

(Ngaboh-Smart, 1986, p. 9).

The Ngawovɛi can thus be seen to perform a function broadly similar to the tales of the Griots in Sene-Gambia. Narration is usually restricted to elders or family heads, children and young people being excluded. The level of artistic expression involved in narration of Ngawovɛi is also very limited, for as Ngaboh-Smart says,

> The Ngawovɛi is narrated with no attempt at dramatization. The interpolations which punctuate the narrative flow are those of ordinary speech and there is a lack of audience participation

(Ngaboh-Smart, 1986, p. 8).

The most important requirement in this type of narration is, therefore, historical fidelity.

The body of tales which constitute Dɔmɛi presents an almost directly contrasting profile. These are tales of pure fiction which in most cases are the artistic creations of the individual storytellers. Despite the existence, through progressive accumulation, of a large body of these tales in Mende land, the storyteller enjoys immense freedom in the interpretation and recreation of what may be familiar tales. With the Dɔmɛi, unlike the Ngawovɛi, the emphasis is on the ability of the storyteller to capture and hold the attention of the audience. Also, the narration of Dɔmɛi is not restricted to any group of people, but cuts across all classes and age groups.

Storytelling or narration of Dɔmɛi usually takes place in the evenings, during the period between the evening meal and retiring for the night, when men, women, and children congregate in open spaces, on large verandahs, or around a bonfire to chat, drink palm-wine, or play games. Such gatherings are usually most common on moonlit nights in the dry season after the harvest, when there is much to eat and little hard work to do.

Storytelling is generally a spontaneous occurrence during such gatherings, with people taking it in turns to tell stories, but sometimes one or a few acclaimed storytellers within a particular community may dominate such sessions. This is the general background against which storytelling occurs, in informal sessions with amateur performers. There is, however, also a small body of highly skilled professional storytellers in whose performances 'the non-narrative elements not only adumbrate the narrative plot, but in some cases supersede it and actually dominate the performance' (Cosentino, 1982, p. 88). These are the Dɔmɛigbuablɛisia.

The presence of one such performer (called a Dɔmɛigbuamɔi) in a village is enough to keep the whole village up into the early hours of the morning, held captive by the sheer artistic force of his presentation. It is with the work of one such performer, Lele Gbomba, that this paper is concerned, for it is among this rapidly diminishing group of artists that Mende storytelling achieves its fullest theatrical dimension.

Lele Gbomba, whose real name is Joseph Moseray, is now in his late seventies, and has been involved in professional storytelling since his teens. Like a lot of traditional artists, he claims to have been inspired to begin storytelling through a dream, which occurred soon after he had lost both parents while still a young boy (Lele Gbomba, 1987). He has travelled widely through the Mende-speaking region of Sierra Leone, where he is a highly sought-after performer who invariably draws large audiences.

Narrative structure

Lele Gbomba's theatre is one in which pure entertainment is of overriding importance. The narrative structure of the Dɔmɛi he creates is, therefore, subsumed within the non-narrative elements of performance which dominate the event.

I do not intend here to examine the narrative structure of Mende storytelling in detail, for this has been adequately done by other writers. Suffice it to say that the Dɔmɛi does not exhibit a simple linear plot structure, but involves digressions of varying lengths which could occur at any point in the story. These digressions are usually instigated by the audience, prompting through the convention of 'baa nde gula' – a formal challenge from a member of the audience to the performer's creative integrity. In other words, the performer is accused of lying. Usually, such a challenge is responded to by the performer dipping into

> a stock repertoire of absurd ripostes – images of a world in which baboons count to ten, or ancestral spirits dance on your verandah in the morning – which are hurled back at the challenger. In such an insane world, argues the riposte, how can my Dɔmɛi be accused of lying?
>
> (Cosentino, 1980, p. 55).

For the Dɔmɛigbaumɔi, such a response is inadequate, and he at times fashions a secondary narrative that could outstrip the original in length and complexity. Lele Gbomba is highly skilled at this.

Frederick Borbor James, in referring to the narrative structure of Lele Gbomba's performances, says, in the introduction to a collection of the performer's stories, 'He normally starts with what he refers to as the Mother Story (the main story). The Mother Story later gives birth to short stories' (James, 1987, p. 3). Whether the stories given birth to by the Mother Story are shorter stories, as James suggests, is arguable, for these 'children' themselves give birth at times.

This results in Gbomba's storytelling sessions exhibiting a rather convoluted structure on the level of plot development. This is, it seems, deliberately engineered by Lele Gbomba as a basis for exhibiting his virtuosity as a performer and as a means of engendering laughter, for his is a comic theatre where exaggeration and farce hold sway.

The performance

Mende storytelling sessions usually begin with a prologue. This accomplishes a verbal break from reality and an introduction to the world of the Dɔmɛi. For the ordinary performer, the recitation of the simple formula, 'Dɔmɛi O Dɔmɛisia', to which the audience responds, 'Jaa Kɔnde', successfully accomplishes this compulsory transition. For the Dɔmɛigbuamɔi, however, the prologue may be used as a personal 'signature tune', a function which the simple opening formula cannot perform.

Songs are the most popular of these non-formulaic openings, although riddles and jokes are also used, and Lele Gbomba usually opens his performance with one of three songs with which he has come to be identified. Each has a melancholy tone, and – with Gbomba seated on a mat, eyes downcast, exuding a mournful air – establishes the image he apparently wishes to project, of a wise old melancholy recluse.

Gbomba thus ceases to be himself immediately the performance starts. He becomes the Narrator, a wise old man allowing the audience to benefit from his wisdom. This transformation is aided by his adroit use of costume, as we shall discuss. One of his performances, recorded by the People's Educational Association of Sierra Leone, began thus:

Chorus: (*Clapping and Singing*)
O, when he is agitating, the last of children
O, when he is agitating, the last of children
O, women, is this your number?
Ah, the stranger who did not bring his own food with him will suffer
    today.
We are no beauties in our family but we abide by instructions.
O, women, is this your number?

Gbomba: Be silent! (*The singing and clapping stop*). I always tell you these tales for your own wisdom tomorrow. The sooner we assemble, the sooner I will begin to tell you some truths. Hey! When a woman is more talkative than her husband, the husband becomes thinner and thinner. All the weight that men lose is not for nothing. It is because their wives are more dominant than they are. When your wife is all mouth, you are always in trouble. Your heart jolts each time you want to touch her private-parts. That is how the men get their blood percentage reduced. Your heart jolts very often because you don't want your wife to yell at you. One woman became very, very wealthy … (Lele Gbomba, *The Bossy Wife*)

And so he launches into his narration. Gbomba thus introduces his audience to the theme of his story before beginning the narration proper. His prologue, through which he achieves the required break with reality is, therefore, a combination of the verbal and the visual, the verbal also being a combination of song and speech.

Performance space

The performance usually takes place in a large open space. This could be either the 'court barri' (the village meeting place where formal disputations take place), or out in the open. Wherever it is staged, the shape of the performance space for Lele Gbomba's performance is, more often than not, the arena – people sitting or standing in a circle, leaving a large enough playing area for the performer.

Somewhere within this playing area, usually around the centre, Gbomba places a large mat, which he proceeds to use as centre stage where most of the narration of his dramas is located. But he does not confine his movements to the restricted space of the mat: while he stands or sits on the mat when playing the role of narrator, he ranges freely over the whole arena when playing the role of a character in the drama.

Lele Gbomba's use of space displays a high level of understanding of the dynamics of theatre. Being the master actor he is, he not only faces in all directions so that the audience can fully appreciate his performance regardless of their own location, but also moves about in such a way that each segment of the audience is fully involved in the unfolding drama throughout. Through his use of space, the audience are drawn into the world of the Dɔmɛi as active participants, and Lele Gbomba thus establishes an actor–audience relationship which ensures that the flow of messages is a two-way process, so fluid that breaks in communication seldom occur.

Performance style

Lele Gbomba's theatre, in consonance with most traditional African theatrical forms, is one where music, song, dance, mime, and mimicry are fused in such a way as to produce a vibrant performance which brings the tales to life.

Most writers on Mende storytelling have noted the use of gestures in the form of facial expressions and hand and body movements as important elements of the art form. The use of voice modulation has also been acknowledged. Lele Gbomba has mastered all of these. His body and voice have been honed into finely tuned instruments whose flexibility enables him to produce a wide range of notes. His portrayal of character is thus extremely convincing on both visual and aural levels.

In addition, his ability to change swiftly from one character to another is remarkable: at one moment he is the narrator, at another the irate husband, at yet another the promiscuous wife about to be caught with her lover. His ability to conjure up a wide range of animals is no less expressive of his skill.

In addition to his abilities as an actor, Lele Gbomba also excels in the songs and dances which form an integral part of his performance. The use of songs is generally acknowledged as a very important element in all Dɔmɛi performances, both amateur and professional, but there appears to be some disagreement as to their exact function. While Cosentino states that

> the Dɔmɛi song is only tangentially related to the plot; its deeper purpose is to mark the impact of particular events in the unfolding drama through the powerful and peculiar emotions engendered only by music
>
> (Cosentino, 1982, p. 108)

and that most songs could be entirely eliminated from the performance without the plot suffering, Ngaboh-Smart insists that

> the songs in most oral narratives are neither static embellishments nor are they tangential to the general movement of the story. They are an indelible part of the entire structural edifice, an organic device that unifies disparate elements – character, moral, or themes and events ...
>
> (Ngaboh-Smart, 1988, p. 48).

In relation to Lele Gbomba's performance, Ngaboh-Smart's statement is the more accurate. Not only does he use songs as a means of commenting on the action being portrayed and as inspiration and background to character portrayal, he also uses them to reveal elements of plot. Thus, in a story about a man whose bossy wife drives him, through fear of her lashing tongue, to go out at night searching for a place to farm, Gbomba introduced the following song at the point where the man is searching in an area in the sacred bush where there is a cave inhabited by the dead who dance day and night. Here, the chorus represent the dead singing in the cave under the man's feet.

> *Chorus:* Gbimanjo-o, I go to Bembe the place of merriment.
> Gbimanjo-o, I go to Bembe the place of merriment ...
> *The man:* (*dancing*) What trouble is this? Can rice do well here?
> *Chorus:* Gbimanjo-o, I go to Bembe the place of merriment.
> *The man:* This is not a place to farm, O!
> *Chorus:* Gbimanjo ...

During this, the man falls into the cave which has opened up to swallow him.

Lele Gbomba also uses songs as mood music – for example, as background for most of his extended characterizations. At times, the characters, through the performer, engage in dialogue with the song going on in the background. At others, individual characters make statements related to the plot which enhance character portrayal while the chorus is being sung. In addition, songs are also always used as musical accompaniment for the various dances.

Commenting on the use of dance in Mende storytelling, Cosentino states that 'unlike its sister, music, ... dance is not an important element' (Cosentino, 1982, p. 108). Most performers, he says, confine themselves and their audiences to simple movements like clapping and swaying. This he sees as being due to a fear of losing control, for the animating potential of dance is such that the narrator may not be able to redirect the attention and energy of the audience to the narrative. However, Cosentino does acknowledge that some performers, particularly those of Dɔmɛigbuamɔi status, do make use of dance, either themselves or by involving the audience.

In Lele Gbomba's performances, all the dancing is done by him, and is generally used as an aid to character portrayal. His dances are usually either exemplifications of the movement-patterns of the characters being portrayed or demonstrative of specific actions of the characters – paddling a canoe, or pounding rice in a mortar.

One vivid example of the use of dance in this way occurs when he is playing the role of a woman smuggling her lover out of the house by hiding him in her lappa (a wrapper tied around the waist like a long skirt). He uses a member of the audience as the lover, and with the lover crouched on the ground, straddles him across the shoulders while both dance round the arena, simulating the dancing of the woman with the lover hidden in her lappa.

Costumes

In this sphere, Lele Gbomba's performance is unparalleled in Mende story-telling. As Cosentino rightly observes, costuming plays no part in the ordinary Dɔmɛi performance (Cosentino, 1982, p. 114), or only to a very limited extent, to establish a persona by which the Dɔmɛigbuamɔi becomes known. Lele Gbomba uses costume much more extensively, as an effective aid to visual representation of the characters he wishes to create.

His wardrobe consists simply of a lappa and a headtie, but his dexterous use of these items transforms them into apparel to suit a wide variety of characters. The performance usually opens with Gbomba dressed in everyday attire – a shirt or T-shirt, a pair of shorts, a pair of sandals. However, during the singing of his prologue, he divests himself of everything but the shorts, which serve as costume for most of his male characters and animals.

Even with this scanty item of clothing, Lele Gbomba achieves variety. For example, in a story about a man afflicted with a wide variety of diseases, including leprosy, he creates a comic visual representation by the simple act of rolling up one leg of the shorts.

Female characters are denoted by tying on the lappa and headtie, the impression of aggressiveness in some of the female characterizations being created by tying the lappa above knee level. Although used mainly to represent female characters, Lele Gbomba uses the lappa and headtie in a variety of other ways to aid the creation of certain specialized male characters. For example, in one performance he uses the lappa as a cape thrown across his shoulders with his arms jutting out at the elbows to represent a village chief radiating an aura of great dignity. In glaring contrast he ties the lappa across his chest with the loose ends flung over one shoulder, the way Ghanaian men tie the Kente Cloth, to represent the village gossip. This, combined with the mincing walk with which he endows the character, enables him convincingly to visualize a rather shifty individual.

Lele Gbomba's theatre, then, is highly visual. While the importance of the symbols and images created on a verbal level cannot be overlooked, it is my contention that the visual representations of these symbols and images is of equal if not more significance, for in the context of performance the visual often over-shadows the verbal as a communication channel. It is the recognition and under-standing of this principle on the part of this *nonpareil* among Dɔmɛigbuablɛisia that has earned him the admiration of audiences.

The audiences

The audience at any Lele Gbomba performance is very actively engaged in the movement of the dramas – a characteristic of all Mende storytelling sessions. However, the extent to which he involves his audience in the narrative process is unusual even for other Dɔmɛigbuableisia.

The audience for Lele Gbomba is usually a heterogeneous one made up of both sexes, all age groups, and the various classes within a particular community. He therefore has to fashion his dramas to appeal to as wide an audience as possible, and one accordingly finds that in any one performance Lele Gbomba negotiates a wide repertoire of tales.

From among his audience, Gbomba draws his musicians and singers, a situation common to all storytelling sessions. Gbomba, however, always performs with a kellie[1] player and a sieguneh[2] player, to provide the instrumental music. He usually also has a singing chorus made up mainly from the women in the community who, together with the instrumentalists, sit or stand in one part of the arena, although not separated from the rest of the audience. This group does most of the choral singing during the performance, although the rest of the audience are free to join in, and usually do.

The whole audience are also usually encouraged to provide rhythmic accompaniment to the singing through hand-clapping, an activity they engage in with gusto. Audience involvement also includes direct intervention in the narrative flow through the 'baa nde gula' convention.

In addition to these various levels of audience involvement, which are roughly similar to those of other storytelling sessions, Lele Gbomba usually succeeds in assigning character roles to his audience. He achieves this in two ways. He might simply ask for a volunteer to assist in dramatizing a particular sequence. For example, during the narration of a story about a very jealous husband always sniffing around his young and pretty wife, he will get a member of the audience to enter the centre of the arena and play the role of the wife. They then engage in dialogue and action which successfully brings the story to life – though most of the burden of performance rests on Lele Gbomba, since his co-performer is a spontaneous volunteer, and the performance therefore an improvisation.

The second way in which Lele Gbomba assigns character roles to his audience is by moving right up to a particular individual and addressing him or her as a character in the drama. Although in a majority of cases the individual does not respond verbally, and is apparently not expected to do so, in some instances individuals do respond, assuming the character being thrust on them and engaging in dialogue with the performer.

The audience is thus fully involved in the drama at every moment of its unfolding. The relationship between performer and audience is so intimate that lines of demarcation become blurred. In this type of theatre, there are no spectators: everybody is a participant.

Notes

1 The kellie is often referred to as a 'slit-log drum'. It is a hollow log with lengthwise slits of varying lengths played with two beaters, and produces a range of three or four tones.
2 The siegureh is a stalked gourd surrounded by a network of beads, buttons or shells on strings. The ends of the strings are held in one hand and the stalk of the gourd in the other. Rhythmic movements of the gourd produce a rattling sound by the beads striking the gourd.

References

Cosentino, Donald. 'Lele Gbomba and the Style of Mende Baroque', *African Arts*, XIII, No. 3 (May 1980), p. 54–5, and 75–8); *Defiant Maids and Stubborn Farmers* (Cambridge University Press, 1982).

Finnegan, Ruth, *Limba Stories and Story-telling* (Oxford: Clarendon Press, 1967).

Gbomba, Lele, interview with author, Bumpe, 2 September 1987.

Innes, Gordon, 'The Function of the Song in Mende Folklore', *Sierra Leone Language Review*, IV (1965), p. 54–63.

James, Frederick Borbor. Preface to *The Bossy Wife*, collection of stories by Lele Gbomba (Freetown: People's Educational Association, 1987).

Kilson, Marion, 'Social Relationships in Mende Dɔmɛisia', *Sierra Leone Studies*, III (1969), p. I–II.

Ngaboh-Smart, Francis. *Mende Story-Telling* (Freetown: People's Educational Association, 1986); 'Method in Chaos: the Structural Basis of Mende Folk Tales', *New Journal of Approaches to Language Arts*, VIII (1988), p. 42–9.

13 The language of anglophone Cameroon drama

Asheri Kilo

Literature as a process of thinking in images utilizes language and draws upon the collective experience – history – embodied in that language. In writing one should hear all the whispering, and the shouting, and the crying, and the loving, and the hating of the many voices in the past and those voices will never speak to a writer in a foreign language.

(Ngugi, 1981: 60)

The choice of language for a Cameroonian playwright lies between French, English, Pidgin and over three hundred indigenous languages of Cameroon. French and English are the official languages and education, technology and cultural development, as well as international communication, are in these languages. No indigenous language is enough to meet the needs of Cameroon as a nation, for each is only spoken by a small group of people. As we see in the opening quotation, Ngugi Wa Thiong'o argues that foreign languages can never fully evoke the realities of life on the African continent. Chinua Achebe, too, asserts that:

For an African, writing in English is not without its serious setbacks. He often finds himself describing situations or modes of thought which have no direct equivalent in the English way of life. Caught in that situation he can do one of two things. He can try and contain what he wants to say within the limits of conventional English, or he can try to push back those limits to accommodate his idea. The first method produces competent, uninspired, and rather flat work The second method can produce something new and valuable to the English language, as well as to the material he is trying to put over.

(Achebe, 1977)

Whilst writing in the metropolitan languages may not allow a full reflection of the realities of the African continent, the many indigenous languages on their part are restricted in their geographical spread. African writers are in search of a tongue that combines their varied attributes without their weaknesses and limitations.

Theatre and language in Cameroon

Cameroon anglophone drama distinguishes between the language of the literary 'elitist' dramatists and the language of a wider theatre. Among the 'literary dramatists' are Bole Butake, Jikong, Bate Besong and Sankie Maimo. Popular among the university students, their plays make up part of the students' syllabus in drama studies at the University of Yaounde which has by and large, become the determinant of the 'elitist' culture where university lecturers select the drama texts for study by the students of drama, as well as the plays the students audiences watch. It is within this university context that the concept of 'elitist' theatre has developed.

Some English language playwrights: Bate Besong, Bole Butake, Jikong, Sankie Maimo

Bate Besong's use of English is as difficult for the native speaker of English as it is confounding to the Cameroonian audience. Words become weapons, tools with which he ploughs his path through the dense jungle of his message. This use of language which has been variously described as avant-garde, elitist, obscurantist and egoistic, and summarizes his standpoint as a playwright. He believes his plays are addressed to the few in society who possess the intelligence to understand them.

In his play *The Most Cruel Death of the Talkative Zombie,* the use of symbols and images is extreme. 'Zombie' is used metaphorically in this play in which lepers are synonymous with 'zombies'. To ordinary people the play is a confused rambling of political ideas and symbols coded in language which renders it turgid to read and irritating to watch. Disparate ideas are forcefully fused to accommodate his expansive political imagery.

He employs lots of deliberate coinages such as 'babacracy', 'touralogy', 'touracracy', as well as bizarre phrases like 'the intriguer-on-high of Gaullist Africa'. What emerges is a dramatic language which reflects more the singular thought processes of its creator than on any conscious attempt to put thoughts and ideas into the mode of English syntax. This deliberate complexity and obscurantism only comes through as a pretentious exhibition of 'elitism'. He prides himself on being an 'avant-garde' dramatist but, even to drama students who study it, his play is neither accessible or comprehensible. He appears as a lone non-conformist who makes his own rules and none but himself knows when he breaks them. Such pretentious theatre is uninteresting for an audience who come to the theatre to relax, be entertained and, sometimes, instructed.

Most Cameroon playwrights have chosen to write in a language that is neither Pidgin nor a Cameroonian language, but in a form of English that is influenced by their mother tongue:

> … the price a world language must be prepared to pay is submission to many different kinds of use. The African writer should aim to use English in a way that brings out his message best without altering the language to the extent that its value as a medium of international exchange will be lost. He should

aim at fashioning out an English which is at once universal and able to carry his particular experience.

(Achebe, 1975: 61)

Cameroonian standard English bears characteristics of the structures of the native languages of Cameroon and whilst playwrights have followed the syntactic categories or norms of the English language, they have deliberately coloured the sentences with Cameroonian vernacular speech patterns which feature the apt use of proverbs, imagery, metaphor and other rhetorical features of Cameroonian discourse.

> In Jikong's *I Did So Swear, But. ...*, the Paramount Chief, in addressing his subjects, says: It is not for nothing that I have invited all of you here today. I have invited you with a reason. What is the reason? The reason is that we have a heavy load on our heads. The heavy load which we are carrying on our heads has to be put down without breaking our necks. What is this heavy load? The heavy load is the problems of our people. Our people have problems, what are these problems?

Jikong, Butake and many others try variously to represent the educated Cameroon person's speech or a translation of the villager's patois or vernacular into English. In the plays of Butake we see how his deliberate and sustained effort to give a Noni colouring to Engish by rendering some traditional kinds of poetry is very effective. One such example is in the speech of Shey Ngong during an invocation in *And Palm Wine Will Flow*:

> ... let their heads be crushed like pumpkins
> and let their brains be licked by dogs!
> Let their bones crack and their members
> be torn each from the other until they lie
> scattered in the devastating fire ....

Other African dramatists such as Soyinka, J. P. Clark, Ola Rotimi, Aidoo and Sutherland also render into English, speeches from the vernacular, while retaining much of the native flavour without submerging the meaning and mood intended.

Bole Butake, a deliberately literary dramatist, is as much at home capturing nuances of the speech of his Noni-speaking people in his drama, as he is portraying a western educated tongue. He has the ability to closely observe a character, capturing mannerisms, pronunciation, rhythm and other details which dramatists of lesser talent might deem inconsequential, leaving a feeling that the speech is true to life.

In his play *And Palm Wine Will Flow,* Shey Ngong, the chief priest of Nyombom, and his friend Nsangong discuss in a language that captures their world view:

Shey Ngong:	Where are you coming from, so agitated, like a monkey that has missed the hunter's bullet?
Nsangnong:	The Fon is mad at you and has sworn ...
Shey Ngong:	That I will hear from him before the sun goes to sleep. Not so?
Nsangnong:	So you know already? Did the tortoise really beat the hare in the racing match? ...
Shey Ngong:	The cat, no matter how full his stomach is, will never spare the rat.

Butake's dialogue and style is one whose concession to its metropolitan foster-parent is in its grammar, syntax and lexis, remains rich with metaphoric language, embracing features in English, in pidgin and in the local Noni language, as reflected in character and place names. Again in *And Palm Wine Will Flow,* for example, when Kwengong answers her husband she says, 'My ears are on the ground husband' or in his *Lake God* when the chief priest of the lake insists that he must be given kolanuts he says: 'Where is Kola? My cowries don't speak with an empty mouth' and later: 'Worse things are yet to come. Did you notice that all the cowries have been falling on their bellies?'.

One of his achievements in this resourceful use of language lies in the fact that he lures the non-African reader into a distinctly Cameroonian world through the aptness of his imagery and the colourful atmosphere he evokes with it whilst at the same time, he gives the Cameroon audience a sense of familiarity which arises from the harmony of setting, character and situation. This is further enhanced by the simplicity of language which allows for a wider readership for his works than those of his counterpart Bate Besong.

In Butake's *Lake God,* for instance, where the action is set in the remote village of Nyos, the characters know little English. They are Bum and Noni speakers and whatever English they speak is the translated effort of Butake himself. The same can be said of the language of the characters in *The Survivors* and *And Palm Wine Will Flow.*

By comparison, it is in the area of the contrast between language and setting that the playwright Sankie Maimo gets most of the unfavourable criticism that meets his plays. In *Succession in Sarkov,* for instance, we are told that the setting, is Sarkov, which, like Nyos in Butake's play is a remote village where Fais (chiefs) and people are known to speak nothing other than their native language, Lamso. It is rare to find them speaking Pidgin, as they have little knowledge and understanding of this language. When Maimo writes the speeches of these local people, he makes them speak in verse and on certain occasions recite some 'Shakespearean style' lines. Yet this is probably justifiable because when elderly people speak Lamso they do so with such poetic richness that it is comparable to Shakespeare's language. He maintains the names of the characters in Lamso, except for Winny Bongfen and her husband Joseph Kubena. Whilst it would be authentic in tone for the educated Kubena to think that his countrymens' answers are 'either evasive, equivocal or simply incomprehensible or inconceivable', it is less so for the uneducated character, Yuri, to talk about:

An un-impeachable evidence of the life of the great lady,
Of the Caucasian stock with sophisticated conventions
For you to draw your own conclusions as a noble lady.

or as she philosophizes when she advises Bongden, wife of the Fai (chief):

What is life after all Winny
But a continuous sharing of this and that
With or without our consent?
You should be magnanimous.

Later, Sitan, the son of the late Fai, speaks in an echo of Shakespearean verse:

On a night like this Bisen was killed in Rokov.
On a night like this Binsen was killed.

Maimo's insistence on writing in an elite, formal style of poetic verse contrasts
with Butake's apt use of proverbs and idioms and the consistency with which his
imagery is anchored in the natural landscape, beliefs, and practices of his people.
When asked why he wrote the play the way he did his response was:

I am not apologetic, I am not out to create stupid people, I am not writing to
get pot-boilers, not for any Tom, Dick and Harry. All my characters carry my
ideas.

(Maimo: 1989)

In Butake's *Lake God* by comparison, even when a character is European, the
language is hardly devoid of African flavour so that Father Leo speaks a variant
of standard English when he addresses the women of Nyos during a sermon:

Yensi, Kima'a and the other devils are taking you on a fast and easy ride on
the big motor road to Lucifer's kingdom … You were in the Fibuen, not so?
And you too. And even you.

Unlike Maimo who does not use language to localize character and setting, or
distinguish between a character's language registers to correspond to social types
and status, Butake maintains a marked difference between Father Leo's English
and that of the other characters in this play. All Maimo's characters share the
same linguistic code.

Butake's insistence on a distinction in language usage reflects the cultural
implication of the use of words in Cameroon traditional society. People in this
society are respected if they have *'the palm oil with which words are eaten'* – that is,
the ability to manipulate language as the occasion demands. Proverbs are
reserved for the old and wise, who have the linguistic competence, maturity and
intelligence to unwrap the message when used in a special context. Butake comes
out as the expert in employing the full range of the traditional Cameroon

repertory , from pithy proverbs to riddles, from gnomic and cryptic sayings of chief priests, to developed figurative language and the skilful techniques of women's speeches. What Butake has done complies with Timothy Wangusa's assertion:

> English could be beaten into submission and made to express African reali-
> ties ... the African writer should listen to the speech of his people, 'to the
> ring of dialogue in his home language' and struggle to find an approx-
> imation of the English equivalent.
>
> (Wangusa, 1989: 33)

If the language of Cameroon drama it is to perform its social function effectively, it must be the language of the people.

Pidgin is one such language.

The case for Pidgin

When we talk of Pidgin in the Cameroonian context we distinguish between it and broken English on the one hand, and between other interlingual manifest-ations in the English spoken by some Cameroonians on the other. One has also to be careful to distinguish what is now Cameroonian English from plain errors in standard English expressions. I mention these problems because it is increasingly difficult to determine when Pidgin is being used and when some hybrid between what one can call Pidgin and standard English is being used. Added to these are different *varieties* of Pidgin depending on which part of the country the speaker comes from.

Pidgin is part of an African society in which people have developed many new, African, ways of living, in response to a new urban situation. Cameroon language variety includes the educated with a good command of English, French or both, as well as those Cameroonians who, having abandoned the villages, still have little command of the official languages of the country. For the latter group, Pidgin may be the most important expression of their neo-African status.

Educated Cameroonians who have at their disposal at least three media of communication – English or French, Pidgin, and their language of ethnic reference, tend to use the ethnic language, in traditional settings, the official languages in formal settings and in communication with Europeans, and Pidgin for the informal Cameroonian situations.

Cameroon Pidgin, also referred to as 'Kamtok' (which originates from 'Cameroon-Talk'), has remained largely a spoken language, indeed it does not yet have a fixed orthography or spelling and has not been standardized. Hence one finds variations in the attempts at writing it. It is this varying application of the language that makes it appear humorous and, to some, 'unserious'.

Primarily an urban language, for since most villages are monolingual, the need does not arise there for a secondary medium of communication, it is also very popular among students as an informal code. Pidgin is used for story-telling, for preaching sermons in churches, in the market and sometimes on radio.

Pidgin has found a haven amongst artists of all sorts. Playwrights may write complete plays in Pidgin, while others who make very minimal use of it, have nevertheless at one point or another put it in the mouths of characters. As there is not just one Pidgin, but several, the choice of a particular Pidgin is determined by the setting, the subject matter of discourse, and the relationship between the characters involved.

Some Pidgin language playwrights: Victor Musinga, Epie Ngome, Jt. T. Menget

Amongst the playwrights, Victor Musinga is one of those who sees Pidgin as the most viable means of reaching the theatre-loving Cameroonians. Through his choice of language, his whole repertoire is a demolition of the myth of inferiority which has been directed at Pidgin. If people do not find *The Tragedy of Mr No-Balance* or *Mr Director* plausible in terms of language, it is only because they have strayed too far from their roots and from the environment which nourishes ideas. Musinga takes the educated, but culturally alienated, elites from the narrow confines of the universities and shows them what they are missing in the drama of real living people. His preferred audience however, is his immediate neighbour for whom he feels so much sympathy:

> ... the presentation of subject matter and sometimes the choice of it are very much influenced by the particular audience which the writer has in mind; that is, he takes into consideration the literary taste and sensitivity of the audience that he wants to address.
>
> (Egejuru, 1978: 15)

Since the aesthetics of these playwrights is one of reality imitated, their success is to be measured by how accurate their audiences judge their imitation to be. Theatre as vital, vigorous, and with as large a following as Musinga's, must be taken seriously. To dismiss these plays as gimmicky, conservative, without progressive views, is misguided for the popularity of Musinga's plays is an indication that audiences find in them things that they value.

Musinga's playtexts, are 'working scripts' which are then modified through improvisation. In performance, the story is brought to life by highly dramatic action and improvisations which makes for great entertainment, and at the same time, the loosely scripted drama also leaves room for audience participation, meeting their expectations as so many people enjoy participating in performances.

Musinga's characters, whether they are children, such as the young boy Oko in *The Trials Of Ngowo*, office boys such as Keke in *Mr Director* or Mrs Zawo in *The Cup*, or Njema's mother in *Njema*, use Pidgin strategically in the action of the play as when Njema's mother suspects that Njema is pregnant:

> Look here my pikin Njema, ma heart no glad no small as you so-so sleep plenty dis time and you bobi grow big-big.

(Listen Njema, my child, I am not happy about the fact that you sleep a lot and that your breasts grow big.)

Similarly, in *The Tragedy of Mr No-Balance,* the self-conscious, culivated Bih labours to speak good English in the court scene, but later reverts to Pidgin, a language in which he can more freely express himself.

In *Not the Name* by Epie Ngome, Dugeh, Nlinde's mother, converses in Standard English with Salle, the local MP, but occasionally switches to Pidgin:

'Shame sef i no dey for wona'.

In another instance, in response to her husband's loud call, she protests,

'Na who don die? Ewange, you go make man fall for banda with this kind call weh you de like for call man. I de talk you no de hear.

Similarly Nlinde and her friend Diengu will switch to Pidgin when they discuss exciting news of their adventures with men in hotels. 'Boh how now?' is their friendly greeting, meaning, 'My dear friend, how are you?' Here we can distinguish through language use, when the two girls are relaxing among themselves and when they are engaged in more serious matters for Nlinde, who speaks mainly Pidgin, talks to her father, whom she regards with great respect, she speaks faultless English.

Through the use of Pidgin, characters speak a language that is appropriate to their status in life and to distinguish and differentiate mood in the same character.

Like Victor Musinga, J.T. Menget promotes the use of Pidgin in his dramas and has always insisted on presenting Pidgin as a literary language by writing poems, short stories, folk tales and plays in Pidgin. In an early play, *The Confession* (1980), using Pidgin, he exposes the mercantile and exploitative role of church leaders who expropriate not only financial but carnal rewards from the singing congregation. In this play he established the functional importance of Pidgin in unifying both the European priest and the Cameroonian parishioner. In persuading his parishioners the priest must speak in Pidgin:

All Christian no pay contribution some lef am Church. My good friends you must be careful Satan i bin too powerful. Many people sin. Dem tell lie, dem steal, fornicate and dem envy.

Pidgin in Cameroon drama is not an aberration, something to be laughed at on account of its quaintness, a language that is bound to die as more and more people become proficient in the English language. However, both Menget and Musinga who have treated very similar themes in their drama, have explored Pidgin in a humorous way. Comic situations abound in Menget's play, *Mimbo Hos.* One instance is when the character Munde analyses the name of the beer they are drinking, he sees that it is SPECIAL, a brand of beer which he spells out to mean, 'Special People Enjoy Cameroon Independence After Labour'. This leads them further:

Sita: How for Guiness?
Munde: *(Laughs)* Girls Under Ill-health Never Enjoy Sex Sufficiently.
1st Customer: Tell me about ma Goldharp.
2nd Customer: Some people say na 'good heart'. But I check say na 'cold heart'.
Munde: No be so. Goldharp mean say Get One Lady Daily, Have Another
                Reserved Permanently.

The playwrights – in serious jest – are cleverly pointing out ways in which men persistently degrade women.

Amongst the most striking qualities of Pidgin is its flexibility. Its vocabulary is limitless, as more and more words are being coined, and as the language comes in contact with ever more languages and dialects, the humour stems from the manner in which these languages are blended for the purpose of communication.

Varieties of Pidgin used in Cameroon English and Pidgin language drama

In Cameroon drama, different varieties of Pidgin are used by different speech communities as, for instance, the variant spoken by the Fulani cattle herders, Dewa in Butake's *Lake God* and by Ardo Duda in Jikong's *I Did So Swear, But ...* In both cases the herdsmen are in trouble because their cattle have destroyed foodstuffs of local farmers, but they have a means of bribing those in control of situations. When we first meet Ardo Duda he is saying that:

> Me come look Bigman for some palaver weh yi komot for ma cow. Dat bush pipi for Fak tok seh me cow don chop dem corn. Me don go seam. Na daso simol dem chopam. Dat bush Chief Galam tok seh me must pay plenty money. Na yi me come look Bigman .... Na so Bigman. Me don biring Bigman some simol ting. Me don see Bigman.

Bigman's dialogue with the illiterate Duda continues in Pidgin but when he addresses Chief Galam he switches to standard English. In the same vein, in *Lake God,* the Fon (chief) switches to Pidgin as he addresses Dewa who, in self-defence, says:

> Kai! me no talkam no noting mbe .... Allah! me no talkam no noting. Cow dong go dirinki water for Ngangba sai wey ka kontiri for Bororo.

These excerpts illustrate the idiosyncrasies of the Fulani Pidgin as compared with those quoted above by non-Fulani people. The non-uniformity in Pidgin orthography can be seen in the case where Butake, in representing the same Fulani group, spells differently from Jikong.

Finally and briefly, another variation of Pidgin that is recorded in anglophone Cameroonian drama is the incorporation of francophone Pidgin. In *Accountant Wawah,* Musinga distinguishes this in the speech of Wawah's friend, Felicia:

You fit change your heart. Je m'en fou. Plenty them dey. Bot apres tous, na you call me for Njomba.

You can change your mind. I don't care. There's plenty others. In any case you asked me to be your girlfriend.

It is a vehicle for drama, songs, witticisms and liturgical teachings and is the most frequently heard language in Cameroon.

Pidgin, as Solomon Ndikvu says,

> drips from the lips of its speakers tap tap tap like roba fall for kop for meunja ... mek we sabi say god whe i gif man korokoro na i go gif finga for kracham

> drips from the lips of its speakers tap tap tap like rubber falls into the measuring cup... Remember that when God gives man an itch he gives him a finger to scratch it.

(Ndikvu, 1965: 167)

Bibliography

Achebe, Chinua 1975. *Morning Yet on Creation Day.* London: Heinemann.

—— 1977. 'The role of a writer in a new nation', in Killam, G.D.(ed.) *African Writers on African Writing.* London: Heinemann.

Amvela, Ze. 1989. *Epasa Moto* (Buea) 1.

Arnold, Stephen. 1986. 'A comparative view of the career and aesthetics of Victor Musinga. Cameroon's most popular playwright', in *African Theatre Review* (Yaounde), 1.

Egejuru, Phannuel 1978. *Black Writers, White Critics.* New York: Exposition Press.

Etherton, Michael 1976. 'The dilemma of a popular playwright' in *African Literature Today'*, 8.

Fonlon, Bernard 1984. Interview in de la Taille, G., Werner, K., Tarking, V. (eds.), *Balason.* London: Longman.

Gilman, Charles. 1979. 'Cameroon Pidgin English – a neo-African language', in Hancock I.F. (ed.), *Readings in Creole Studies.* Ghent: Story-Scientia.

Lee, Mary Hope 1979. 'Ethnographical statement in the Nigerian novel with special relation to Pidgin', in Hancock, I. F. (ed.) *Readings in Creole Studies.* Ghent: Story-Scientia.

Maimo, Sankie 1989. Interview on Cameroon Television programme 'Focus in Art' by Mutia, Babila and Tangwa, Godfrey.

Ndikvu, Solomon 1965. 'Lingua Franca for Cameroon', in *ABBIA* (Yaounde), 8.

Ngara, Emmanuel 1985. *Art and Ideology in the African Novel,* London: Heinemann.

Ngugi Wa Thiong'o 1981. 'Return to the Roots', in *Writers and Politics.* London: Heinemann.

—— 1986. *Decolonizing the Mind.* London: Heinemann.

Spencer, Julius. 1990. 'Storytelling in Sierra Leone, the Example of Lele Gbomba', in *New Theatre Quarterly,* 7.

Timothy Wangusa 1989. Quoted by Omole, J. O., in 'National literature and Nigeria's language dilemma', in *Epasa Moto* (Buea) 1.

Todd, Loreto 1991. *Talk Pidgin.* Leeds: Tortoise Books.

—— 1981. *Language and Society,* London: Routledge and Kegan Paul

—— 1974. *Pidgins and Creoles.* London: Routledge and Kegan Paul.

Wali, Obi. 1963. 'The Dead End of African Literature', in *Translation* 3.

14 Congolese playwrights as cultural revisionists

Emmanuel Yewah

The Central African sub-region has a well-developed literary history. Although such countries as Cameroon and Zaire have been the region's literary vanguard, the Congo presents a rather fascinating case study given its size, population and its incredible contribution to national and African literature. Roger Chemain insightfully notes: 'De toute l'Afrique dite "francophone", le Congo compte le plus fort pourcentage d'écrivains par rapport à l'ensemble de la population au point qu'il peut prétendre à être l'un des "pôles" culturels de cette partie de l'Afrique, au même titre que le Sénégal ou le Cameroun, pourtant beaucoup plus peuples.'[1] Indeed, the Congo has produced some of the continent's most innovative and daring political writings. In the theatre, a number of playwrights have attempted to take issue with post-colonial dictatorships and cultural assumptions inherited from African traditions and colonialism.

In order to effect these cultural revisions, playwrights have developed various strategies. Some reinterpret concepts such as 'the hero', emphasizing the collective advancement of the community over personal achievement. For these playwrights, the hero is no longer defined by his physical prowess but, more importantly, by his conceptual abilities. Other dramatists concentrate on power relationships as they are shared by the ruler and the people, or 'exercised at the micro-level of society', rather than wielded by authorities 'in a top-down model of power'.[2] These playwrights create recalcitrant characters whose opposition to authority highlights the inherent capacity of any system of power to generate counter-forces. In some plays, cultural revisionism takes the form of super-imposing African paradigms, such as the traditional court, on colonial structures, thereby subverting both structures and creating a new and authentic one. More-over, by showing a certain ambivalence toward their African traditions, presented both as sources of inspiration and as forces that stifle progress, some of the playwrights try to raise the consciousness of their audience to the need to revise some of the elements of tradition in the light of today's realities. Some plays, for instance, reassert the idea of freedom in what are clearly totalitarian states.

Our investigations of the dramatic form should not overshadow sterling contributions made by Congolese writers in novel, poetry, short stories, and detective fiction. Even a cursory overview of literary history shows remarkable production in all genres. However, the sheer number of plays and the mushroom-ing of theatre groups in the 1960s and again, very recently, in the early 1990s, would seem to give theatre pride of place in the Congo. As Amadou Koné, the Burkinabe novelist, observes, drama's interactive nature may well account for all of this attention:

> Le théâtre me semble être un des domaines littéraires et artistiques qui permettent le plus à l'écrivain d'être en contact avec son public. En contact pratiquement physique, puisque la pièce est jouée devant un public vivant qui réagit et, d'autre part ... le théâtre est, probablement, le genre littéraire qui permet de mieux exprimer ses préoccupations, de mieux se faire entendre ... parce que c'est un genre de groupe ... un genre plus africain que le roman.[3]

In this light, actor-activists and their audience can interact and reconstruct the hegemonic discourses inherent in both traditional and modern structures.[4] Moreover, the theatre is the site *par excellence* for the individual 'I' or 'je' of the actors to give way to a collective 'I'. Caya Makhélé's comments on Sylvain Bemba's plays might accurately be applied to Congolese drama as a whole:

> Le théâtre est sans conteste, pour Sylvain Bemba, le retour nocturne de la communauté autour du feu, remplacé par les projecteurs. C'est le retour à la communion. Par le personnage principal, cette communauté évacue ses angoisses, devient un personnage collectif et social le temps d'une représent-ation à travers une identité culturelle.[5]

Congolese playwrights also investigate traditional customs and elements that made their traditions vulnerable to the type of cultural, economic, and human exploitation that has characterized contacts between African and Western cultures. On a more general note, the theatre has served as an open window onto the Congolese, and by extension the African world, i.e. an introspective examin-ation of culture in an attempt to dramatize its problems and, in the process, raise the consciousness of the masses, silenced first by an indigenous culture that inhibits free expression, and then by the colonial adventurism of European powers. In the words of Colin Granderson, the theatre serves as a rallying cry, 'a call to collective action, an invitation to the public to participate in and translate action into reality'.[6] Such a call for collective action has been directed against leaders inspired by their African heritage or strongly influenced by colonialist and post-colonialist systems of government.

A closer look at these models reveals their tendency to breed a dictatorial culture. Indeed, certain aspects of traditional culture were reinforced by European colonialism as it systematically destroyed African civilizations, and subverted their political customs by introducing distorted pictures of indigenous values or simply by inventing new traditions. Subsequently, individualism displaced community-oriented thinking, individual achievement outweighed collective action and reward, Christian monotheism dislodged African polytheism. In politics, the chief as the spiritual link between his society and the ancestral world was replaced by one absolute colonial ruler whose physical distanciation from and spiritual omnipresence in the colonies through colonial administrators mirrored exactly the status of the African chief in his traditional society. The post-colonial era has seen the emergence of dictators from this political tradition. Typically they share with colonial rulers and traditional chiefs a predilection for absolute political and spiritual powers, individualism, cult of personality, physical distanciation from the people and an overwhelming spiritual omnipresence in society.

Congolese playwrights have portrayed and denounced the multiple faces of colonialism and dictatorship. Their commitment reverberates in the words of a character in *La Parenthèse de sang* (1981), by Sony Labou: 'Je ne suis que cette force de dire: à bas la dictature: celle des hommes, celle des choses, celle de Dieu si elle existe.' (48–9) Many Congolese plays focusing on dictatorship reinterpret the old saying 'uneasy lies the head that wears the crown' within the context of today's African political realities as 'uneasy lies the head that dictates'. These plays portray their monster-dictators as neurotic and solitary psychopaths and megalomaniacs, trapped in their own diseased imagination, as, for example, the President in Maxime N'Debeka's *Le Président* (1970). N'Debeka, a military electronics technician by training, a politician and one-time political prisoner turned poet and playwright, brings all his experiences to beat on this biting satire on personal power.

Le Président is set in an imaginary African dictatorship. A new president has just been elected. In his inaugural speech to the people, he details his political philosophy, by declaring, 'L'État, c'est moi; je serai le dieu; le vol est naturel; la propriété privée c'est le vol; si je vole le voleur, je vole moins que d'autres; je vole les plus grands de mes sujets, je m'occuperai des petits plus tard.' (27) The dictator's words offer stringent commentary on arbitrary government, to which he adds, 'gouverner, c'est toujours voler' (27). In addition, the powermonger has a high-sounding plan to transform the world, but his actions unmask him as a possessed figure, an evil spirit fighting against the progressive forces spear-headed by his own son, the only incarnation of virtue in this totalitarian state. The latter will eventually be killed because, in the words of François Salien, he believes strongly 'à la bonté, à la pureté, à la dignité, à la justice, à la bienveillance, à la tendresse',[7] ideals that had already helped to marginalize him from the society controlled by his father. The dictator wants to be deified and at the same time maintain unchallenged control over the material world, 'j'aime bien qu'on m'adore plus que les dieux, mais je préfère encore l'or' (27). However, in his effort to upset the status quo and remake the world, he sets in motion a process that eventually leads to his demise, leaving his country even more chaotic than during his reign.

Tchikaya U'Tamsi develops a similar diagnosis of the dictator's isolation. Born Gérald Félix Tchikaya, he adopted the pen name Tchikaya U'Tamsi, which, in the words of Janheinz Jahn, means 'the little bird who sings from home'.[8] In the 60s, U'Tamsi was already well-known in the francophone world for his numerous poetic compositions described by Hans Zell as surrealistic, 'oblique, fluid, suggestive, and replete with private symbols and symbolic motifs'.[9] More recently, he ventured into theatre with plays such as *Le Destin glorieux du Maréchal Nnikon Nniku, Prince qu'on sort* (1977) and *Le Zulu* (1979), his own retelling of Chaka the

Zulu legend. In *Le Zulu*, Chaka, like N'Debeka's president, is portrayed as a power-hungry, solitary figure. Although he complains, 'on meurt seul d'être seul' (III, viii, 109). Chaka's obsession for power leads to generalized violence. In an apocalyptic atmosphere, he spills much blood, 'j'ai égorgé Noliwé .... J'ai égorgé Nnandi. À qui léguer un tel héritage. Le sang est répandu? À qui léguer un rêve qui a tourné au cauchemar .... Je suis venu avec la nouvelle du renouveau ....' (III, xv, 130) In this gory nightmare, the dictator-general's distrust leads him to kill his own mother who, in his distracted mind, embodies the enemy. Inspired by his African traditions that tend to celebrate the cult of personality, Chaka puts himself at the centre of the political regime: 'Et si j'instituais un culte .... Le culte de Chaka, représentant de l'Umzikulu! .... Ce totem, je veux qu'on le voie partout!' (II, iii, 66) He is consumed by the quest for power, but worried by his sick conscience.

He sees himself more like a god than a blood-thirsty tyrant, but his neurotic mind is haunted by his deeds and a paranoiac fear of a conspiracy and assassination. Having failed in his utopian vision to change his people into Zulus, symbol of military prowess, Chaka creates an imaginary battle in which the sounds of cannon, flying swords, and gunshots eclipse him, and bring to an end his delusions of creating his own breed of loyal Zulus.

Labou Tansi's dictator in *Antoine m'a vendu son destin* (1986) recalls the antagonistic Chaka as he laments on the solitude of power, 'pas de peuple! pas d'alliés. Pas d'amis. Mais je n'avalerai pas cette méchanceté. Je refuse d'entrer dans ce néant.' (255) In his African political tradition where the chief acts as intermediary between his people and their deities, Antoine has distanced himself from the community. Having tried to deify himself, Antoine makes a desperate appeal to God. He needs to overcome his isolation born of disassociating himself from the people in order to dominate them more absolutely:

> Dieu! J'écrase mon exil dans tes mains. Sois mon allié, ma route – si tu veux. Je te choisis en guise d'avenir. Donne-moi quotidiennement le temps de saccager l'arrogance de ce monde. Donne-moi la force d'envoyer mon pied à la face ou dans le cul de ce monde.
>
> (255)

The leaders discussed so far draw on their African heritage for models of government; however, other despots, like 'le Maréchal Nnikon Nniku' in *Le Destin glorieux du Maréchal Nnikon Nniku. Prince qu'on sort*, the old scientist in *Conscience de tracteur*, (1979) with his scientific approach to remaking Africa, and Walante in *Qui a mangé Madame d'Avoine Bergotha?* (1989) rely on European examples. Western educational, political, and social thinking dominated colonial Africa, and in the wake of independence the West's control over bank loans, debt repayment, food-aid and its exploitation of African raw materials continues to dictate political and economic policy. In *Le Maréchal Nnikon Nniku*, a 'sinister farce' and a 'pun-filled satire', U'Tamsi further probes 'contemporary African dictatorship'.[10] Maréchal Nnikon Nniku – 'ni con, ni cul' ('neither ass nor asshole') – the supreme Guide, has taken power in a military coup with his cohorts Nkha Nkha, Don and Mphi Ssans Po in a fictitious country called Mutulufwa. Nnikon Nniku's political philosophy of 'Nnikonnicunisme' echoes the 'isms' of both Eastern and Western political thought and suggests the President's partiality for foreign ideologies. He defines his outlook in these terms,

> Le Nnikonnicunisme est la symbiose structurelle de deux éléments moteurs que je traduirai en langage simple: avec l'unité, c'est la symbiose (*ovation*). Je ne saurais trop vous encourager à l'étude de notre philosophie idéologique, création géniale du peuple Mutulufwa, éclairée par son Grand Timonier, moi-même!
>
> (90)

In a press conference, Nnikon Nniku summarizes his political platform: 'priorité à l'agriculture, à la discipline, incorporer tout le peuple dans l'armée pour lui apprendre la discipline' (36). Paraphrasing this philosophy, Salien highlights the perverted logic inherent in such an authoritarian regime:

> Le régime du Maréchal, Guide Suprême, Timonier et père de la Nation, abolit le travail – ce qui évite le chômage – a pour objectif d'appauvrir la pauvreté et s'est fixé pour finalité le régressisme social: dans les temps anciens, les gens vivaient de cueillette et d'eau de pluie. Pas d'usine, pas de pollution! Radicalisons la pauvreté![11]

In his conclusion, Salien quotes Nnikon Nnniku, 'je combattrai la merde par la merde' (37). Nnikon Nniku's attempt to create a new economic order on the ruins of the old reveals his total lack of understanding of economic indicators and seems to mirror uncannily and ironically the old order that he tries to destroy:

> Nous nous sommes appliqués à approfondir, à radicaliser notre pauvreté. Notre revenu par tête d'habitant était, lors de notre accession au pouvoir, voisin de celui des moins riches des pays riches. Aujourd'hui, notre PNB tend vers le zéro absolu (*ovation*). Le ministre des Finances m'a assuré ce matin qu'il était très voisin de zéro. (90–91)

The President's regressive economic philosophy resembles the various 'philosopher-dictators' of 'Authenticité', 'Renouveau', 'Pragmatisme Communautaire', 'African Socialism', and so on, which infest the African political scene today and who, more than thirty years after independence, have taken their societies back to the agrarian period. In an ironic *mise en abîme* of Nnikon Nniku's philosophy, his leadership slumps to ground zero. His complete loss of power and self-destructive policies are symbolized by his crumbling effigy.

Sony Labou Tansi is another Congolese playwright who dramatizes the attraction of African leaders and pseudo-intellectuals to imported political and scientific ideologies. In the last decade, Labou Tansi has emerged as one of the continent's most creative, innovative, and politically engaging writers with works marked by fiercely anti-colonialist, anti-dictatorial rhetoric. He appropriates the French language by consciously transgressing its rules and subverting its grammar to convey his own view of humanity abandoned to itself, caught in a cycle of crude violence in an oppressive inhuman world 'qui fout le camp'. In *Conscience de tracteur*, an old scientist, fascinated by scientific methodology, undertakes an apocalyptic but utopian project to flood the world and start all over again: 'recommencer le déluge, pour sauver le genre humain du genre humain. Un déluge de sang, de feu, d'espoir aussi.'

The scientist unleashes a wave of mayhem which destroys the world, but, like Noah, by building an ark for himself and his specimens he generates a selective rebirth. In imitating God and Noah, he assumes qualities which, together with his claim to control the means of production and scientific knowledge, give him absolute power over life, death, and over the new world. In his satiric parody of the bible, Labou Tansi denounces the totalitarian potential that is unleashed when scientific and political power are concentrated in the hands of one individual.

In a similar vein, Walante, the dictator in *Qui a mangé Madame d'Avoine Bergotha?* is called 'l'omniscient', 'le sage des sages', 'le divin', 'père et fondateur de la paix', 'l'inséminateur suprême'. He symbolizes misogynist patriarchy by embarking on a grandiose project to create a woman-only island. The exclusion of his potential male rivals from his political kingdom gives Walante the chance to assert himself as the supreme man. He will thus control the women, mere procreators, whom he will personally inseminate to produce a new breed of humans loyal to him. The constitution of the island reads:

> Les hommes sont démis de leurs fonctions en tant que peuple. / Moi Walante, je les remplacerai, personnellement, / dans toutes leurs fonctions. / Moi Walante, je me programme et me planifie / avenir / espoir / et volonté personnelle du peuple! Gérant et garant de ses consciences, / son inséminateur unique ...
>
> (35–6)

In the words of one of the characters, 'Walante s'apprête à égorger tous les mâles de l'île!' (21) However while Walante wants to get rid of all the men, the women, who are the source of the male power struggle, are not mentioned. Even Madame Bergotha, Walante's object of seduction, the protagonist of the drama, actually a man in disguise, is rarely seen or heard. Like the other women in the play, 'she' is a voiceless, absent other. So, while this play functions as a commentary on personalized power, it also raises issues about the way women have been used as silent pawns and absent participants in the dramatic creation of new meanings.

The male heroes conceived by the playwrights we have discussed above dramatize the call to a new beginning made by the Guide Suprême in Labou Tansi's novel *La Vie et demie* (1979):

– Nous voulons reprendre!
Et la foule de répondre:
– L'homme à zéro!
– Reprendre!
– L'Histoire à zéro!
– Reprendre!
– Le monde à zéro!

(39–40)

Starting over from nothing would be a way of closing an excessively painful chapter in African history and would help to exclude colonialists and neo-colonialists from the process of producing new knowledge. It would also banish the dictator from the stage where, in the past, he spawned human suffering and observed the unfolding events, with an amused and unconcerned countenance. Consequently, any clean break with the past has to surpass the misgovernment of general-dictators who have left the continent in a perpetual state of retardation and stagnation. To borrow from Labou Tansi in *Conscience de tracteur*: 'le monde sera peut-être fini que l'Afrique n'aura pas commencé' (10). In this play, a scientific dictatorship replaces the military one, as the general suggests: 'Si je comprends bien, professeur, nous [dictateurs] n'étions pas prévus dans votre paradis?' (II, vii, 111) The professor's reluctance to answer implies a marginaliz-ation of the dictator and others who hold an abusive monopoly over knowledge of traditions. At the same time, pseudo-scientific projects of death and selective re-birth will not surmount Africa's problems. What Africa appears to need is a new breed of heroes, leaders, scientists, thinkers, indeed visionaries inspired by both their indigenous and received traditions of governance who can con-ceptualize a new continental order. For, as Henri Lopes succinctly puts it in the introduction to *Conscience de tracteur*, 'les héros, les leaders et savants ne suffisent pas pour la Grande Marche de l'Afrique, il faut aussi et surtout des maîtres à penser et à sentir' (12).

The attempt to create a new breed of heroes and the experimentation with the concept finds its fullest expression in *La Parenthèse de sang* (1981). The setting is a totalitarian state. The action centres on Libertashio, a revolutionary figure whose omnipresent spectre haunts the authorities after his death. Libertashio's ghost transforms him into a menacing consciousness, but the military crackdown leads only to bloody violence as the authorities discover to their dismay that Libertashio, their tormentor, is simply a product of their imagination. Since Libertashio is nothing but a virtual being, it is impossible to destroy him. Even though he never physically appears in the play, he remains engraved in the authorities' consciousness.

Labou Tansi thus conceptualizes the hero as a process rather than as a physical entity. And since the hero is not confined to a given time and place, he is less vulnerable to society's rampant corruption. And through constant redefinition and reflection, the heroic element operates as an ideal of resistance and change and avoids the pitfalls brought by success through physical prowess and tactical skills.

In *Je soussigné cardiaque*, Labou Tansi offers another version of revolutionary heroism. Perono, a Portuguese imperialist, has a firm god-like grip on the political structure: 'Ici personne ne résiste. Personne. Je distribue le droit à l'oxygène. J'écrase tout le monde.' (I, iii, 96) He seems to be so many things at once, 'le drapeau, la loi, la liberté, le droit, la prison, le diable et le bon Dieu enfin. Si bien que toute la région m'écoute et m'obéit aveuglément.' (I, iii, 93–4) However, his all-encompassing, inflated self-image nullifies him since he is both sides of everything: 'je suis le bonheur, le malheur, l'amour, la haine, le drapeau, la loi. Je suis le bien et le mal.' (I, iii, 99)

He uses his power to deride and annihilate the opposition. He boasts, 'j'ai des sous, et je me'en sers à dégonfler les autres' (I, iii, 97). However, by reducing everyone to nothing, he rules over an empty society: 'Depuis longtemps je n'ai jamais eu que du vide devant moi. Du vide en face. Un vide vierge. C'est énervant le vide.' Mallot the schoolteacher fills the void in Perono's universe as Perono makes clear to Mallot, 'vous êtes le seul qui allez m'obéir parce que je commande' (I, iii, 95). Yet Mallot's obedience merely veils the emptiness surrounding Perono. The total lack of popular legitimacy undermines any kind of authority that he thinks he has.

Despite Mallot's subservient position, he challenges the omnipotent Perono by being disobedient in front of others. Perono fears that this will inspire opposition: 'Tu m'as humilié devant ce gosse, devant mon cuisinier et devant moi-même. Ils en parleront dans tout le village et tu deviendras le héros.' (I, iii, 100) Ultimately, Mallot's resistance leads to his death, but the ideals of freedom that his life embodied will fuel future struggle. Appropriating the oppressor's language the people call for sustained rebellion, 'aluta continua!'

Through cultural revisionism, Congolese playwrights reconceptualize heroes within the context of the African people's historical struggle against dictators and colonial hegemony. Some plays subvert both indigenous and imported structures by superimposing one structure on another and thereby creating a new and original organization. For instance, Antoine Letembet-Ambily's *L'Europe inculpée* (1977) and a lesser-known play *Les Conjurés du 17 janvier 1961* (n.d.) by Kodia Noël-Ramatta take the form of court trials in which Europe and its accomplices are accused of, among other things, cultural genocide and the invasion of African spaces (physical, political, intellectual, religious, …). *L'Europe inculpée* develops as an allegory in which Noah is brought back to earth to testify in a lawsuit brought by Cham, the father of Africa, against his grand-children Europe and America, accused of turning Africa into:

> Le théâtre de la haine, de la discorde, de la honte,
> De l'oppression de la douleur, du châtiment
> De l'exploitation, de l'esclavage, de l'asservissement,
> Du vol, de la spoliation, de la frustration,
> De l'ivrognerie, de l'alcoolisme.

> (60–61)

Les Conjurés du 17 janvier 1961 also puts Europe on trial before an international court for the assassination of Patrice Lumumba. This event changed the course of

Congolese and, by extension, African history given Lumumba's strong nationalist views and his Pan-Africanist vision of a united Africa countering all neo-colonialist adventurism on the continent and competing as a giant economic block on an equal footing with other world economic systems. In both plays, the court-room setting is a semi-circular traditional court superimposed on a Western-style tribunal. By merging both structures, the playwrights create a new, somewhat decolonized, space, where characters highlight the pains of coloniz-ation and slavery. In the process, they stifle European colonialist and neo-colonialist domination by denying the 'masters' of yesteryear a voice to defend themselves in an African court. The tables are turned on European and American colonialism which had denied Africans their humanity, meaningful represent-ation, and participation in the legal, political, and educational systems. As the other continents judge the impact of European and American domination an alternative, a collective vision is created.

Drawing their inspiration from Congolese socio-political history, today's playwrights explore 'le fleuve essentiel'. One of the great role models for young writers is the prolific and versatile Sylvain Bemba. A man of numerous pseudo-nyms, described as 'un garant de la mémoire collective dans la littérature congolaise', he has led the literary vanguard in re-evaluating both indigenous and received cultures through incisive inquiry into the political culture of the Congo and Africa.[12] Sony Labou Tansi dedicates *La Vie et demie* and *Les Sept Solitudes de Lorsa Lopez* (1985) to him, and gives the name Martial, Bemba's theatrical pseudonym, to his revolutionary heroes in *La Vie et demie* and *La Parenthèse de sang*. Labou Tansi's dedication is testimony to the special place that Bemba occupies in the Congolese literary tradition; a tradition in which the imaginary is nourished by political, social, economic, cultural, and linguistic realities. As Bemba puts it:

> J'adhère pleinement à cette forme de réalisme, qui ne s'appuie pas sur les mythes populaires ou sur l'inconscient collectif pour perpétrer l'obscuran-tisme, mais part au contraire du réel, des vocables les plus expressifs et des croyances du peuple pour les dynamiser et les projeter dans une vision du monde qui libère l'homme de ses chaînes.
>
> (97)

In his preface to Bemba's *Une Eau dormante* (1975), J.B. Tati-Loutard identifies two major trends in Congolese and African drama: 'il exalte la mémoire des héros nationaux de la période coloniale ou se livre à la critique des mœurs' (9–10). In their critique of mores, Congolese dramatists show their ambivalence toward their African heritage. On the one hand, traditions have shaped the African mind, personality and identity, and they provide the ethical and moral basis of his being, hence Bemba's reference to a certain 'fierté ancestrale'. On the other hand, traditions are viewed as a 'prison', a mechanism of enslavement, especially in the hands of unscrupulous village chiefs, 'griots' and other leaders. The prison metaphor implies both physical and mental isolation from society, and stresses the type of moral, spiritual, cultural and behavioural codes prescribed by those who claim some knowledge of traditions.

In *Une Eau dormante*, Olessa, the fisherman, characterizes tradition as incarceration declaring: 'l'esclave c'est toi, c'est ce griot, c'est l'homme du village enchaîné à la tradition, à la coutume même quand celle-là et celle-ci ne répondent pas exactement aux conditions actuelles' (XVII, 90). And Véritas concludes, 'Vous avez été paralysés par la coutume, pris aux filets de la tradition alors que le chef Oluo était le seul juge de celle-là et de celle-ci. Vous étiez une eau dormante. Réveillez-vous.' (97) Though trapped by their tradition, these authority figures, nevertheless, harness elements of traditional culture in order to impose their own conception of traditions as fixed principles to be possessed, personalized, and manipulated in the name of selfish ambition.

Olessa's words echo those of the 'griot': 'le monde', he asserts, 'est divisé en deux parties: ceux qui possèdent et ceux qui n'ont rien. Ceux qui n'ont rien n'ont que le droit de se soumettre à la tradition.....' 'Avez-vous déjà vu un chien sans puces?' he asks rhetorically. He concludes his peroration, 'il en est de l'homme par rapport à la tradition, comme du chien vivant avec ses puces. Un chien qui essaierait de secouer ses puces serait ridicule tout comme un homme qui tenterait de s'affranchir de la tradition.' (X, vii, 87–8) When questioned about the objects of possession Perono replies, 'Posséder quoi? Eh bien, soi, les autres et le monde!' (I, iii, 104) In addition to his narcissistic notion of possession and the materialistic view underlying his possession of 'les autres et le monde', one must read in Perono's answer a claim to a certain authority over traditional knowledge and the production of meanings. As chief Oluo puts it, 'la justice est une fille respectueusement soumise à sa mère. Ce n'est pas la justice qui fait la tradition, c'est la tradition qui fait la justice ....'

By equating the relationship between justice and tradition with that of a daughter respectfully submitting to her mother, the chief subjects justice to malleable and self-serving interpretations of tradition. Moreover, by depicting justice, one of society's guiding principles, as a female relationship in a society where tradition has silenced and marginalized women, Oluo shows how his society has emptied justice of all its shared meanings. Doubly exploited by both the owner of the fish pond where he works and the chief who lends him money at exorbitant interest. Olessa, the chief's interlocutor, asserts, 'la justice c'est ce qui ne récompense pas les gens pour leur travail' (II, 20). Clearly, the chief as traditional guardian and spiritual link between his society and the ancestral world has attempted to impose his own conception of justice on his people as if it were *the* concept, conditioned or defined by tradition. However, Olessa opposes the chief, by contending that, 'la justice ou tout au moins ce qu'on appelle ainsi c'est le fait de ceux qui possèdent à tort devant ceux qui cherchent à posséder' (I, iii, 104). He acts as a cultural revisionist by showing how chief Oluo has devalued justice and calling for the reassertion of justice's original collective meaning.

Like other playwrights discussed here, Bemba portrays the culture's propensity for breeding monster-dictators who usurp power and warp collective history to serve their own ends. Bemba shows how this unequal power relationship creates pockets of resistance from which popular heroes emerge. However, Bemba's heroic concept is founded on the community as the hero embodies the whole society. The individual 'I' becomes a collective rebellious 'we'.

By the end of Bemba's *L'Homme qui tua le crocodile* (1972), Henri Balou, a schoolteacher who fights the economic tyranny of a rich and powerful business man, N'Gandou,[13] emerges as a 'metonymic hero' incarnating the collectivity. The action has two theatrical facets. In the background, N'Gandou pits his local and economic power against Balou's accusations of corruption. N'Gandou makes loans to the people at exorbitant interest rates, seduces married and single women, even under-age girls, and controls access to the river, the lifeline of the population. At N'Gandou's house, Balou denounces this exploitation of the people. He paints N'Gandou as a blood-sucking man eater: 'Vous mangez vos semblables, vous les nettoyez jusqu'aux os.' (I, iii, 22) Though a forced symbiotic relationship seems to exist between N'Gandou the lender and his perennial debtors, Balou uncovers the skewed terms of the relationship. His ironic food metaphor captures N'Gandou's destructive parasitic existence where he sucks his victims dry then picks their bones clean.

This unprecedented challenge to his authority prompts N'Gandou to deviant counter-action. He sends Django, one of his henchmen, to seduce Balou's wife in the mistaken belief that she would fall prey to his money. This act would both reinforce N'Gandou's omnipotence and undo Balou's family structure. But the wife resists the temptation and Balou beats the seducer. Subsequently, N'Gandou has an anonymous letter sent to Balou's wife accusing her husband of infidelity. Though this causes a temporary separation, reason wins out over passion as the couple is reunited. The power play concludes as N'Gandou's daughter uncovers some incriminating documents detailing her father's involvement in corrupt wheeling and dealing, and sex scandals, and this compelling evidence sends N'Gandou to jail.

While the storyline develops behind the scenes, an 'amuseur public' or clown, an omniscient narrator, relates highlights of the tale to an audience in a setting similar to a storytelling session in traditional societies. The public's questions and choral responses collectively sustain the story, and the dictator is finally ousted from power not by the resistance of a single individual endowed with exceptional leadership skills but by the joint action of Balou, the audience, Balou's wife and son, N'Gandou's daughter, and especially the clown with his acute sense of humour and effective use of proverbs, irony, metaphors, riddles and jokes.

In the process of challenging N'Gandou the people become aware of the vulnerability of those who appear powerful, and learn to stand up against today's home-grown and neo-colonialist oppressors. By extension, they are alerted to the authoritarian structure embedded not only in slavery but also in materialism and the cycle of dependency on foreign aid handouts and imported ideas which have contributed immeasurably to Africa's stagnation and underdevelopment.

Like Labou Tansi, Bemba works with the conception of hero rather than presenting an individual's heroic resistance against a subjugating system. He creates a situation propitious for the emergence of a hero, and calls upon the audience to participate in the shaping of the hero. For example in the pro-vocatively titled *Tarentelle noire et diable blanc*, Bemba creates a Manichaean world in which actions generate not only from conflictual relationships between a father's blind submission to the dictates of tradition and his rebellious son, but also from tension between interacting dualities: black/white, good/evil, god/satan, light/dark, soul/body, master/slave, superior/inferior, exploiter/exploited, producers of knowledge/consumers of knowledge. The dualities serve as a commentary on a world in which binary opposition renders things mutually exclusive. A hero does not materialize but, in the process of 'undoing' or deconstructing the dualities, a refractory concept emerges. Out of the attempt to negotiate these conflicting situations, Bemba evokes the need to go beyond the cycle of alternating domination, where the oppressor becomes the oppressed, and reconceptualize human drama.

Set on a rubber plantation, *Tarentelle noire et diable blanc* indicts colonialist exploitation of African raw materials and manpower through the incorporation of the African agrarian economy into a capitalist system with its monetary basis. The destabilizing effects of money is acknowledged by chief Oluo in *Une Eau dormante*: 'L'argent est venu défaire ce qui était fait, désunir ce qui était uni, famille, conscience familiale' (II, 19). As a colonizing agent, the introduction of money creates haves – the colonialists and their African satraps – and have-nots – the oppressed masses. Whereas other playwrights discussed here create a space in which to develop anti-colonialist discourses that marginalize the colonialist, in *Tarentelle noire et diable blanc*, Bemba uses the direct approach to denounce the evils of colonialism.

By reinterpreting the concept of a hero, denouncing some elements of tradition and the dehumanizing effects of colonialism, and creating a stage for neurotic dictators to dramatize their buffoonery, the Congolese playwrights endeavour to raise their audience's consciousness to the internal and external factors that have contributed to the present economic quagmire, political stalemate, intellectual bankruptcy, and lethargy in Africa. In so doing they appeal for collective action on the part of the disenfranchised masses, and a revision of cultural assumptions that have led to the rise of dictatorships. However, to effect such action, the need to close the parenthesis on the past as a condition for a leap forward remains imperative. To this end there seems to be a general call to start at ground zero.

Despite its progressive stance, the appeal could still lead to ever more vicious cycles of renewal. What is needed, therefore, is not just a call for a new beginning, but effective ways to close the cycle and, from the point of closure, make a tangential move from whence a new world could develop. Furthermore, conditions have to be created that allow the new breed of humans, heroes, and thinkers to create a new order for the African world which accounts for the multiple factors that have so far shaped the African mind or destabilized the environment.

In spite of the appeal of drama to a broad audience, these plays have unfortunately remained a means of entertainment and education for very few African audiences, because they are written in a foreign language. As a result, they have, for the most part, been staged in French cultural centres, and capital cities of former French colonies, where, besides having an audience educated in the French language and history, some people can afford the luxury of paying to watch the plays. Ironically, most of the plays discussed were created in the context of the Concours Théâtral Africain, an annual drama contest organized by Radio France Internationale, one of the voices promoting French cultural hegemony. National radios in French-speaking countries aired a selection of these plays written by newly independent Africans. Of all the playwrights discussed, Labou Tansi seems to have been more successful in reaching a wider international audience due in part to his innovative style, his virulent critique of institutions, systems and cultural assumptions, and his creative subversion of the French language. More importantly his success comes from the fact that as a stage director himself, his theatre group, Le Rocado Zulu Théâtre, has staged most of his plays both in Africa and Europe, where they have found an audience willing to call into question history and prejudices, and engage in a complicitous relationship with the plays and playwrights to destabilize and re-evaluate certain cultural assumptions and structures. In so doing, Labou Tansi's plays, like others discussed here, have raised the consciousness of the audience to the need to revise elements of both indigenous and received traditions.

Notes

1 Roger Chemain, 'Introduction', *Tarentelle noire et diable blanc* (Paris: Editions P.J. Oswald, 1976), p. 5.
2 Dominic Head, 'Gordimer's None to Accompany Me: Interregnum', *Research in African Literatures* (Vol. 26, No. 4, 1995), pp. 46–57. Head is here paraphrasing Foucault's ideas expressed in 'Of Other Spaces' (*Diacritics*, 16.3, 1986), pp. 22–7.
3 Günter Bielemeier, 'Interview avec Amadou Koné', *Bayreuth African Studies Series*. 8 (Bayreuth, 1986), p. 50.
4 By hegemonic, I mean any discourse by an individual or group that conditions behaviour, perceptions, and shapes, modes of thinking and other aspects of life in a given society. Hegemonic here also applies to cultural forms, indigenous or imposed, that predominate over others.
5 Caya Makhélè, 'Wylvain Bemba ou le syndrome du miroir brisé', *Notre Librairie* (92–3, mars–mai, 1988), p. 97.
6 Colin Granderson, 'The Chief in Contemporary Black African Theatre of French Expression', *The Theatre in Africa*, edited by Oyin Ogumba and Abiola Irele (Ibadan: Ibadan University Press, 1978), p. 85.
7 François Salien, *Panorama du théâtre africain d'expression française*, II (Bandundu, Zaire: CEEBA Publications, 1983), p. 92.
8 Janheinz Jahn, *Who's Who in African Literature* (Tübingen, 1972), p. 377.
9 Hans Zell, *A New Reader's Guide to African Literature* (New York: Africana Publishing Company, 1983), p. 503.
10 Zell, p. 285.
11 Salien, p. 95–6.
12 Makhélé, p. 97.
13 N'Gandou, the name given to the arrogant, exhibitionist, tyrannical business man is the Congolese word for 'caïman'; but 'l'amuseur public', gifted as he is, has used his creative abilities rather sarcastically to add a new dimension to the name thereby transforming it to that of a more ferocious creature 'crocodile'. He does this by combining the conjugated phonetic forms of the verb 'croquer', that is 'croc', bite or eat, with the name of one of the female victims of N'Gandou's sexual escapades called Odile. Juxtaposed the words give us the title of the play *L'Homme qui tua le crocodile*.

References to plays

Sylvain Bemba. *Tarentelle noire et diable blanc* (Paris: Editions P. J. Oswald, 1976).

—— *Une Eau dormante* (Paris: O.R.T.F., 1975).

—— *L'Homme qui tua le crocodile* (Yaoundé: CLE, 1972).

Noël-Ramatta Kodia. *Les Conjurés du 17 janvier 1961* (Brazzaville: Editions Héros dans l'Ombre, n.d.).

Sony Labou Tansi. *Qui a mangé Madame d'Avoine Bergotha* (Bruxelles: Editions Promotion Théâtre, Théâtre en Tête, 1989).

—— *Antoine m'a vendu son destin* (Paris: *Revue Equateur*, no. 1, octobre/novembre, 1986).

—— *La Parenthèse de sang*, suivi de *Je soussignè cardiaque* (Paris: Hatier Monde Noir en Poche, 1981).

—— *Conscience de tracteur* (Dakar/Yaoundé: NEA-CLE, 1979).

—— *La Vie et demie* (Paris: Le Seuil, 1979).

Letembet-Ambily, Antoine. *L'Europe inculpée: drame en quatre actes* (Yaoundé: CLE, 1977).

Maxime N'Debeka. *Le Président: drame satirique en trois actes* (Paris: P.J. Oswald, 1970).

U'Tamsi Tchikaya. *Le Destin glorieux du Maréchal Nnikon Nniku. Prince qu'on sort: comédie-farce-sinistre en trois plans* (Paris: Présence africaine, 1979).

—— *Zulu*, suivi de *Vwène le fondateur* (Paris: Nubia, 1977).

15 Purity and pollution in Freetown masked performance

John Nunley

Police in Big Clash with Masqueraders

Bloody Mary Arrested

As the feast of Eid-Ul-Adha was celebrated yesterday, Freetown was not without its incidents of drama.

It was a test of strength and will power between the police and masqueraders who went out to defy the ban on street performing.

As the defiance continued police pounced.

Scores of arrests were made and heavily armed policemen patrolled the streets the whole of the day.

The mask of the popular "Bloody Mary" devil was seized by police at Fergusson Street as the group masqueraded in the street.

As the devil was grabbed, the followers fled.

Along Mountain Cut and Kroo Town Road, Siaka Stevens Street and Campbell Street, dancers were out as early as Monday night, the eve of the holiday.

Much alcohol flowed as the night progressed and in the morning the streets were a sea of broken bottles.

The police were put on the alert and the war of Wills began.

And yesterday, by midday, teargass [sic] was used at a number of points.

– We Yonne, 23 November 1977

Confrontation – the power of one Ode-lay masking society of Sierra Leone against another, the government, or the police – extends from the aesthetic/ spiritual realm into everyday reality, where violence often goes along with successful performances. Ode-lay groups such as Firestone, Rainbow, Bloody Mary, Civilian Rule, and Juju Wata have grown up in the tough urban environment of Freetown and have claimed the streets for masked performances. The success of these performances depends both on their location in the streets and on the risk of danger. In contrast, an unsuccessful masked performance by the Firestone group in 1977 was restricted to a given area by government permit. It was apparent that what ordinarily occurred outside this area – namely in the streets – was missing in this instance. The location and the risk are both essential to successful performance, as well as potential causes of violence.[1]

Ode-lay originated in the Yoruba masking societies of Nigeria, introduced to Sierra Leone from 1807 to the middle of the century. Yoruba culture – its music, masked performances, religion, and medicine – played a central role in a long-standing political dialectic which currently manifests itself in the relationship between the Ode-lay groups and the Sierra Leone government (Peterson 1969: 44–47). The government often depends on the political patronage of masked societies, yet it is fearful of the aesthetic intensity generated by their processions.

Hunting masks are the prototype of Ode-lay. They consist of *eri* (a horned headdress); *asho* (a loose-fitting smock and baggy panteloonlike pants); and the most powerful part of the costume, *hampa* (a vestlike garment worn over the smock). The hampa may be covered with a variety of materials including wooden spoons, tortoise shells, and small gourds studded with quills that protect the maskers from witches. Dried and gutted sea porcupines stuffed with leaves containing medicinal properties are placed on the back of the hampa to help maintain its shape, and mirrors are attached to the garment so that attendants can see the reflection of witches. Also attached are bushbuck horns dipped in poison, wooden combs, monkey and dog skulls, empty pasteboard shotgun cartridge casings, and cowrie-lined red cloth sacks filled with medicine.

The Hunting costume honours Ogun, the deity of hunters, who was introduced to the colony by repatriated slaves, sixty thousand in all, most of whom were Yoruba. With horror and evangelical frustration, missionaries describe the appearances of Ogun in his Hunting costumes. Traditional Hunting associations formed a solid institution which helped establish the Yoruba Creole class as the cultural elite of the then British colony.

Throughout the pre-World War II era, native sons applied for and were denied membership in the Yoruba Hunting Societies. For this reason, during the mid-1940s the so-called Alikali maskers formed their own groups based on Hunting Society traditions. About 1950, Michael Banton photographed one Alikali group at the west end of Freetown. The performer is surrounded by participants in paramilitary dress. A few of them hold up a banner. The formation of the group and its militant posture strongly resemble the present-day Ode-lay society masquerades.

The 1978 Easter Monday outing of Juju Wata at Hastings exemplified a successful Ode-lay performance. Their objective was to establish a strong reputation for devil processions on the east side of Freetown. Since most of its members were Internal Security Unit troops (ISU), some of whom were trained in Cuba, it was important that they stage a successful masked performance. The fancy aesthetic of the costumes was intended to compliment the fierce reputation of the ISU. Ode-lay representatives from nearby towns were invited.

Sometime during the preceding night, a sacrifice of uncooked rice in a bowl of water, a bottle of rum, and a 45 rpm record in its paper sleeve (symbolizing the record-breaking beauty of the devil), were spread before the assembled costume. With more early-morning sacrifices, members drank rum from a glass offered by the society's female officer called the mammy queen.

At 8.30 AM, a bush mask which had been used the previous year caroled through the town to announce the procession of the Juju Wata 'devil' (Krio term for maskers). The bush devil costume was decorated with porcupine quills and hunter's raffia, displaying a few fancy materials like the hunter's costume. But the headpiece was much more elaborate. The procession moved from house to house until noon to the accompaniment of snapping sounds of rhythm sticks similar to those used by the Hunting societies.

By 1.00 PM most of the Juju Wata Society members and their girlfriends had gathered around the house of the *agba* (society leader). The women wore long uniform dresses of brown print; their hair was decorated with cowrie shells to complement the fancy mask. A flag carrier paraded up and down the road with a town crier who rang an assembly bell to announce the procession. The men wore jeans and printed T-shirts which bore the name of the group along with a variety of designs and slogans. The air was charged with excitement. At the shrine enclosure several members in *ashoebi* (society dress) and tennis shoes, along with the mammy queen in black satin pants and blouse, served portions of rum in the bottlecap. Other members carried phonograph records in honour of the event. Several broke 78 rpm discs hung from a flagpole. Meanwhile, the group's sponsors paced back and forth waiting to begin.

Expectation and tension mounted as word spread that the Bantus Mailo Jazz Band would not play until it received a cash advance. This is a method often employed by bands to guarantee payment. After reaching a compromise, the Juju Wata leader signalled the jazz band that the devil was prepared to dance. As the band struck up the first notes, the masker crashed through the mat enclosure, dancing for a few moments before he was carefully led down a hill and across the rocky path of an old rail bed. On the opposite side of the rail bed, women, flag carriers, the Bantus Mailo Jazz Band, and society members moved toward the devil. The music and singing intensified as the crowd and masking party converged.

Once the two groups met, the procession turned toward the home of the society's financial sponsor, where the devil danced for several minutes. Then the group departed for the homes of other important society members and townspeople. At 2.00 PM the party made its way to the village headman, who made a contribution to the society and gave a speech lauding the beauty and restraint of the procession. The procession then returned to the agba's house to change dancers and refresh the musicians. An hour later the Juju Wata group was prepared to play until the late evening. By 10.00 PM the jazz band and the society members were exhausted. Returning to the abga's residence for rice, meat sauce, and drink, the band jammed through the early morning while several society members played the mouth organ, triangle and *mbira* (the so-called African thumb piano) – a jam session the group called 'back off'.

The Juju Wata performance met the expectations of its members and, indeed, all of Hastings. The village headman requested that he be considered a grand patron for the society's next performance. As the celebration was a record breaker, the agba smashed numerous discs at several points along the procession route.

In contrast, the 1977 Firestone Society performance was a failure. At that time the Ode-lay society claimed about 90 members and over 3,000 supporters who gathered annually for Eid Ul-Adha at the end of Ramadan in order to attract Muslims. The head of the group, *ashigba*, maintains the shrine of Ogun, the Yoruba deity of war. The power and danger of Ogun, as conceived by the Yoruba, have effortlessly lent themselves to an urban toughness and concern for militancy expressed in Ode-lay masked performances.

When the government rejected Ode-lay requests for public permits for Eid Ul-Adha in November, Firestone selected the first week of December of that year to present their devils *off* the street. The main Firestone costume was built in the same three-part construction as the Hunting costume previously described, though the headpiece was strikingly different. Yet despite the expertise of the artist who made it and the aesthetic quality and completeness of his creation, Ode-lay maskers must be placed at risk to be successful. The performance must be dangerous.

Restricted to a confined and private space, the performance failed to reach its potential intensity, and the disappointing first night resulted in the cancellation of the remaining presentations. Roger Abraham's theory of enactment helps explain what went wrong (1977: 80). He defines enactment as any cultural event that brings people together to employ multivocal and polyvalent signs and symbols to heighten ritual experience. Such enactments may include performances, games, rituals, and festivities. These four components are interpenetrating, as, for example, the coin toss and national anthem *rituals* in the *game* of football. In Ode-lay, the masked *performance* may be interrupted by the *play* of the *kaka* (shit) devil mask who mocks the main performance. Overlap is also evidenced in the post-masking *festivities* when members *play* at kung fu.

Abrahams notes that these four components are highly stylized, each marked, or framed, to foreground the form and movement of the participants (1977: 98). With the appropriate frames and their most effective editing, the organizers of Ode-lay enactments have at their disposal a mechanism for structuring masked performances in order to heighten individual experience.

By identifying the frames of Ode-lay enactment and by assigning affective significance to each one, successful performances may be compared with the failed Firestone event. From several successful Ode-lay performances, I developed a list of primary sequential frames.

1 *Officers of the society meet and select the days for masking.* In the larger group, celebrations occur at fixed times of the year, such as New Year's, Muslim and Christian holidays, and political celebrations such as Independence Day. In special circumstances, a group will 'pull' its devils for elections and political demonstrations. Performances have also been staged to challenge other masking societies.

2 *A permit is requested from the police.* This is one of the most difficult tasks set before Ode-lay societies. Their officers decide which political contacts to use for obtaining permits. Occasionally a politician will visit a group and give a progress report. The police will invite society leaders to headquarters to discuss permits in general. Rarely, society members will lobby with leading politicians on this issue.

3 *The general membership meets to collect funds.* This event occasions mistrust among members. Questions of how much to raise, what each member should pay, and how the group's leaders spend the money are a source of tension. Sometimes challenges and accusations result in physical confrontation.

4 *Styles of costumes are discussed and selected at a special meeting.* The minutes of one Ode-lay society shown to me by G. T. Coker of Paddle Society indicated vigorous debate over the type of headpiece, cloth, and other applied materials. In some cases the intent of a particular performance determines the style. The first time Bloody Mary took to the streets, the society decided that because it was on a mission of revenge the style should be fierce, similar to Hunting society maskers, with horns and other animal parts and a bag-cloth asho. On other occasions, when violence is not the expressed goal, fancy costumes are made (Shaft 1978).

5 *Several officials visit the artist while he works on the commission.* At the first meeting, society officers may present a drawing or illustration of the kind of costume they want. It can be an elaborately detailed rendering of the headpiece or a chromolith featuring such images as Hindu deities. These sessions are private and held in hushed voices.

6 *The artifacts are collected from the artist a week or so before the public display.* Usually this frame is performed late at night under the protection of darkness. The delegation arrives in an automobile and takes the costume to a protected space.

7 *A mailo jazz band is selected at one of the meetings.* The term 'mailo' (milo) derives from mailo gin, a locally distilled beverage with an alcoholic content high enough to render it as 'hot' as mailo's musical inventor, Dr. Olu of Freetown, who assembled the first group in the 1960s. Mailo ensembles include a bass box drum, *sangbai* (single-headed drums); *keling* (a wooden slit gong), and *agoogoo* (a double metal gong often carried on the waist and struck with wooden mallets). Such ensembles are capable of making or breaking the masked performance – if the music lacks the appropriate rhythm and tempo the dancer will perform poorly. The explosive staccato rhythms and hypnotic ostenato beats establish the tempo for the dancing.

Mailo music compels dancers to move pell-mell down the streets with an unpredictability that ensures risk and danger for anyone unexpectedly confronting a masker. With dance steps such as 'Pole to Pole', the masker nearly crashes into one telephone pole after another; 'Banga Banga' confronts moving vehicles straight on; and 'Gutter Anse' trips along the deep trench gutters paralleling the streets. Everyone is poised for action. Nothing is safe, and surprise predicates danger.

8 *A flyer announcing the society program and crediting its organizers is prepared at a party the night before the performance and then distributed by mail.* Its prose style, a Krio-English mix, helps set the participants' expectations.

9 *Sacrifices to the dead are offered at the local cemetery the morning of the performance.* Sacrifices of kola nut, rum, and uncooked rice are offered to the costume, which is positioned on a mortar some Ode-lay members associate with Shango, the Yoruba deity of thunder and lightning. On one Bloody Mary

visit to the cemetery, John Shaft, an important society member, and a couple of *jeweni* (medicine men) aroused two spirits. The first one, according to Shaft, was evil and manifested by a forceful wind. The other was a Muslim man wrapped in white cloth with his thumbs and big toes tied in submission to Allah. The spirits were asked to prevent those 'funny arguments' and fighting that occur before the masker appears in order to ensure that the performance would be peaceful.

10 *On the morning of the festival there is a parade (caroling) of a fancy mask or a bush devil.* After a sacrifice of kola nuts and rum, this devil and several society members proceed through the town collecting money to buy food and drink for the main masker. Children spread the word in their neighbourhoods.

11 *Women prepare food.* Not all societies allow women to participate in the festivities, but in such groups as Juju Wata the wives and girlfriends of society leaders prepare ground-nut soup, sauces, rice, and fish stews for the final entertainment at the end of the day.

12 *Members dress in the fashion predetermined at society meetings.* In some groups, men choose stenciled T-shirts, jeans, and sneakers, while in others they select more elaborate costumes such as brown army uniforms and red berets accented with stripes of red ribbon over the shoulders and on the cuffs. Invited women participants purchase cloth for making long dresses and carefully fitted, wraparound gowns. Hairstyles and head wraps are also specified.

13 *Alcohol and marijuana are consumed from early morning.* Drinking among the membership may vary somewhat, from formal toasting with a specified beverage to sparingly distributed liquor in the bottle cap. Drinks include Remy Martin, champagne, Sierra Leone factory-bottled gin, mailo, and various beers and soft drinks. Marijuana is rolled in large quantities in six-inch paper wrappers occasionally seasoned or cured with rum, the favorite drink of Hunters.

14 *The* soweh (*or* saweh: *medicine*) *is applied to the costume.* Within the confines of the mat enclosure the medicine man, the agba (head of the society), and invited guests spread soweh over the costume. Meanwhile, attendants carefully check the costume to determine if all its parts are securely attached and in place.

15 *Reception of the mailo jazz band(s) usually involves heated debate over the amount of payment and its method of dispersal.* In a Seaside Firestone festival the mailo jazz band waited nearby an outdoor bar for cash payment before agreeing to play. Messages went back and forth between the agba and the band's leader, building tension among the general membership. Resolving the dilemma, the band approached the shrine, urging the devil to dance. Finally, at a distance of a few yards, the masker could no longer resist the mailo sound and burst out of the mat enclosure. The two forces – aural and visual – were consummated.

16 *Members and maskers are doused with* soweh *from this point throughout the performance.* To receive the medicine, members move to form an inner circle where society strongmen protect the devil.

17 *The masked dancer is replaced in the costume three or four times.* These are very

dangerous moments because both the costume and dancer are stripped of their 'covers' and are thus susceptible to the malevolent acts of diviners and competing societies. The masked dancers, known as the *onifakun*, are selected at the group's meetings. After strengthening their own medicine with sacrifices, the performers are closely watched to see if their dancing is correct and if any part of their body becomes exposed as a result of their athletic actions.

18 *The society encounters and confronts competing groups and the police.* With colorful, yet accurate description the press covers the conflict. One *Sunday We Yone* article entitled 'Bloody Mary Under Arrest' (11 December 1978: 1) describes that group's encounter with Firestone:

> Also involved in the gunshot incident was one Oram Moses of 15 Wellington Road, Kissy Mess-mess, who was treated and discharged at Connaught [hospital]. The incident which led to the arrest of the 'Bloody Mary' was a fight at Krootown Road involving a rival masquerade group known as 'Firestone'.
>
> Earlier, the two groups had engaged in a battle along Siaka Stevens Street. In the fighting along Saika [sic] Street, the situation got so desperate that supporters of the 'Bloody Mary' were reported to have boarded a taxi and give [sic] chase to supporters of a rival group when in a bid to avoid trouble, they decided to leave in taxis.

19 *The mask is retired at the society settlement.* The dancers and supporters funnel through the small threshold of the shrine where a few members assist the dancer with removing the costume.

20 *The members eat and recount the day's events.* During this time, mailo or recorded music entertains members. Younger boys play around and practice martial arts, including kung fu. Courtship also occurs.

22 *Press coverage is read.* Throughout the week members living in and near the society headquarters collect news articles about themselves. Bloody Mary members sit around Johnny Shaft, who recites them with dramatic verve, at times slapping the paper with his fingers to stress a particularly exciting episode with the police or another society. The press reports reaffirm the aggressive character of the Ode-lay societies while fostering the fierce aesthetic of its maskers.

23 *Confiscated costumes and jailed members are retrieved.* Society leaders make frequent trips to their local police stations to request the return of their devils, asking how police can arrest a spirit or whether they have the right to interfere with something that is sacred. Frequently members will seek the advice and cooperation of politicians.

Compared with this ideal scenario, the Firestone celebrations of 1977 lacked several frames, including 16–18 and 20–22. Just as notes missed in a song or unexpected gaps in a melody leave listeners questioning its legitimacy as song, missing frames of the Firestone performance left participants unconvinced of its enactment as enactment. There are intrinsic qualities in each missing frame which account for the affective failure of the Firestone event. These inherent qualities are explained with reference to Mary Douglas's work on purity, danger, and social pollution (1966) and Gregory Bateson's on play and fantasy (1972).

Douglas introduces a primary assumption: 'Rituals work upon the body politic through the symbolic medium of the physical body' (1966: 128). In the Sierra Leone case, the symbolic notions essential to the body ritual were located primarily in the missing frames, and therefore these notions were not manifest in the Firestone masked performance or its body politic, and vice versa.

Douglas identifies four types of social pollution which inspire body ritual: (1) pollution which presses on external boundaries; (2) pollution which transgresses internal lines of a system; (3) danger in the margin of lines; and (4) danger from internal contradiction – i.e., basic postulates denied by others (1966: 122).

Ode-lay as well as Hunting society members express fear and anxiety especially over the first two kinds of pollution. These shared anxieties are expressed in individual body ritual, projected onto the masker, and passed on to the body politic. Hunters and Ode-lay members fear *fangay* (harmful medicines which cause skin rashes, scabs, and other skin disorders) on what Douglas calls external boundaries. Skin pollution is countered by soweh, a Mende-derived, creolized term for medicine.

The other major pollutant feared by members is medicine that penetrates the stomach or, in Douglas's terms, internal boundaries. Stories and practices related to the stomach and medicine abound. From the day an initiate joins a society he must take the *oogun* (medicine) of his group and swear to maintain its secret. Should he reveal the secret, his belly would swell and kill him seven days after his initiation. Related to this stomach anxiety are stories in the newspapers and in neighborhood gossip pointing to lethal stomach poisoning by witches. One of the most powerful Yoruba-descended diviners in Sierra Leone once described how the repatriated slaves carried medicines in their stomachs on ships (Brown 1978). Hunters and Ode-lay members believe that the stomach is vulnerable: although it contains the purity of society medicine, it can swell and eventually kill its carrier if he should pollute that medicine by revealing its secret or by taking another medicine. In short, body rituals in the urban societies of Freetown pertain to purity and pollution of the skin and stomach.

The soweh man applies medicine to members' skin for protection against fangay pollution. As if by analogy, he uses a broom applicator to sweep clean the polluting agent. Hats, shoes, and long pants also protect the participants' skin. To safeguard the stomach, members eat and drink sacrifices prior to performance.

These body rituals, if provided with the proper framing, are projected onto the masker, especially through parts of the costume: the asho, eri, and hampa. The asho covers the entire body except the head, which is protected by the horned eri. As an additional layer, the asho protects the skin. The most powerful part of the costume, the vestlike hampa contains medicines which protect the dancer's stomach area. Like newly initiated members who consume the society's medicine and forever carry it in their stomachs, the masked dancer likewise carries the medicine in his hampa. The masker's skin and stomach must be inviolate to impurities inflicted by outside sources.

The empty shells, sea porcupine bodies, skulls, tortoise shell, shotgun casings, horns, and small sacks which make up the Seaside Firestone Ode-lay costume are all filled with medicine. Like the stomach, they are medicine containers. Maskers and society members are homologically served from these containers with carved ladles which hang on the back of the hampa.

Only two of the eight missing frames in the Firestone celebration – the morning parade and the postmortem news reports – were not directly related to concerns about pollution. It is the street processions that provide participants the opportunity to apply medicines for protection from malevolent diviners and members of competing societies. The government's refusal to grant procession permits preempted this option, preventing the necessary intensity for achieving the desired heightened experience.

Though societies abhor pollution, they are bound to it by paradox. Purity cannot be defined without knowing impurity in the same way that a feast cannot be appreciated unless the daily menu of a particular society is known (Abrahams 1977: 105). In rituals, games, performances, and festivities, participants can attain the purity of heightened experience only by becoming susceptible to pollution. Taking the mask to the streets provides the necessary susceptibility.

Moreover, the concept of individual pollution is projected onto the masker and the body politic. The Ode-lay procession suggests an anthropomorphic formation which expresses individual fear of the two pollutions. At the head of the procession the flautist, or flagman, directs the masked dancer through the streets. He is the eyes and ears of the dancer. Second is the *bila* man who, with carved gun or stick in hand, protects the masked dancer. He is its hands. The masked spirit itself symbolizes the stomach of the procession with the large, medicine-filled hampa. Members protect the stomach (hampa) by forming a semicircle around the masker. These participants are fully dressed in ashoebi (society dress), which collectively constitutes the social skin of the body politic.

Denied the fear-inspiring aesthetic experience which accelerates as it moves in a reverberating manner from individual concerns to those of the masker and the body politic, Firestone members could not protect their personal concerns about pollution and its dialectical partner, purity, onto the group or the masker. One explanation for the participants' inability to identify with the Firestone performance concerns the type of communication available *off the streets*. Play, threat, and histrionic behavior are based on the dancers' ability to communicate by recognizing signals and map-territory distinctions. Occasionally during these periods signals go unrecognized. When this happens play changes to mood-sign behavior and nip becomes bite. Bateson comments:

> [T]he discrimination between map and territory is always liable to break down and (for example) the ritual blows of peace-making (among the Andaman Islanders) are always liable to be mistaken for the 'real' blows of combat. In this event, the peace-making ceremony becomes a battle.
>
> (1972: 182)

Ritual may be mistaken for the real thing and with that reality another kind of heightened experience is obtained by the participants.

In the region where art, magic, and religion overlap, humans have evolved the metaphor that is meant. To see how the 'metaphor that is meant' comes into play, Bateson provides a useful classification of messages. In the message he calls the mood-sign, the parties are nonreflective during the message-sending phase. If they exhibit biting behavior face to face they take real action and bite. Here the map and territory are the same. The second message simulates the mood-sign and, by exhibiting a set of behaviors called play, the nip instead of the bite results. The remaining type of message allows the receiver to discriminate between, or to equate mood-signs and those who resemble them. The third message asks the question: Is this play? The equivocation introduced by this question allows the Ode-lay participants, in this case, to confirm the 'metaphor is meant' and its resultant potent experience (see Bateson 1972: 189).

At times playful Ode-lay behavior turns to the mood-sign. Then nip will become bite and people get hurt. The confusion of nip and bite is seen in the relationship between Ode-lay groups and the police. Whereas members may parade with a coffin in front of police, playfully warning them not to interfere with its procession, the taunting of law enforcers may result in their use of tear gas, or more, to stop the play. In this instance the police equate map and territory. In the failed Firestone event, the absence of particular frames preempted the third type of message. Without it, map and territory could not be equated; therefore, the real metaphor and the heightened experience that results from it were denied (see Bateson 1972: 191).

The labile nature of Ode-lay signaling or message-sending during street processions is the axis on which its affective success turns. The 'metaphor that is meant' creates excitement and nonanalytical Gestalt perception of the enactment. In successful Ode-lay masked performances, members become the masked spirit; the spirit becomes the membership; the spirit becomes the medicine. The achieved aesthetic diminishes the participant's sense of being separate. 'We are Ogun', 'We are the god of Iron', 'We are inviolate', are pronouncements that express that collectively. It is as if to say, 'Our external and internal boundaries are pure and protected in the collective purity of the body politic'. At this juncture Bateson's words are appropriate: 'here we can recognize an attempt to deny the difference between map and territory, and to get back to the absolute innocence of communication by means of pure mood-signs' (1972: 183).

Unlike Firestone, the Juju Wata and Seaside Firestone performances were able to *take it to the streets*, therefore achieving success. By masking in the streets, societies such as Juju Wata risk spiritual and physical pollution of each member, masker, and the rest of the group – i.e., the body politic. By experiencing all of the frames they achieve ritual purity. The excitement generated by the masked dancers breaking through the mat enclosures onto the public streets, the sacrificing along the routes, the vulnerable changing of the dancers, and the performing before important personages on route all add to the ritual intensity.

In Ode-lay masked performances, the open air and the streets provide a wide variety of contrasting qualities of texture, color, motion, and sound. The Juju Wata costume featured an electric-blue, female face-mask with red lips. The mask was surrounded by soft, fuzzy, shiny, hard, and dull materials in pink, red, gold, and yellow. Such surfaces reflect the intense, direct African sunlight and actively engage the retinas of participants; no doubt modifying everyday perception. At the same time, shouts, screams, keening, song, footsteps, bells, and mailo jazz establish a cacophony of sound on the streets. These aural elements impact qualities of action, thus inspiring carefully studied musical steps, circle dancing, marching, rushing, and the general success of performance. The complexity of sound and costume helps determine everyone's body movement. At certain times during the procession leaders such as the bila man jump with spread legs while holding their guns or staffs straight. At the height of their ascent they draw their feet together and execute a scissor kick, returning to earth with both feet together. Countering the weight of the jump, they squat to the ground in a shock-absorbing action. Other members of the group maintain fixed expressions: mouths open in a circular shape with tension focused on the muscles connected to the lips, eyes cast downward. Since the qualities of these performances frequently appear as oppositions I speculate that there is something about oscillation between polarities that excites human beings.

Firestone members attributed the failure of their performance to the government's refusal to grant permits. They did not explain the disappointing celebration in terms of purity, danger, pollution, mood-sign and the 'metaphor as meant', or qualities of opposition: however, they did sense that what was lacking had to do with masking in the streets.

The All People's Congress (APC) has wisely established a patronage system which includes the major Yoruba secret societies and the Ode-lay groups. It has done so to strengthen the positions of party members. In the case of young men's societies it has used this system to keep a close watch on a potential breeding ground for political radicalism. Ode-lay associations like Firestone, Bloody Mary, and Paddle have demonstrated for the APC on election and nomination days and in 1978 for the referendum to declare the one-party state, instituted in April of that year. With such active Ode-lay support, why do government officials insist on controlling the movements of the maskers by permit? Mistrust prevails on both sides. During the Ode-lay masked performances, societies support their patron, yet the affective experience they obtain extends beyond the political realm and into the religious and sacred. Such ambiguity is not well-tolerated by governing institutions that rule by establishing clearly defined roles, governing departments, and the black-and-white letter of the law. Ode-lay performance expresses a worldview whose foundation was established well before the advent of institutionalized religions and nation states.[2]

Notes

1 The research for this paper was sponsored in part by a Fulbright-Hays Post-Doctoral Research Fellowship for 1977–78 to Sierra Leone and a Joyce Foundation Fellowship, Summer 1979, University of Illinois at Chicago. I wish to thank members of all Ode-lay societies for their help in this project.

2 For a complete coverage of Ode-lay societies, their history, rituals, and performances, see Nunley 1987.

References

Abrahams, Roger 1977 'Toward an Enactment-centered Theory of Folklore'. In *Frontiers of Folklore*, edited by W. Bascom, 79–120. West Boulder, CO: Westview Press.

Bateson, Gregory. 1972. *Steps to an Ecology of Mind*. San Francisco: Chandler Publishing

Brown, David Nelson. 1978. Personal communication.

Douglas, Mary 1966 *Purity and Danger*. London: Routledge and Kegan Paul.

Nunley, John. 1987. *Moving with the Face of the Devil: Art and Politics in Urban West Africa*. Urbana and Chicago: Univeristy of Illinois Press.

Peterson, John. 1969. *Province of Freedom: A History of Sierra Leone, 1787–1870*. London: Faber and Faber.

Shaft, Johnny. 1978. Personal communication.

16 Comic Opera in Ghana

E. J. Collins

Since the Second World War, one of the most vital folk arts in Ghana has been the concert party, a contemporary roving comic opera. Like many features of Ghana today, this theatre can be considered a syncretic fusion of Western and indigenous elements, created out of the impact of Western musical and dramatic influences on the traditional performing arts.

The 'party' is a professional organization composed of a central core of founding members and an ever-changing periphery of band-boys. The concert play is a slapstick musical comedy containing a prominent moral tone, performed in the Akan language. Music punctuates the speech of the actors, and song lyrics are relevant to the plot of the play. Highlife is the primary music used, itself a syncretic fusion of West African and European music. The concert actors portray in a humorous and exaggerated fashion situations and stereotypes familiar to their audience; the audience responds with a great sense of participation.

The early history of the concert party is closely tied to traditional West African performances in which the music, enactment, and dance are blended together and the distinction between audience and performer is limited. Traditionally the drama is not a discrete event here as it is in the Occident; in West Africa it is generally found encapsulated within a whole range of rites and ceremonies. It would be incorrect, however, to assume that there has been no specialization within West African drama. In the savanna regions there is a long tradition of professional historians-cum-entertainers (the *griots*), and in the forest areas, drama has been developed to a high degree within the masquerades of the secret societies and in association with the art of storytelling. The latter tradition is particularly important as a formative agent on the Ghanaian concert party, for it was in the Akan-speaking areas of southern Ghana, with its wealth of spider stories (*Anansesem*), that the concert party evolved. In these *Anansesem*, the narrator has traditionally used different voices for the various characters and has sometimes dressed up as well.

Western dramatic influences, introduced to coastal Ghana from the turn of the last century, also contributed much to the formation of the comic opera. As the name 'concert party' suggests, the genre originated from the school concerts performed on Empire Day. Many prominent concert actors began their careers by acting in these shows. The idea of a stage (i.e. a physical barrier separating performers from the audience) was introduced to the concert party through these school plays, as well as through Cantatas, church-organized morality plays. A third foreign influence on early concert was silent films, which started appearing in Ghana around the First World War. After World War I, Afro-American music, dance and comedy were brought to the port towns by Black American seamen and comedians.

Ghana's first concert actor was Teacher Yalley, the headmaster of a Sekondi elementary school, who began acting in his school's Empire Day concerts in 1918. In these, he used to joke, sing, and dance, wearing a fancy dress, wig, false moustache and the white makeup of a minstrel. His shows were in English, and tickets were expensive; consequently the audience consisted mostly of the educated Black elite. The show opened with a hired brass band that campaigned around town and ended up outside the theatre. Inside the theatre, Yalley performed his comedy sketches with the assistance of a trap drummer and a harmonium player, who provided an assortment of then-current popular Western dance-music, such as Black American ragtimes, and ballroom styles like the foxtrot, quickstep and waltz. The famous Fanti comedian Bob Johnson was a boy at this time and recalls that Yalley's shows lasted three hours and that the audience consisted of 'official people and gentlemen,' including a small number of Europeans.

Bob Johnson's own acting career started at shows performed at his Sekondi Methodist school, after the Empire Day parade around town. His group became known as the Versatile Eight, the main characters being the joker, the gentleman and the lady impersonator. Bob Johnson played the joker, and did it so well that this concert role has since been known as 'the Bob.' This character, a central one to concert, usually wears bizarre and often ragged clothes and uses the white makeup of the minstrel. Although he clowns around mischievously, the audiences adore him as he is really a theatrical continuation of Ananse the spider, the popular but self-centred hero of Akan folk stories. Ironically, the 'Original Bob' Johnson's real first name is Ishmael. He told me that he obtained the nickname 'Bob' from the Afro-American seamen who visited the Optimism Club opposite his home in Sekondi. He used to hang around that place watching and listening to Liberian sailors singing sea-shanties and highlifes to the accompaniment of guitar and musical saw, and Afro-Americans performing comedy sketches and singing foxtrots and ragtimes. It was they who called him Bob; in fact, he recalls that the Black American sailors seemed to call everybody Bob.

Another Afro-American influence on Johnson was the shows performed between 1924 and 1926 by the Black American couple Glass and Grant who were brought to Accra by Mr Ocansey, a film distributor and cinema-hall owner. Johnson saw them in Sekondi and was impressed by their boldness on stage (i.e., their professionalism). Their shows, high-class affairs like Yalley's, began with a silent film before the comedy act and a dance afterwards. The act was vaudeville, with Glass the minstrel and Grant his wife, joking, tap-dancing and singing ragtimes. This pair also influenced Ga actors like Williams and Marbel so that when the Americans returned to the United States, the 'Accra Vaudeville' continued. By the mid-twenties, concerts had separated into two distinct variations: the upper-class shows of Yalley and the Accra Vaudeville on the one hand, and Johnson's sixpenny shows on the other.

In 1930 Johnson went professional when he formed The Two Bobs and Their Carolina Girl. Their shows were publicized by a masked bell-ringer wearing a billboard, and they commenced with a half-hour introduction consisting of an 'Opening Chorus' of quicksteps, danced and sung by the three comedians, followed by an 'In,' during which one of the Bobs sang ragtimes, and closing with a 'Duet' of joking by the two Bobs. Music was supplied by the group's trap-drummer, who was usually helped by members of a school orchestra hired for the night. The play proper, or 'Scene,' that followed the introduction lasted an hour and was performed in English, with an occasional translation into Akan; this concert audience was less educated than its high-class counterpart. Yet another difference between the two varieties of concert was that Johnson incorporated, in addition to popular Western songs, a few highlifes sung in pidgin English.

In 1935 Johnson became the joker for the Axim Trio, the concert party that eventually became a prototype for succeeding parties. E. K. Dadson played Susanna, their lady impersonator, and Charlie Turpin was the gentleman; they acted to the accompaniment of harmonium and drums.

CONCERTS FORMED BEFORE 1955
Teacher Yalley – (Sekondi) 1918
Versatile Eight – (Sekondi) 1922–30
Accra Vaudeville – (Accra) 1920s–1930s
Two Bobs – (Sekondi) 1930–42
Axim Trio – (Axim) 1935–55
Happy Trio – (Aboso) 1937–46
Dix Covian Jokers – (Dix Cove) circa 1938
West End Trio – (Sekondi) circa 1940
Keta Trio – (Keta) circa 1940
Saltpond Trio – (Saltpond) 1942–44
Jovial Jokers – (Aboso) 1946–54
Burma Jokers – (Elmina) 1946–48
Yanky Trio – (Suhum) 1946–48
Ghana Trio – (Elmina) 1948–69
Fanti Trio – (Sekondi) 1952
Akan Trio – (Accra) 1952
Abuakwa Trio – (Apedwa) 1952
Kwaa Mensah's Concert – (Cape Coast) 1953
Jungle Jokers – (Adoagyiri-Nsawam) 1954
Kakaiku's Concert – (Aboso) 1954
Jaguar Jokers – (Adoagyiri-Nsawam) 1954

Their first engagement was a tour of Nigeria, during which they were joined by the 22-strong Cape Coast Sugar Babies dance-orchestra. The Trio's normal practice in Ghana, however, was to supplement their two musicians with a brass band or Konkomba group, hired for the night. (Konkomba was a choral highlife popular in southern Ghana between the thirties and fifties.) Their shows consisted of an Opening Chorus, In and Duet, followed by a two-hour long play. The plays they performed between 1935 and the mid-fifties (when the Trio dissolved) included:

The Coronation of King George the Sixth; The Bond of 1844; The Ten-Foot Man; The Downfall of Adolph Hitler; Kwame Nkrumah Will Never Die; Love is the Sweetest Thing and *Kwame Nkrumah is a Mighty Man*. In the course of its career, the Trio conducted two trips to Nigeria, extensive tours of Ghana, and also visited Liberia, the Ivory Coast, and Sierra Leone.

The high-class concerts died out before the Second World War. In contrast, the Axim Trio became so popular that by the early forties, five other concerts had modeled themselves after it. In 1937 Bob Cole formed the Happy Trio in the Western Region. Cole had played the piccolo as a boy and became leader of his school band; he started his group after seeing the Axim Trio perform. Like the Versatile Eight, this was a schoolboy affair, playing for pennies and sticks of plantain. About the same time the Dix Covian Jokers and West End Trio were formed; they, too, were from the Western Region. In fact, the only concert not based on this region was the Keta Trio, formed by Ewes from eastern Ghana.

World War II had its effect on the concert profession, as several concert actors performed for the troops. Concerts were even held for the African troops in India: between 1943 and 1946 an African theatre was set up within the West African Frontier Force based there. Bob Vans was the leader, and with six other Ghanaians they played at camps and hospitals. The language they used was pidgin English and the music Konkomba. Vans was influenced by Black American comedians he met and when he returned to Ghana he formed, along with other Ghanaian ex-servicemen, the Burma Jokers. Due to nationalist sentiment, his group was later renamed the Ghana Trio.

This brief history of the concert party would be incomplete without a discussion of the growth of highlife music, for these two syncretic art forms have merged together. The high-class concerts included highlifes in the dances that closed the show; the Axim Trio even used an occasional one in the play itself, but this music never became fully integral to the acting until E. K. Nyame formed his Akan Trio in 1952.

Like concert, highlife music grew up around the turn of the century in the coastal Fanti area. It was based on the acculturation of traditional recreational music with Western musical influences; the resulting syncretic dance-musics, the most important being Osibisaba, became known collectively by the 1920s as 'highlife.' By that time, three varieties of this music were in evidence: that played by the brass bands; that by acoustic guitar bands; and that by prestigious dance-orchestras. The orchestras created a very Westernized variant of the music aimed at a wealthy audience, and it was out of this milieu that the term 'High Life' was coined.

It was the guitar-band style of highlife, however, that became particularly associated with the concert play, an innovation pioneered by E. K. Nyame. Nyame was the leader of a guitar band for some years until 1952 when, encouraged by the Axim Trio's popularity, he formed the Akan Trio from among his bandsmen, taking the role of gentleman for himself. His synthesis of highlife and concert, plus the fact that Akan Trio was the first to perform exclusively in Akan, made his group an instant success, and within a few years most of the other guitar bands followed suit. Conversely, concerts already operating expanded their small musical section to a full-scale guitar band.

The Akan Trio has become the prototype for the present-day concert, of which there are now at least fifty in Ghana. Their immense popularity and relevance to contemporary life has recently led to an upsurge of interest in concert parties by film directors, television producers and academics. In the latter part of 1973, the Arts Council of Ghana presented a ten-day National Festival of Concert Parties, the first of its kind in the country.

The evolution of the concert party has seen continual multiplication and diffusion of groups, and a consequent change in the performances. Early concert parties were formed in coastal towns. Apart from the schoolboy Versatile Eight, they were performed for a literate and affluent urban audience; it was not until the Axim Trio that concert spread into the rural hinterland. By World War II, the vaudeville concert had died out and there were a handful of groups modelled on the Axim Trio; by 1954, there were ten (see p. 236). In 1960, when concert actors and musicians organized the Ghana National Entertainments Association, there were thirty concerts, all staged in the Akan language and employing guitar bands. The change from the early concert to the present one can be attributed to the three groups that served as prototypes for their successors: Teacher Yalley's, the less-Westernized Axim Trio, and the post-war Akan Trio.

Feedback of ideas from Black American theatre and music has been a major influence on concert history. The most direct source of this influence was Glass and Grant. Less direct were the cinema minstrels such as Al Jolson; here one finds the ironic situation of Ghanaian actors copying white actors who in turn were copying the humour, dress, music and dialect of Southern plantation slaves of the United States. Even ragtime, the music of early Ghanaian concert, originated from the Black American slaves.

In addition to a causal relationship, there are also parallel features present in Black American theatre and Ghanaian concert which are illuminating to compare. Both are low-brow comedy performed without script and both provide humorous satire for a newly-urbanized and polyglot audience. (Black theatre, that is, minstrelsy and its derivative, vaudeville, originated in mid-nineteenth-century North America, a period of high immigration and rapid urbanization.)

Also significant to comic opera history is its relevance to social change. Political involvement and criticism in the form of musical and dramatic satire, which has a long tradition in West Africa, has been carried through to contemporary syncretic theatre. For instance, during the 1945 Nigerian general strike against the British, Yoruba Hubert Ogunde wrote a play for his concert called *Strike and Hunger.* A later play called *Yoruba Ronu,* with its allegorical plot based on the 1964 power struggle in Western Nigeria, was considered so inflammatory that it was banned (Adedeji 1967). In Ghana, there were a number of concert plays that came out in open support of the independence struggle. The Axim Trio's *Nkrumah Will Never Die* and *Nkrumah is a Mighty Man* have already been mentioned. Another play taking a political stand was *Kwame Nkrumah is Greater Than Before,* which they staged in 1950 and then donated part of its proceeds to the Convention People's Party fund (*Gold Coast Evening News,* July 5, 1950). In 1952 S. Sackey presented a concert called *Bo Hu Ke Ono Aba* (Wait Until Your Turn Comes), which defended Nkrumah's constitutional reforms (*Daily Graphic,* December 7, 1952). Indeed, the government-financed Workers' Brigade bands and their concert parties, formed in the late fifties and sixties, became organs of C.P.P. propaganda. In the latter part of Nkrumah's rule, when disenchantment set in, concerts became less inclined to support the government, although none were overtly critical. In fact, openly political plays have been rather the exception in Ghana, their reflections on the existing order being more in the form of social criticism and morality tales. For instance, Osofo Dadzie, one of the most popular concerts today, specializes in plays about corruption and inefficiency in high places – such as a hospital.

These roving theatres, bringing new ideas and the attractions of city life to even the most remote areas, have contributed to the process of urban pull. Their importance has been appreciable, for television and rural cinema are only fairly recent in Ghana. Comic opera is, of course, also popular in the ever-expanding towns and cities; but rather than catering to a high-class audience as they did in the twenties, they are now aimed predominantly at newly-arrived rural immigrants, i.e., first generation city-dwellers. In the ethnically heterogeneous urban areas, the plays and songs act as a humorous mechanism for releasing psychological-cum-social tensions – a dramatic *lingua franca*. The concert shows, in portraying stereotypes and situations found in city life to both rural and urban audiences, are agents of urban socialization, as they educate the audience to the complex multiple roles met within modern Ghanaian life.

In order to illustrate the workings of contemporary concert parties, the second half of this article will examine the history, structure, and plays of one particular concert party, the Jaguar Jokers, with whom I have worked for six years as a musician and researcher.

The leader of the Jaguar Jokers (J.J.'s), Mr Bampoe, began his acting career at eleven years old performing in his elementary school plays based on Ananse and Bible stories. About the same time (1946), influenced by the Axim Trio who regularly lodged at his home in Suhum (40 miles north of Accra), Bampoe and some of his school friends formed the Yanky Trio. After completing elementary school and spending a short period as a tailor, Bampoe joined the City Trio. In 1954, he and two other Fantis, the Hammond Brothers, formed the Jaguar Jokers. The band's name was chosen because Jaguar (pronounced Jagwah) was a word that was popular in Ghana in the 1950s that represented the quintessence of modern urban life.

A major difference between the J.J.'s and the earlier Yanky and City Trios was that the J.J.'s modeled itself after the Akan Trio and therefore staged in Fanti and Twi (both Akan languages), rather than in English. Also, instead of hiring out Konkomba groups for the night, the J.J.'s established their own guitar band. At the beginning, they played highlifes, foxtrots, quicksteps, ragtimes and West Indian calypsos, the last being very popular in Ghana during the 1950s. In the 1960s the band incorporated into its repertoire Western pop music (Elvis Presley, the Beatles, James Brown, Wilson Pickett, etc.) and Congo music, a syncretic form that grew up in the Congo after World War II. The latest addition is Afro-beat, a sort of African soul music, pioneered by Nigeria's Fela Ransome Kuti since 1970.

The J.J.'s have reached an enormous audience in twenty years; besides extensive tours of Ghana and parts of the Ivory Coast, the group has been making radio broadcasts since the late fifties (Radio Entertainment in Akan) and regularly appears on television today.

Like other concert parties, the J.J.'s are a professional group composed of an executive committee and wage-earning artists. The J.J.'s executive committee numbers six (all actors) including a secretary (Bampoe), a chairman, and a treasurer. The other performers are paid between thirty and sixty dollars a month (1974 wages), and after all expenses have been settled, the remainder of the group's income is divided among the executive members.

In 1974, the band consisted of 23 members, plus a driver and mate. Most had received an elementary education, and their previous occupations included cobbling, house construction, electrician-work, farming and pharmacy. There were 13 actors, 9 musicians and a pioneer-man (the band's own promoter); two were Ewes from southeastern Ghana and the rest were from the various Akan-speaking areas. Members ranged in age from their early twenties to their late thirties.

The J.J.'s have unwritten rules and practices. Bandsmen can be fined and expelled by the executives for fighting and drunkenness on stage or other misconduct. On the other hand, if a member becomes sick, the band pays his hospital fees; if one of his family dies, the J.J.'s contribute toward the funeral expenses; and if a member himself dies, the band will supply the coffin.

The group travels in a hired mini-bus and makes seven or eight major tours (treks) a year, covering the entire country. Each trek begins on payday (the end of the month) and lasts three weeks, during which time the band moves from town to town playing every night. During the rainy season (May to August), they make a series of short local treks, with long periods of rest and rehearsal at their base town of Adoagyiri, twenty miles north of Accra. The theatres used by the band vary from place to place: they may be cinema halls, night clubs or, in a village, a private compound-house containing a crude wooden stage in the courtyard.

The J.J.'s prefer that their treks be planned by their own pioneer-man, who goes ahead of the group to advertise, hire theatres and obtain police permits and chiefs' permission. Most treks, however, are arranged through private promoters who pay all the costs, take all the gate receipts and pay the band an agreed price. The J.J.'s, like many other concerts, are often forced during the quiet rainy season to borrow money from these promoters, who then bond them during the lucrative Christmas cocoa season. The huge profit-making by the promoters of the concert business has stimulated the formation of a concert union. (Mr Bampoe played a role in the formation of the Ghana National Entertainments Association, and since its collapse after the 1966 coup, he has been involved in several attempts to revive the union.)

When the J.J.'s arrive at a town or village, some of the musicians campaign around the area in the mini-bus, making announcements and playing music through a battery amplifier. When they return, the musical equipment and lighting are made ready; in the areas where there is no electricity, a portable generator is used. An anteroom is curtained off behind the stage to provide a place for the actors to change and make up. Mr Bampoe has told me that many bandsmen put magical potions in their face-powders to increase their popularity on stage, while others have taboos against eating specific foods when 'on trek.'

The show itself begins at about 9:00 p.m. with a dance for which the band plays a cross-section of currently popular Ghanaian dance music: highlifes, Congo numbers, Afro-beats, rock-and-roll, soul, and reggae. The play starts when the theatre is full, usually around 11:00, and lasts three hours. After this, the band plays again for a short while, the night's show rarely finishing before 2:00 a.m. The bandsmen sleep on the floor of the theatre and are up early in the morning to travel to their next station.

The concert audience varies from place to place, although it always embraces both men and women, the old and the young, including babies slung on their mothers' backs. In the rural areas, the audience is composed primarily of farmers and their families; in the cities, poorer urban dwellers, often first generation migrants from the countryside, attend. Because of its audience, concert is considered by the more sophisticated and wealthy urbanites to be rather 'bush,' even though fifty years ago it started off as a posh affair. Mr Bampoe has told me that the low esteem in which his profession is held creates many problems. Concert actors and musicians are treated as rascals, and occasionally a school even forbids its pupils to attend a show. This situation is fortunately beginning to change as Ghanaians are coming to realize that this folk theatre is a legitimate part of their country's cultural heritage.

The plays performed by the J.J.'s consist of an Opening, followed by a Scene, the play proper. The Opening was originally an hour long, and, like the Axim Trio's, was composed of an Opening Chorus, In and Duet, in which the actors, with whitening around the mouth and eyes, tap-danced and sang ragtimes. The Opening today is only twenty minutes in length, but still contains many features borrowed from the Axim Trio, including one of its songs. It is within the Opening that the early vaudeville influences have been retained.

The Scenes, of which the J.J.'s had fourteen in 1974, are each about three hours long, although in the group's early days they were shorter. Music for the plays is supplied by four musicians on drums and guitars. The plays are basically morality stories with a pronounced religious content, an influence from the cantata. They also have many traditional features, including performance in a vernacular language, indigenous music and dance, and the portrayal of traditional figures such as chiefs, elders and priests.

The characters in the plays represent a cross-section of stereotypes found in Ghana today: rural figures such as the illiterate farmer and the village elder; and urbanites such as doctors, lawyers and teachers. The young urban literate is also depicted, wearing the latest stylish clothes and speaking contemporary urban slang. Some of the lady impersonators (there have never been actresses in the J.J.'s) play the role of the adventurous 'high-time' girls who leave their villages for the cities. Different ethnic groups also appear: the northern policeman speaking a mixture of Hausa, Twi and pidgin English; Lagosians with strong Yoruba accents; and Accra marketwomen speaking Ga. Mr Bampoe always clowns in the role of Opia, an Ananse-like imp loved dearly by the audience.

As with traditional Ghanaian performing arts, there is a great deal of audience participation in the form of applauding, weeping, jeering, and throwing food or coins on stage. Sometimes spectators are so moved by an actor's portrayal of an unfortunate character that they will go up to the stage with food and money; or they may stick coins on the moist foreheads of popular actors and musicians.

The importance of these plays bringing new ideas to the rural population must be stressed, for the performances give a glimpse of urban life and its problems to rustic audiences. Themes of sociological interest that recur in the stories include the following: (1) *Urban migration.* At some point, the plots usually describe the plight of young, single men and women who leave home to go to the cities. They turn to crime, drunkenness and prostitution and return with no respect for the old ways. (2) *Social stratification.* Unemployment and poverty in the cities is portrayed, and the humble, hard worker is contrasted with the avaricious man who destroys friends in his scramble for money and position. (3) *Cash crops.* New wealth has increased divisive tensions within the extended family system (especially among the matrilineal Akan), manifested in inheritance disputes. The plays often contain themes of the witchcraft accusations and poisonings resulting from such disputes within a family group. (4) *Changing sexual norms.* Women are becoming increasingly emancipated; they are rejecting polygyny, obtaining a Western education, experimenting with family planning and becoming wealthy traders. Consequently the authority of the husband is being undermined, a topic treated humorously in the plays. (5) *Generation problems.* The ever-changing influx of new ideas on the youth is graphically portrayed, and loss of respect for traditional authority criticized.

To illustrate how these themes are handled and what type of music is played, printed below are synopses of two plays performed by the Jaguar Jokers during 1973 and 1974.

Opia Hia Mmoa (Man Needs Help) 2 hours 25 minutes

Kofi, a farmer's son, has been educated and goes to Accra to find work, followed later by his wife, Comfort. After settling in a job, Kofi's parents come to visit and he gives them gifts. He also gives a small gift to his Aunt Amakom, who is so ungrateful that she curses him. Kofi falls to the floor in agony and Comfort calls in three fetish-priests. They perform a wild dance, strip Kofi of his clothes and leave Comfort with medicine to rub into his body. After some weeks, Comfort's friend Selena, a high-time girl, persuades Comfort to leave the still-sick and helpless Kofi. He is left in the care of his mother and his friend, Opia. Because the traditional medicine does not work, they bring a Christian priest to the sick man. The priest, through prayer, drives out the evil spirit and obtains a repentance from the aunt. After Kofi's recovery, one of the fetish-priests is seen wearing the clothes taken from Kofi and never returned. The unfortunate priest is drilled around the stage by Opia and taken away by Corporal Bobo, a Hausa policeman. Opia, pointing at the dishevelled aunt, gives a long soliloquy on how witches in a family can cause barrenness, drunkenness, debt and general bad luck. Kofi naturally divorces Comfort and then remarries. He does so well for himself that the spoiled Selena and Comfort decide to visit him, both at the same time. They fight and are thrown out by Opia. The play ends with Kofi's father advising the new wife on her duties and Kofi on his need to be humble and involve himself in the community projects of the town in which he has decided to settle.

The 32 songs played during the course of the show included: 23 highlifes, ranging from slow, sad renderings to a fast song accompanied by crazy and scatty dancing: one *calypso*, sung in English; two *'swing' songs,* both in English, one of which was invented for the play, the other entitled 'Chattanooga Choo Choo'; four *traditional songs,* including music of Akan royalty (the Adowa), one traditional drunkard's song, one traditional Akan lament, and one song played on conga drums and gong during the fetish scene, accompanied by a full-scale fetish-dance; and two *Apostolic hymns,* sung in the Akan (the Apostolic Church is nominally Christian but has many African features like spirit healing and possession; in other words, like highlife and concert, it is syncretic).

Awisia Yi Wo Ani (*Orphan, Do Not Glance Enviously*)
3 hours 15 minutes

Mr Johnson is a building contractor who works away from home most of the time. He has three children, one by his dead wife, and two by his domineering second wife, Comfort. Whenever he is away Comfort favors her own children, the arrogant King Sam and the high-time daughter, Dansowa, over the unfortunate and humble orphan, Kofi Antobam. Opia is brought to the house as a servant to help Comfort, but she feeds neither him nor Kofi. Finally she decides to remove Kofi altogether by sending an evil spirit to him, but he is saved by three angels singing Apostolic hymns. Mr Johnson is so disturbed by his wife's actions that he sends Kofi to Kumasi to complete his education out of harm's way. Some years pass, and while Dansowa and King Sam waste their lives in beer-bars listening to pop music, Kofi is working hard at school and is rewarded by passing the Common Entrance Exam. He becomes a postmaster, marries and travels home to introduce his wife to the family. He arrives to find King Sam harassed by women and expelled from school. Kofi's wife gives advice to girls about how they should go about looking for husbands. The couple then distributes gifts to everyone and promises to help Sam continue his education, if he changes his ways. Mr Johnson sings the closing highlife, in which he points out the problems of having children by different wives, referring particularly to preferential treatment of children by their own mothers and maltreatment by their stepmothers. He also advises young people to respect their elders and, if unsuccessful in life, to move on and try their luck elsewhere.

This show had 40 songs in total, including: 29 *highlifes;* one *Akan funeral song,* sung in Fanti, an Akan language; one *quickstep,* called 'Cry Baby Cry,' sung twice in English; two *Apostolic hymns,* sung in Akan; two *Presbyterian hymns,* sung in Akan; one *rock-and-roll song,* not sung but danced to by King Sam and Dansowa, graphically demonstrating how spoiled they are; *one soul song,* called 'Funky Funky' sung and danced to by King Sam and later parodied by Opia; and one *Congo number,* not sung but danced to by Dansowa at the opening of the play.

17 Folklore and tradition in the drama of Cliff Lubwa p'Chong

Sam Kasule

Lubwa p'Chong is the leading Uganda playwright in English. His works include *Generosity Kills* and *The Last Safari* (1972),[1] and *The Minister's Wife* (1982).[2] Yet to be published are *The Bishop's Daughter* (1988)[3] which discusses moral decadence and hypocrisy in the church today, *Do not Uproot the Pumpkin* (1987)[4] a stage adaptation of Okot p'Bitek's *Song of Lawino*,[5] *Kinsmen and Kinswomen* (1988)[6] which deals with issues of extended families, and *The Madman* (1989).[7] He has described all these plays as being 'very, very political'.[8] He has also published a collection of poetry, *Words of my Groaning* (1975).[9] He is a realistic and direct dramatist who belongs to the 'song school'. The 'song', being emotive and the most popular traditional performance genre, became the major motif of the writings of Okot p'Bitek and many Ugandan writers. This form adapts and transforms idiomatic expression into English making the end-product appeal to literate and semi-literate audiences alike. It develops the stylistic features of traditional orature as a means of re-awakening communal and collective responsibility in society. Lubwa p'Chong's sensitivity to socio-political issues and 'humaneness', as alternatives to political absolutism, is evident in the play texts discussed in this article.

Generosity Kills

Generosity Kills,[10] like *The Last Safari*,[11] a dramatization of a legend, belongs to Lubwa p'Chong's earlier works contextualizing the disorder in Uganda's history. It was written for performance during the Makerere Arts Festival Week of 1971. In the plot, Latina discovers a new recipe for beer and, in her excitement, she brews it and generously serves the whole community. The chief of the village consumes a substantial amount and passes out and is mistaken for dead. On waking from his stupor he demands to see Latina to congratulate her, only to be informed that she has been killed, an act fulfilling the Acholi proverb 'Generosity kills the generous ones.' Latina's brewing skills, her inventiveness and generosity lead to her death. Lubwa p'Chong adapts the form and structure of the folktale illustrating how excessive well-meaning behaviour can be detrimental to an individual.

The Prelude to the First Movement begins with excitement as a group of people drink beer at Latina's house. It is a traditional evening setting complete with story-telling, dance, and music. The characters in this scene are only referred to as 1st Man, 2nd Man, 3rd Man, who are villagers or representatives of a community whose voices may easily be mimicked by the narrator. On behalf of an Elder, who arrives too late to share the brew, the Boy warns the Girl to '... leave a remnant/In the bottom of the pot'. After goading the Elder to explain how 'generosity' which has '... no hands/For holding knives, stick or Spears/To kill ...' could have killed Latina, the Elder becomes the Narrator-cum-Diviner and the scene is transformed into a re-enactment of Latina's legend. He uses a diviner's 'cloak' and 'gourd rattles' to invoke the spirits of Latina and her adversaries. Weird sounds signify the response of the spirits to the invoking sounds of the rattles. In performance the Elder and his audience join the secondary audience in the circle off the stage to witness the re-enactment of the legend. The Elder, as Diviner, appeases Latina's spirit approaching earth from the underworld beckoning her to 'Come in peace ... Slowly, slowly ...'. Latina, and her daughter, Lawino, appear centre stage and are later joined by Oluma the husband. After Lawino has accomplished her 'creation', Oluma drunkenly dances and laughs while Lawino yodels to climax.

Dramatic irony is achieved when Twon-coo and other neighbours initially dismiss the brew as 'soppy bread' or 'the sickly vomit of a dog' only to discover its potency. The point to note is the communal spirit of the society which collectively responds to the alarm (ululating) – this time resulting from excitement – and are willing to share the achievements and shortcomings of their neighbours. Latina observes communal ethics when she takes her brew to the Chief for,

> ... our people say
> If you kill an animal, however small it may be
> One leg belongs to the Chief.
> Chief ... here is your share.

> (p. 15)

The Chief gulps the drink and talks wildly, reciting his heroics to the background of exciting music. Lubwa p'Chong's ridicule of the Chief is highlighted in the following extracts.

> (*He [the Chief] again drinks it non-stop. He begins to sway. Gets up, dropping the calabash, and begins to talk wildly*)

> I went to hunt,
> A buffalo came,
> It came as if singing:
> 'Children, children, children.
> See, see, see,
> My liver, my liver, my liver ...'

> (p. 16)

and later,

(*He looks at one of the court jesters who is not even standing near any of the Chief's wives*)

Chief: You, you, what are you doing?
The Court Jester: Nothing, Nothing, Chief.
Chief: Nothing, Chief, nothing, Chief.
      Do you think I am blind?
      Do you think
      I did not see
      What you were doing?
      (*staggering towards him drunkenly*)
      How dare you, a commoner.
      Touch the Chief's wife?

(p. 1)

Laughter is provoked from the audience by his attempt to chase the Court Jester round the stage. As the Chief strikes the Court Jester the latter ducks and he falls on the floor. More laughter is 'milked' from the audience by his abortive attempts to stand before he finally lies prostrate, dead drunk. Like a 'commoner', he is embarrassingly awakened from his stupor by the throbbing drums and the cold water poured over him. The awe, embarrassment, shock and communal guilt is expressed by the silent moment, as the Chief looks round searching for Latina. The projection of the Chief in this state is meant not only to criticize chiefs who behave in a manner contrary to their positions of responsibility in the community, but to caution people against the evils of taking strong drink.

Lubwa p'Chong intends to recapture in English the aesthetics of Acholi. The poetic effect of the play is realized through images, symbols, similes, proverbs and metaphors which relate to the cultural environment and are very much part of the audience's life. For example, describing the potency of the beer, the 3rd Man says, 'See how it [the beer] vomits clean froth.' Latina describes Lawino's emerging breasts as 'pawpaws'. The lyrics in the language are highlighted in Oluma's description of the brew as,

      ... not *gasia* (*tastes*)
      This is sour-sour. (*tastes*)
      Bitter-bitter. (*tastes*)
      Sweet-sweet. (*shakes his head*)
      Strong-strong ...

(p. 8)

Similes, praise-names and other images are used by the characters to describe each other, such as Oluma's description of Latina as, '... the mother-in-law of birds ...' whose mouth has been beaten with 'the testicles/Of a he-goat'.

Glorious mention of one's roots by the naming of clan and praising of parents is an instinctive response in the people's daily life. It is done to summon one's courage in moments of danger, to show pride, warn off potential antagonists and display determination:

Oluma: Woman shut up!
Let me drink this drink in peace,
(*Drinks and belches*)
I am the son of my mother!
I am the son of the woman
Whose teeth are white
Like dry season moon!
I am your wife beat you with pestle ....

(pp. 9–10)

It is the praises, and the subsequent cajoling adjectival phrases, which make the scene in which Oluma's neighbours share his brew light-hearted, humorous and memorable.

Oluma holding the calabash in one hand, shakes hands with him [Twon-coo]. They call each other praise names.

Oluma: Yaa Twon-Coo!
Twon-Coo: Yaa Oluma *yaa!*
Oluma: Yaa a dog urinated in your wound!
Twon-Coo: Yaa your wife beat you with pestle!
Oluma: How are you man?
Twon-Coo: Healthy as sunrise.
Oluma: Put your buttocks down man.
Twon-Coo: (*sitting*) Thank you, friend.
　　　　What are you drinking?
Oluma: We are drinking millet bread
　　　　Which our child dumped in water.
Twon-Coo: So you drink *Gasia*, rubbish?

(p. 1)

In juxtaposing ritual, divination, invocation, and legend Lubwa p'Chong transforms the traditional story-telling genre into a theatrical mode. The result is a mutually shared experience of the legend by both audiences – the primary audience assisting the narrator to animate the story and the secondary audience watching the dramatization.

The Last Safari

This is a dramatization of a folktale existing both in Acholi and Buganda, centred on Ketimo (or Mpoobe in Buganda), a hunter of great repute, who defies the ominous signs of fate. When Ketimo goes hunting, he ends up in the Kingdom of Death in the underworld. Death releases him on condition that he should never reveal his experiences. When he breaks the promise Death strikes him.

Lubwa p'Chong focuses our attention on the spear, the strongest symbol of the homestead in many Ugandan communities. It is the pride of the homestead, source of food, and 'guard/over all!' Neglected and rusty, the spear is discovered by the Young Man who raises the alarm, calling the whole cast to the stage. The Old Man interprets the sacrilege as the cast bursts into a mournful dirge indicting the community for having neglected the 'shrine of my father' and left the 'hippo-spear sleeping out'. The Old Man proclaims that social chaos, disorder, rape and robbery will prevail and the community will have to pay the price. The dirge highlights the shared social guilt. It is a dirge for a community plunged into chaos by reckless individuals who should have been guardians of the people's conscience, physically symbolized by the ancestral shrine. The whole community has participated in the erosion of the human essence, the cultural mores which made it whole. The state of the neglected spear is parallel to the state of a community which has become powerless, defenceless and helpless.

The First Movement is full of ominous signs such as the sounds of cock-crow, hoots of the owl, and Ketimo's sneeze as he cleans his hunting spear. His wife, Binen, dreams of Ketimo sitting under a 'big *Kituba tree*/While young men were digging a grave' (p. 27). Contrary to her interpretation of the dream – Ketimo should not go hunting – Ketimo predicts a successful hunt. Further, Binen draws her son's attention to the multiplicity of ominous signs hovering over the homestead:

> *Binen:* Mh, my son, do you call that
> success.
> Don't you know
> Meat is red
> Like grave soil?
> To make the matter worse,
> An owl was hooting
> Just before you sent for me.
> When owls hoot at dawn.
> It means death, sure death.
> Therefore, this owl
> Was announcing someone's death;
> And that person
> Must be close, close,
> For the owl was sitting on your
> roof.
>
> (p. 30)

It is signals such as these that Lubwa p'Chong exploits to create a fresh indigenous theatrical shorthand.[12]

The play is a multidimensional reconstruction of Acholi attitudes, thought-systems and social ceremonies relating to death and human destiny. Tragedy is a communal concern to be shared by friend and foe. Through imagery Lubwa p'Chong reminds the audience that they should not laugh at victims of death like Cock:

Elder: (cock crows) Diki Wang ca rommo neno pala!
A Man: Tomorrow the knife
will sink past
The ram's throat!
Clan Leader: And the ram answers:
In kono ibi dok kwere ki abila pa kwara?
A Man: What about you, cock.
How will you escape
Being sacrificed at the ancestral
shrine?
Clan Leader: (addressing everybody) The death
That killed your brother
Will be the death
That will kill you.

(p. 41)

The ubiquitous nature of death (fate) is further expressed in the extended eulogy by Binen and the thematic content of the dirges. Binen, using hyperbole, refers to her tragic loss of a son as,

… the sharp axe
Of death, the unkind one
Has felled Ketimo …

(p. 39)

and

Then my son must be dead.
My clansmen. Come and see me.
This cruel world has knelt on me
And crushed me completely.

(p. 39)

She personalizes death, drawing a picture of a cruel, beastly, and blood-thirsty person who fells people like trees. Okot p'Bitek[13] notes that, among the Acholi, Fate is described with hunting images of 'kneeling and crushing'. These derive from the manner in which a wounded buffalo, for lack of strength, falls and crushes its victim with its massive weight.

The climactic conclusion to the tragedy is a synchronized mime of omnipresent Death and his assistants dancing to the rhythm of an Acholi dirge, stalking, shouting and wooing Ketimo to his Death. The Acholi metaphysics visualize Ketimo being locked in battle with death while his people helplessly watch him receding beyond the horizon. The audience may

… just sit there stone still in their seats though alive in every fibre of their being to every little movement or sound or impression that is being projected to them by the actors … intensely silent, but intellectually and emotionally active [in] participation …[14]

The ritual presented in its entirety in the play is the blessing of the hunters' spears by Binen. Ketimo and his friends hold their spears and stand forming an arc, while the elders stand behind them. A liturgical prayer intended to placate the ancestors, inspire the hunters and woo animals to their traps, is chanted in a litany. As Binen sprinkles ritual water on the spears, she leads the chant and the elders respond with the last line of her incantation. The hunters do not respond till the last lines of the prayer. Binen prays to the ancestors to bless the spears so that they may 'Drip red with animal blood'. She asks the evil spirits which live in rivers, big trees, dark mountains, shady forests, caves and holes to give way to the hunters. This part of the prayer illuminates the metaphysical and cosmic nature of Acholi belief and the possibility of communing with evil as well as good ancestral spirits.

Sacrifice and ritual are important facets in the development of the plot. Ketimo's return from the bush is a representation of a funeral crowd 'unfearingly' speaking their minds for the good of the victims of death and the community. The elders emphasize to Ketimo the importance of instant sacrifice for falsely shed tears – to be instantly washed away with a bull's blood – else he would end up in the 'stomach of the earth'. Using mimicry, the Elders recall Lekamoi's words:

> I still do not have a bull,
> I still do not have a bull ...
> Now where is the young man?
> Is he not in the stomach of the earth?

> (p. 45)

The men led by the Clan Leader use strong images to make their point.

> *Clan Leader:* If you want to kill a snake
> safely, kill it in the egg.
> Don't wait till it breathes.

> (p. 45)

and

> *Elder:* Evil is like
> Dog's dung, [it] must be removed
> From the floor
> While it is still steaming.
> *1st Man:* True, if you wait till it gets
> cold,
> It stinks.

> (p. 45)

Lubwa p'Chong uses language with intensity, as in the speech when Binen mourns her son's death with the poetry of a funeral ceremony declamation. She draws attention to her plight by dramatizing her sorrow as she imagines her son. '... rotting/Somewhere in the grass/Like a dog!' (p. 39). In anguish she decries the hyenas, bald-headed vultures and worms laughing at her son's body, breaking bones, eating out the intestines, burrowing into his beautiful eyes, ears and mouth (p. 40). She further carries the audience into the abyss by alternating images of Ketimo's body being ravaged by land as well as aquatic creatures. The images used by Binen intensify the tragedy because they are within the immediate social experience of the people as, again, they are allegorically referring to their experiences under the Amin regime.[15]

The Madman

This play, written after an interlude in which Lubwa p'Chong changed his style, marks his maturity as a playwright able to mix the contemporary and myth, legend and fantasy. His argument in *The Madman* is that ultra-egotism and myth-making have contributed to the state of dictatorship and the gun culture endemic in Uganda's politics. The play laments Fruits of Independence, *Matunda Ya Uhuru*, which have not been delivered thus causing a paralysis in a society where human and temporal clocks have stopped:

> The clock at the prestigious Mulago Hospital's eye–nose–throat clinic reads 4:56. On the tower of Makerere University's administration building the clock reads 12:20. Above the main entrance to the high court in downtown Kampala it reads 11:14. Inside the main post-office it reads 12:27. All over Kampala clocks have stopped – at different times.[16]

It is a society where the élite at the national university drive their '... Mercedes on the sidewalk right up to the door of their office building ...'.[17] In Uganda the euphemism for this institutionalized madness is '*Aminism*' or '*Oboteism*'.

In *The Madman*, the legend of Walukagga has been so dramatized that at each stage the equation with the modern situation can be recognized (the same legend has been treated by Eli Kyeyune in *Bemba Musota*). In style and form, the play illustrates the theatrical trend in Uganda by which artists use folklore, pre-colonial themes and traditional structures to interpret and criticize contemporary conditions. As in the earlier plays, the Narrator plays a central role in the plot. He outlines the conflicts in the plot underlining the fear experienced by the villagers, '... for each morning the sun rose with news of some new orders ... and nobody's life was safe' (p. 5). He highlights the misdeeds of the Chief, noting his manipulation of the people through plunder, torture and murder. His warrior vigilantes follow his instructions without '... caring about right or wrong ... They operated anywhere at any time, and in full public view ... ran wars of intimidation and terror ... looted and destroyed property, killing and maiming, raping young and old women ... widows ... sowing yaws [AIDS]!' (p. 6). The people reached their nadir when the royal warriors, in executing their 'painful duty' of collecting human tears and hair, broke bottles and used the pieces to shave heads. In the end 'popular anger' forced the Chief to relinquish power to a committee of elders. The end-form of folktales in Buganda is used by the Narrator when he describes how the people celebrated the Chief's downfall:

... I came away to tell you the story. (*Plays a tune briefly [on his bowl-lyre]*) And up to this day in Uganda, there is a proverb which says: A man will take his problem to a madman when sane men fail (*Wokubira omulalu mu kyama nga omulamu gwolaba*).

(p. 109)

One of the characters in *The Madman* is Walukagga, the Blacksmith who, in *Ganda* printed literature is a folk figure.[18] Lubwa p'Chong exploits the conflict between a megalomaniac, self-centred Chief and the peasant Walukagga. The latter represents the *Will* of the people, the unspoilt elements of harmonious communal existence and humaneness. The Chief represents despotic rulers.

Chief mistrusts crowds and only visits at short notice. When he eventually appears on stage he rolls his 'frightened ... eyes terribly' to frighten the villagers. This parodies the manner in which both Obote and Amin faced their audience at the ebb of their rule. Using phrases and words relished by dictators, he orchestrates forced applause from the villagers. The people are his 'masters' and he is their 'humble servant', the '*shamba* boy', labouring in their gardens for their own good. For this reason they are 'fat' and *must* 'Clap for your happiness'. His images and metaphors are beastly and obscene, showing a person whose brain has been crippled by power, wealth and innocently spilt blood. For example, he illustrates his contribution to the welfare of the villagers, by comparing their physical state at the beginning of his reign to 'chickens drenched by some heavy rains ... cows suffering from dysentery' (p. 23). But now they are 'sleek like lion's cubs! ... like well-fed puppies ... bubbling with life like well brewed *kwete* beer!' (p. 24).

Chief's intellectual dwarfism and gullibility is further exhibited in the riddle he gives the women to solve. He is oblivious to the sufferings of his people, failing to interpret the women's answer to his riddle in which they echo the suffering unleashed on the community because of his greed. They tell him, that after eating a lot of 'saliva-bringing food', his hunger goes to a poor person in his kingdom, and so does his illness after he is cured of an illness. The women's solution to the riddle means that the Chief's rule has merely putrefied society. Chief makes a decree that no one else in his Chiefdom is to be referred to by the title 'CHIEF'[19] any more, and all holders of the title will henceforth be called 'Clan-overseers, Village Heads, [and] Communal organisers ...' (p. 25). Dramatic irony is effected when we realize that the 'Chief Hunters' will effectively become '*Head* Hunters'. The pun is not lost on the audience as the villagers, at 'spear-point' (gun-point), chant refrains parallel to contemporary party songs, 'One Chiefdom, One Chief.'

The ritual of peasants offering gifts to visiting 'dignitaries' is structurally used to precipitate the conflict between Chief and his people. Village Head 1 offers a 'Hammer' to the Chief. Village Head 2 offers a 'Chain'. Village Head 3 a '*Panga* (Matchet)' and Village Head 4 offers a 'Spear'. Chief is the 'Chief Murderer', the master blacksmith, forging dead bodies out of his human subjects. The audience is aware of the apparent misuse of these symbols of torture and cruel death, so that the euphemism for Amin is 'Matchet' (*Kijjambiya*) and his regime is the 'Matchet's reign' (*Omulembe gwa Kijjambiya*). The intended parallelism of the Chief's regime with Amin and the post-Amin state security organs (Head Hunters) is quite clear.

Chief, incensed by the display of praise for Walukagga, dares, '… our clever blacksmith [Walukagga] … to forge me a man who can eat and starve, can cry and laugh, can love and hate, can kill and be killed …' (p. 39). Because jealousy, rivalry, ambition and greed have become a way of life in the community, abductions and extermination of work-mates, neighbours and relatives are commonplace. In the conflict between Walukagga and the Chief, the latter is supported by the evil blacksmiths. Walukagga's adversaries preoccupy themselves with mud-slinging, spreading '*ladit*' (nepotism and corruption), backbiting, bickering, gossiping and rumour-mongering.

Lubwa p'Chong's dramatic vision is evidenced by his choice of folklore material from east, west, south, north and central Uganda to represent the 'various types of madness of our time and place'.[20] In an interview given after the première production of *The Minister's Wife* he remarked that '… particularly after the fall of Amin … about 90 per cent of Ugandans' heads are not correct …'[21] In using 'madness' as a motif he is contemplating the plight of Ugandans who continue to suffer at the hands of a few mad politicians. He traverses post-independent Ugandan history identifying positive and negative forms of 'madness' in society. His target is the negative and destructive madness of politicians which has moved the leadership in Uganda from reconciliation to intimidation, to the systematic elimination of citizens in the Amin regime, and the near-genocidal massacres under Obote. The addition of the madman in the play is a thematically important feature. He represents the people's past, present and probable future. He is a living example of those people who have paid a price for resisting the Chief's orders. He enters, '… wearing some human bones around his ankle like ankle bells, and carrying a human skull in one hand laughing at (and) with the skull' (p. 52). He cross-examines the human skull, his only companion, and the symbol of death and terror existing in society:

> To whom did you belong? What was your sex? Place of birth?
> Age? Work?
> Tribe? Religion? Marital status? How did you meet your end?
>
> (p. 52)

The question about the 'skull's' identity echoes the statement made by a former Ugandan Vice President to the effect that he should not be charged with the atrocities (in the 'Luwero Triangle') because the skulls in Luwero are unidentifiable.[22] The drum is replaced by the skull as the symbol of the kingdom. The Madman

> … (*lifts up the human skull*) This is Chief's royal drum! (*beats it briefly …*)
>
> (p. 61)

The substitution of the skull – which he presupposes to have belonged to his wife who with his children 'disappeared'[23] from his home – as 'the Reality of this chiefdom', marks the denouement.

The character of the Madman has multi-layered metaphorical significance in this play. Like Serumaga's Majangwa (in *Majangwa*),[24] the Madman is the 'conscience' of society, indicting the audience for mis-treating the sick in their midst. They

> ... throw cruel jokes at me! You set your dogs on me! One of you one night scratched me all over the body with his barbed arrow for sleeping on his verandah! Your children throw stones at me but you don't' reproach them! A bad animal comes from a bad bush. You and your children are the same: mad! You are like Chief! Mad! You enjoy inflicting pains on people. Like Chief! ...
>
> (p. 61)

He underlines the 'mad sense of humour' prevalent in the community which makes people.

> ... *Nyah, nyah, nyah, nyah!* (*laugh*) at the misfortunes of others, at everything .... Even when Chief says or does something that pulls our hair, and makes anger choke us, we burst out, *nyah, nyah, nyah! Nyah, nyah, nyah, nyah ... nyah!*
>
> (p. 68)

Society expunges its frustration, moral and physical corruption, on the mentally sick, turning them into 'carriers' of evil. There is dramatic reversal when the Madman comments that the 'madness' in society has reached such abominable depths that ancestral prayers relating to society's cosmology have changed.

> North is [now] south, and south is now north. The sun rises in the west and sets in the east ...
>
> (p. 60)

Contrary to the Acholi world-view by which people pray for evil to descend with the setting sun, the prayer asks:

> All the evils
> That are coming,
> Let the setting sun
> Take them down
> In the East!
> And so they are taken down
> In the east!
>
> (p. 60)

The Madman's image of the 'man' who can effectively tackle Chief is Lubwa p'Chong's metaphor for a strong ruler, capable of purging the country of all the evils symbolized in the Chief. He offers Walukagga a solution to his dilemma through a riddle to be given to the Chief. Sarcastic about Walukagga's troubles, he states that Chief's virility may be on the wane otherwise he would not require a 'man' forged from steel. In this mood he requests Walukagga to:

... forge us a man who will tackle Chief head on. A real man who will wrestle with Chief and throw him down. (*Grabs Walukagga and throws him down*) Like that! To teach Chief some sense. Stupidity has built a permanent house over Chief[25] ... a man not with two balls only but five balls, who will grab Chief's big balls and pull them hard for us. Chief has fondled our balls for too long!

(p. 56)

If Chief wants Walukagga to forge a man, he must provide him with 'a full five big sacks' of charcoal burnt from human hair and five big pots of 'human tears'. Chief orders his warriors to collect the items from all '... four corners of the chiefdom ... today before the sun sets' but they only manage to collect a pouch-full of hair and a bowl of tears. Dissatisfied, Chief orders everybody to 're-shave hair, and re-shed tears'. Should the villagers refuse, the warriors must

> ... slaughter all the people therein! Raze their huts and granaries to the ground! And drive all their livestock to the royal herd!.... Kill everyone then hang yourselves on the nearest tree! I must see only corpses tomorrow!
>
> (p. 86)

This is the turning point in the plot, for 'popular anger' turns the villagers against the Chief and they demand his resignation. In spite of promises for reform, Chief and his Chief Murderer Ssenkoole are tied up and elders take over the reins of the state. Lubwa p'Chong is optimistic that society will one day say 'NO' to dictators.

The use of indigenous images and phrases makes it easy for Lubwa p'Chong to make believable his themes and effectively communicate with the audience. Two women in the play (called Woman 1 and Woman 2) give us the impression that the issue of a multitude of edicts, decrees, legal notices and pronouncements is the Chief's delight.[26] Ethnicity is used by the Chief to manipulate his subjects as illustrated by his latest order by which everyone must stick to their places of ethnic origin. Woman 2 graphically describes the divisive and isolationist strategies of the Chief as a game of 'dividing, sub-dividing and sub-sub-dividing' society. The women are sarcastic about the nature of obedience prevalent in society:

Woman 1: Our children are now like little machines ...
Woman 2: When Chief presses Button A ...
Woman 1: They move ...
Woman 2: When Chief presses Button B ...
Woman 1: They stop ...
Woman 2: Like well-oiled little machines!
Woman 1: Obedience!
Woman 2: Obedience!
Woman 1: Obedience has become madness in this chiefdom.
Woman 2: We have become obedient like bulls trained for ploughing.
Woman 1: We are submissive!

Woman 2: So subordinated that even Chief's favourite expressions have become fashionable throughout the chiefdom.
Woman 1: Everyone wants to be his Master's voice!
Woman 2: Everybody dies to talk like Chief!
Woman 1: To smile like Chief!
Woman 2: To walk like Chief!
Woman 1: To stand like Chief!
Woman 2: To dress like Chief!

(p. 12)

The climax of the 'play-in-play' is achieved when both women turn to the audience and in unison consult it on whether they should turn their Chief into a 'Chiefdom deity [President for Life]'. The scene illustrates the power with which Lubwa p'Chong uses folklore motifs and expressions to enhance his drama.

Absolutism and the demagogic position of the Chief in society is symbolized by the 'stick' he carries, for every person straying from 'the herd ... is beaten back'.[27] Implied in this image is the contemporary African leaders' ridiculous use of fetish-like paraphernalia such as sticks, fly whisks, and handkerchiefs. Talking through riddle and metaphor, the women satirize the maddening aspects of power, comparing it to the fangs of a poisonous snake.

Woman 2: ... the longer the person stays in power the longer his fang grows.
Woman 1: Until it grows out of his mouth like the teeth of a warthog.
Woman 2: Yes, power possesses man, with evil spirits!
Woman 1: And when a man is possessed with some evil spirits of power, he can wake up one day and tell the people under him, 'I want this mountain levelled down!
Woman 2: Yes, when power has possessed a man in power, the unthinkable becomes thinkable!
Woman 1: The impossible becomes possible!
Woman 2: And the useless becomes useful!
Woman 1: I tell you, power turns us into mad people.
(*They both burst out laughing*)

(p. 22)

The theatrical devices include music, song and dance. Most outstanding is his use of the Luganda (sacred) folk song 'Walugono'. The villagers perform this song during the preparations of the village ground for Chief's visit. Walugono is a pugnacious god whose relationship with the community is as demanding and retributive as Chief's. In: '... mother's womb/Walugono twists babies' hands/He enlarges heads of babies/When they are born/They are deformed' (pp. 16–17).

Throughout the performance the actors involve the audience to imply that they share the guilt for the country's decadence and must therefore help to remove the ogres in their midst.

Lubwa p'Chong effectively articulates the problems of society. However, because he writes in English his plays have a limited audience and one can only hope that they will begin to be translated into Acholi, Luganda and other indigenous languages.

Notes

1   Cliff Lubwa p'Chong, *Generosity Kills* and *The Last Safari* (Nairobi: East African Publishing House, 1975).
2   Cliff Lubwa p'Chong, *The Minister's Wife* (Kampala: New Expression Press, 1982)
3   Cliff Lubwa p'Chong, *The Bishop's Daughter*, (Unpublished, 1988).
4   Cliff Lubwa p'Chong, *Do not Uproot the Pumpkin* (Unpublished, 1987).
5   Okot p'Bitek, *Song of Lawino and Song of Ocol* (London: Heinemann, 1984).
6   Cliff Lubwa p'Chong, *Kinsmen and Kinswomen* (Kampala: Crane Publishers 1988).
7   Cliff Lubwa p'Chong. *The Madman* (Unpublished, 1989).
8   Lubwa p'Chong made these comments in a letter to the present writer in May 1991.
9   Cliff Lubwa p'Chong. *Words of my Groaning* (Nairobi: East African Publishing House, 1975). (Dates in text are of first performance).
10 Lubwa p'Chong. *Generosity Kills*.
11 Lubwa p'Chong, *The Last Safari*.
12 This style is close to that used by Okot p'Bitek and Tom Omara.
13 Okot p'Bitek, *Horn of My Love* (London: Heinemann Educational Books, 1974): 150.
14 J. C. de Graft, 'Dramatic Questions' in *Writers in East Africa*, eds. Andrew Gurr and Angus Calder (Nairobi: East African Literature Bureau, 1972): 33–67.
15 Forests, lakes and rivers became dumping (burial) places for victims of state terrorism. Namanve, eight miles from Kampala City on Jinja Road, is a forest reserve which was the most favoured dumping spot. After the fall of Idi Amin it was declared a 'National Cemetery' by President Binaisa in 1979.
16 Adolf Enns, 'The Clocks Have Stopped in Uganda', in *Crisis in Uganda*, eds. P. Dodge Cole and Paul D. Wiebe (Oxford: Pergamon Press, 1985): 53–6.
17 Enns: 54.
18 Sir Apollo Kagwa, *Engero za Baganda (Baganda Folk stories)*. (London: Sheldon Press, 1956): 1–7. Zirimu's translation is quoted by Lubwa p'Chong in the introduction to the *The Madman*. Eli Kyeyune uses the same legend for his play, *Bemba Musota*.
19 This echoes Idi Amin Dada's Decree which forbade anybody other than himself to be referred to by the title, President.
20 See Lubwa p'Chong's Introduction to *The Madman*.
21 Interview with Alex Tetteh-Larley of the BBC African Service Programme, *Arts on Africa*, (London) 7 June 1985.
22 The statement was made in 1989 before the 'Uganda Human Rights Commission' by Paulo Muwanga, a former Vice-President and Minister of Defence in Milton Obote's government.
23 'Disappeared' (*yabula or yabuze*) is a euphemism coined to describe the method used by the state of exterminate its opponents. For more information see, Ali Mazrui, *Soldiers and Kinsmen in Uganda* (California: Sage Publications, 1975): 161.
24 Robert Serumaga, *Majangwa and A Play*, (Nairobi: East African Publishing House, 1974).
25 Here Lubwa adapts and directly translates the saying, '*Obusiru bumuzimbyeko akayumba*', in popular use at the time of the writing of *The Madman*.
26 This is a parody of the 'unconstitutional' laws imposed on Ugandans under the umbrella of 'Presidential Decrees'. We note that whereas Amin rules by 'decrees', the post-Amin liberation governments have used 'Legal Notices' to impose laws outside the rule of parliament.
27 King Bemba earned the title of *Musota* (Snake) because of his murderous character and, the saying, 'King Bemba never pays a friendly visit, he always raids' was coined to describe his reign.

18 Horrific comedy

Cultural resistance and the *Hauka* movement in Niger

Paul Stoller

Few things can be more memorable than those occasions when everyday routines are shattered abruptly by shocking experiences. One of my most shattering experiences occurred in 1969 in the Republic of Niger. I had been teaching English in the secondary school of Tera, a town of 1000 in the heart of Songhay country. For three months my routine at the school was to teach from early morning to noon and then go to the dusty bar in town to drink beer with my French colleagues. The same routine was repeated at the end of the working day. We came to spend a great deal of time at Chez Jacob, the establishment of a Yoruba trader, one of the few non-European beer drinkers in town. The beer was usually lukewarm due to the temperamental flame of Jacob's kerosene refrigerator. But neither the temperature of the beer nor the stark décor, a hard bench against a mudbrick wall, kept us from maintaining our European rituals in a strange and distant land. What we did not know about Chez Jacob was that it bordered upon the compound of a *zima*, a ritual priest of the local possession cult. One afternoon, however, we discovered, to our dismay, the violent nature of the *Hauka*, one of several 'families' of spirits in the pantheon of the Songhay people of the western regions of the Republic of Niger.[1]

In the late afternoon some three months after we had begun to frequent Chez Jacob a crowd began to form. One musician played a one-string violin and two others were beating on overturned calabashes with bamboo drumsticks. Having never witnessed such a dance we left the hot stuffiness of the bar and joined the crowd. Suddenly, a young man, who had been standing only a few paces from me, vomited up a black liquid. I thought he was about to die. Like the other members of the audience, I gave this man room to maneuver. He threw himself to the ground, threw sand all over his body, and then put large amounts of sand into his open mouth. Sand in mouth, he stood erect and peered at people in the audience. Seeing me, he spit sand in my direction. Seeing the Songhay members of the audience, he jerked his body toward them and attempted to strike them, but attendants of the local cult restrained him before he had the chance to strike anyone. He turned around and I saw him clearly for the first time. His eyes were bulging and a blood vessel in his forehead was throbbing. He groaned like a beast and saliva was frothing from his mouth. He began to come at me and I retreated quickly to Chez Jacob, shaken. 'Is the man crazy?' I asked someone in my inchoate Songhay. 'Oh no,' responded another member of the audience. 'He is not a man; he is one of the *Hauka*. You must go up and greet him. He will not harm you.'

At first I refused the man's invitation, but he insisted. And so I approached this terrifying *Hauka* who thrust his open hand toward mine. 'How are you?' he asked in Pidgin French. 'Fine,' I answered, still afraid. 'Your mother has no tits.' This provoked great laughter. 'Yes she does,' I protested. 'Your father has no balls.' This provoked even more laughter from the audience which was being entertained at my expense. The man who had accompanied me suggested that I say goodbye to the *Hauka*, and so I did, having had my first exposure to horrific comedy.

Six years later I returned to the Republic of Niger to conduct anthropological research. During that year of field study I learned that *Hauka* in the Hausa language meant 'craziness,' which was not terribly surprising. I also learned that the *Hauka* were supposed to be funny as well as horrifying. Based upon my previous experience, this revelation was also not surprising, for while the *Hauka* were undoubtedly a terrifying sight, they were also aping the ways of the European. Dressed in their pith helmets and carrying their swagger sticks, I often observed the *Hauka* take the roles of European army generals who speak to their troops in pidgin French or pidgin English. This mockery, in my experience, has precipitated fright in impressionable children and has provoked laughter among seasoned adults.

In this paper I consider the *Hauka* movement of Songhay possession dance as a dramatic form in which the deities practice horrific comedy. This comedy, I suggest, provides a symbolic means by which the Songhay anchor themselves culturally in a world which the way of the European is rapidly changing. By aping the European they have resisted culturally the way of the European and have expressed metaphorically their preference for the traditions of their ancestors. In so doing the Songhay have used symbolism to protect their cultural identity from the ever expanding encroachments of European civilization (see Ranger 1975; Mitchell 1956).

Comedy and cultural resistance

Roger Bastide (1978: 156) defined cultural resistance as 'an endeavour not to let the vital values inherited from … ancestors perish, but to reestablish them through symbolic or military means.' There is a vast literature on the rebellion of enslaved populations in the new and old worlds. But when military aspects of cultural resistance fail, as they did in short order when the Songhay confronted the colonial armies of France around the turn of the century, people must resort to symbolic means to protect the vital links to their ancestors, the essence of cultural identity.

Since the times of Aristophanes, writers have used paradoxical comedy to express their sociocultural protests. Aristophanes himself poked fun at Athenian society, 'criticizing the weaknesses of her citizens and praising the simple manly existence of another age' (Perry 1968: 6). In royal France 'a long succession of farces copied matter from political and social circles so strikingly that at length

Henry IV had to restrict subjects to private life' (Miles 1971: 5). The French farce gradually developed into 'avant-garde' theatre around the turn of the century and the 'theatre of the absurd' in more recent times. As Wellwarth (1971: x) suggests, the disparate plays of the avant-garde and the theatre of the absurd are remarkably similar in that they share a common theme, social protest, as well as the common technique of paradox. Powerless, the creators of the theatre of the absurd

> can no longer scream because they can no longer hope. They can no longer speak directly to their hearers because they can no longer believe that they are heard. They can only express themselves indirectly in sardonic paradoxes.
>
> (1971: x)

But the comedy of paradox has served perhaps a more significant purpose for those powerless peoples whose cultural identities have been threatened by contact with powerful Others. For groups such as the Songhay of the Republic of Niger the comedy of paradox as it is expressed in the *Hauka* movement 'has helped them to overcome the strange and the terrifying' (Courtney 1974: 121). In so doing the comedy of paradox can reaffirm a people's link to their ancestors and allows them to create new cultural forms which stretch with the expansion of their experience. 'If a cultural institution is laughed at, its meaning cannot be taken at face value. Laughter must be regarded as a denial of cultural automation and the affirmation of a complex human freedom to follow, change or create culture' (Codere 1956: 349–350). The comedy of paradox is therefore a major tool which can be used by people to resist culturally the influence of powerful foreigners.

Colonization and Songhay society

The coming of the French to Songhay country in 1898 marked a significant turning point in Songhay experience. Before the colonial era, the traditions of the Songhay had never been threatened significantly by military or cultural invasion. During the incessant wars of the 19th century, for example, the victors would take their slave-prisoners or their tribute and return to their own lands. The combatants in these precolonial wars were unconcerned about such European notions as cultural evolution. With the onset of French colonialism, however, the Songhay confronted the way of the European, a path of progress culminating in 'civilization.' To rescue the African from his uncivilized ways, the French introduced a colonial policy of 'cultural renaissance.' The colonial policymakers designed this policy to train a small educated elite and to instil in the masses a deep shame of their ancient ways. 'Cultural renaissance' succeeded in radically transforming the social and political foundations of the precolonial social order. Out of this decay, however, there emerged a revolutionary cultural phenomenon, the *Hauka*, a new 'family' of Songhay spirits. Through their outrageous mockery of such colonial identities as *King Zuzi* (the colonial chief justice) and *Gomno Malia* (the governor of the Red Sea), the *Hauka* burlesqued the European and his ways. Because of their bold contempt of French culture, the *Hauka* became popular in colonial Niger. In the ruins of the old order, the *Hauka* symbolically resisted the cultural invasion of the French and protected the last vestige of Songhay cultural identity – their links to their ancestors. In what follows I describe the essentials of the colonial policies which devastated the precolonial Songhay social order.

French colonial policy and the chiefs

Before the coming of the French, the chiefs of the Songhay principalities held full authority over their polities. They were military leaders and could declare war against their neighbors. They could form alliances with other Songhay states or with other ethnic groups. They were judges in both civil and criminal disputes and under the right circumstances they could impose the death penalty. They also preserved the right to collect taxes from their subjects.

But the chief was more than a major political operator and more than a great warrior; he was responsible for the fate of his people. Indeed, as Olivier de Sardin (1983) has written of the Songhay: 'The chieftaincy can be considered first as a symbolic institution the roots of which can be traced back to magic and divination.' Military success and prosperity, it was believed, depended upon the chief's links to his ancestors which were maintained through ritual sacrifice.

Through their colonial policy the French usurped the power and authority of chiefs. Chiefs were stripped of their military independence and retained only judicial authority over minor civil disputes. The French also took from the chiefs those military and symbolic aspects of the chieftaincy which gave the polity a political foundation and a cultural identity. And to add insult to injury, the French made the chiefs agents of taxation whose special charge was to recruit their own people for forced labour. 'These functions were largely responsible for the changeover of the position of chief from the symbol of the collective unity of his people to the most hated member of that community' (Crowder 1968: 187).

French colonial policy and slavery

Slavery was the principal pillar of the foundation of most precolonial societies in the Western Soudan.[2] The importance of slavery for the precolonial Songhay principalities was paramount (Olivier de Sardin 1969, 1975, 1976, 1983). One of the major reasons for the incessant warfare in the 19th century in Songhay country was to procure more slaves. By consequence, all of the Songhay slaves theoretically could trace their descent patrilineally to a prisoner of a precolonial war. A Songhay noble could sell his prisoner-slave, *benya* (*benyey*, pl.), but once the *benya* had produced offspring, the offspring (*horso*) became farmers who tilled the soil for noble patrons, or skilled specialists (weavers, bards, blacksmiths, musicians, and healers) who became the clients of noble patrons.

In 1901 the governor-general of French West Africa, William Ponty, abolished slavery in the French Soudan. This edict, however, did not bring about the immediate disappearance of slavery. In many regions of Songhay country, for example, the ties between nobles and their former slaves remained important, for slavery was an institution deeply embedded in the social structure of pre-colonial Songhay society. The social importance of slavery was sharply reduced, however, because colonialism brought with it new economic opportunities, especially for men who had once been '*captifs*'. With the official abolition of slavery, many former slaves were freed to travel and seek their fortunes in distant markets. In fact the departure of slaves from the lands of their former masters was much greater than the French had anticipated. By 1908 French colonial officials estimated that some 200,000 slaves in the Western Soudan had left their patrons. In 1911 Governor-General Ponty suggested that 500,000 slaves had liberated themselves. And in a report circulated in 1912 French colonial officials estimated that one of every three slaves in the Western Soudan had fled from his master (Roberts and Klein 1980: 393). The end of slavery brought about the beginning of significant labour migrations from the steppes of the Soudan to the forests of the Guinea Coast. Many Songhay slaves travelled to Ghana to seek their fortunes. When they returned as men of worldly experience, they significantly transformed the social category of slave.

As Crowder (1968: 184) writes, 'Once a domestic slave decided to quit the family that owned him traditionally, the master could not reclaim him.' And thus the dynamic interdependence between master and slave, of which Hegel wrote, was forever undermined. As the Songhay slaves liberated themselves by choosing to travel to Ghana, the foundation of the Songhay master-noble identity was compromised. While the nobles and slaves continued their routine as though nothing had changed (and to this day, this pattern continues) the most important foundation of the precolonial stratified society had disappeared. In the wake of its disappearance a new social structure began to emerge.

French colonial policy and education

While the French were undermining the old social order of precolonial Soudanic societies through their policies on slavery and their official relationship with chiefs, they sought to expose some of their new subjects to a European universe of meaning. The French policymakers wanted to use education to create new Frenchmen out of colonial populations. The education policy sought to give instruction to the masses and to educate a small African elite to help in the governance of the new colonies.

French colonial policy on education was ironically called 'cultural renaissance'. As Governor-General Jules Brevie stated:

> However pressing may be the need for economic change and development of natural resources, our mission in Africa is to bring about a cultural renaissance, a piece of creative work in human material, an association of the two races which can be brought about only by a free and wholehearted acceptance of the African by the French.
>
> (Mumford and Orde-Brown 1935: 96)

Brevie's rhetoric masked the ultimate policy goal: to destroy the cultural foundations of African society.

In Songhay country there was large-scale indirect resistance to French education. Education among the Songhay as well as many other Islamized peoples in French West Africa was not an isolated phenomenon. Centuries before the coming of the French soldiers, Koranic schools flourished in Songhay country. Detailed non-formal education was also given by fathers to their sons and mothers to their daughters. Given the previous educational experience of the Songhay, why would they resist French education? One major reason is that the Songhay believe that the ways of the foreigner, especially if the foreigner is Christian and White, can pollute the mind. A child who goes off to school, learns French, and studies about European society can never again be a pure Songhay, for the child's mind will have been forever altered. The French, hoping to create an elite with traditional claims of leadership, established schools for the sons of chiefs. The Songhay saw no boon to elite leadership in these schools, and instead sent to be enrolled children of slave origin. An overwhelming percentage of the population of students in French schools in Songhay country were of non-noble origin (Seybou Harouna, personal communication).

French education, together with the policies on slavery and chiefs, created a climate of irrevocable change. The chiefs, once the powerful symbols of their ancestors, became hated tax collectors. The slaves, once the bulwark of the precolonial social order, became free people and they travelled to the edges of their worlds in search of adventure and money. When they returned they were free men of wide experience who transcended the narrow definition of their precolonial social positions. There also emerged a new educated elite, many of whom were of slave origin, which began to play an increasingly important role in the colonial administration on the local level and an increasingly significant role in the local-level politics which was to lead to independence.

Colonialism brought on radical and unsystematic change to the Africans living under French rule. In the decay of the old order, there arose not only the beginnings of a new order, but also a deep despair. In Songhay country and elsewhere in French West Africa, people

> had their old life broken by the shock of European contact; the old order of tribal society, with its cohesion based on unquestioned rule of custom, has been forced into the background; and the native, deracialized by the shattering of everything which has previously guided him, drifts disillusioned and despairing now knowing no hope, and now with the insane joy of the iconoclast aiding the outside forces in rending his life from top to bottom.... The future is not clear because the native, here a French citizen and there a mere 'subject' does not know where he can fit in. Seeing neither a place for himself nor hope for his children, he drifts in reckless despair or gives way to carefree insouciance.

> (Roberts 1963: 312–313)

While the remark which I quote above is overstated and paternalistic, it does touch on the well-known fact that when peoples are faced with rapid social change, when they are uprooted from the comforts of centuries-old traditions, they tend toward despair (Kiev 1972). But what the author fails to realize is that people possess a great stock of cultural resources which they can manipulate to cushion blows to their social and cultural vitality. In what follows, I shall describe how the Songhay resisted culturally the ravages of French colonial rule.

Genesis of the *Hauka* movement

The Songhay possession dance (*holey hori*) has been a continually evolving aesthetic form. From its humble beginnings at the dawn of Songhay civilization it grew in importance and complexity to become, along with Islam, a major religious force of the precolonial social order. Possession dances have been always staged in the same manner. The *zima* or priest of the possession cult organizes the dance which features the music of the monochord violin (*godji*) and the calabash drum (*gasi*). When the music of these instruments is combined with the sound of the sacred verse of spirit praise-poetry and the movement of dancer-adepts, the spirits are lured from their domain in the heavens and take the bodies of their mediums on earth. When the spirits arrive in the social world, members of the cult give them food and drink and dress them in their respective costumes. Attendants also give them objects which are associated with their respective roles in the spirit world.

At the onset of French colonial rule, the possession cult of the Songhay, which did not yet include the *Hauka*, was a well-organized social institution consisting of an elaborate cult-on-earth and a pantheon of five spirit 'families' which mythically reflected the socio-cultural experience of the Songhay. Possession dance, in large measure, had been the sociocultural institution which, through the expression of its complex of symbolic forms, had maintained links between the Songhay and their ancestors.

The onset of colonial rule, as we have seen, devastated the economic and social bases of most of the societies of the French Soudan. Songhay was no exception. The first inclination of the Songhay was to militarily resist the armies of the French. There was a revolt against the French in 1905–06 (Kanya-Forstner 1969). This resistance, however, soon proved to be ineffective. While there was scattered military resistance in Songhay country, most of the Songhay reconciled themselves to French military superiority. By 1922 the French had firm control over Songhay country.

As the French began to consolidate their power in Niger, the *Hauka* movement emerged. During the course of a dance of young adults in 1925, the first *Hauka* took a medium. As Jean Rouch's informant, *El Hadj* Mohammadou of Filingue said:

> It all began during a dance of girls and boys. During the dance, a Soudye woman, Zibo, who was married to a Timbucktu *sherif*, began to be possessed by a spirit. They asked her who it was. It said: 'I am *Gomno Malia*' (Governor of the Red Sea). The people said that they did not know this spirit. Then others came and took the bodies of some of the young boys. They too spoke

their names, and the people did not know them. The spirits said: 'We are the *Hauka*, the guests of *Dongo*.' This occurred at Chikal, very close to Filingue. A few days later, all the boys and girls of Filingue had been possessed by the *Hauka*.

(Rouch 1960: 73)[3]

Appalled at this strange turn of events in the ritual life of his town, the chief of Filingue, who had enjoyed the support of the French administration, sent word to Niamey, the capital of the Niger territory, that the woman Zibo had ruined his community with her crazy *Hauka*. The commandant of Niamey, a Major Croccichia, received the message and gave the order that all these *Hauka* should be arrested and brought to Niamey. The Filingue chief presented the 60 participants to the French officials who brought them to Niamey. They were immediately put into prison and kept there for three days. When Croccichia allowed them to leave prison, the young people began to dance until the *Hauka* came into their bodies. Zibo's body, as in other episodes, began to shake from the presence of *Gomno Malia*. Upon learning this, the commandant of Niamey ordered his soldiers to bring Zibo to his headquarters. He slapped her and said: 'Where are the Hauka?' He continued to slap Zibo until she said that there was no such thing as the *Hauka*. Then the other *Hauka* were brought to Croccichia and he and his soldiers began to slap them until they, too, admitted that there were no *Hauka*. Finally, the commandant sent them back to Filingue. But Zibo and her cohorts found no peace; they were expelled from Filingue. When they travelled to other villages, they established new *Hauka* cults. In this way the *Hauka* movement began to spread.

The development of the *Hauka* movement

The *Hauka* movement spread rapidly. By February 1927 the French administration noted that there were *Hauka* adepts in all the villages of the Filingue district. Indeed, the colonial administration considered the *Hauka* movement to be hostile to the local *chefs de canton*. The *Hauka* themselves were considered rivals 'of the established order, represented by the chieftaincy, the backbone of the administrative system created by the French' (Fugelstad 1975: 204).

The old chief of Filingue, Gado Namalaya, died in March of 1927. The French supported the candidature of Chekou Seyni, one of the sons of Gado. Chekou, however, had less than the unanimous support of the population. The *Hauka*, manifesting themselves as a political force, supported another candidate. This action was a bold, if not intolerable affront to French authority.

Because of these accumulating incidents, the *Hauka* movement grew in size and in importance. In uninhabited areas of the bush, the *Hauka* founded their own villages and set up their own society which was overtly anti-French.

The French found in the *Hauka*

a clear opposition to the traditional chieftaincy. They discovered the presence of an open dissidence, a society the members of which openly defied the social, political and religious order. It is here that we discover the most original aspect of the Hauka movement: their total refusal of the system put into place by the French.

(Fugelstad 1975: 205)

The harsh intervention of Major Croccichia, the French commandant of Niamey, accelerated the diffusion of the *Hauka* movement. The brutality which Major Croccichia ordered against Zibo and her group left such a searing memory that Croccichia was soon deified as a *Hauka* himself, *Korsasi*, the wicked Major and one of the most violent of the *Hauka*.[4]

As time passed by, the *Hauka* family and the mythology which reinforced the place of the *Hauka* in Songhay cosmology took form. In all cases, the deities and identities associated with the *Hauka* aped French colonial society. Continuing to assert that they were from the Red Sea and the guests of *Dongo* in Songhay country, the following characters emerged as the most important of the early *Hauka* deities:

1 *Istanbula*, who lives in Istanbul and who is both a pious Moslem and the chief of all the *Hauka*.
2 *Gomno*, the colonial governor (of the Red Sea).
3 *Zeneral Malia*, the general of the Red Sea.
4 *King Zuzi*, the king of judges or the colonial chief justice.
5 *Mayaki*, the warrior or great soldier.
6 *Korsasi*, the wicked Major who sometimes kills his mediums.
7 *Sekter*, the secretary or clerk.
8 *Kapral Gardi*, the corporal of the guard who is the assistant Korsasi and who knows how to break iron with his hands.
9 *Babule*, the blacksmith.
10 *Falimata Malia*, the wife of *Zeneral Malia* who had her son *Cemoko* with *Kapral Gardi*.
11 *Cemoko*, the young boy who knows how to pull silver out of the ground.

(Rouch 1960: 74–75)

Given the great migrations from Songhay country to the Gold Coast during the colonial period, many of the adepts of these deities travelled far and wide. And as they confronted new experiences, new deities manifested themselves in the bodies of adepts. In the Gold Coast of colonial times, the *Hauka* received two new deities, *Kafrankot*, the corporal of the coast, and *Hanga Beri* (big ears), who runs locomotives. Just as the colonial administration had become more complex, so the family of *Hauka* became populated with new deities which reflected the more complete expansion of colonial authority. These were *Hauka* who represented highly placed civil servants: *Minis de Ger* or minister of war, simple ministers, or *minis*, and *Prazidan di la Republik* for President of the French Republic. The *Hauka* also parodied the French colonial army with deities who were colonels, captains, lieutenants, and sergeants, as well as the foot soldier, *Bambara Mossi* (many of the foot soldiers were either *Bambara* or *Mossi* in ethnic origin). Local administrative identities were not spared from the theatrics of the *Hauka*. There are *Hauka* lawyers (*Wasiri*) and doctors (*Lokotoro*) who inject people with their syringes. These new *Hauka* came into being in the exact manner as the original group in Filingue in 1925. During the course of a dance, an adept would be taken by a new deity which would not be known to the members of the cult. The cult members would then ask for the name of the deity, and upon learning the name, this new deity would become a member of the *Hauka* family (Rouch 1960: 76–77).[5]

The cultural messages of the Hauka in performance

The *Hauka* movement challenged the supremacy of French colonial rule. As a complex, the bizarre and brazen behavior of the *Hauka* expressed clear and boldly critical statements about the nature of the colonizer and his behavior. The verbal statements were made in a mixture of Pidgin French, Pidgin English, and Songhay. Having *Gomno* or *Korsasi* speak to his audience in Pidgin, which continues to be a stigmatized linguistic form in both Francophone and Anglophone West Africa, constituted a negative message about the colonial authorities. Imagine a French colonial administrator being aped by a possessed Songhay. The medium's body is contorted. His eyes are bulging, and like all *Hauka*, he froths at the mouth. And to add insult to injury, he speaks a mixture of Pidgin French and Songhay. The result of this complex of symbolic messages is a combination of fright, for the *Hauka* is a terrifying sight, and burlesque, for the *Hauka* mocks the identity which he or she represents.

The *Hauka* take the bodies of their mediums at possession dances in Songhay country during which deities representing the other spirit families of the Songhay pantheon may be enticed to journey from the spirit to the social world (see Rouch 1960).[6] These dances are always staged in the same manner. Essential participants in the dance, as I have mentioned, are the *zima* or the ritual priest who is the impresario of the possession cult, the ritual musicians who play monochord violins (*godji*) or calabash drums (*gasi*), the *sorko*, the praise-singer of spirits whose sacred incantations create a metaphorical bridge between the social and spirit worlds, and the mediums themselves (*hol'isey*), the dancers whose bodies may be 'taken' by their spirit.[7]

The possession dance itself consists of two frames. In the first frame any person can enter the dance area, usually a flat sandy plain within the compound of the ritual priest, which is encircled by an audience. A hangar, under which the musicians produce their sacred music, stands at the edge of the dance grounds. This frame is called *hori* which literally means 'to play' in Songhay. During the *hori* the people at the dance have a good time, competing with one another to see who are the best dancers. The best dancers are rewarded with praise: a member of the audience, inspired by a particular dance sequence, will leap into the dance area and present the dancer with a sum of money. The dancer will then give the money to the musicians who are the keepers of the possession dance kitty. After two hours or more of *hori*, the *zima*, with a flick of his wrist, signals transformation from a social occasion to a serious religious ritual. Now only known mediums, all of whom have undergone an initiation, can enter the dance area. When the music begins again, the musicians play only those rhythms associated with the spirits they wish to entice to earth. These are sometimes the *Hauka*.

There are only two occasions when the *Hauka* alone are summoned. The first is when many members of a community have been suffering from witchcraft, for the *Hauka* today are, among other things, the principal adversaries of Songhay witches. In these circumstances the *Hauka* take the bodies of mediums and then pick up burning bushes and brandish them over their heads – a sign that the witches of the community should be wary of the presence of the *Hauka*. The second circumstance for an all-*Hauka* possession occurs when a novice who has been possessed initially by a *Hauka* goes through his or her initiation – an initiation similar to those of the other spirit families of the Songhay pantheon. Despite the fact that the *Hauka* constitutes only one of the six spirit families of the Songhay pantheon, it and it alone has deities which burlesque horrifically the identities associated with the colonial epoch of Niger.

To illustrate the combination of horror and humour in *Hauka* possession dances, let me describe two cases from my field notes. The first encounter involved *Lokotoro*, the European doctor, which I recorded in December of 1976 in the Songhay town of Mehanna.

> I join the audience in the evening. From a distance I see two possessed adepts carrying burning bushes above their heads. These are *Hauka*. One of the *Hauka* throws down his burning bush and takes a torch which he holds to his bare chest with no effect at all. Someone in the crowd tells me that the two *Hauka* are none other than *Zeneral Malia* and *Lokotoro*, the Doctor. *Lokotoro*, who is wearing a pith helmet, carries a hypodermic syringe. He approaches me and extends his open hand.

Lokotoro:	Sha vas?
	'How is it going?'
Stoller:	Ça vas?
	'How is it going?'
L:	Sha vas?
S:	Ça vas?
L:	Me ne doctor
	'I am called doctor.'
S:	Ni doctor?
	'You are a doctor?'

Our exchange is interrupted by laughter. The members of the audience in my vicinity find this hilarious because I am mocking *Lokotoro*. The dialogue continues:

S:	Alahumdu lilaahi. Enchanté.
	'Praise be to God. Enchanted (to meet you).'
L:	Sha vas?

S:	Ça vas?
L:	To anasara hinka. Tu as connay?
	'Okay, (there are) two Europeans (here). Do you know it?'
S:	Tu as connay?
	'Do you know it?'

This comment brings more laughter. *Lokotoro* is ridiculing the Europeans, and I am mocking him, which is appropriate in this context. We are both being obdurate, playing out the exaggerated roles of two Europeans, which the audience appreciates greatly. A *sorko* breaks into our conversation.

Sorko:	A ne ni anasara no n'inga manti anasara no.
	'He says that he is a European and that you and he make two Europeans.'
S:	Wo anasara no? To, enchanté.
	'This is a European? Good. Enchanted.'

This, too, provokes laughter. Before me is a black man frothing at the mouth and holding a syringe. He tells me he is a white European. I play along with this ridiculous charade, stating that he is indeed a white European. Then I code-switch into French to signify my recognition of his European status and say that I am enchanted to meet him. We are participating in a veritable theatre of the absurd which precipitates uproarious laughter.

Lokotoro leaves me to examine a small girl who had been ill. The girl's mother explains to *Lokotoro* that she had taken the child to the Islamic healers, to the nurses and to the non-Islamic healers in Mehanna. None of their remedies, however, had cured the girl. *Lokotoro* looks at her, blows on her arm, and injects her with his syringe which contains a milky fluid. *Lokotoro* returns to me.

S:	Ah *Lokotoro* ka
	'Ah, the doctor has returned.'
Sorko:	(To *Lokotoro*). Ci wala. Ni ma ci wokom ni ga ba
	'Recite then. You must tell (him) what you want.'
L:	To l'argen'
	'Okay, (I want) money.'
S:	L'argen'? To a go ka. Ay ma cece l'argen'. Ay ma no *Lokotoro* se l'argen'. *Lokotoro*, boro hano no.
	'Money? It's coming. I need to look for it. I should give money to the doctor. The doctor is a good person.'

I give *Lokotoro* 100 francs. He takes the money and puts it in his pocket.

L:	Anasara, sha vas?
	'European, how is it going?'
S:	Ça vas.
	'It goes.'
L:	Mershi.
	'Thank you' (for the contribution).

In this last sequence of interaction, *Lokotoro* addressed me as *anasara*, which signifies that we are no longer in the same social category. 'Anasara, ça vas?' is a linguistic device the Songhay use to distance themselves from the European. We are suddenly in different categories because he had asked me for a contribution. This sudden shift is a comic slap in my face.

And so we have here the terrifying possessed figure of *Lokotoro* burlesquing a European doctor and equating himself with the only white person in the audience. This is a ridiculous situation; it is also a means of defining the Songhay vis-à-vis the European colonizer. The interaction creates and maintains distance between the encroaching European civilization (me, in this instance) and the essentials of Songhay cultural identity.

The second *Hauka* encounter I wish to describe occurred in the town of Tillaberi in June of 1981 during a *yenaandi*, the rain dance during which the Songhay make offerings to the spirits who control the heavens. The Songhay believe that if they make offerings to these spirits, the spirits will bring enough rain during the planting season (June through September). A good rainy season usually insures a good millet harvest in October. The *yenaandi* is primarily a *Tooru* dance, for the *Tooru* is the family of deities which control the winds, the clouds, lightning, and thunder – forces which are associated with rain. When the *Tooru*, the nobles of the Songhay spirit world, come to the social world they travel with an entourage of lesser spirits. When there are visiting *Tooru*, those *Hauka* who personify French soldiers swoop down to earth, take the bodies of their mediums and serve as sentries to the *Tooru*. The following slices of interaction took place when the *Tooru* held court during this rain dance. The *Tooru* were seated on overturned mortars and received the people of Tillaberi. Before approaching the *Tooru* to receive advice, however, the townspeople had to endure the horrific comedy of the *Hauka* whose role it was to bring the people to the masters of the heavens. *Commandant Bashirou* (CB) and *Lieutenant Marseille* (LM) were the two *Hauka* who provided this escort service.

CB: (Goose-steps from centre of dance ground to audience. Stops in front of Young Woman [YW]. Slaps his legs together and salutes YW.) You are a fool, young woman. (Sprays saliva in her face.)

YW: (Recoils)

CB: (Grabs her hand and yanks her away from audience)

YW: (Falls to the ground, and as she is dragged) I don't want to go. I don't want to go.

CB: (Stops. Stands on one foot and looks at the audience). You are all stupid Songhay. How can you resist? (Looks at YW and smiles). Come, you daughter of a donkey (He laughs, audience laughs and he pulls YW to standing position and takes her to the *Tooru*.)

(Minutes Later)

LM: (Starts toward the crowd and stands on one foot gazing at the audience for a few moments. Then he struts toward a Young Man [YM] and salutes him). In the name of the army, in the name of God, in the name of the spirits, in the name of the Tooru …

YM: In the name of idiocy? (General laughter.)

LM: (Extends his hand to YM) You … you, the one with the limp penis. Come and seek a solution. (More laughter.)

YM: (Pointing at LM and laughing) And you with the empty head?

LM: (Grabs the arm of YM and shoves him toward the Tooru.)

From these brief accounts of *Hauka* Songhay interaction we see again the bizarre mixture of fear and comedy. The *Hauka* are incredibly strong. Besides being able to pick up burning bushes with their bare hands and touch themselves with burning torches, I have seen them knock down thick mudbrick walls with their fists. Since the *Hauka* are anything but gentle, when they summon someone to the *Tooru's* court, members of the audience are quite concerned about bodily injury. These roughhouse tactics, however, are coupled with such ridiculously exaggerated military behaviors as goose-stepping and saluting, during which the *Hauka* holds his hand to his forehead for as much as two minutes as he froths at the mouth and stares at the person he is saluting. And so in imagery alone we have a spirit who demonstrates great strength as he mocks the French military. To lighten the context even more the *Hauka* resort to typical Songhay ritual insults. *Commandant Bashirou* calls the young woman the daughter of a donkey, a Songhay ritual insult which in most contexts precipitates laughter (see Stoller 1977). When *Commandant Bashirou* says 'You are all stupid Songhay', this, too, precipitates laughter. This kind of direct insult is not taken seriously. Real insults in Songhay are usually indirect statements. The direct ritual insult therefore precipitates laughter.

Lieutenant Marseille engages in the same kind of horrific comedy as *Commandant Bashirou*. He approaches a young man and salutes him in an exaggerated form. He mocks the formality of military custom, saying 'In the name of army, etc. …' The young man, however, is taking none of this and mocks *Lieutenant Marseille*, saying 'In the name of idiocy?' The Songhay immensely enjoy this kind of mutual mockery for it corresponds to the verbal duel, a favourite activity of young Songhay. After this verbal duel, which also precipitates laughter, *Lieutenant Marseille* escorts the young man to the *Tooru*.

The *Hauka* in contemporary times

Scholars of the Songhay have suggested that the *Hauka* movement represented mainly the era of colonialism; it was a reflection of the confrontation of Songhay with colonial society (Rouch 1953, 1960; Gado 1980). After 1960, the year that France granted independence to the Government of Niger, the *Hauka*, according to Rouch (1978), had less of a following than during colonial times. Having lost their colonial *raison d'être*, it has been suggested, the *zimey* accelerated the process through which these outlaw spirits were incorporated into the mythology of the *holey*.

So *Dongo*, the god of thunder is now considered their [the *Hauka*] father. And the story is that *Bilali*, another aspect of *Dongo*, when he was in Mecca had a lot of sons who came to Africa. They say that *Bilali* actually sang *Hauka* songs and did *Hauka* rituals when he was in Mecca. The *Hauka* were the *enfants terribles* of *Bilali*, but now they are with us, and we are all together in the same family. And even today in the very remote village the *Hauka* still play an important role.

(Rouch 1978: 1009)

The expressive role of the Hauka

With Nigerien independence and their putative acceptance into the Songhay spirit cult, one might think that the expressive symbolism of a *Hauka* frothing at the mouth has been relegated to the background of social perception. But when the *Hauka* takes the body of his medium, there continues to be ribald comedy and terrifying drama: a manifestation, perhaps, of ongoing contact with the European 'force'.

There is no longer a separate *Hauka* movement as there was in 1927, a movement directed against the rule of the European. After all, opposition to European rule ceased to be a viable role for the *Hauka* when France granted independence to the Republic of Niger. But just as the conceptual residue of being a slave remains today among the former slave populations of the Songhay (see Olivier de Sardin 1969, 1976, 1983), so the psychological yoke of colonialism has remained with many of the peoples of the Republic of Niger (see Memmi 1962). While Europeans are no longer the political administrators of districts in the Republic of Niger, they still hold many important positions both in the capital city of Niamey and in the more rural regions of Songhay country. Europeans are the technical advisors to various Nigerien ministries. Europeans comprise a large part of the staffs of the national and regional hospitals in the Republic of Niger. Europeans are the technicians responsible for the progress of a wide variety of development projects. And Europeans have been teachers in Niger's secondary schools and in Niger's university.

The European population of Niamey is large and visible. Most Europeans live in one section of Niamey, the Plateau. Niamey has French shops, grocery stores, bakeries and butchers. Europeans, often living on generous 'hardship pay' allowances, lead elegant lives compared to those of Nigerien civil servants and peasants. And so the continued popularity of the *Hauka* is a kind of cultural resistance to the ongoing European presence. Much to the delight of audiences, the *Hauka*, despite the absence of a colonial government, continue to ridicule the European with their pretentious and outrageous mockery. The 'force' of the European continues to be strong in all the regions of the Republic of Niger. And the need of the Songhay to make sense of this 'force' remains equally strong.

Joking, cultural resistance, and the *Hauka*

Radcliffe-Brown (1940) and Evans-Pritchard (1949) have characterized the outrageousness and pretentiousness of joking as 'privileged license' and 'permitted disrespect'. The mediums of the *Hauka* take the exaggerated roles of Europeans only in the frame of possession dance activities. During possession, they make hilarious statements which form the foundation of a comedic role. Why the persistence of this comedy, especially at the expense of the European?

A partial answer to the question lies in considering the parallels between the *Hauka* movement and the way American Indians joke about the White man. In both cases, the White man, someone who held a vastly different world view, came in contact with peoples whom he subjugated. In the American and the West African cases, moreover, the White man created a 'colonial situation' (Wallerstein 1961) which overturned the worlds of the colonized peoples. In both cases, the colonized peoples reacted to the cataclysmic change by telling jokes about the White man. In the case of the Songhay, there came into being a 'family' of spirits which mocked the colonizer. In both cases it is the powerless who have ridiculed the powerful. As one Canadian Indian put it:

> The biggest of all Indian problems is the whiteman. Who can understand the whiteman? What makes him tick? How does he think and why does he think the way he does? Why does he talk so much? Why does he say one thing and do the opposite? Most important of all, how do you deal with him? Obviously, he is here to stay. Sometimes it seems like a hopeless task.
>
> (H. Cardinal quoted in Basso 1979: 3)

The greatest problem for the Songhay is no longer the European; it is rather the European's way. The European no longer rules in Songhay country, but the ideas of the European, his language, his system of education, and many of his values have influenced the lifeways of young Songhay. And when this happens Songhay elders consider these young people no longer to be Songhay, but Frenchmen with black skin. And so the *Hauka* continues to ape the European, continues to mutilate the French language, and attempts through burlesque to make sense of a rapidly changing world in which the European continues to play a major role. The European will remain in the Republic of Niger, and so will the *Hauka*, forever resisting through mockery the influences of foreigners and forever protecting those values which are central to the cultural identity of the Songhay.

Acknowledgements

The research upon which the present paper is based was conducted in the subprefectures of Tera and Tillaberi in the Republic of Niger in 1969–71, 1976–77, 1979–80, and in the summer of 1981. The research was made possible by a Fulbright-Hays Doctoral Dissertation Research Fellowship (GOO-76-03659), a Grant-in-Aid (#3175) from the Wenner-Gren Foundation for Anthropological Research, a NATO Postdoctoral Fellowship in Science, and a Grant-in-Aid (#1569) from the Johnson Fund of the American Philosophical Society. A Faculty Research Small Grant and an Equivalent Time Teaching Load Reduction Award from West Chester State College have provided me time and support in the preparation of this manuscript. I thank all of these institutions for their generous support. I would also like to thank H. E. Colonel Seyni Kountché, President of the Republic of Niger, for granting me research authorizations for ethnographic research in Niger. I would like to acknowledge Cheryl Olkes for her extensive comments on the manuscript, as well as Susan Pevar and Joanne Saunders, my graduate assistant and undergraduate assistant respectively, for their assistance in gathering research materials. An abridged version of this paper was read at the Northeastern Anthropological Association's annual meeting which was held at Princeton University, March 18–21, 1982.

Notes

1 There are some three million Songhay speakers in the Republics of Mali, Niger, and Benin. The Songhay continue to be primarily millet farmers in most regions and both millet farmers and rice cultivators in riverine areas. The society is divided into three general groups of unequal status: the nobles, who trace their descent patrilineally to Askia Mohammed Toure, King of the Songhay from 1493 to 1528; former slaves, who trace their descent patrilineally to prisoners of precolonial wars; and foreigners, peoples who have migrated into Songhay country in the distant or recent past. (For more detailed information on Songhay society see Rouch 1953, 1960; Gado 1980; Olivier de Sardin 1969, 1976, 1983; Stoller 1980, 1981).

2 The 'Western Soudan' refers to the French colonial territory of West Africa. The colonial Soudan was composed of Senegal, Mali, Niger, and Upper Volta.

3 *Soudye* refers to an ethnic group which today lives in the area of Filingue, some 180 km to the northeast of Niamey, the capital of the Republic of Niger. The *Soudye* live on the border of the Hausaphone (Songhay) Zermaphone speech areas. Songhay and Zerma are dialects of the Songhay language.

4 There are numerous versions of the incident involving Major Croccichia. The version cited here presents a reasonably accurate view of the birth of *Korsasi*, the wicked Major.

5 From the beginning of the *Hauka* movement, the mediums have been of both sexes. But as the movement grew in size and importance the number of male initiates began to out-number that of the females. The mediums of the *Hauka* have come from a variety of ethic groups and represent the broad swath of Nigerien social experience. *Hauka* mediums are Songhay, Zerma, Peul, Bella, Hausa, and Kanuri in ethnic origin and may be poor peasant farmers living in isolated rural areas or wealthy merchants living in the crowded cities of independent Niger. As was the case in the first *Hauka* initiation in 1925, the new initiates have almost always been adolescents and young adults.

Despite the fact that the *Hauka* deities reject the way of the European, some of the mediums have worked diligently to become French-speaking nurses, soldiers, administrators, and scholars in independent Niger. Once wedded to their spirits, these educated mediums know that they will harbor them for the rest of their lives. These educated mediums keep their distance from the music and sacred words of possession dance festivities because they fear that the intoxicating sounds of possession dance could bring on their *Hauka* and compromise their social positions. Unlike their fellow initiates in the countryside, the educated mediums walk a narrow tightrope between the private world of their deep-seated beliefs and the public world of their social roles in a developing society. The impact of colonialism notwithstanding, the traditions of the ancestors are still close to the hearts of even highly educated Nigeriens.

6 The other spirit 'families' of the Songhay pantheon are: the *Tooru*, the deities of the sky and the water; the *Genji Kwearey*, the 'white spirits' who are the Islamic clerics of the spirit world and who advise human beings about social problems; the *Genji Bi*, or 'Black spirits,' who represent the original Voltaique speaking peoples who first mastered the forces of the land; the *Hausa genji*, or spirits of the east who precipitate illness,

especially paralysis; the *Hargay*, or spirits of the cold who are associated with death; and, of course, the *Hauka* themselves. There are roughly 150 spirits in the Songhay pantheon.

7 Each medium must be initiated. The spirit first identifies its medium through the manifestation of illness. The proposed medium becomes ill and the afflicted person responds neither to traditional nor western medical therapies. Members of the family of the afflicted person consult a *rinna*, a ritual priest, for his or her opinion. If the *zima* senses that the spirit possessing the afflicted person is a member of the Songhay pantheon, he proposes to stage an initiation festival (*horendi*). The initiation festival spans seven days, during which the novice gradually becomes acquainted with his or her spirit (see Stoller n.d.). On the seventh day, the spirit takes full control of the novice's body and reveals its identity to the community. Thereafter the novice will be known as that spirit's horse. Once the ceremonies are over the spirit leaves the body of the novice and the novice regains his or her health. And if the initiation festival has been flawlessly staged, the spirit will return to the body of its medium only when it has been beckoned by the music, dance, and word of a possession dance.

References

Basso, Keigh. 1979. *Portraits of the Whiteman: Linguistic Play and Cultural Symbols Among the Western Apache*. London and New York: Cambridge Universiy Press.

Bastide, Roger. 1978. *The African Religions of Brazil*. Baltimore: The Johns Hopkins University Press.

Codere, Helen. 1956. The Amiable Side of Kwakitl Life. *American Anthropologst* 58, 334: 351.

Curtney, Richard. 1974. *Play, Drama, and Thought*. New York: MacMillan.

Crowder, Michael. 1968. *West Africa Under Colonial Rule*. Evanston, Ill.: Northwestern University Press.

Evans-Pritchard, E. E. 1949. Nuer Curses and Ghostly Vengence. *Africa* 19(4): 288–294.

Fugelstad, Finn. 1975. Les Hauka: Une Interprétation Historique. *Cahiers d'Études Africaines* 58: 203–216.

Gado Boube. 1980. *Le Zermaterey: Contribution à l'Histoire des Populations entre Niger et Dollol Mawri*. *Études Nigériennes* No. 45. Niamey: Institut de Recherches en Sciences Humaines. Université de Niamey.

Kanya-Forstner, A. N. 1969. *The Conquest of the Western Soudan*. London: Cambridge University Press.

Kiev, Ari. 1072. *Transcultural Psychiatry*. New York: The Free Press.

Memmi, Albert. 1962. *The Colonizer and the Colonized*. New York: Orion Press.

Miles, Dudley Howe. 1971. *The Influence of Molière on Restoration Comedy*. New York: Octagon Books.

Mitchell, J. Clyde. 1966. *The Kalela Dance: Aspects of Social Relationships Among Urban Africans in Northern Rhodesia*. Manchester: The Rhodes–Livingstone Papers, No. 27.

Mumford, W. and G. St. John Orde-Brown. 1935, *Africans Learn to be French*. London: Evans Brothers.

Olivier De Sardin, Jean-Pierre. 1969. *Structures Économiques et Structures Sociales: Les Wogo du Niger*. Paris: Institut d'Ethnologie.

—— 1975. Captifs Ruraux et Esclaves Impériaux du Songhai, *L'Esclavage en Afrique Précoloniale* (C. Meillassoux, ed.), pp. 99–135. Paris: Maspéro.

—— 1976. *Quand Nos Pères Étaient Captifs*. Paris: Nubia.

—— 1983. Women and Slavery in Africa, in Robertson, Claire and Klein, Martin A. (eds), Madison, WI: University of Wisconsin Press.

Perry, Henry. 1968. *Masters of Dramatic Comedy and their Social Themes*. Washington, D.C.: Kennikat Press.

Radcliffe-Brown, A. R. 1940. On Joking Relationships. *Africa* 13: 195–210.

Ranger, T. O. 1975. *Dance and Society in Eastern Africa*. Berkeley: University of California Press.

Roberts, Steven. 1963. *The History of French Colonial Policy 1870–1925*. London: Archon Books.

Roberts, Richard and Murry, Kein. 1980. The Banamba Slave Exodus in 1905 and the Decline of Slavery in the Western Soudan. *Journal of African History* 21(3): 375–395.

Rouch, Jean. 1953. *Contribution à l'Histoire des Songhay*. Mémoire No. 29. Dakar: Institut Français d'Afrique Noire.

—— 1960. *La Religion et La Magie Songhay*. Paris: P.U.F.

—— 1978. Jean Rouch Talks about his Films to John Marshall and John W. Adams. *American Anthropologist* 80: 1005–1022.

Stoller, Paul A. 1977. Ritual and Personal Insults in Songrai Sonni. *Anthropology* 2(1): 33–38.

—— 1980. The Negotiation of Songhay Space: Phenomenology in the Heart of Darkness. *American Ethnologist* 7(3): 419–431.

—— 1981. Social Interaction and the Management of Songhay Socio-political Change. *Africa* 51(3): 765–780.

—— n.d. *The Way of the Ancients: Cultural Resistance and Songhay Possession Dance*. Unpublished ms. (in author's possession).

Wallerstein, Immanuel. 1961. *Africa and the Politics of Independence*. New York: Academic Press.

Wellwarth, George. 1971. *The Theater of Protest and Paradox: Developments in Avant-Garde Drama*. New Yok: New York University Press.

Part IV

Spectators, space and time in performance

19 South African theatre in an era of reconciliation

Zakes Mda

> The best thing that could happen to a storyteller is
> to be born in South Africa.[1]

Six years ago I was asked to address the subject of theatre and reconciliation in South Africa by a journal of the Yale School of Drama and Yale Repertory Theater[2]. I observed at the time that one of the features of the burgeoning theatre for reconciliation in South Africa was a very loud silence in history. I further commented on my compatriots' antipathy to the habit of memory.

After six years the fear of memory persists, although faltering movements to confront the past can be seen on our stages and on the pages of our literary works in the wake of the Truth and Reconciliation Commission (TRC).

The TRC itself was a unique experience that brought the excesses of the apartheid past into the living rooms of South Africa through television screens. Here we saw victims of gross human rights violations re-living their torture in the presence of their squirming torturers. We saw the tears of the TRC commissioners as the narrative of wheelchair-bound survivors unfolded and as mothers who lost their children wept and wailed openly. We saw erstwhile torturers confessing their activities, sometimes contrite, and at other times stubbornly standing their ground that the demands of war drove them to commit whatever crimes they were being accused of. Yet others blamed the elders. They were pawns of the elders; footsoldiers that carried out the orders of the government of the day, the very rulers who were now being rewarded with fat pensions, while the minions had to answer before a commission set up by the victors of war. We saw torturers demonstrating how they suffocated their victims, smothering them either to confession or to death, how they ran electric currents through their testicles and how they roasted corpses of those who were not strong enough to survive on open fires while they enjoyed fireside beer and laughter.

Here was drama to top all drama.

The TRC emasculated many storytellers. Their fiction could never compete effectively with the real-life theatre that was unfolding every night to millions of viewers. It was the theatre that was making many of my white compatriots sing in unison: 'We did not know that these things were happening.' At the same time they were recoiling at the very act of resurrecting the ghosts of the past. The past is another country, they were saying, and it should remain so.

There is indeed an attempt in some sectors of South African society to erase the past in order to reconstruct a new collective identity – from race and ethnic-bound identities to a new South African national identity. This fear of the past manifests itself in the outcry in our various media, especially in radio talk shows, whenever the legacy of the past is cited, or whenever national television screens documentaries or drama that depict the atrocities of apartheid and the resistance that finally brought us to a new democratic dispensation.

A new collective identity at the expense of memory is, in my view, not feasible. Memory is vital to identity. Memory loss leads to loss of identity, because who we are is fundamentally linked to memory. In any event, South Africa is currently pursuing policies that recognise and respect diverse cultural identities. The beauty of South Africa lies in its many cultures, each with its own history. Then there is, of course, our collective history that emanates from the interactions of those cultures. The memory of each peculiar past can only enrich our present. We should rejoice in our multiple identities – among which is a national identity – instead of trying to achieve an impossible state of affairs, which would not have been desirable even if it were achievable.

After apartheid, which expropriated the reality of multiple identities for the purposes of oppression, segregation and exploitation, it is understandable that we should feel threatened by the very thought of giving due recognition to multiple identities.

There is a demand from some of my white compatriots that since we have now attained democracy we should all have collective amnesia, because memory does not contribute to reconciliation. Our new identity-in-the-making is threatened by memory. We should, therefore, not only forgive the past, but we should forget it as well. However it is impossible to meet this demand, for we are products of our past. We have been shaped by our history. Our present worldview and our mindset is a result of our yesterdays.

For South Africa to survive and prosper reconciliation is absolutely essential. But true reconciliation will only happen when we are able to confront what happened yesterday without bitterness. We cannot just sweep it under the carpet and hope that all of a sudden we shall live in brotherly and sisterly love in a state of blissful amnesia.

For those of us who are survivors of the past it is important that we do not forget. We owe it to future generations that what happened to us must never happen again. It must never be repeated by those who oppressed us before. But most importantly, we ourselves must never assume the new role of oppressor. And only history can teach us those lessons – provided, of course, we are capable of learning from history.

We must never forget, but this does not mean we must cling to memory, as some of us are wont to do, and blame our own inertia and our present failures on a disadvantaged past, for that would make us perpetual victims of our past. We only look back in the past in order to have a better understanding of our present. And it is a present that is informed by our strong commitment to reconciliation.

Contrary to what many people think, the era of reconciliation did not pass with the presidency of Nelson Mandela from 1994 to 1999. Reconciliation was, indeed, the dominant discourse in South African society during his presidency. He went out of his way to reach out to various communities, assuring them that there was a place for everyone in a liberated South Africa. At the same time he tried to rehabilitate the Afrikaner in the imagination of a South Africa that was still bleeding from the wounds inflicted during the divisive reign of the members of that white African ethnic group.

Although reconciliation is no longer the dominant discourse in society, the quest for reconciliation continues in various forms. It may not be articulated as much as it was during the Mandela era, but it is in the content of government and civil society programmes that recognise the identities and the rights of minorities while affirming the previously disadvantaged majorities such as women and black people. Indeed, the current president's (Thabo Mbeki) definition of an African in parliament has been inclusive of the members of all racial and cultural groups that call South Africa their home.

Like all artists, South African theatre practitioners get their material from society. Their theatre is informed by the dominant discourse in society. And those who are influential enough may even inform the discourse in society, in a symbiotic relationship. Perhaps I should explain that I use 'theatre practitioners' here because many of our playwrights are not just writers. They are directors, designers, actors, and sometimes even musical composers and choreographers. They are total theatre practitioners.

The post-apartheid theatre that was created soon after our liberation in 1994 was indeed preoccupied with the themes of reconciliation. I wrote in the cited Yale journal that during this period practitioners of protest theatre such as Athol Fugard turned to a new theatre of reconciliation. His play, title *Playland*, created and staged during this period, depicts a confrontation between a white man, a former soldier of the apartheid regime who had killed a number of black people in the 'operational area', and a black man who had served fifteen years in jail for killing a white man who had raped his fiancée. Both these men are haunted by the murders they committed. By the end of the play these characters have both agreed that it is futile to dwell in the past and to harbour hatred. They resolve to lead a new life that is not haunted by the past.

There were other plays too, that dealt with reconciliation, and these were seen in the city purpose-built theatres, in the township venues where community groups grappled with the subject, and at festivals such as the National Festival for the Arts in Grahamstown. *My Life* was one such play. Athol Fugard and five teenage girls from the different racial groups of South Africa jointly created it. The play, referred to as 'an allegory for reconciliation', premiered at this festival in July 1994, and featured the five girls who told the stories of their lives through a series of dramatic vignettes.

Athol Fugard is not the only voice in South African theatre that has addressed issues of reconciliation. I, however, focus on his plays for two reasons. Firstly, he was a pioneer of the protest theatre movement in South Africa. Before Fugard there was a wealth of theatre in the towns and townships of that country, but none of it overtly dealt with political themes. Fugard was able to position himself within this wealth of theatre, and through his collaboration with black theatre practitioners such as Zakes Mokae, John Kani, Winston Ntshona and a host of others in such groups as the Serpent Players of the coastal city of Port Elizabeth, he generated a new energy that drew from the politics of the time. Apartheid provided the stories. The less generous have even gone to the lengths of saying without apartheid there would be no Athol Fugard. He himself has said that without Zakes Mokae, John Kani and Winston Ntshona he would not have become the writer he is.[3] Secondly, Fugard has been one of the many writers in South Africa who have found the new dispensation quite harrowing.

Recently he confessed to a theatre writer of one of our newspapers that after 1994 he had stumbled across the landscape of South Africa, lost, unsure of his relevance, and depressed that he might have lost his purpose as a human being and writer. He told the journalist: 'After the democratic transition, I had a sense that I had outlived my time and become redundant, because I was a voice that plugged into the energy and the conflicts of the old South Africa. I can't deny that. Those conflicts – those rights and wrongs, dos and don'ts – were a very energizing factor in my writing.'[4]

Fugard further says that he was able to rescue himself from the wilderness of redundancy by redeeming his essential identity: that of a storyteller rather than a politician. Recently a new play by him, *Sorrows and Rejoicings*, opened in Cape Town. Many writers in my country – those who were very active during the apartheid era – have not managed to rescue themselves. The landscape of South Africa is strewn with the corpses of authors who were not able to survive liberation.

To understand this phenomenon one needs to recognise the fact that apartheid as a system was so absurd that it was possible to take a slice of real-life and put it on the stage or on the page without doctoring it and have a great piece of the theatre of the absurd. In the workshop method of creating plays that was made famous by such practitioners as Barney Simon, actors went out to the community, observed what was happening, seasoned it a bit with their own personal experience of apartheid – for indeed apartheid touched every aspect of everyone's life – and jointly with the directors created a great piece of theatre. Rarely did imagination interfere with the process.

This brought about the death of the author as apartheid appropriated to itself the role of creator. As a result many of our writers never learnt to use their imagination. They became mere reporters of the great drama that was being created by the absurdist creator of all – apartheid. When apartheid died, they died with it.

Besides being a great absurdist creator apartheid delineated a world of good and evil. And as always, that was the stuff of great conflict. Often unidimensional conflict, but conflict all the same. In my travels in Europe I met a German film-maker who told me: 'We really envied you during apartheid because you could draw from such a clear-cut world of good and evil whilst we had to struggle to interpret a complex society that was replete with ambiguities.'

In the post-apartheid era South Africa is no longer just black and white. There are shades of grey. We are now faced with complexities and ambiguities that we need to interpret. We have become normal and ordinary. To create an exciting drama from the daily narrative of our lives we need to draw from the depths of imagination. But we never really learnt to use our imagination. A newspaper theatre critic observed: 'The strong contrasts of good and evil, us and them, right and wrong, made for boldness that today's complexities and ambiguities don't. Opposition stimulated creation: social compliance has not.'[5]

The content was the thing. It was enough for many of these writers to create the kind of theatre that uttered the correct sentiments and shouted the most popular of slogans. Solidarity audiences overlooked any flaws in form and structure. Theatre was a mobilisational force, and for many a practitioner, supported by an audience eager to be rallied to action, it was fulfilment enough that the theatre effectively served that function.

It is a telling fact that the most vibrant theatre in South Africa today emanates from practitioners who had not reached any measure of maturity at the height of apartheid. They are able to plug into the energies of a new South Africa with ease, and to address new themes, while exploring new creative forms. They were never really part of the old culture of reportage and of sloganeering.

Many of them continue to draw from the workshop methods developed and refined by the old practitioners. But since the world is no longer just black and white, and there are shades now that present complications that need further examination and reinterpretation, the new practitioner cannot but draw from the well of imagination to create riveting theatre. An example of this was *Fong Kong*, a play created by the students of the Market Theatre Laboratory and performed at the National Festival of the Arts in Grahamstown in July 2000 and on the professional stages of the Market Theatre in August of the same year. It has since had a number of revivals, the most recent being at the United Nations World Conference against Racial Discrimination, Xenophobia and Related Intolerances in Durban from August 31 to September 7, 2001.

The play is about the new scourge that has attacked the cities of South Africa: xenophobia. Xenophobia is prevalent mostly among working class and un-employed South Africans who blame foreigners for every woe that beset the country, ranging from crime and AIDS to the theft of their jobs and of their women by the hordes that are descending from the north. But South Africa's xenophobia is of a peculiar kind. It assumes a racist complexion. South Africans are not bothered by the influx of white foreigners from Eastern Europe, and to a lesser extent the immigrants from Pakistan and China. The foreigners that black and white South Africans hate are the black ones from other African countries and from the Americas. And the darker they are the less acceptable they become in South African society.

This should be understood in the context of the hierarchy of colour that was established by the apartheid system. In spite of themselves South Africans have internalised the values that place whiteness at the top of a pyramid, followed by people of mixed blood known as Coloureds in South Africa, then people of Asiatic extraction, and at the bottom of the pile the indigenous black people. Some of those blacks who were lighter in complexion played Coloured in order to access more resources in the form of employment and educational oppor-tunities, and those Coloureds who were quite fair played white for access to even greater resources. The residue of this mindset persists even though we would very much like to deny that. The fact that on average the Africans from the countries north of South Africa are perceived to be much darker in complexion than the 'normal' black South African reinforces black South Africans' complexes of superiority.

The ruling classes and the intelligentsia claim to have been greatly embarrassed by this racist xenophobia. A few years ago the United Nations High Commission for Refugees and a statutory body called the South African Human Rights Commission launched the Roll Back Xenophobia Campaign. But it is obviously receiving half-hearted support from other crucial government organs. Rarely does one hear government ministers speak out against xenophobia. Instead one has seen television programmes where black South Africans are complaining bitterly about black Americans who have come into the country in great numbers since 1994. And the irony of it all is that the very people who are complaining are the community leaders from various spheres of South African life who shout the loudest about the African Renaissance. This tells us that racial xenophobia is not only confined to the ranks of the unemployed in search of a scapegoat, but it is an ailment that is also found among the national elites. The second irony is that there has never been any television programme about the presence of white Americans who have come to South Africa in even greater numbers for the same purposes – mostly business – as African Americans.

The title of the play, *Fong Kong*, refers to the fake Nikes and Reeboks from China that have found their way into the sidewalk markets of Johannesburg and other cities of South Africa. By extension *fong kong* refers to anything that is not genuine, including immigrants – illegal and otherwise – who have flocked into the country from other African countries and from such diverse countries as Bangladesh and Bulgaria.

The director of the play, Richard Manamela, says the seed for the play was planted one morning in the inner-city area of Johannesburg called Hillbrow when he saw a black policeman rudely pushing an old black woman and called her *kwerekwere*, a very derogatory word for black people from African countries north of the Limpompo River which separates South Africa from Zimbabwe. The starting point of the play was the word itself.

Actors came together and shared stories and presented their own experiences of xenophobia. They read newspaper stories on the subject and invited refugees from other African countries who are on the receiving end of xenophobia to share their experiences.

The result was a very entertaining play created in the highly stylised mode of theatre that was made famous by the Market Theatre in the years of apartheid. Fifteen actors – five females and ten males – took the audience through the journey of a South African who poses as an immigrant from Malawi with the hope of deriving certain benefits, only to find that he is seriously regarded as one, and is subjected to a harrowing treatment, including detention at the infamous Lindelani Centre where illegal immigrants are locked up for weeks on end before they are deported to their countries. The play is both poignant and humorous. It presents the problems without providing any answers because its creators merely wished to put xenophobia on the agenda. Manamela says, 'We left it hanging so that people should start thinking about xenophobia and decide where we go from here.'

Hallelujah! is another play that addresses, among other issues, xenophobia. Unlike *Fong Kong*, which uses the workshop method whereby the director and actors come together to jointly create a play, this one was scripted by a single author, Xoli Norman, a young playwright who has emerged from the loins of the Market Theatre. Unlike the fast-paced and energetic performance styles that have come to be associated with South African theatre created by black practitioners and their white collaborators such as Barney Simon, Norman's play relies on a more naturalistic setting and acting style. It is variously an angry and a celebratory play. Its anger is directed at black people who are full of self-hate, manifested through the way they rape and kill each other, and the way they mistreat other black people from foreign countries. Black people's merciless self-examination and self-criticism caused quite a stir when this play was performed at the Market Theatre. A minority of black opinion leaders objected to it, claiming that it was 'exposing' blacks to those white compatriots who are of a racist orientation, who would seize at the message to reinforce their racist agenda.

The majority view of the play was very positive. Hence it performed to full houses throughout its six-week season and received rave reviews, especially in all the media that are run by blacks, and are targeted primarily at black consumers.

Performed by three actors who portray a poet, his mentor and his fiancée, and a three-piece jazz band, the play also celebrates our performance poetry culture and the thriving culture of jazz – particularly the South African brand of jazz. The playwright, an accomplished trumpeter, also composed its original music.

The two plays I have mentioned here illustrate quite vividly that even more than the necessary reconciliation between black and white South Africans, there is a need for reconciliation among blacks themselves. This is an area that has been neglected by the political establishment. Hence there has been no attempt to heal the deep wounds that the blacks have inflicted on one another, and on themselves, in response to even deeper wounds inflicted on them by the apartheid system. These wounds remain unattended today. Many of them are embedded very deeply in our psyche, while on the outside one may see scars that look quite healed. The damage manifests itself in our physical and sexual abuse of those we profess to love, who also happen to be those who are deemed less powerful than us: women and children. By 'us' here I am obviously referring to the black male, who wields the political power but is still grappling to regain some measure of economic power.

The plays further illustrate that one essential ingredient of reconciliation is tolerance. This is very crucial in a society that recognises diverse cultural identities while fiercely protecting individual rights. The constitution of the country itself places individual rights above group rights. It protects, for instance, an individual's gender, an individual's religion or lack thereof, and an individual's sexual orientation, above the rights of groups that may have strong views one way or the other on issues of gender, religion and sexual orientation. Individuals are free to reject inherited cultural identities and adopt new ones. Therefore the respect of multicultural identities does not necessarily imply a guarantee of the survival of any culture, even though political rhetoric may suggest the government is out to preserve cultures that are perceived to be endangered. This would be an impossible task.

In my view the diverse South African theatre that attempts to address these issues is more of a theatre of reconciliation than the theatre that dominated South African stages in the Mandela era, that went out of its way to deal with reconciliation as a theme. And it is a dynamic theatre that is not only seen at the so-called mainstream venues in the cities, but in the townships and villages as well. It is seen at national and community theatre festivals. It ranges from the highly physical theatre of Andrew Buckland and Bheki Mkhwane in *Makana*, to Athol Fugard's wordy confessional in *Sorrows and Rejoicings*, and to the varied works of the playwrights who feature in the annual Barney Simon Young Writers' Festival at the Market Theatre.

Makana opened at the National Festival of the Arts in Grahamstown at the end of June 2001, and transferred to the Market Theatre two months later. In a performance style that is forceful, fast, supple and athletic the play retrieves from the horn of plenty that is history the story of Makana, an amaXhosa prophet of the early 19th century who was incarcerated on Robben Island in 1819 and later drowned while attempting to escape by swimming across the channel. Through a combination of spoofery and seriousness the four actors who assume a myriad of roles show us how Makana is removed from his mother by the Christian missionaries after the death of his father, and how he is converted into Christianity and later gets disillusioned with a religion that is oppressing his people and grabbing their lands for colonial settlement. He prepares for war against the English and attacks Grahamstown to reclaim the land that was stolen. The battle that follows is presented as a present-day boxing match. In the ring we have the British and the Xhosa slugging it out, with a ringside commentator giving a blow-by-blow account of the historical battle as interpreted by the boxers in the ring. With the assistance of the Khoikhoi people the British defeat amaXhosa and Makana is shipped to Robben Island where he is preoccupied with building a boat in order to escape back to his people.

Makana is a mixed-media play, relying not only on the effective use of the bodies of the actors, but on song, on isiXhosa praise poetry, on noise, and on art installations that function as sets on which hang scanty costumes and props. The play also relies on African ritual, some of which would be regarded as sacred by its practitioners in its real-life social context. For instance the ritual of initiation where boys are circumcised into manhood is enacted. So is the ritual of slaughter of the beast that is sacrificed to the ancestors, and that would indeed send the Society for the Prevention of Cruelty to Animals in a frenzy, as has happened on many occasions in the previously all-white suburbs where middle-class blacks now reside and continue to practise their age-old customs of slaughtering beasts as a sacrifice to the ancestors.

My observation is that generally white playwrights are the only ones who have ventured into using African ritual on the theatrical stage. Blacks still hold these rituals in awe. Hence there was an outcry when another white playwright, Brett Bailey of the Third World Bunfight Company, featured real-life traditional healers, who are also religious figures in African communities, in his play titled *iMumbo Jumbo*. They performed the ritual dances outside their social context and in the context of the fictive world of the play. To many people this was tantamount to blasphemy.

Sorrows and Rejoicings opened at the Baxter Theatre in Cape Town at the end of August 2001. The American production moves to New York this December. It tells the story of Dawid, an Afrikaner poet who returns to South Africa after an exile of seventeen years. He had been an anti-apartheid activist at one of the major universities in South Africa, had married one of his students, and had left for London in the early 1980s in search of freedom 'to speak and be heard, to write and be read.' But exile drained him. He dried up and was unable to create poetry anymore. He hankered after his home in the Karoo semi-arid region of the southern tip of Africa. He identified strongly with his homeland. He even regarded the mispronunciation of his Afrikaner name Olivier into English Oliver as an erosion of his Afrikaner identity. (Issues of identity are emerging very strongly in South African discourse today.) He is diagnosed with leukaemia and returns to South Africa to die. In fact the whole play happens after his funeral. The three women in his life – his estranged wife, his coloured mistress with whom he has an illegitimate daughter, and the resentful daughter – gather in the living room of his Karoo house to piece together the story of his life. He features in memory sequences.

Another playwright, Anthony Ackerman, writing an assessment of the play for a publisher, says that the importance of this play lies in the fact that it links our political past to our political future. Although the play has very little intrigue and not much subtext or complexity, it signals Fugard's 'move away from dramatic realism to a style in which more "theatrical" devices, such as the above-mentioned memory sequences, could be deployed.' He concludes that this play is a testimony that Fugard has indeed reinvented himself.

Black playwrights have re-invented themselves too, as reflected by the plays in this year's Young Writers' Festival at the Market Theatre. One finds less of the themes that are overtly political and more on relationships. When politics are dealt with it is politics in a broader sense, such as the hypocrisy of religion and the politics of sex and sexual orientation. Remember that our constitution has freed gays and lesbians to be who they are. Prejudice, of course, remains in the minds of the people, in the same way that racism still exists even though it has been outlawed.

In conclusion let me reiterate that theatre is alive and well and living in South Africa. It does not only happen at the Market Theatre but at many other venues throughout the country. In Johannesburg alone it is possible to see two new plays every week for one whole year, with the average season of a play lasting six weeks. And here of course I am not talking only of those plays that are performed in purpose-built venues in the cities. The most vibrant yet under-funded theatre happens in makeshift venues in the marginalised areas of the city – in the townships and informal settlements.

Of course you will hear us moaning and whingeing that theatre is dying in South Africa. The truth is that South African theatre is dead only at venues like the Johannesburg Civic Theatre. This used to be one of the most important theatre venues. It is a glittering glass palace built for millions of rands by taxpayers' money – since it is owned by the city of Johannesburg. In an effort to have the theatre self-sustaining it was given over to a management that undertook to run it on business lines. The first thing the new management did was to change its name to Times Square at the Civic, creating, according to a local critic, 'the impression that the complex is being turned into a little corner of New York.'[6] Although the main stage is named after Nelson Mandela, the rest of the stages and restaurants carry such New York names as Off-Broadway Bytes and Spencer's ShowBiz Bar. This renaming, which suggests that the management of the institution is no longer interested in developing serious local theatre, is accompanied by the actual practice of sidelining local productions for imported ones, or for locally-produced Broadway and West End shows.

The Civic Theatre clearly reverses the gains that have been made by South African theatre internationally since apartheid. Here we see an institution that is owned by local government opting for short-term financial gain at the expense of long-term investment in South African products that have proved to be of high and exportable quality. We see government reinforcing American cultural hegemony in South Africa, seen already in the proliferation of American cultural products that are threatening to suffocate South Africa's. In their defence the management has declared that it is not in the business of 'arts and culture' but of 'entertainment', and in their view a Broadway worldview is more entertaining than a South African one. Yet the Civic Theatre management cannot escape the fact that they are purveyors of culture – American culture.

Theatre is alive and well in South Africa. It has merely adapted to the new conditions. It has not adapted enough though. The constitution of the new South Africa recognises eleven official languages. Yet almost all our theatre is created in English, and to a lesser extent in Afrikaans. This becomes the case even in the most marginalised areas, where English is in fact a foreign language. There is an unwritten law that theatre is only theatre if it is in English or at least in Afrikaans. The theatre practitioner takes his cue from the politician. Our political leaders address the masses in English deep in the rural areas of the Eastern Cape. Ordinary villagers never really understand what these politicians – born and bred in local communities and quite fluent in the languages of those communities – are trying to convey to them. All the villagers can say is, 'Hey, uyakhumsha lomfo!' – Hey, this man can really speak English. In parliament the members use the indigenous languages apologetically, and only to greet the Speaker of Parliament and to introduce the subject, and then the rest of the speech is in English.

The fact that community development begins with communication escapes our politicians. So does the fact that languages develop and grow with greater utilisation. Afrikaans, for instance, is a much younger language than Sesotho, isiZulu or isiXhosa. Yet today Afrikaans is a highly developed language of science and technology because it was utilised as a medium of instruction from the first year of schooling to post-doctoral level. It was also used extensively in commerce and industry, in the public sector, in literature and in theatre. Of course we know that some of the methods that were used to enforce it were quite coercive.

In a democratic South Africa the insistence on Afrikaans and English excludes the majority of the people who speak neither of these languages from the democratic process. It also takes the theatre further away from the people, and turns it into an elitist activity that it has become in the Western world. In South Africa we need to reach a stage where it is not a curiosity to see a play like *Wangishiya Wangesheya* by Mncedisi Shabangu which was all in the isiSwati language and *KaMshangana* by Obed Baloyi which was mostly in the Shangaan language. The fact that each one of these plays had a full season of six weeks of full houses at the Market Theatre tells us that the most effective theatre of reconciliation will be performed in the languages of the people.

Notes

1 Fugard, Athol, *People of the South*, television interview, South African Broadcasting Corporation, SABC2 TV, September 30, 2001.
2 Mda, Zakes 'Theater and Reconciliation in South Africa', *Theater* Volume 25 Number 3, 1995, Yale School of Drama/Yale Repertory Theater.
3 Fugard, Athol, *People of the South*, television interview, SABC2 TV, September 30, 2001.
4 van der Walt, Judy 'Fugard finds his voice in the new South Africa', *The Sunday Independent*, August 19, 2001.
5 Greig, Robert 'From revolt to anachronism', *The Sunday Independent*, September 23, 2001.
6 Kakaza, Luvuyo 'Broadway in Braamfontein?' *Hola* supplement to *The Sunday World*, September 9, 2001.

20 Masks and secrecy among the Chewa

Kenji Yoshida

Despite a recent marked increase in the literature on African masquerade and initiation, our understanding of those traditions in East Central Africa remains limited. Few reports have been written on those of the Chewa.[1] In this article I hope to offer new insights into Chewa masking traditions as well as the issue of secrecy and its role in delineating gender boundaries. My discussion focuses on rituals practised by men, but for a thorough understanding of these activities one must place them in the wider context of male–female interactions. Thus I conclude with an account of women's rituals, especially those associated with the girls' initiation ceremony, which is based on data collected by my wife, Mariko Yoshida.

Although masked rituals are practised throughout Chewaland, details of these traditions and the styles of masks differ from one area to another. My discussion derives from field research carried out between 1984 and 1986 in and around the village of Kaliza located in Chadiza District in the Eastern Province of the Republic of Zambia.[2]

Chewa society

One of the so-called Bantu peoples, the Chewa (pl. Achewa) live in the area where Zambia, Malawi, and Mozambique meet. Their total population is well over one million, and according to the 1969 census, those residing in Zambia numbered approximately 150,000.[3]

The Chewa are primarily farmers who grow mainly corn and raise some livestock as well. Only a few men hunt and then only sporadically, although some elders said this activity used to be more common. The basis of the Chewa social system is matrilineage. In the past, residence was uxorilocal, but in recent years many newly married couples have settled in the husband's home village. Husbands and wives retain their lineage affiliations; children are affiliated with the group of their mother and mother's brothers, in accordance with the principles of matrilineal inheritance and descent.

Almost all Chewa in Zambia are under the authority of a paramount chief called the Karonga Gawa Undi. There are also more than twenty regional chiefs, each region containing about one hundred villages with their own headmen, *mufumu*.[4]

Nyau as a semi-secret association

Nearly every Chewa boy between the ages of 12 and 15 is initiated into a masked association, and males are not considered to be adults until they join. Each village has its own association, but membership gained at one village holds good at any other. The association and its maskers are called *nyau*. The major function of the association is to perform masquerades at funerary rituals; these are accompanied by five male drummers and a women's chorus.

The masks used by *nyau* are divided into three types. The first is a feathered net mask and the second is a wooden face mask. Generally those who dance these masks are considered to embody the spirits of the dead and may simply be called *nyau*. They can be divided further into more than fifty characters, each with its own name, songs, way of dancing, mask, and costume. People identify each *nyau* character by its name and the content of the accompanying song. The mask is not necessarily helpful in this regard; my informants told me that even though some of the *nyau* characters have masks of specific forms, dancers are free to replace them with feathered masks.

The third type of *nyau* mask is a large zoomorphic basketry structure that envelops the entire body of the dancer. Because many of these structures turn around and around in their dance, they are collectively called *nyau yolemba*, '*nyau* that draw (circles on the ground).' There is a large variety of *nyau yolemba*, most of them portraying wild animals.

Women and children are taught that *nyau* are dead people who have been revived and that *nyau yolemba* are real wild animals. When they ask what the *nyau* is, men simply answer: '*Nyau ni nyama*' ('The *nyau* is an animal'). They do not say the *nyau* is a dead person, since they consider the zoomorphic *nyau yolemba* to be more important than the other *nyau*. In any case, the existence of the masks themselves is kept secret. For almost one year after settling in a Chewa village, I was treated in the same manner as women and children: the men did not tell me anything that had to do with masks. The secret adamantly kept by association members is that the *nyau* is a man in disguise. It was revealed to me only after I was initiated into the association on May 25, 1985.[5]

The men have devised various means of keeping this secret: by using falsettos and nasalized voices for *nyau*; by making the masks, including *nyau yolemba*, in the bush distant from the village; and by giving special names to materials and tools used in making masks. Such secret terminology enables the men to conceal the content of their conversation from women and children. Finally, members use riddles to determine whether a newcomer is really a member of the association.

A member of *nyau* is not supposed to divulge to outsiders anything he sees or hears while engaged in association activities, including the special terminology and the riddles. If he should reveal the secret, it is said he will be cursed by a *nyau* instructor (*nyamkungwi*) and bleed to death from the nose.[6]

Nevertheless, in reality there are always men who try to seduce women by offering to reveal the secret, and it is quite common for a husband to disclose it to his wife. In practice, then, women do at least know that the *nyau* is a man. If, however, this disclosure is discovered, both parties to the affair are punished severely, regardless of gender (though probably not to the extent of death), and they are required to surrender substantial numbers of cattle. In addition, the woman concerned is forced to join the association. For this reason, women pretend to the last that they do not know the actual identity of the *nyau*. It may safely be said that Chewa society as a whole connives in constructing a pretense concerning the reality of *nyau*.

I do not mean to imply that the *nyau* dance is a mere performance. *Nyau* dancers believe they are possessed by the spirits of the dead or of the animals portrayed by the masks they wear. They say, 'We feel hot and light when we dance,' which indicates that their bodies have acquired some attributes of the spirits. This type of spirit possession differs from that which causes trance, for the dancer is still able to recognize every movement of the audience. Yet it is no less genuine. Appealing to *nyau* is considered to be equivalent to appealing to the spirits of the dead they embody. This is why *nyau* perform at funerary rituals.

The funerary ritual: description

The funerary ritual starts with *utaya*, the burial rite, and is completed by *bona*, a rite that takes place after the harvest of corn in the subsequent year. *Utaya* today is largely Christianized: the Bible is read and prayers are offered even when the deceased was not a Christian. Although elders said that *nyau* used to carry the corpse from the village to the grave on a stretcher, they now play no role in *utaya*. Burying the corpse, however, is still done only by members of the association, although they no longer disguise themselves as *nyau*.

By contrast, the *nyau* dance is indispensable to the rite of *bona*, which marks the end of mourning.[7] *Bona* is performed along with beer brewing. According to the Chewa, the beer is not only for the people attending the rite, but also for the spirits of the dead embodied by *nyau*. *Bona* takes place after the corn harvest because of the large quantities of the grain needed to produce the beer. First the corn is soaked in water for about two weeks until it germinates. The germinated corn, *cimera*, is the fermenting agent. When the *cimera* is ready, the actual brewing commences, a process that takes an additional two weeks or so. During this period the central part of the *bona* rite takes place. *Nyau* masqueraders come to the village every day to participate in the brewing.

On the evening before beer brewing is to begin, several groups of *nyau* dance in an area of open ground called *thambwe*, on the outskirts of the village. In front of men and women gathered there, a *nyau* leader declares the commencement of the ritual, saying, 'Tomorrow, women will start pounding corn in the village, and men will open a *dambwe* in the bush.' The *dambwe* is the secret place where men make the zoomorphic *nyau yolemba*. Women are told that men 'fish up' *nyau* out of water there. The day after the declaration, men and women begin their different tasks: making *nyau yolemba* and brewing beer.

That night the ceremony for initiation into *nyau* usually starts in the bush. In principle, the initiation must be performed along with a funerary rite, especially *bona*. While *nyau* are dancing in the *thambwe*, the initiates (*namwali*) led by an instructor (*nyamkungwi*) leave the village and head for the *liunde*, a place deep in the bush, where men have disguised themselves as *nyau*. As the group approaches, the instructor shouts to the distant darkness, 'We are bringing the dead,' referring to the *namwali*. *Nyau* members, some of them masked and others not, shout back in falsettos, 'The dead, the dead, ayi, ayi, ayi.' Crying these words, the group of *nyau* attack the *namwali* and beat them relentlessly with switches made of branches. Next there is an exchange of whipping between the *nyau* and the instructor trying to protect the *namwali*. Afterward the *namwali* are gathered in one place. *Nyau* members stand in front of them and admonish each in turn by recounting a novice's past wrong doings and then whipping him severely:

> Today you have seen us at the place of *nyau*. From now on, stop being childish. Never again step inside the bedroom of your mother and father. Never touch cooking pots used by women. Stop your childish behavior. You sneaked into your uncle's field and stole some sweet potatoes, didn't you? Never do that again. Otherwise you will die.

On the same night the instructor appoints a tutor (*phungu*) for the *namwali*. Thereafter the *namwali* lodge with the tutor, and in the daytime they stay in the bush with the men preparing for the funeral. In this way they learn the secret *nyau* terminology and riddles as well as how to make masks, including *nyau yolemba*. The *namwali* should never be seen by women or children during the initiation.

The first riddle taught in the initiation is '*Nyau ni ciani? Nyau ni muntu*' (What is the *nyau*? The *nyau* is a human).[8] For the boys who until then had been taught that the *nyau* is an animal (*Nyau ni nyama*'), and would have been subjected to severe punishment for using any other word but *nyama* to describe the *nyau*, the new teaching implies a complete reversal of their view of the world.

It is customary for every member of the association to make his own feathered or wooden mask and to wear it on appropriate ritual occasions as long as it lasts. Although a mask might be commissioned from a man with a well-known talent for carving, there are no professional carvers as such. *Nyau yolemba*, on the other hand, are jointly made by members of the *nyau* every time there is a *bona*, and are burned when the ritual is over. The method of making *nyau yolemba* is as follows. First, the perimeter of the bottom of the structure is drawn on the ground, and branches are planted along the outline at equal intervals. By tying crosspieces to the branches, a sort of basket is made to serve as a frame. The men then cover the frame with grass, attaching it by passing strings crosswise and lengthwise. Up to this point the method is an application of the technique used by men in roofing. Finally, husks of corn are placed between the strings to cover the entire structure. It takes at least three days to make a single *nyau yolemba*, and most of the time is spent tucking the husks between the strings.

While the men are involved in making *nyau yolemba* and educating the novices in the bush, the women are brewing beer in the village. Every time the brewing process reaches a new stage, a small number of *nyau* called *kasinja* appear in the village to help. *Kasinja* wears a mask of loose net covered with the feathers of guinea fowl and chickens, and a short skirt made of torn bark. Female relatives of the deceased wail when they come, because *kasinja* is said to embody the spirit of the deceased (*ciwanda*), which is believed to stay on the earth and roam in and outside the village even after the corpse is buried. The feathers, particularly of guinea fowl and chickens – both ground birds – allude to the elusive but earthbound nature of the deceased's spirit.

After helping with the brewing for a while, *kasinja* start ridiculing some of the women by mentioning and making joking references to their genitals. Those ridiculed in turn make fun of the *nyau* in the same way. These exchanges occur every time *kasinja* come to the village, and they continue for hours. For the Chewa, referring to the genitals of another person is the greatest insult. In everyday life the mere use of such words would stir public discussion. However, these insults are considered acceptable between relatives in a joking relationship, especially between cross cousins. As the preferred form of marriage is between cross cousins, the exchange of insults between *kasinja* and women suggests that the living, represented by the women, and the spirit of the deceased, embodied by *kasinja*, have entered into a very close relationship, similar to that of joking and marriage partners. This is supposed to console the spirit of the deceased.

During the brewing period, *nyau* named *kang'wing'wi* also appear in the village occasionally to chase away women and children, steal livestock for the men staying in the bush, and collect corn husks for making *nyau yolemba*. While *kang'wing'wi* looks just like *kasinja* and is also considered to embody the spirit of the deceased, this masquerade is characterized by his high voice and fierce behavior.

On the night before the last day of brewing, at a special place set inside the village, all the available *nyau* and *nyau yolemba* appear and dance one after another until dawn. *Kasinja* and *kang'wing'wi* appear most frequently. Others include *kalamba*, *makanja*, and *cayakamoto*.

Kalamba, which means 'old man', is said to portray an old man who died long ago. He wears a wooden face mask and a piece of animal skin tied around his waist, and holds a stick in his hand. His appearance is designed to resemble that of a typical Chewa male elder. This is an example of the song to which *kalamba* dances:

> *Mau yanga wano*
> *Nkuti, nkaimba*
> *Na chule womwe*
> *Mang'ombe*
>
> My own voice
> If I say, if I sing,
> Even a frog answers

Makanja dances on stilts, a feat that requires much training. Although *makanja* is supposed to wear a wooden face mask, its dancers frequently don feathered masks used by *kasinja*. Many Chewa who report having seen spirits say, 'The ghost was so tall that I had to raise my eyes to see it.' Some, therefore, consider that stilt-dancing *makanja* portrays such a spirit. Others, however, say *makanja* represents a kind of water fowl with long legs, because he sometimes dances to a song in which a water fowl is mentioned.

Cayakamoto means 'that which is on fire'. The dancer sets fire to numerous strings attached all over his body and runs around in the dark. He is supposed to portray a sorcerer who has concealed himself in the flames.

Various kinds of *nyau yolemba* appear along with these *nyau*. The men have spent many days in the bush constructing them for this particular night. Praising their effort, a *nyau* leader makes an announcement like this one whenever a *nyau yolemba* appears on the scene:

> Be quiet, be quiet,
> This, this, this, this, this, animal.
> This one has come from Lavu village.
> It is the heart of Joseph, a son of Mrs. Dyenji.

The women respond,

> Aaaa Joseph,
> That is wonderful, in his house.
> Joseph. Joseph eeee.

The leader thus announces the name of the central person involved in the making of the *nyau yolemba*. Although to association members, the line 'It is the heart of Joseph' means 'It is Joseph who made the *nyau yolemba*', the women are supposed to interpret the same sentence as 'It is Joseph who has caught hold of the animal'. That is why they answer, 'That is wonderful (to keep such a big animal), in his house.'

The *nyau yolemba* that appear include *mkhango* (lion), *fisi* (hyena), *fulu* (tortoise), *galimoto* (automobile), *nswala* (impala), *ng'ombe* (cow), *kacala* (fingers), and *kasiya maliro* ('that which abandons the deceased').

On one occasion *galimoto* appeared on the assumption that the deceased, who used to drive a car when he was alive, would come back from the grave to the village by car. A *kasinja* that embodied the spirit of the deceased 'drove' *galimoto* but got out of it occasionally to dance. It is reported that in some other areas, this type of *nyau yolemba* appears together with a *nyau* portraying a European (Makumbi 1963: 60; Faulkner 1988: 31).

The *nyau yolemba* known as *kacala* (fingers) derives its name from the long fingers at the end of the arms extended from its cone-shaped body. The Chewa believe that the sorcerer who uses medicines to curse people to death digs graves open with his long fingers and eats the flesh of the victims. *Kacala* portrays the sorcerer.

Around midnight the *nyau yolemba* called *kasiya maliro* appears. *Kasiya maliro*, 'that which abandons the deceased', is built in the form of an eland. When it comes the women present sing a song like the following:

> *Iwe edee*
> *Wakwenyerera*
> *Suuja umakana kale*

You
You have finally come close,
Though you always said you
didn't want to

Kasiya maliro is normally taken into the house of the deceased that night and left there. At dawn, as the all-night masquerades begin to come to an end, *kasiya maliro* comes out of the house, dances before the people, and returns to the bush, where it is immediately burned. The house of the deceased may also be destroyed soon after.[9]

As I said earlier, according to the Chewa the spirit of the deceased (*ciwanda*) remains on the earth after the burial to roam in and outside the village. Many people say they have actually seen ghosts, and rumours circulate of sightings of the deceased transformed into an animal. In contrast, the Chewa believe that ancestral spirits (*mzimu*), which are invisible like the wind, are freely moving around the world. *Kasiya maliro* is kept in the house of the deceased to capture the lingering *ciwanda*. When *kasiya maliro* is finally burned and its smoke disappears into the wind, it is thought that the spirit of the deceased also disappears into the wind and becomes an ancestral spirit.

The *namwali* eat the ashes of *kasiya maliro* as medicine to make them immune to the hotness of the deceased's spirit. This is the reason why initiation into *nyau* is normally held along with funerary rituals.[10] After the ashes are administered, the *namwali* are taken to their parents by the instructor (*nyamkungwi*) and by *kang'wing'wi* masquerades. At each *namwali's* home, the parents say to their child:

Today, you have grown up. From now on, you should not step into the bedroom of your parents. You should build your own house and live there on your own. Also, you should never touch cooking pots. That is the business of women. Watch your manners. You have grown up. From now on, you can take part in the funerary rituals as a full-grown man.

This last line signifies that the boy has been officially accepted as a member of *nyau*, whose activities are mostly performed in the course of funerary rituals.

The *namwali* are normally sent home on the day following the all-night masquerades. This is also the day when the beer matures. The people, having danced and sung all night, drink beer all day. Masquerading resumes shortly after noon. This is the only occasion during the *bona* when organized masquerade performances occur during the day. It is thought of as an opportunity for the dead to return to this world to welcome their new member. The performances on this occasion include the appearance of a *nyau* called *mbiyazodooka* ('a broken pot'), which portrays a person returned from the grave, holding a fragment of the pot that was buried with him. Red earth peculiar to the graveyard is smeared on the entire body of the dancer, who wears no mask.

The last day of the ritual is the day for *kaole dothi*, the discarding of ashes. Ashes produced by the beer brewing are left by *kasinja* at a dump outside the village. These *nyau* then visit each of the deceased's relatives, a practice called *utambitsa*. Their arrival prompts the female relatives to wail, for it is believed that the spirit of the deceased is coming to say good-bye. Having seen all the relatives, the *kasinja* leave the village and disappear. Women are not told that the *nyau yolemba* containing the spirit of the deceased was burned; for them, the final departure of the deceased from the world is signified by the *kasinja* vanishing into the bush.

The funerary ritual: exegesis

The central part of the funeral ritual is the all-night performance at which a number of *nyau yolemba* appear. An elder explained to me the reason *nyau yolemba* in the form of wild animals appear on this occasion:

> God (or the Creator, *mlengi*) originally created humans and animals. Humans and animals therefore lived happily together in the very old days. Even when humans got hungry, they only had to look up in the sky and say, 'Shomo *mlengi*' (God have mercy), and animals would die of their own accord and provide meat. However, because humans started feeling jealous of one another and began using sorcery, God became angry and separated animals from humans. Since then, it has become necessary for humans to chase and hunt animals when they get hungry. Animals, on the other hand, started running away from humans, and if they encountered humans by chance, they began hurting them or causing them illness. But even today, during the *bona* rite, that is, when the deceased return to God, animals remember the old days and come back to the village. Then they cry for the deceased together with humans.

This mythic narrative recalls the lyrics of the song sung when *kasiya maliro* appears in the village: 'You have finally come close, though you always said you didn't want to.' It is supposed that when the spirit of the deceased, which has remained on the earth, finally returns to the place 'where it originally came from, that is, to God, the world itself is also restored to its original state in which humans and animals live in harmony. This is why the zoomorphic *nyau yolemba* are instrumental in sending the spirit of the deceased back to God.

The idea of returning to an original state is also implied by the way space is organized for the ritual. Throughout the period of brewing beer, almost all men remain in the bush, and women in the village. The distinction between bush (*thengo*) and village (*mudzi*), or inside (*mkati*) and outside (*kubwalo*) the village, is rigorously observed. In particular, *nyau yolemba*, constructed in the bush, never enter the village until the last stage of the ritual. Before then, any performances by *nyau yolemba* occur in the open ground (*thambwe*) on the outskirts of the village.

There are, however, some *nyau* that commute between the bush and the village almost every day throughout the weeks of beer brewing. They are *kasinja* and *kang'wing'wi*, which embody the spirit of the deceased. As already noted, the Chewa believe that while the body of the deceased is buried in the graveyard beyond the bounds of the village, the spirit, once separated from the corpse, keeps returning to the village. The commuting by *kasinja* and *kang'wing'wi* corresponds to this belief.

The other *nyau*, which are said to portray the dead of the more distant past, as well as animals, sorcerers, and Europeans, dance in the *thambwe* together with *nyau yolemba*, but they do not play major roles during the brewing period. Association members explicitly said that at the beginning they had few types of *nyau* and that they have created many new ones since then. The functional difference found among *nyau* might be the result of a historical proliferation of *nyau* characters.

In considering the whole context of *nyau*, the women who brew beer with masqueraders and sing songs for them must also be taken into account. The world of *nyau* consists of three parts: *nyau yolemba* (wild animals), standing for those living outside the village; *kasinja* and *kang'wing'wi* (the spirit of the deceased), which enjoy a dual existence both inside and outside the village; and the women, representing those who live within the village.

On the occasion of the all-night masquerading, when *nyau yolemba* make their appearance, the distinction between 'inside' and 'outside' the village is denied. On that night, *kasiya maliro* enters the deceased's house, captures his spirit, and returns to the bush the next morning. The spirit of the deceased, which was violating this distinction, is thus removed from the village by a wild animal. Taken out of the village, it is then separated from the earth in fire and smoke, and becomes an ancestral spirit. Considered in regard to the deceased, the funerary ritual is a means of transformation into an ancestral spirit; considered in regard to the living, it is a process for re-establishing the border between village and bush.

This helps to explain why there are exceptions to the general definitions of *nyau* and *nyau yolemba*. *Nyau yolemba*, which are said to portray only wild animals, include representations of cattle, automobiles, and sorcerers; and *nyau* which are said to portray the dead, include representations of sorcerers and Europeans. Association members themselves say that cattle and cars are 'things which originally did not exist in the Chewa village'. Indeed, cattle were not introduced until the end of the nineteenth century, when the Chewa were conquered by the pastoralist Ngoni. Therefore cattle and cars are seen as being not of the village, but rather of the bush, and thus, belong to the same category as wild animals. The same applies to sorcerers portrayed by *kacala* and *cayakamoto*; viewed as beings to be ousted from the village, and thus belonging in the bush, they are also classified with wild animals. Europeans are similarly categorized, for neither do they have their place in the village. In sum, any *nyau* that do not fit either of the prescribed definitions of *nyau* as 'the dead who have been revived' or of *nyau yolemba* as 'wild animals' are classed as exterior to the village.

The creation of *nyau* characters always upholds the distinction between village and bush. New characters can only take the form of types external to the village, a fact that explains the eclecticism of *nyau*. The recent introduction of Europeans and cars into the range of *nyau* characters does not signal the destruction of traditional culture by modernity; it is rather to be understood as a development quite in accord with inherent principles of *nyau* tradition.

Finally, there remains one question. Why, of all *nyau yolemba*, is the one built in the form of an eland called *kasiya maliro* ('that which abandons the deceased'), and why is it in charge of transforming the deceased's spirit into an ancestral spirit – the ultimate purpose of the funerary ritual? In reality, the *nyau yolemba* of the eland is occasionally replaced by the one of the impala (*nswala*), another antelope, but never by any other *nyau yolemba*. Why then are antelopes selected for such an important task?

Unfortunately, I have not been able to obtain an answer to this question from the Chewa themselves. Nevertheless, considering the position of the antelope in their taxonomy of animals, the answer can to an extent be deduced as follows. The antelope is a wild animal of the bush and the source of a large quantity of delicious meat. The process of bearing the spirit of the deceased away from the village must be entrusted to an animal living outside the village, in the bush. In addition, since it must invite the spirit of the deceased into itself, the animal must be of the kind the spirit would be willing to approach. Furthermore, because the ashes of the *nyau yolemba*, which bore the spirit of the deceased, are 'eaten', or taken as medicine by the novices of *nyau*, the animal portrayed by the *nyau yolemba* must be an edible one. It follows that the animal most suitable to the task is the antelope, which lives deep in the bush and is difficult to capture, but whose meat is considered as delicious as that of cows and goats. The antelope would easily attract the spirit and take it far into the bush.

The Chewa say that if the dead are merely buried, they cannot be born again, being tied to the earth. The role played by the *nyau* at the *bona* ritual is to enable the spirits of the deceased to leave the earth and return to God; as ancestral spirits, they can be reincarnated in the bodies of their descendants. Among many dances performed by the Chewa, the *nyau* dance is distinguished by its name, *gule wamkulu*, 'the great dance'. Although words of prayer are never uttered by the participants in the dance, it is also called *pemphero lalikulu*, 'the great prayer', precisely because it is considered the most effective means of controlling the spirits of the deceased.

Men in charge of death, women in charge of birth

We have seen how Chewa men organize the *nyau* masking association to perform funerary rituals, and how these rituals also provide boys with the opportunity for initiation into manhood. There is also a girls' initiation ceremony, *cinamwali*. Just as knowledge about *nyau* masks is kept secret from women, so the teachings given in *cinamwali* are kept secret from men. In this way, the world of men and that of women are clearly differentiated. A brief investigation of *cinamwali* will help place the activities of the *nyau* in a wider context.

During *cinamwali* a girl who has reached the age of puberty is secluded in a house for a certain period of time and is taught the manners and accomplishments required of an adult woman.[11] Like the *nyau* novice, the girl to be initiated is called *namwali*. The other participants in *cinamwali* are limited to women who have already gone through the ceremony. For this reason, the data on *cinamwali* was mostly collected by my wife.[12]

When a girl has her first menstruation, a tutor (*phungu*) is selected for her from among the adult women in the village. The tutor educates and takes care of her throughout the ceremony. The first word said to the girl after she has been secluded is *mwakula*, meaning 'You have grown up'. The girl is then taught how to use a piece of cloth during menstruation and told never to let the cloth be seen by men. She is also warned not to reveal to men any of the things she will learn in the ceremony. The content of the teachings, presented mostly through songs and dancing, can be classified into two types: instruction in womanly manners and practical instruction in sex and childbearing.

In the past the *namwali* were taken to the bush for the last stage of the ceremony. There, clay figures (*vilengo*) were made by the tutor, and the *namwali* were taught to dance around those figures. We asked two elderly women in Kaliza village to reproduce *vilengo* after about a forty-year break in their manufacture.

Most of the figures they made had something to do with water: a python (*nsato*), a snake called *tunga*, a crocodile (*ng'ona*), a tortoise (*fulu*), and a vessel for drawing water (*kacifulu*). They were made the same way women usually make pottery. Every figure was decorated with red, white, and black dots, in imitation of the spotted pattern of the python.

No such clay figures are made in today's *cinamwali*, which has adopted many elements of another girls' initiation ceremony, *cisungu*, practiced by the neighboring Nsenga people.[13] However, when the girl returns to her parents, her body is painted with red, white, and black dots, and she is welcomed by the other women with this song:

> *Dzaone nanga dzaone*
> *Namwali dzaone*
> *Ukaone cili kumbuyo*
> *Cati mwanga ngati nsato*
> *Dzaone nanga dzaone*

> Look, hey look!
> It's the girl who has grown up, look!
> Look at the one on the back
> She has the colours and pattern of the python
> Look, hey look!

The python is considered a messenger (*wamthenga*) of God (*mlengi* or *cauta*) who brings rainfall and ensures the fertility of the land and human beings. Through *cinamwali*, girls are initiated into a condition of existence like the python's, and hence the fertility of the land and human beings.

It is clear that the major concern of *cinamwali* is reproduction. This is in sharp contrast to the men's *nyau* association, which is in charge of funerary ritual. The men of the *nyau* actually say, 'Because women make a secret of birth, we make a secret of death.' Chewa men are excluded from witnessing births and are never told how a child is born. That information belongs only to the women who have completed *cinamwali*. On the other hand, that men 'make a secret of death' means that funerary rituals are controlled by the men of the *nyau* association and that the process of transforming the spirit of the deceased into an ancestral spirit is concealed from women.

While the fact that women are in charge of birth is a biological inevitability, that men are in charge of death is a cultural invention. Interestingly, according to a legend known to *nyau* members, *nyau yolemba* were originally created to imitate the clay animal figures made by women at the *cinamwali* ceremony. In addition, *nyau* members proudly say, 'The women's figures do not move, but the *nyau yolemba* we make can be worn and made to dance.'

It is difficult to tell whether the legend suggests a historical process in which men start making *nyau* masks. However, considering men's pride in their masks, it may safely be said that by making masks and controlling funerals, men are still trying to emulate the self-evident role of women in childbirth. It is as if through these means men meant to establish themselves in the cosmological cycle of life and death.

Victor Turner makes somewhat similar observations about the Ndembu, with whom the Chewa are supposed to have historical connections:

> It is interesting that the main theme of Mukanda [the boys' initiation ceremony in which masquerades are performed] should be productive activity (i.e. hunting), while that of Nkang'a [girls' initiation ceremony] should be reproductive activity. Women's economic activity, which is, when all is said and done, essential to the existence of the community, is hardly ritualised at all, while that of men is steeped with ritual.
>
> (Turner 1967: 8)

As David Binkley has already noted (1990: 157), many scholars, including Turner, discuss masquerade either as an expression of gender differences or as a means of releasing tensions that arise between men and women. However, I would suggest an alternative scenario for the Chewa: masquerade is a means of creating differences between men and women, rather than a mere representation or arbitrator of existing gender differences. It is through an active process of contrasting the *nyau* masquerade and *cinamwali* ceremony that the experience of manhood and womanhood, of death and life, is realized.[14]

Notes

Field research for this article was carried out between March 1984 and March 1986, when I was affiliated with the Institute for African Studies (I.A.S.), University of Zambia. My research was made possible by a 1983 Noma Asian and African Scholarship.

I would like to express my heartfelt thanks to all who supported me in this long-term field research, especially to Dr Steven P. C. Moyo, then Director of I.A.S.; Mrs. Ilse Mwanza, Research Affiliate Officer of the same institute; and Dr Mwesa I. Mapoma, then Director of the Centre for the Arts, University of Zambia. I would also like to thank Dr John Picton, Head of the Department of Art and Archaeology, School of Oriental and African Studies, University of London; Dr John Mack, Keeper of the Museum of Mankind (the Ethnography Department of the British Museum); and Mr Christopher Spring, Curator of the Museum of Mankind, for reading and commenting on the first draft of this manuscript.

I am also grateful to Mr Moses Gabriel Phiri, my assistant throughout the period of the research, and the people of Kaliza village and its vicinity, who warmly received my wife, Mariko Yoshida, and me. Lastly, I wish to note the generosity of Chief Mwangala and the members of *nyau* and *cinamwali* in his region in allowing me to disclose some of the secrets of initiation.

1 They include those by Hodgson (1933), Rangeley (1949, 1950), Marwick (1968), Blackmun and Schoffeleers (1972), Schoffeleers (1976), Kubik (1987), and Faulkner (1988). Mapopa Mutonga, a Zambian scholar, has also written a dissertation on Chewa masked rituals (Mapopa 1980). Unfortunately, it remains unpublished.

2 The article's 'ethnographic present' refers to the 1984–86 period of research.

3 To prevent so-called tribalism the census of the population of each ethnic group in Zambia has not been published since 1969.

4 Chewa words are written in italics, and nouns are given in one form, usually the singular. The spelling of Chewa words follows the prevailing convention in Zambia. Notable departures from the usual English pronunciation are limited to the following: *c* is pronounced as in *church*; the *h* in *ph*, *kh*, or *th*, adds an extra puff of breath to these consonants.

5 I went through the initiation ceremony into the *nyau* association with three boys. It began on May 25 and lasted until May 27. The ceremony was performed basically as described in the text, except that it was held independent of the funerary ritual (see note 10).

6 Since I have obtained permission to reveal some *nyau* secrets for 'educational purposes', I believe that the *nyau* instructor at Kaliza village will not curse me.

7 Although *nyau* dance only at the *bona* of members of the association and distinguished personages in the community, the Chewa people consider that the masquerade at a person's *bona* can also deal with all the recently deceased members of his or her family.

8 To avoid any disclosure of the secrets of the *nyau* not directly required for the purpose of exposition, the other riddles and confidential terminology are not presented here.

9 If the bereaved express their wish to keep the house of the deceased, *kasiya maliro* is not taken into it. Instead, it dances over and over again in front of the house. It is believed that the dance enables *kasiya maliro* to absorb the spirit of the deceased.

10 Increasingly in recent years, masquerades are performed independent of funerary ritual, on the pretext of entertaining ancestors. Some initiation ceremonies are conducted on these occasions. However, boys initiated into *nyau* through ceremonies unconnected with the funerary ritual are not considered fully qualified members of the association until they take the ashes of *kasiya maliro* in the *bona*.

11 The length of the period of seclusion, that is, of the *cinamwali* ceremony, depends on how fast the girl learns and how well she behaves; roughly speaking, it is between three weeks and three months.

12 First she received the necessary education privately from an elderly woman of the village of Kaliza, and then she participated in the ceremonies held in the neighbouring villages. The proceedings of the ceremonies were all, with permission, recorded on tape, and I am responsible for the translation and analysis of the collected data.

13 As has become well known through the work of Audrey Richards (1956), the Bemba of Northern Zambia also call their girls' initiation ceremony *cisungu*. This type of ceremony is widely practised among the so-called Eastern and Southern Bantu.

14 For further discussion of *nyau* and *cinamwali*, see Yoshida 1992.

References

Binkley, D. A. 1990. 'Masks, Space and Gender in Southern Kuba Initiation Ritual', *Iowa Studies in African Art: The Stanley Conferences at the University of Iowa*, 3: 157–76.

Blackmun, B. and J. M. Schoffeleers, 1972. 'Masks of Malawi', *African Arts* 5, 4: 36–41, 69, 88.

Central Statistical Office, 1973. *Census of Population and Housing 1969, Final Report, vol II(c) – Eastern Province*. Lusaka: Central Statistical Office, Zambia.

Faulkner, L. B. 1988. 'Basketry Masks of the Chewa', *African Arts* 21, 3: 28–31, 86.

Hodgson, A. G. O. 1933. 'Notes on the Achewa and Angoni of the Dowa District of the Nyasaland Protectorate', *The Journal of the Royal Anthropological Institute of Great Britain and Ireland* 63: 123–64.

Kubik, G. and M. A. Malamusi, 1987. *Nyau – Maskenbünde im südichen Malawi*. Vienna: Verlag der Österreichischen Akademie der Wissenschaften.

Makumbi, A. J. 1963. *Maliro ndi Myambo ya Achewa*. London: Longman.

Mapopa, M. 1980. 'The Drama of Gule Wamukulu: A Study of the Nyau as Practiced by the Chewa of the Eastern Province of Zambia'. M.A dissertation, University of Ghana.

Marwick, M. G. 1968. 'Notes on Some Cewa Rituals', *African Studies* 27, 1: 3–14.

Marwick, M. G. 1965. *Sorcery in its Social Setting: A Study of the Northern Rhodesian Cewa*. Manchester: Manchester University Press.

Rangeley, W. H. J. 1952. 'Two Nyasaland Rain Shrines', *The Nyasaland Journal* 5, 2: 31–50.

Rangeley, W. H. J. 1950. 'Nyau in Kotakota District', *The Nyasaland Journal* 3, 2: 19–33.

Rangeley, W. H. J. 1949. 'Nyau in Kotakota District', *The Nyasaland Journal* 2, 2: 35–49.

Richard, A. I. 1956. *Chisungu: A Girl's Initiation Ceremony among the Bemba of Northern Rhodesia*. London: Faber & Faber.

Schoffeleers, J. M. 1976. 'The Nyau Societies: Our Present Understanding', *The Society of Malawi Journal* 29, 1: 59–68.

Turner, V. 1967. *The Forest of Symbols: Aspects of Ndembu Ritual*. Ithaca and London: Cornell University Press.

Yoshida, K. 1992. 'Masks and Transformation among the Chewa of Eastern Zambia', *Senri Ethnological Studies* 31: 203–73.

21 Tourism and social change among the Dogon

Paul J. Lane

With the steady growth in international tourism, anthropologists, art historians, and others have become increasingly interested in the ramifications of this form of culture contact, especially where small-scale, nonindustrial societies are concerned. A variety of issues have been studied, ranging from the effects of tourism on local economies to its influence on indigenous values and artistic traditions.[1] Most studies not only perceive tourism as an agent of social change, but also consider such changes as detrimental. While such sentiments are understandable, they also lead to a specific analytical perspective that I wish to take issue with here.

The problem, it would appear, lies in our attitudes toward material goods, which in certain contexts are viewed as an index of prosperity and well-being, and in others as signs of cultural debasement (Douglas 1982: 16). Typically, the growing preference for goods of industrial rather than indigenous manufacture, the adoption of new artistic and cultural practices, and the growth of a waged economy in small-scale societies have all been treated as part of a more general process of 'Westernization.' Indeed, as elsewhere, many of these features are more prominent now in Dogon society than when anthropological work began in Sanga region of Mali during the 1930s. The houses of younger people contain a higher proportion of artifacts of industrial manufacture than those of their seniors (Lane 1986). More men, and even some women, spend time engaged in waged labor, and equally, more people are involved in tourism in some way. New art forms have also emerged and traditional genres been adapted to suit the interests of tourists (Imperato 1971).

Despite a history of colonial administration, and more lately, growing tourist activity, it would be entirely inappropriate to regard all these changes as comparable parts of a process of Westernization. There are two basic weaknesses in generalized concepts of this kind. They fail to document the specific historical conditions under which the new developments occur, and they place too great an emphasis on exogenous forces of change (Moore 1987: 86–87). Consequently an indigenous response to a particular set of changing circumstances tends to be portrayed at worst as one of passive reception and at best as opportunistic adaptation to events beyond the control of local inhabitants. In the case study outlined here, I shall discuss aspects of tourism in the Sanga region, with particular reference to the masked dances of the Dogon. Unlike Pascal James

Imperato in a similar study (1971), I shall focus less on the perceived effects of tourism on 'traditional' dances and more on the choices and strategies of the individuals involved.

For the Dogon, as for many other peoples, mass tourism is a post-World-War-II phenomenon. The popularity of the Sanga region rests on the appeal of a specific set of features rather than on any desire among visitors to experience Dogon society in its entirety. This is a common characteristic of tourist trips to societies of the developing world, and one that Duncan has gone so far as to describe as 'the social construction of unreality' (1978). It is, nevertheless, important to emphasize this point, since it is toward the reproduction of this international and popular model that most tourist activity is geared.

Essentially, the model used to promote tours to the Dogon comprises elements of the geographical situation of the region, the local landscape and architecture, Dogon mythology, and especially the more spectacular aspects of the traditional masked dances abstracted from their broader regional and social contexts. To a certain extent the main components of this model are drawn from the anthropological studies of Marcel Griaule and his students, in particular the emphasis placed on the exegesis of Dogon society through a detailed understanding of their mythology. When this is combined in travel brochures with colorful descriptions of the scenery of the Bandiagara escarpment, an image of the mysterious, exotic, and remote society can be skillfully created. Visitors arrive in the Sanga region with expectations based on this imagery. Since independence there has been greater state involvement in tourism through the auspices of the national tourist board, La Société Malienne d'Exploitation des Resources Touristiques (SMERT). Most visitors to 'le Pays Dogon', roughly 6,000 in the 1982–83 season, are offered much the same kind of deal, irrespective of whether they arrive alone or as part of a package tour group.

Guided tours vary in extent and duration. Most popular are the short trips around the village of Ogol to look at some of the more intriguing architectural forms, usually taking in a visit to a vendor of wooden sculptures, carvings, and souvenirs. Slightly longer tours to the edge of the escarpment, or even down into the cliff-line villages of Banani, are also popular. Round trips along the foot of the escarpment via several villages, which take at least a day, can also be arranged. If the guide is good, tourists will be given an accompanying commentary on Dogon myth, history, and beliefs, which closely follows some of the more publicized anthropological summaries. Although some boys play truant from school to act as guides for shorter trips, most guides are registered with the tourist agency. Indeed, the agency often attempts to levy a tax on visitors who employ one without stopping at the local SMERT office first. Financial remuneration for the guides is not great, since tourists pay SMERT a fixed sum that varies according to the extent of the tour. In turn, the board pays the guides a percentage of this fee. They may also accept tips and other gifts.

The numbers of those involved in tourism vary from village to village. Where the bulk of my own research was carried out, four men regularly worked as porters on the longer treks, and only one person had much regular direct contact with tourists. In effect, he monopolized the flow of visitors through the village, which over the course of a year can amount to 1,000–1,500 people. He saw himself as a vendor of tourist objects and putative antique carvings, and a supplier of services as well. All visitors who wished to spend the night in the village were accommodated in his compound, and he would frequently call upon one of his wives to prepare a meal for a group passing through. He continued to farm with the rest of his lineage, however, for the proceeds from these activities alone would not support even his nuclear family. Several other men were also engaged indirectly in tourism through the production of engraved calabashes and other souvenirs. Engraved calabashes appear to be a fairly recent innovation, and it is interesting to note that the motifs used are predominantly drawn from the repertoire of traditional mythical figures and mask types. As with other aspects of the local tourist industry, the favoured representational forms help to reinforce images of the Dogon that are already held in the Western world.

Whereas the topography and architecture are permanently on display, and carvings, ancient or modern, can always be found for sale, the masked rituals for which the Dogon are famed are sporadic. A form of masked dance can be staged at tourists' request. In his study of these, Imperato described some of the main differences between the ritual and theatrical forms, and suggested that some of the characteristics of the latter were beginning to appear in the former. I want to propose an alternative explanation.

The ritual dances are performed by members of the Awa, or society of masks. Each village has its own Awa, composed of circumcised, initiated males, whose members perform a range of dances at funerals and spirit-raising ceremonies (*dama*) that follow. Most dancers are in their late teens to early thirties, while the masters of ceremonies, the *imina giru*, who appear unmasked, are middle-aged. The number and types of masks possessed by any particular Awa vary, and no specific ruling governs who can use a particular kind of mask. Griaule recorded sixty-five different types, divisible into six categories: mammals, reptiles, birds, Dogon personages, non-Dogon personages, and things (Griaule 1938).

Several points should be made about funeral and spirit-raising ceremonies. Masked dancers appear according to criteria related to the deceased's identity. They do not perform for deceased women or juvenile males. Moreover, a greater number of dancers will appear in ceremonies for older than for younger men. A single ceremony is often held for several deceased men, when one was a senior male and the others were younger men from the same village who had died after him.

The social identity of a deceased male is frequently marked by ceremonies specific to that identity. For example, special rites and dances are performed for hunters or cattleherders as part of the general sequence of a funeral ceremony. This marking of social differences does not occur for women. Finally, it should be noted that the dances are only a part of the *rites de passage* connected with death, mourning, and the transition to ancestorhood.

Dances held for tourists or for visiting dignitaries take much the same form but are highly abbreviated. Only the more spectacular portions involving maskers are retained. Furthermore, the performances are not held in a residential area, as happens when maskers visit the house of the deceased and dance on his roof. Neither do they take place in the village square, as during the latter stages of the traditional ceremonies. In Ogol, for example, they are put on in front of the local post office on the edge of the village.

Nowadays the dances are supervised by a tourist board official, who sometimes intervenes to instruct performers to dance more energetically, something the *imina giru* never do. The audience is composed of people who have no familiarity with the genre or its significance, and the sexes are not segregated as they would be at a funeral or a *dama*. Also, the dances can be held at any time during daylight hours, and without regard to other rhythms of activity and sequences of events. Finally, they are more staged and closely choreographed, and the arrival of performers is markedly different. Instead of approaching an assembled crowd by a sinuous route, in single file through the village, the dancers generally gather beside the arena well before the visitors arrive. After the performance they often stand around waiting to be photographed instead of leaving the area immediately, as they would in a ritual context.[2]

Some features of the ritual performances are, however, retained. For instance, care is generally taken not to let women see the masks when in transit from their place of storage to the area where the dancers get into their costumes. Although in Sanga women walk by with little regard for the dancers, when one was staged in my research village all of the women who wished to watch the performance took refuge from the masks by climbing onto rocks and house roofs, as they would at a funeral or *dama*.

Imperato noted several differences between the ritual performances of masked dances in the late 1960s and those described by Griaule. He suggested that the mock combats had diminished in scale; the night-long vigil on the roof of the deceased's house was often omitted; the *bago bundo* part of the funeral rite, in which the *sirige* mask performs, was frequently deleted; and there was a general shortening of the dances and the entire ceremony. Like Griaule before him (1938: 322) Imperato perceived these changes in the traditional ceremonies as evidence of encroaching alien values. The implications of his argument, though not explicitly stated, are that the initial tourist adaptations have since been incorporated in the traditional rituals themselves.

Like Imperato I noted the frequent omission of the *bago bundo* part of the funeral rite, and more rarely the night-long vigil on the roof of the deceased's house. Since Griaule (1938) does not provide sufficient comparative data on funeral ceremonies, it is not possible to say whether these elements were omitted on occasions in the 1930s as well. Comments from my own informants would suggest that, for them at least, the inclusion of the *bago bundo* rites was partly related to the status of the deceased.

The deceased's status can also influence the scale of mock combats and the ceremonies as a whole, although other factors are involved. For instance, the sample of mask forms held by an Awa society of a particular village is entirely independent of that held by the Awa of another village, since it results from individual choices of the dancing members of the society. Once these members pass the age of thirty they perform less frequently, and eventually cease altogether. Meanwhile, new members have joined the society and acquired masks of their own, which need not be of the same form as that of an immediate predecessor. Thus the inventory of forms used by the members of particular Awa changes from ceremony to ceremony, even during the course of a single year.

For example, during my research the number of dancers present at various ceremonies in the locality differed on each occasion. At a *dama* in June 1981 there were four antelope maskers, a Fulani and a cow masker (these dance as a pair), and two *satimbe* (beautiful woman) maskers, drawn from my village's Awa. At another in July of the same year, there were five *kanaga*, the Fulani and cow pair, two antelopes, and two *satimbe*. In October 1982, at another village, only three *kanaga* and a single *satimbe* appeared. In January 1983, at yet another village, four *kanaga* and the Fulani and cow pair from my village were present.

Several reasons could be advanced to explain these differences. The scale of funerals and *dama* ceremonies varies according to the status of the deceased. The older the deceased, the greater his status and the larger the ceremony. A man's social position is also contingent on his achievements during his life. Lineage size is also important; the larger the lineage, the greater its resources and network of kin on which to draw for material contributions. Since one of the additional consequences of these ceremonies is the renewal of links between affines and the fulfillment of reciprocal obligations through the provision of beer and food, bigger, more spectacular ceremonies, with participants drawn from a large area, have a wider importance. By demonstrating its extent and economic resources, a lineage can reinforce its reputation as one capable of providing for in-marrying women, potentially enhancing its reproductive goals and network of affinal kin.

The other reason for this variation in the number of dancers from a particular village has to do with the personal strategies of the individuals concerned. A man's temporary absence from the village to work in the nearby Séno plain as a subsistence farmer or in places such as Mopti, Bamako, and Abidjan as a wage laborer provides him with an opportunity to amass resources or capital to finance his marriage or to support other activities aimed at keeping a wife or wives. Rarely are all men eligible to dance at a ceremony in the village at one time. The scale of a funeral ceremony or *dama* can often vary simply on account of the number of dancers available. While there has certainly been a steady increase in the number of men temporarily absent from their villages, this practice has been going on at least since the 1930s and probably longer.

It would appear, therefore, that contrary to Imperato's view, several factors unrelated to the attitudes of young Dogon men toward traditional values can have a marked effect on the size of funeral and *dama* ceremonies. It is even questionable whether the ritual and theatrical genres are at all comparable. Tourist dances have developed against a broader historical context of changing Western images of the Dogon and, more generally, small-scale African societies. The ritual dances, on the other hand, are enmeshed in a web of mythological significances and interlineage strategies.

Partly because the two types of dance are performed for different audiences, their meaning also differs considerably. Though tourist audiences cannot interpret the dances of funerals and *damas*, they are perfectly capable of responding to the drama of a staged dance, and of reacting unfavorably to a performance they consider substandard. Also it would be highly presumptuous to suggest that they perceive tourist dances as if they were real rituals. In other words, the two categories of dance differ in modes of representation. The theatrical presentation should be seen as a new genre, and however close the formal similarities, should not be confused with a ritual performance whose participants' belief has diminished or been abandoned. The two types are employed to quite separate ends. While the ritual ceremonies are the subject of interlineage competition, tourist dances are used by young men as an expression of their own identity. Older, senior men, all of whom occupy specific ritual positions, are responsible for the Awa society and control the representational production of its members.[3] While they have the freedom to choose their own masks and while good dancing is acknowledged by the watching crowd, younger men, as dancers, remain masked. Their identity is obscured and is subject to the controlling influence and instruction of the senior officials of the society. In the context of tourist dances, however, they have far greater control over the production. Despite the guiding influence of the SMERT official, it is their choice to participate and their own abilities that gain them reputation.

Within the context of a ritual dance there is little desire to be recognized, but in a tourist dance performers are happy to be singled out and to be photographed. The young men are willing to be identified because here they are in control, not because their respect for Dogon traditions is declining. The decision to engage in tourist production, like that of seeking waged employment in distant towns, is aimed at being modern, at marking differences between younger and older generations, and at strategies of accumulation. When temporary migrants return to their villages with quantities of goods such as cloth, sunglasses, hats, umbrellas, and bicycles, these objects of non-Dogon origin are used to construct an identity, a reputation for 'being wealthy', for 'being able to provide'. This reputation is deployed to attract marriage partners. The fathers of these men returned from Kumase and Accra, also laden with 'exotic' cloth and other paraphernalia.[4] At least since the 1930s, then, there has been a kind of youth subculture that represents itself as modern, not in the eyes of the world but in those of other Dogon. In this respect, the rising participation of the young men in tourism has simply meant the substitution of one way of demonstrating their suitability as marriage partners for another.

However, a more fundamental change has arisen, bringing with it the potential for a restructuring of the present relationship between authority and control of knowledge. Today's youth have become responsible for presenting their own society and for providing an exegetical commentary to the outside world. This is an entirely novel role for young men, since traditionally the responsibility for presenting Dogon traditions lay solely with the male elders. In certain contexts, as in the ritual dances, this group still maintains a strong hold over these duties. However, now that young men are in a position, through engagement in tourist-related activities, to control the content of specific representations of Dogon culture, they are also in a position to give new meanings to those representations. Indeed, younger men, as much as elders, are intensely proud of being Dogon, and take great pleasure in depicting their society through representational forms. The content and effect of tourist dances and tourist artifacts should be seen not as evidence for diminishing beliefs but as a novel metaphor for the culture itself.

Notes

Fieldwork was carried out with the permission of the Office of the Directeur General des Enseignements Supérieurs et de la Recherche Scientifique, permit nos. 0626/DNERS and 1596/DNERS. I would like to thank Dr. Klena Sanogo, Directeur de l'Institut des Sciences Humaines, Bamako, for his assistance. My thanks, also, to Mr. Domion Girou, Mr. Ana Dolo, and Mr. Missidon Dolo for their help in the field.

Earlier versions of this paper were presented at seminars held in the Department of African Studies, University of Cambridge and the Centre for Urban and Regional Studies, University of Birmingham. I would like to thank Dr. Susan Drucker-Brown and Mr. Nicholas James, respectively, for the opportunities to do so. Responsibility for any errors remain my own.

1 See, for example, Graburn (1983) for a general summary, and Nolan and Nolan (1978) and Wagner (1977, 1981) for more specific studies concerning the cultural impact of tourism.
2 My own observations of the form adopted by 'tourist dances' are similar to those of Imperato (1971: 31, 69–70).
3 In this context, the term 'representational production' refers not only to the fabrication of the masks and associated costumes, but also to the dances and their setting, the sequence in which dancers from different Awa societies appear, the length of time allowed to elapse following the burial of the deceased, the time of year the ceremonies are held, and the ritual knowledge required for their successful performance.
4 See for example the comments on 'Les Goldcoast' in Lifchitz and Paulme 1936. All the older men in my research village who had spent some of their youth outside the region confirmed that they too returned with quantities of non-Dogon objects. Some had even managed to retain their most prized acquisitions, which they now keep hidden in their personal stores.

References

Douglas, M. 1982. 'Goods as a System of Communication,' in *In the Active Voice*, ed. M. Douglas, pp. 16–33. London: Routledge & Kegan Paul.

Duncan, J. S. 1978. 'The Social Construction of Unreality: An Interactionist Approach to the Tourist's Cognition of Environment,' in *Humanistic Geography, Prospects and Problems*, eds. D. Ley and M. S. Samuels, pp. 4–57. London: Croom Helm.

Graburn, N. H. H. 1983. 'The Anthropology of Tourism,' *Annals of Tourism Research* 11: 9–34.

Griaule, Marcel, 1938. *Masques dogons*. Université de Paris, Travaux et Mémoires de l'Institut d'Ethnologie, no. 33. Paris: Institut d'Ethnologie.

Imperato, Pascal James. 1971. 'Contemporary Adapted Dances of the Dogon,' *African Arts* 5, 1: 28–33.

Lane, P. J. 1986. 'Settlement as History: A Study of Time and Space among the Dogon of Mali,' Ph.D. thesis, University of Cambridge.

Lifchitz, Deborah and Denise Paulme, 1936. 'Les fêtes des semailles en 1935 chez les Dogon de Sanga,' *Journal de la Société des Africanistes* 6: 95–110.

Moore, H. L. 1987. 'Problems in the Analysis of Social Change: An Example from the Marakwet,' *Archaeology as Long-Term History*, ed. I. Hodder, pp. 85–105. Cambridge University Press.

Nolan, S. D. and M. L. Nolan. 1978. 'Variations in Travel Behaviour and the Cultural Impact of Tourism,' in *Tourism and Behaviour*, ed. V. L. Smith, pp. 1–17. Studies in Third World Societies, Williamsburg.

Wagner, U. 1981. 'Tourism in the Gambia: Development or Dependency,' *Ethnos* 46: 190–206.

—— 1977. 'Out of Time and Place – Mass Tourism and Charter Trips,' *Ethnos* 42: 38–52.

22 Theatre and social issues in Malawi

Performers, audiences, aesthetics

David Kerr

All over the Third World aesthetic conventions are being overthrown. Audiences and performers are transforming the codes which govern the relations between them. This is happening not so much when westernized intellectuals react against the outworn aesthetics of the North, but when workers and peasants ally themselves with some committed intellectuals in an attempt to find a cultural weapon for articulating collective grievances.

This article attempts to trace some of these transformations as they apply to popular theatre experiments in Malawi. The analysis will be very tentative, a caution necessitated by two contrasting imperatives: I am simultaneously both too much of an outsider and an insider.

My outsider's role is easy to define: as a British-born expatriate working in Malawi, many of the popular theatre techniques I describe go against the whole aesthetic grain of my conventionally elitist university training. On the other hand, I have been associated with popular theatre in Central-Southern Africa for the past seventeen years, for the last ten of which I have worked directly with, or for, working-class and peasant communities. This involvement causes problems of finding equilibrium and distance from the creative effort in order to reflect on the social, political, and aesthetic implications of the work.

Popular African theatre describes drama created by peasants and workers or by intellectual cadres in close association with the people, usually through collective improvisation, in order to clarify or articulate people's issues and viewpoints. This is not the place to trace the development of such a theatre mode in different countries. Well-documented accounts have already been made and are not very difficult to obtain.[1]

My purpose is rather to initiate an analysis of the ideological implications of such popular theatre, particularly as these affect (or are affected by) the aesthetic forms of the theatre. Popular theatre's nexus of ideological/aesthetic categories is part of a dialectical interaction with existing ideological imperatives, many of a neo-colonial nature. It makes sense, therefore, for African popular theatre to be partly defined by what it is *not* – that is, by contrast with a Northern theatre tradition.

Against the European tradition

There are two major elements of Euro-American drama which have largely been negated by popular African theatre. These are individual authorship, and the separation of the audience from the performers. I am aware, of course, that these two elements are not inherently Euro-American, and that there have been many attempts within twentieth-century Euro-American theatre to break away from their limitations. But they have developed mainly, though not exclusively, as aspects of the rise of capitalism: and for African economies, which have related to capitalism in complex ways through the process of imperialism, it is the aesthetic correlative of capitalism which is being negated by an emergent anti-imperialist popular African theatre.

Authorship in Euro-American art is linked to a nexus of economic, philo-sophical, social, and cultural determinants which constitute a dynamic and complex ideology. Economically, the dominating influence is that of indi-vidualism. Even after the entrepreneurial stage of capitalism which had given rise to the classical Ricardian notion of individual economic liberty had been superseded by monopoly capitalism, the ideology of liberalism continued to dominate Northern culture.

In the cultural field, collectively-created forms such as the ballad and the folk play were superseded by more private, individually-authored forms such as the lyric and the novel. In drama a mode of theatre production evolved in which the author's script became the dominant creative input, to be interpreted by a whole production team which, with its specializations and craft restrictions, corres-ponded to the hierarchical structure of capitalist industry.

Laissez-faire capitalism had another powerful impact on Euro-American theatre – the increasing distance from the seventeenth century onwards between the performers and the audience. The elimination of the orchestra in the neo-classic stage and the growing dominance of the proscenium arch were archi-tectural techniques which did for theatre what capitalism was doing for industry – making a clear distinction between produce and consumer. This was reinforced by economic determinants of the box office, expressed architecturally by audience divisions reflecting the class divisions of society.

In the twentieth century, as capitalism has been attacked both by revolutions and by growing internal contradictions, the aesthetic categories of authorship and audience/performer separation have become less ideologically secure. In the theatre itself there have been experiments in improvisation, group techniques, ritualism, and audience-participation, as well as an architectural revolt against the proscenium arch.

The modernist urge to deconstruct the traditional theatre by attacking the categories of the *auteur* and voyeuristic audiences has been championed by the French philosopher Jacques Derrida. He imagines a stage:

> where the spectator presenting himself as spectator, will no longer be either seer (voyant) or voyeur, will efface within himself the difference between the actor and the spectator, the represented and the representer, the object seen

and the seeing subject .... That public festival will ... have a form analogous to the electoral meetings of a free and legiferant assembled people.[2]

I believe that utopian vision has in no way been achieved in the theatre experiments of Artaud, Brook, or Grotowski, but that something approaching it was inherent in some African indigenous performing arts and, as I hope to show, is occasionally strived for in modern African popular theatre.

The African context

The impulse towards ritual forms in some avant-garde European theatre movements was far from the preoccupations of the literary theatre exported from Europe to Africa during the colonial period. In Africa the cultural lag which is common under imperialism has meant that the cultural values which dominated colonial theatre in Africa (and after formal independence the expatriate-dominated 'little theatres') was an archaic bourgeois aesthetic, very little influenced by modern avant-garde movements. Similarly, media imports have mostly been what Mahama Traoré calls 'vehicles of violence, sex, and a culture that is alien to us'.[3]

Even in the black African art theatre many of the colonial aesthetic categories survived. Despite experiments like Mbari Mbayo in Oshogbo, Ori Olukun in Ife, the Drama Studio in Accra, and Chikwakwa Theatre in Lusaka, most theatre architecture in Africa has followed a debased and tawdry version of the proscenium arch model.

Creatively, the play script, backed up by publishing houses (some African like Ibadan, Ravan, Présence, or East African Publishing House, but many multinational like Heinemann, ORTF, or Longman), have supported a tradition of individually created authorship which goes against the grain of indigenous collective aesthetics. Playwrights like Dadié, Rotimi, Serumaga, and Soyinka have produced brilliant, poetic, individually crafted texts which, though often in sympathy with popular sensibilities, reinforce an alien tradition of the heroic *auteur*.

Despite the achievements of the literary theatre, the collective participatory theatre modes found in indigenous African performing arts like *Egungun*, *Kotetlon*, or *Makisi* were not entirely destroyed by colonialism. Syncretic performing arts have also arisen such as the Concert Party, Yoruba Travelling Theatre, and *Kwagh-hir* in West Africa, *Vichekesho*, *Beni*, and *Muganda* in East Africa, and *Pungwe* and township musicals in Southern Africa.

These are nearly all collectively created, improvised forms of theatre which, despite different functions and social bases, share the use of dance, mime, song, and structured stereotyping to mediate some of the contradictions arising from modern life.

In recent years, however, another type of theatre has arisen which elsewhere I have called 'induced' popular theatre, meaning theatre which has not emerged 'naturally' in the manner of syncretic theatre forms, but whose birth has been 'induced' by educated development-oriented cadres.[4] The theatre examples from Malawi which I cite are of this induced type.

Experiments in Malawi

Since 1981 theatre workers at the University of Malawi have been involved in experiments where drama has been used as a communication device for focusing on such issues as health, literacy, working conditions, nutrition, urbanization, and agriculture. The idea of the theatre is for the catalyst group (of theatre teachers and students) to research problems found in a particular peasant or proletarian sector of society and to use theatre as a way of allowing the community to debate these issues and hopefully act to overcome problems.

The early experiments which Malawian theatre cadres made in 1981–82 were marred by the dominance of the catalyst group, so that the audience did not genuinely participate in the analysis of the issues. The organizers realized that they had much to learn from the experiences of popular theatre workers in other parts of the world, and the theories of Augusto Boal arising from his Latin American work, the experience of the Kamiriithu Cultural Centre in Kenya, the *Wasan* Samaru organized by Ahmadu Bello University in Northern Nigeria, and the Morewa Drama workshop in Zimbabwe all made contributions to a far more democratic and participatory theatre process.

This called for a methodology in which plays were not simply created by catalyst groups from participatory research into peasant and working-class communities, but where the catalyst group initiated a theatrical process which communities could appropriate for their own use at all levels – theoretical, organizational, and aesthetic. What was needed, in other words, was a theatre serving as a cultural tool for communities to monitor, analyse, and criticize their own ideologies and social structures.

The theatre process I am describing started in November 1985 and is still gaining momentum as I write this article in September 1987. Students and teachers of theatre at the University of Malawi's Zomba campus joined forces with the Primary Health Care Unit (PHCU) of the Liwonde Agricultural Development Division (LADD) for a primary health education campaign in certain areas of Liwonde District. The first 'target' area was Mwima, a busy trading area and centre for a cluster of ten villages.

Economically, the area depends on subsistence farming and fishing, with the nearby River Shire and the asphalt road from Liwonde to Mangochi allowing the area considerable articulation with a cash economy and urbanized cultural values. Internal male migration to tobacco estates in the Central and Northern Regions has caused women to face a heavy burden of being major food producers, in addition to onerous domestic duties.

The area has one of the lowest per-capita incomes in Malawi and a very high mortality rate owing to the low-lying swampy terrain, which provides easy access to such diseases as malaria, diarrhoea, cholera and typhoid. Childbirth-related diseases and infant malnutrition are also serious health hazards.

Politically, the area is controlled by the local branch of the Malawi Congress Party (Malawi is a one-party state with a heavily centralized network of district, area, and village sections). Extension services are supplied by the ADD in Liwonde, with additional local authority provided by a network of traditional chiefs and headmen.

The area is culturally heterogeneous – ethnically a mixture of Yao, whose religion is Islam, and Mang'anja/Ngoni, who are mostly Christian, though among both Muslims and Christians strong animist beliefs persist. Indigenous values are strong concerning kinship systems, communal work patterns, and attachment to traditional beliefs such as faith in spirit mediums.

The main performing arts are oral narratives and *Majini*, a spirit-possession dance for mental and physical therapy. Both these use a high level of audience participation and collective creativity. The dominant language is ChiYao, but the national language of ChiChewa is also widely spoken and universally understood. All the plays created in the PHC campaign have used ChiChewa as the main language.

Creating a first play

Initial participatory research by the catalyst group, conducted in December 1985, indicated that the community around Mwima identified specific aspects of sanitation and access to water as a major cause of health problems in the area. However, the people were also aware of more ideological causes, particularly concerning the difficulties in mobilizing the community to protect its own health.

The problems of mobilization arise from the marginalization villagers feel owing to their distance from political centres of power, and more specifically from health and other services in Liwonde, perceived as neglect by urban bureaucrats of their rural peasant community. The feelings of marginalization and dependency have led not to increased solidarity but to jealousies and mutual distrust.

The constraints identified by community spokespersons upon self-mobilization confirmed the experiences of the Liwonde PHCU, which had found it very difficult to encourage villagers to promote their own health. This seemed to reflect a general apathy and cultural fragmentation in the community, at least when there was need for involvement in development projects.

The catalyst group's intention was to keep their own input to a minimum, allowing the Mwima community as much creative involvement as possible. At the beginning, however, since drama (as narrative through dialogue) was a new medium in the village, it was necessary to make some simple sketch, if only as a dialectical statement to be negated.

The catalysts chose to centre their sketch on hygiene and water problems in Mwima, particularly concerning wells. At Mwima there were two shallow wells in common use, one half way between the headman's house and the main road, and one about a kilometre away, on the road itself, next to a shop in the trading area.

Both wells were very dirty owing to the water which slopped on to the bare earth being subsequently trampled by barefooted women and by domestic animals. The villagers identified the wells as an obvious source of disease, claiming that community discord and lack of materials prevented them from being cleaned up with a cement apron. The Liwonde PHCU promised free cement if the community could organize themselves on a self-help basis to build the cement aprons around the wells. Drama was intended to help mobilize this activity.

The catalyst group created a sketch through improvisation, which was untitled but for convenience called *Chitsime* (*The Well*). It dealt not so much with the problem of the dirtiness of the wells but with who had responsibility for their upkeep. The basic conflict was between the headman, who wanted a proposed new well (for reasons of prestige and convenience) near his own house, and a petty-bourgeois shop-keeper who (for the same reasons) wanted the well at the trading area.

These two characters represented two different types of authority structure – the traditional, and that arising from economic wealth. In the end a compromise was reached, reflecting the siting of the *real* well, which pleased the whole village.

Reactions and resentments

The first 'performance' was in a village about two kilometres from the trading area. It took place in the *bwalo* (open space used for village court cases and community dances/music). The main parts played by a university lecturer (the headman) and three students (the shopkeeper and two vocal villagers).

They used a technique of throwing questions to the audience in order to open up the play to audience participation, and this proved phenomenally successful. The audience responded to questions and comments with approval, disapproval and even fairly complex analysis of the issues.

The women (who are the users of wells in Malawian villages) were particularly articulate in voicing their opinions, and it was also notable that the audience was not cowed by the presence of the real headman and party chairman in the audience – who in a regular *bwalo* meeting would have expected and normally have achieved total submission from the villagers, especially the women.

One point which emerged from the play process was an urgent sense of resentment about the upkeep of the real well at the trading centre. That well is owned by a relatively wealthy shopkeeper who allows villagers to use the well so that they will be encouraged to buy from his store. However, he refused to allow the villagers to clean up the well or to build a cement apron to improve hygiene.

Performing the play allowed the villagers to articulate their resentment against that particular shopkeeper, although there was also a shadowy feeling of solidarity, an incipient class-consciousness, against the structure of power represented by the Mwima Trading Centre.

It was one thing to express that resentment in a performance in the village. It was quite another to articulate the resentment to the traders themselves. The villagers decided to do this by performing the play at the trading centre. In order to clarify the issues, they first performed the play again in the village, with the main parts taken by villagers – which led to the interesting situation of a commoner playing the part of the headman, while the real village headman took the part of a commoner. This second performance helped the villagers gain the confidence to take the play to the Trading Centre.

At the Trading Centre there was a well-established *bwalo* under the shade of a huge and beautiful *msolo* tree, used for community gatherings of the surrounding villages. *Chitsime* was performed in-the-round there to an audience of over 200 people, including traders from the local stores, one of whom was the recalcitrant owner of the well referred to in the play.

The performance was extremely lively with active and sometimes acrimonious participation from the audience, the traders' and villagers' viewpoints being debated with a frankness unimaginable outside the context of theatrical role-play. By the end of the performance the owner of the well at the trading centre had rather shamefacedly agreed to allow the villagers to work on refurbishing his well, a task which was accomplished a few days later.

The success of this theatre process gave the villagers near Mwima a great incentive to continue using theatre as a tool of analysis. It allowed them to explain mistakes made in the past, to articulate grievances, and to strategize about future community action.

Dramatizing other problems

Two more 'plays' were created over the next few weeks. For convenience these could be called *Chipatala* (*The Hospital*) and *Chimbuzi* (*The Lavatory*), since they dealt respectively with the problems faced by villagers in travelling long distances to the under-staffed, overcrowded hospital in Liwonde, and with domestic conflicts which arise from campaigns to dig pit latrines.

The creation of the plays was part of a larger process whereby the community analysed its own health problems, and with the help of the Liwonde PHCU, health committees were elected for every village in the Mwima area. Interestingly, at least half of the elected committee members were women, some of whom had health skills as traditional birth attendants. These committees were so active, and became so keen on theatre as a mode of communication, that they set up their own theatre group in the village, independent of the original catalyst group.

Actors from the Mwima group (who were also all health committee members), along with some of the original catalyst group, then went to a different area. Mbela near Balaka, where a quite fresh approach was made to animate discussion about local health problems. There, plays concentrated on themes such as the failure of government bureaucrats to staff a clinic built by villagers on a self-help basis, and problems of role conflict between established authorities (such as the village party chairman) and the newly elected health committee, as well as the unwillingness of men to listen to the views of women elected to the committees.

In brief, the setting up of the village health committees has helped to solve some problems but has created a whole series of new conflicts and problems which the process of mobilization through theatre has to address. At the time of writing this article, the theatre process, linked to the spread of the health committees, is continuing and expanding rapidly, not only in Liwonde District but in Zomba and Machinga too.

Some aesthetic implications

I would like now to turn to some of the ideological and aesthetic implications of this work, particularly as these relate to the elements of text and of audience/performer relationships.

In the Malawian popular theatre work I have described, the Northern category of division between audience and performer is almost completely discarded. To start with, there is no 'theatre' as such, in the sense of a specially designed plant cut off from the real world and serving as a dream-palace for the creation of illusions.

The *bwalo* is an integral part of the community and there are no admission charges. The rough benches or mats used for the audience are the same ones used for domestic purposes or for such functions as dances, court cases, and public meetings. There is no special scenery or lighting. The backdrop is that of trees, village houses, or maize gardens. Real life is not something 'out there' beyond the lobbies and magical lights of the theatre: it impinges on the performance itself.

As an example I could cite the performance of *Chibudzi* at Mwima Trading Centre. The actor playing the dynamic and public-spirited headman referred to the real *msolo* tree under which the audience was sitting as a significant part of the community's history. (It was planted in 1906 by villagers in order to cover the *bwalo*, and they resisted attempts by traders to have the market built beneath its shade.)

At another stage of the performance, when a lorry from Liwonde to Mangoche stopped by the roadside, the actor playing the headman rebuked the audience for being distracted by the vehicle. The hear-and-now theatricality of the event and its relation to the real world was constantly kept before the audience's consciousness.

This is not, of course, to say that there is no suspension of disbelief. The temporary abeyance of normality which allows commoners to play important people in their society is an essential feature of popular theatre, but this is in a situation where the gaps between reality and illusion are constantly being blurred, corresponding to the flux and potential transformations taking place in society.

A major reason why illusionism is deconstructed is the unembarrassed participation of the audience in the plays. The performance tradition in the villages, such as oral narratives and *Majini*, allows the audience not only to participate (for example in songs), but even in some cases to modify the flow or structure of the performance.

This indigenous tradition could be perceived in the structure of the plays. For example, the motif of the trickster being outwitted, common in oral narratives, dominated the texture of the *Chimbudzi* play. Perhaps a bigger influence was the tradition of village court cases being judged by the chief or headman with the active participation of the whole community at the *bwalo*. This determined much of the moral structure and forensic format of the plays.

Such traditions made the acceptance of a participatory, development-oriented theatre relatively easy. In the *Chipatala* play, for example, members of the audience spontaneously queued up for 'treatment' from the actor playing the irascible and harassed doctor. More important still, whenever a debate over moral or ideological issues broke out the audience actively joined in the debate and urged the actors on towards the collective choices.

It is the collectivity of the creation and performance of these plays which gives them a direct, morally coercive power rarely found in Northern theatre. The village court tradition uses *manyazi* (shame) as an incentive to urge individuals to respond to the collective will. The popular theatre use of *manyazi* (for example, in *Chitsime*, persuading the real trader to allow the villagers to refurbish the well at Mwima trading centre) is one which gives the popular will a chance to counteract some of the power exercised by influential individuals in the community. The rural problems arising from modernization – bureaucratic red tape, bribery, patronage, and exploitation – require new popular social and cultural tools of analysis.

Against specialization

The way such plays transform the Northern notion of 'text' is implicit in the participatory techniques I have just described: the whole creative process is one which encourages collectivity rather than individualism. The catalyst group may occasionally use some writing (usually a few rough notes on a chalk-board) to clarify the scenario, but the dialogue itself is created through improvisation in a collective way.

Obviously, not everybody on stage and in the audience provides an equal creative input. The actors playing the major roles, especially those with a high level of contact with the audience (such as the headman), have a strong influence not only on the dialogue but also on shaping the form and trajectory of the play. But the total effect cannot be attributed to any individual, only to collective creativity of actors and audience.

The plays are always rehearsed by the catalyst group alone and with the village actors. But since an open-ended scenario is used, with set-piece speeches or dilemmas allowing for audience intervention, the plays are always transformed according to the collective will of the audience. If a play is repeated, no per-formance is ever the same, since the audience, time, mood, and sometimes venue are different. In short, the plays do not conform to the notion of a sacrosanct script, served by copyright laws, textual analysis, and literary criticism. The script is disposable: it is merely one stage in a much wider process of group learning and cultural interaction. The performance of a play at Mbela on the history of their self-help clinic led into the election of its own village health committee: the theatre event was not a quasi-magical end in itself, but part of the whole process of social transformation.

Just as there is no role specialization on the creative side, so there is no specialized role of critic: and the most significant evaluation is that made orally immediately after the performance, whether with the whole audience or in small groups. Such evaluation covers aesthetic, technical, and ideological aspects of the process, so that evaluation leads into community action rather than being enclosed within an aesthetic or critical ghetto.

Since this is an 'induced' form of popular theatre, there must always be some doubt about how healthy and enduring the innovation will be. Moreover, since the 'midwife' is a bureaucratic parastatal agency (using West German funds), there must also be doubts whether such patronage can contribute to a genuine popular movement of consciousness-raising. Aid, even with the thinnest of attached strings, tends to create an ideology of dependence.

That point is perhaps illustrated by a play created by the women of Mwima without any guidance from the catalyst group. It presented an interesting contrast between effective modern medicine and ineffective traditional medicine. The catalyst group wondered whether the scapegoating of the *sing'anga* (herbalist) in the play was not a projection of what the local Mwima health committee felt the catalyst group *wanted* to see, rather than a genuine expression of popular sentiment.

On the other hand, the Mwima villagers have shown an increasing confidence in handling drama as a medium. The plays have shown a syncretic vigour and a progressive mastery of theatrical resources. They have also given villagers the courage to articulate grievances and to debate issues with far less inhibition than the authoritarian nature of rural politics in Malawi usually allows. It is not inconceivable that the villagers could make the play process a genuine part of community culture.

One reason the play process has taken off so quickly is that there is no residue of pre-conceptions about Northern drama to interfere with the creation of a new theatre mode. The apparent cultural innovation bears some resemblance to an indigenous tradition of African performing arts, yet is also capable of mediating some of the most critical issues met by peasant communities as their societies are articulated with the dynamics of westernization and urban capitalism. The villagers are beginning to participate in and contribute to a wider third-world movement away from individualism and towards an aesthetic of collective performance.

Notes

1 For a full bibliography of the field, see Ross Kidd, *The Performing Arts, Non-formal Education, and Social Change in the Third World: a Bibliography and Review Essay*. The Hague: CESO, 1981.

2 Jacques Derrida, *Of Grammatology*, trans. G. C. Spink (Baltimore: Johns Hopkins University Press, 1974), p. 306.

3 Mahama Traoré, 'Cinema Must Be a School', *Cinéaste*, VI, No. 1, p. 33.

4 David Kerr, 'Didactic Theatre in Africa', *Harvard Education Review*, LI, No. 1, p. 145–55.

23 Fathers and sons

Politics and myth in recent Zambian drama

Stewart Crehan

At the tenth annual Performing Arts Festival of the Zambia National Theatre Arts Association (ZANTAA), held at a National Service camp outside the old mining town of Kabwe, what seemed to me to be a new theme was manifested in some of the plays presented. It made itself felt even more strongly at the 1985 festival, held at Hillcrest Secondary School in Livingstone, but I realized, on reflection, that it had also been there at the 1983 Mansa festival where, as at Kabwe in 1984 and Livingstone in 1985, I had been invited to adjudicate in the drama section (the only white person, incidentally, among the 1200 participants).

After going through my notes on the 110 plays staged in the last three ZANTAA festivals, I counted 27 in which this theme, hinted at in the title of this essay, was overtly present. Not that there is anything new about the conflict of generations or the revolt of the young against a status quo which, in their eyes, is sustained merely in order to keep them down. There is something less common-place, however about the idea of parents, and of fathers in particular, either killing or being responsible for the deaths of their own children – an idea that was articulated in eight of the plays.

None of this can be understood in western terms: there are no African Bazarovs or James Deans, no skinheads, punks or other western-style youth subcultures (so far) in modern African societies. Respectful, submissive behaviour towards the old in general, and towards one's parents in particular, still has the ideological force of divine law.[1] What makes the 'fathers-and-sons' theme in these ZANTAA plays so central and yet so difficult for a western mind to grasp, is its political and mythical rather than simply its familial dimension. Where, traditionally, the old are the rulers and the ruler is the father of his people, any questioning of the traditionally-accepted ties and obligations between the old and the young, has automatically, serious political and ideological implications.

The conflict of generations acquires a different aspect, of course, when the parents are illiterate peasants and their son is a socially-mobile, educated urbanite. Plays dealing with that kind of conflict (perhaps two per cent of the ZANTAA festival plays), and 'culture-conflict' plays (less than two per cent), now appear more relevant to a period when job opportunities kept pace with educational expansion, and when the new Zambian urban middle class was still in process of rapid formation.[2]

Such plays, if they are still written, tend to reflect the viewpoint of those who benefited vocationally from the post-1964 educational expansion. Gideon Phiri's *The Tragedy of Pride*, produced in 1980 by the Zambian National Association of Writers, and again in 1984 at the Lusaka Playhouse, is one such play – an all-too-familiar story of the young man who goes morally astray in the fast-living, corrupt world of the city, who can no longer communicate with his poor old parents back in the village, and whose fate, inevitably, is suicide (a fate that befalls guilt-torn characters in African novels and plays far more often, in my experience, than it does their somewhat less angst-ridden counterparts in the real world).

I have chosen this single thematic focus because it affords us a unique insight into the larger social process: into the role of ZANTAA itself (bearing in mind its history, organization, and membership), and hence the role of drama in Zambia today; into Zambia's education system, political and class structure, and pre-colonial traditions; and lastly, into certain ideological tensions which a collapsing economy is fast pushing towards breaking point. Theatre in this context is both a living response to a changing world, and a way in which performers and spectators can perceive and feel social relationships ideologically, as 'deep structures' (some perhaps deeply buried in the psyche).

It is the contradiction between these two aspects, which I have somewhat crudely labelled 'politics and myth', that I wish to examine. The ZANTAA plays are symbolizing events within a larger discourse, a discourse generated by what Victor Turner (1974) calls 'social dramas' or 'dramas of living'. Theme, even choice of theme, is determined in the first instance not by the playwrights or the groups who put on the plays, but by objective circumstances. Some account of these circumstances – historical as well as cultural – is therefore necessary before we look at the plays themselves.

Emergence of an indigenous drama

In the 1950s in what was then Northern Rhodesia, all formal (i.e., non-tradi-tional) theatrical activity[3] came under the umbrella of the Northern Rhodesia Drama Association, a whites-only body formed out of the expatriate 'little theatres' along the line of rail. The little theatres saw themselves as cultural outposts of British imperialism: before the building of the Lusaka Playhouse, for example, productions were staged at the Garrison Theatre, inside the army barracks. After 1964 the NRDA changed its name to the Theatre Association of Zambia (TAZ), but retained its identity as a predominantly expatriate association, inviting adjudicators, professional actors, and directors from Britain and South Africa, encouraging the production of Shakespeare in the schools, and mounting all-white West End hits in the playhouses.

In 1966 the University of Zambia registered its first students. A university drama club (Unzadrams) was founded, and in 1969 an expatriate lecturer, Michael Etherton, was instrumental in establishing Chikwakwa Theatre, a University-based group whose long-term aim was the creation of a popular theatre move-ment, an 'indigenous' Zambian theatrical tradition with 'grassroots' support and a democratic mass-oriented outlook.

While Chikwakwa, Unzadrams, and the University drama courses succeeded in producing a number of committed Zambian theatre artists during the 1970s, Chikwakwa's policy of 'taking drama to the people' did not mean leaving it there. The seeds of a genuinely popular theatre movement were not so easily planted: students and staff of Chikwakwa's travelling theatre went each year to the provinces and rural areas, performed there, then returned to Lusaka. If anything, Chikwakwa's most lasting impact was not on the rural areas, the urban compounds, and small provincial towns, but on the minds of university graduates. By the late 1970s popular theatre as an ideology was firmly embedded, even though what it had come to mean was using drama simply as an educational tool for 'community animation' in agency-funded developmental projects.

The current chairman of ZANTAA, Dickson Mwansa, is also an adult educator and popular theatre worker. 'Popular theatre artists', he says, 'believe that local people have the ability to solve their own problems'. The community animateur is there 'to help push up the process of conscientization. *After he has gone*, things should work even without him. The poor should be able to work together and confront all forms of oppressive phenomena – physical, social or economic' (Mwansa, 1984; my italics). Whether things *do* 'work even without him' is, of course, debatable.

In a report on the BAM (Brothers of All Mankind) rural development project in Luwingu district, Katete Kalumba (1982) concludes that the typical self-help project can become 'a form of subsidy by the rural poor to [international] capital without their being involved in the developmental process itself'. Nevertheless, a substantial number of popular theatre workers and resource persons was enlisted for the Luwingu project – one of several theatre-assisted projects that have taken place in Zambia since the Theatre for Development Workshop in Chalimbana in 1979.

When ZANTAA was formed in 1974, not one drama group was functioning independently of the schools, the University, or TAZ. But with the 'Zambianization' of Zambia's schools (Zambian teachers taking the place of European and Asians) and the spread of the Chikwakwa philosophy, the schools became an important training ground for 'indigenous' Zambian theatre. School drama clubs, organized by young Zambian teachers who wanted to produce African or, better still, Zambian plays instead of Shakespeare, began to give ZANTAA the solid base it needed in its struggle against TAZ.

If ZANTAA's cultural nationalism was inspired by the political and ideological mood of the 1970s, its theatrical philosophy and orientation were inspired by Unzadrams and Chikwakwa. Organizationally, however, the new body differed from Chikwakwa in three important respects. First, it was a *nationwide*, umbrella organization like TAZ; second, its roots were in the school drama clubs and among young, independent theatre artists, not in the University; and third, whereas Chikwakwa backed a written constitution and operated on a loose, voluntary, and collective basis rather than through a formal executive, ZANTAA developed its own constitution and electoral procedures, a membership policy, provincial and national executives (all volunteers), and the capacity, despite meagre resources, to mount regular provincial and national workshops and festivals. In due course, it began receiving government funding through the Department of Cultural Services, whose full-time provincial cultural officers and transport facilities were placed at ZANTAA's disposal.

The character of Tikwiza

Yet ZANTAA's rise was slow. Between 1975 and 1980 two independent theatre clubs emerged whose professionalism and discipline, organizing ability and creative skill stole the limelight from ZANTAA's initiatives. One was Bakanda Theatre in Kitwe. The other was Tikwiza Theatre Club, formed in Lusaka in 1975. Tikwiza was dominated by the personality of Masautso Phiri, a publishing editor, playwright, and producer–director who gathered around him a talented core of actors and performers (mostly graduates), whose hostility to TAZ was balanced by their cool if brotherly detachment towards ZANTAA.

Phiri's trilogy, *Soweto Flowers Will Grow*, written and produced after the Soweto uprising in 1976 (and later performed by Tikwiza in Nigeria, Cuba, Botswana, Kenya, and Zimbabwe), has had more influence especially in the schools, than any other Zambian play. Its mixture of poetic recital and factual documentary, of tearful (in performance) lamentation and heroic declamation, using the barest of stages and the minimum of props with the maximum symbolic and emotive power, and demanding of its actor–declaimers either a hypnotizing, immobile stance or slow, stylized gestures and attitudes, has been much imitated, especially in the so-called 'poetry recitals' at ZANTAA festivals.

Yet, whether the theme is the black man's plight, Mother Africa, slavery, the freedom struggle, South Africa, or Namibia, the effect of these abstract protests is unconvincing. Their maudlin self-pity is a far cry from the cathartic intensity of Tikwiza's *Soweto* performances, and this, I think, is borne out in the dutifully polite response of the festival audiences. The genre demands much greater stage presence, voice control, and command of language than most young ZANTAA performers possess.

That aside, there is some validity in the assertion that 'Africanist' protest has never had deep roots in Zambia.[4] The theme: unity-in-blackness; the ossified style: droopy, repetitive wailing, fixed expressions of anguish, pathetic arm-waving and clenched-fist defiance; and the form: ritualized protest that is part-statement and part-narrative, with bits of statement and/or narrative shared by a standing crescent or a prostrate litter of victims – all this seems somehow less 'authentic', less 'Zambian' than the down-to-earth, satirically observant tragicomedies of urban and domestic life in which Zambians have undoubtedly excelled.[5]

If so, this may help to explain Tikwiza's own demise (in 1984, the year of the Nkomati accords). Specalizing in liberation themes, with plays such as *The Island*, *Che Guevara*, and *The Trial of Dedan Kimathi*, perfecting a high-energy, 'revolutionary' style, and breaking down the actor–audience barrier by extending the acting area into the auditorium, Tikwiza became a living contradiction, for within the club itself a kind of stratification had occurred.

On the one hand, there were the graduates, lawyers, accountants, executives, and secretaries in secure parastatal or government jobs – a dynamic, professional elite with good promotion prospects and a flair for leadership and administration. These, as the most vocal and articulate members, dominated the executive and various sub-committees, and played the star roles.

But making up the bulk of the membership were the poorly-paid office workers, factory workers, school students, and unemployed, with a sprinkling of college and University students. These, as the merely loyal, 'footing' members, carried the flats, looked after the drums and props, built and painted the sets, hunted down adverts for the programmes, fixed the lights, and defined the art of coarse acting in roles such as Fourth Freedom Fighter.

Despite its enormous contribution to theatre in Zambia, Tikwiza did relatively little, then, for popular or 'indigenous' theatre, attracting largely middle-class audiences, and preferring West, North, East and South African to Zambian plays, since most of the latter, in the opinion of Mumba Kapumpa, state lawyer and chairman of Tikwiza (1980–83), were not worth including in the club's production schedule. The maintenance of high standards did not, however, prevent Tikwiza's loss of patronage and members.[6] The late Haggai Chisulo, public relations officer for INDECO and a leading Tikwiza actor, commented on the club's demise as follows: 'The core has disintegrated due to the individual pursuance of individual professions.'[7]

Turning point for ZANTAA

Having described (if drastically over-simplified) the character of Tikwiza, we are better able to understand the nature of ZANTAA – in particular, the way in which it has been able to provide expression for what, in a club such as Tikwiza, was either suppressed or ignored. In 1980, Dickson Mwansa's play about prison life, inmates, and conditions, *The Cell*, was performed by Bakanda Theatre. It was best production at the ZANTAA festival, and best original script at the TAZ festival. Plans were made for Bakanda to take the play to the Canadian Festival of Indigenous Performing Arts, but government funds were not forthcoming.

Mwansa's explanation (1982: 34) is that *The Cell* was not the sort of play Zambian authorities wanted to see representing Zambia abroad (in contrast to their wholehearted support for Tikwiza's trips with *Soweto*), since it 'was about Zambia – its loss of conscience, rise in corruption, rush for material things, formation of social classes'. For the Zambian elite, a socially-critical play was something to be feared rather than supported: 'As long as its message is about "the other" [South Africa], a play presents no problem. Problems start when a play starts asking questions about and portraying what is current in Zambia today.'[8]

In this sense, 1980 was the critical year. Independence in Zimbabwe turned attention back to Zambia's growing internal problems. The war across the border was no longer a valid excuse for the continuing poverty, urban squalor, unemployment, commodity shortages, inflation, and high rate of school drop-outs, nor for the corruption, mismanagement, and greed of those at the top.

The year 1980 was also a turning-point for ZANTAA. The association continued to draw most of its support from the schools, but between 1978 and 1980 an important development had occurred, the result both of Tikwiza's example and ZANTAA's campaign to encourage and bring together independent Zambian theatre groups. This was the sudden, unprecedented explosion of independent drama groups in key urban centres along the line of rail, especially on the Copperbelt – an event hailed by Stephen Chifunyise (1981) as the long-awaited triumph of a grassroots, community-based theatre movement. (Coming ten years after the founding of Chikwakwa, it was, it should be noted, an *urban*-based movement.) Although some of these new groups were not averse to competing in TAZ festivals, many affiliated to ZANTAA, thereby transforming the association.

A number of the groups' names followed that of Tikwiza (Tumbuka for 'We are coming'): for example Tithandize ('let us help'); Tabwera ('We have come'); Tafika ('We have arrived'); Tikondane ('Let us love one another'); Tapeza ('We have met'); Zhaninge ('Come!'); Zani Muone ('Come and see!'); and, more recently; Tinabadwa ('We were born'); Twasika ('We have arrived'), and Tigwirizane ('Let us support one another'). Together these sentence-formula names proclaim a shared national and cultural identity, the need for cooperation, and a common purpose.

Significantly, the Lusaka-based groups asserted their *non*-Tikwiza identity, both in name and outlook. Tikwiza rehearsed in a first floor conference room in Findeco House, a 22-storey sky-scraper in the city centre, and performed in established venues. Makishi Theatre 2000 (borrowing their name from the Lozi initiation ceremony in which animal and human characters perform) used a small community hall in Kabwata, on the east side of the city; another group, Pamodzi ('Together'), originated in Kaunda Square, a compound less than two miles from the University, and began using Chikwakwa's neglected open-air theatre for their well-attended performances of comic sketches, dances, and improvised, one-act plays on social issues, all in the vernacular. (The Chikwakwa students, even when performing in the vernacular, had never been able to attract such large local audiences.)

The best-known community theatre group in Lusaka began in 1978 as Taluta Theatre ('We are going'). Using a new community hall in Kanyama, a sprawling, dust-blown (in the dry season) or flood-ravaged (in the wet season) compound on the west side of the city, Taluta produced three plays about slavery, apartheid, and witchcraft in 1978–79. At the end of 1979 the Director of the Department of Cultural Services, Stephen Chifunyise, persuaded the group to turn professional. It changed its name to the Kanyama Production Unit and began touring the provinces as a travelling theatre. The group comprises three actors, all of them Form III school-leavers. The change of name went with a change of repertoire, noted by the *ZANTAA Newsletter* in 1982: 'We see that their theatre is shifting from political issues to social-economic issues. . . . The success of the Kanyama Production Unit will motivate other School Leavers to take up acting professionally.'[9]

Aspects of a young theatre

As Martin Banham (1976: 7) has stated, 'So much of African theatre is *young* theatre.' This partly reflects the fact that in Africa, with its higher birth-rate and lower life expectancy, the population is much younger than in Europe; but it also reflects, at least in Zambia, a social and cultural awakening: unemployed school-leavers, like those in the Kanyama group, have discovered through drama an effective means of voicing their criticism and discontent without bringing the wrath of a one-party state on their heads. (Many have also discovered the effectiveness of allegory and allusion. When, at the 1984 ZANTAA festival, a tramp in Tekumwenzo's play *The Tramp's Whistle* is asked by a passer-by why he lives such a life, and he replies: 'Are we not free here? Look at me – I am free to eat where I want and sleep where I want!' everyone understood the point.)

In a context of high youth unemployment, minimal job prospects, and un-wanted skills, drama not only gives scope for individual creativity and collabor-ative endeavour, it bestows a sense of purpose, a feeling of public recognition and public attention, when in other circumstances only helplessness, dependence, and impotence prevail. From a therapeutic pastime, drama becomes a *necessity*.

The realization that social and personal relationships can be comprehended, criticized, and hopefully changed through their dramatic and theatrical representation is, in this case, profound. Hence, the falsity of the choice between 'art and education', 'aesthetics and didacticism' so frequently invoked by the proponents of what David Kerr (1980) calls 'induced didactic theatre'.

No spokesperson for the groups I have mentioned would probably disagree with Kabwe Kasoma (1978) that 'Theatre which engages in art for art's sake is a luxury in Africa', or that 'Our theatre must therefore be totally committed to national development'. But the 'must' of the university adult educator and the 'must' of the disillusioned school leaver are two different things. When life acquires meaning through the practice of dramatic art, and an improvement in that art is an improvement in one's life, who is to say where 'theatre as art' ends and 'theatre for development' begins?

A persistent feature of these young independent theatre groups is the dominance of a particular personality, a leader-organizer who writes, produces, and directs the plays, and often acts the main role. A more binding factor, however, is the age-set, a group-within-the-group that has grown up and passed through the same school together.[10] One such club, originally consisting of school students, is Tithandize, founded in 1978 by Gregory Lungu and Francis Kapambwe, both pupils at Ndeke Secondary School in Kitwe.

Lungu soon proved to be an outstanding actor and a prolific playwright. In 1980 the club's leading members 'were sent to Kafue National Service Camp as an intact group. Their work in the camp was the production of plays while their mates produced food.'[11]

The new group took the name Kafunase, still maintaining links with Tithandize. In 1983 Lungu and other Kafunase members were transferred to the Zambia National Service Headquarters in Lusaka, where they formed Zanase, winning first prize at the 1983 and 1984 ZANTAA festivals, and still maintaining close links with Tithandize several hundred miles away.

In 1982–83 the ZANTAA leadership, boosted by the affiliation of new urban theatre groups, began calling for the boycotting and dissolution of TAZ, the nationalism of the little theatres (some of which were now Zambianized), and the establishment of a national Performing Arts Council, with ZANTAA as the only association representing the theatre arts. The government's response was revealing. In 1982 President Kaunda called for a merger between the two associations in the name of national unity.

ZANTAA's immediate response was to insist that TAZ had not changed. It was still an 'elitist, racially segregated' association. Any merger would therefore be 'a merger of two diametrically opposed approaches to the promotion of culture'.[12] To some, this was a rebellious act. Countering a decree from the Head of State, the people's father and fountainhead of wisdom, was tantamount to treason and subversion; and it led to ZANTAA being continually mauled thereafter by the media.

In 1983, after strong talk by ZANTAA chairman Dickson Mwansa and Culture Minister Dr. Henry Matipa, Kaunda sent Dr. Matipa to the Zambian embassy in Paris. The Government grant to ZANTAA, meanwhile, was cut by four-fifths. This was no death-blow, since affiliation, membership and festival participation fees, together with non-government sponsorship, had by now become ZANTAA's main sources of funds. In 1984 tripartite merger talks began between the government (represented by a new, *younger*, more enlightened minister, later Prime Minister, Kebby Musokotwane), TAZ, and ZANTAA.

Some rank-and-file ZANTAA members were uneasy; there was even the smell of betrayal in the air. Yet this no longer mattered, for whatever the chief and elders decide is law. How many, if any, of ZANTAA's members perceived the merger plan as the only way the ruling elders could find to strangle a rebellious child is hard to say. At a subconscious level, however, something like that may have been intuited. If so, it was soon to surface at another level – in the ZANTAA plays themselves.

In some respects these ZANTAA plays do not conform to the ideal of popular theatre, summarized in a 1977 Chikwakwa handout as 'unpretentious' drama *in the vernacular*, using 'simple stage settings, in school halls, or outside in village squares with sunlight or tilly lamps for lighting, and with simple, impromptu costumes and properties'. Socially-committed and participatory, popular theatre is 'drawn from local Zambian situations and Zambian problems', using 'Zambian languages, and Zambian culture, whether traditional or modern'.

In the last three ZANTAA national festivals, only one full-length entry has been entirely in the vernacular: an unscripted tragi-comedy in Bemba called *Samala* about a hopeless drunkard of a husband and his hard-working exploited wife, which the Kitwe group Bwanayina (a breakaway form Bakanda) popularized in the compounds and brought to the 1984 festival. Unscripted, improvised drama in the vernacular is usually confined to short, front-of-curtain comic sketches, performed as light entertainment while the stage is being prepared for the next play on the programme. English, the official medium of instruction in Zambia from first-year primary level, thus becomes the inevitable choice in a multilingual context where groups from different provinces compete in a national festival.

Other 'non-popular' elements can however be cited, such as 'atmospheric' stage lighting; the use of curtains (which Tikwiza had opposed); elaborate make-up (for ghosts and witchdoctors); the occasional use of sound effects; specially-designed costumes; and some technically sophisticated props, such as a disco machine and disco lights – all, needless to say, far from the popular-theatre ideal of simple drama for simple peasants.[13]

The fathers-and-sons theme

The 'fathers-and-sons' theme observed in these ZANTAA festival plays has four facets. Firstly, the stereotyped 'romantic love' plot – lovers who defy the traditional custom of arranged marriage, try to escape, fail, then, after much suffering, win their parents' – and a relenting, often repentant chief's – blessing just in time, turning possible tragedy into a happy resolution. In Greg Lungu's *Den of Torment* (Kasama Boys, 1984) the young hero is imprisoned and tortured on the chief's orders, but his sweetheart, the chief's daughter, manages to rescue him, and love eventually conquers death.

Secondly, there is the criticism of traditional, gerontocratic rule itself. Rigid, oppressive, witch-infested and tyrannical, it is projected by (and seems to present itself to) some young Zambian psyches as a source of anxiety, even terror. J. C. de Graft (1976) says that a complete identification of the subject 'with the pulse, the rhythm, the ritual purpose of drama' is perhaps only possible 'for people who believe in the curative power of magic'.

In the case of Bayete Nkosi, a group from the Eastern Province of Zambia,[14] ritual, magic, and witchcraft are represented on stage in order to arouse and so purge *fear*, especially fear of the social order that engenders them. (They are also excellent for sheer Gothic-horror entertainment. During one spectacular production, deliberately chosen as an evening performance, the only illumination in one scene came from oil lamps fixed onto the ram's-horn headgear of some horribly screaming witches. Their chests were painted with red and white stripes, symbolizing access, while living, to the world of the dead.) The witches' victims, or potential victims, almost without exception are the young.

Thirdly, there is what can be called the 'bad parents' theme. Here, lack of parental care and concern is the ostensible target. When, however, through neglect, indifference, or ignorance (less often through deliberate intent) an offspring, invariably male, is killed, dies, or commits suicide, the fourth facet is shown: filicide, or 'sacrifice of the son'.

In a country where Christianity has put down such strong roots, sacrifice of a son is not, perhaps, such a bizzare theme. In this context there are, as I shall try to show, deeper implications.

'Bayete Nkosi' is the traditional Zulu, Ndebele, and Ngoni greeting to a chief or king – an ironic choice of name in view of the thematic emphasis of the group's plays.[15] (All the plays are one-acters, a general rule in Zambian drama. Forty-five minutes is the average length of a ZANTAA play; over an hour is considered long.) *Mulangani* is about a young man whose life is threatened by witchcraft (most Zambian witches, by the way, are old *men*).

Zilole and *Witchcraft in Africa*, two 1984 entries, present a jealous father, a vicious uncle,[16] and other old men as terrifying ogres, witches in disguise who use evil magic to kill young lovers but, of course, fail in the end. *Mist of Africa* deals with the negligence of the old towards the young, while *It Happens* is about the conflict between school discipline and the desire for freedom.

The most original of Bayete's plays, however, is John Mwale's *Tears of Musetambe*, a 1985 winning entry, whose simple set design was strangely reminiscent of Plautine comedy, with the door of the Shumba house (containing daughter Shupe) stage right, and the door of the Mwenzo house (containing son Madzulo) stage left.

Mr. Shumba and Mr. Mwenzo have one thing in common: both are ignorant philistines who hate drama. Madzulo, leader of a local drama group called Musetambe ('Come and watch' in Bemba), brings Shupe home late one night from a rehearsal. Waiting at the door, her father bellows: 'Do you eat drama here?' The stage-struck pair run away rather than face a beating, and Messrs. Shumba and Mwenzo pursue them, armed with hunting gun and knobkerrie. Mwenzo to Shumba: 'I think you just shoot drama'. But, like the anarchist in *The Secret Agent*, who tries to 'blow up astronomy' by planting a bomb in the Greenwich Observatory, the would-be exterminators find that drama cannot be put down.

After some well-executed stage business, in which the partners-in-drama give their slow-witted elders the slip, Madzulo, despairing, reads Shupe a letter addressed to 'My former father'. Shumba and Mwenzo still pursuing, swap weapons and targets – though Shumba, in a moment of anxious concern suggests that his neighbour aim only for his daughter's *leg* if he happens to see her first. What began as a fine-spirited comedy ends, however, in a generic mix-up when Madzulo is accidentally shot and killed by his own father.[17]

The 'bad parents' theme

The 'bad parents' theme occurs in various guises. Twasika's *Parents* (1985) exposed a father's religious hypocrisy and sexual duplicity: father and son share the same girl-friend, a fact neither son nor girl-friend is aware of, and which the father, on discovering, tries to hide from his son. In Kasama Teacher Training College's *A Noble Profession Abused* (1984), a hospital doctor is punished for dereliction of duty as a father as well as a doctor when, ignoring an emergency call from the hospital, he unwittingly allows his own son to die.

In Nkwashi Primary School's *The Honorable Minister* (1985), a top politician who sells organs from dead bodies to Indians, who use them as elixirs (according to common belief), nearly causes the death of his own son when the latter is seized by hired thugs for the same purpose. Unemployed school drop-outs, maltreated orphans, 'mishanga boys',[18] unwanted or adopted children, are common motifs.[19]

The most, extreme statement of the 'bad parents' theme, however, was probably Zhaninge's *Tears in the Shacks*, staged at the Kabwe festival.

Zhaninge, formed in Kitwe in 1980, specialize in strong emotive, hyperbolic statements, harrowing audiences with tales or urban misery and exploitation. After staging *Sacrifice* and *Victims of Misfortune* in 1981 (the titles suggest the nature of the plays), the club withdrew its affiliation from Kitwe District Council and moved into the Zambia Railways Community Centre. 'The group's main problem', wrote the *ZANTAA Newsletter* in 1983, 'is the rude treatment they receive from some heads of institutions who sometimes deny them permission to perform in their institutions without offering any reasons.'[20]

In *Tears in the Shacks*, performed with minimal set, props, and costumes (a true 'theatre of poverty'), two starving brothers are terrorized by their heartless, brutalized parents. Driven from the family's shanty home by his drunken father, one of the boys is later found scavenging among dustbins labelled 'Keep Kitwe Clean'. A council worker (no doubt a symbolic figure) chases the boy away. After a heart-wringing soliloquy (the actor's identification with the role was total), the boy hangs himself. When the body is brought home, the insensitive father – taught to be so, it seems, by his selfish and unfeeling wife – turns suddenly and tearfully repentant.

As a social protest, Zhaninge's play bears witness to an acute ideological as well as emotional crisis. Traditional African society looked after its members according to the ties of kinship. Any son or daughter belonged to the kinship group, not just to a nuclear couple. In the extended family system, the father's brothers are also called 'father', and the mother's sisters, 'mother'; child welfare is thus built into the system. The word 'orphan', like the word 'bastard', has little meaning in such a context.

Urbanization changed all that. Two generations on, we see the urban trauma relived and refracted in hyperbolic melodrama, just as in Bayete Nkosi's image of witch-bound Africa we see the projection of a psychic, in many ways adolescent world. The tone of Zhaninge's play, like that of the speakers in some of Blake's *Songs of Experience*, is one of self-pity, bitterness, and despair.

Ideologically, there seems to be a difficulty in distinguishing personal and moral actions from social and economic causes. It is absurd to imagine that 'bad parents' are to blame for Zambia's street vagabonds, *mishanga* sellers, and young petty criminals, though the breakdown, under capitalist economic pressures, of traditional kinship ties and the fact that little has been done to replace the old humanism with a new welfare system, can create conditions not unlike those portrayed in *Tears in the Shacks*. Ideologically, however, it is extremely difficult for these young Zambian dramatists and performers, in apportioning blame, not to see things in terms of 'them', as parents and/or the old, and 'us' as the young.

Perhaps the most richly-loaded statement of this 'fathers-and-sons' theme is *The Witchfinder* (1985) by Hilary Mbodza, automotive engineer and leader of a new group based on the mines called Mwendalubi, again from Kitwe. The play's traditional setting – an Ngoni village, with every scene but two made up of the chief (Chimutengo, 'Big Tree') and his counsellors – avoided tedious stereotypes such as the slow-speaking, toga-adjusting, fly-whisk-wielding child surrounded by his sagely nodding, head-shaking, cross-legged elders sporting white blobs on their hair. Instead, the chief (played by Mbodza) was vigorous, business-like and energetic; the leopard's tail hanging down in front and the knobkerrie in his right hand (not just held as a sceptre but used for demonstration) symbolized his phallic, patriarchal power. The counsellors likewise were warlike (in the Ngoni mould) and physically impressive.

The play opened with an elder, Mpondolo, complaining, like the suppliants in *Oedipus Rex*, of famine and death, flooded rivers without rain, infertile wives, stillbirths, and pigs laying eggs – all, he says, caused by witchcraft (meaning, here, the breaking of some taboo – again, as in *Oedipus*). The chief, unlike Oedipus, dismisses the stories as old wives' tales, the product of superstition, ignorance, and malice. Chief and elders then drink beer, dance (to some powerful drumming), and sing a song about an ancestral king called Lobongo, who had twenty wives and six hundred children.

During a famine, Labongo resorted to eating his own children. Yet so feared was he, with his elephant-like footsteps, that people held back from killing him. At last they found the courage collectively to rid themselves of this evil by setting fire to the royal enclosure, and killing all those inside, wives included.

Chimutengo, loved and feared as father of his people, is warned by Mpondolo that if he does not bring in a witchfinder his village will break up. Mpondolo champions the women of the village, saying: 'What the women suffer, we also suffer' – at which the ZANTAA audience applauded. 'Miracles' (in Zambian English, a 'miracle' means breaking a taboo, or an event caused by breaking a taboo) are still taking place, he reports.

We next see Chimutengo at night as a witch, creeping up on a sleeping boy and bewitching him with a cow-horn. The boy dies, and at his burial the chief feigns a father's tears for the loss of his 'son'. A witchfinder is brought in, with negative results. Another comes, and finally discovers the witch – Chimutengo himself, who has been hiding his 'vitumwa', or witch's impedimenta, under his throne. (Each one was clearly displayed to the audience while its function was explained.)

The chief's murderous behaviour is entirely motiveless in terms of psychological realism. However, it fits into a magico-mythical view of reality. Poverty, famine, and drought, infertility and 'abnormal' happenings, presuppose a human polluting agent, a crime of which someone, somewhere, *must* be guilty. In singing together of the killing of Labongo, the village elders symbolically share in the primal guilt; Labongo, the polygamous ancestral father, is guilty of eating his own children, but stopping him means killing the father.

Chimutengo, as clan head, thus carries the main burden of guilt, and when things go wrong, it is he who is responsible. Guilt is transferred onto a father-figure whose double crime of parricide (symbolically inherited in a ritual celebration) and filicide points to an endlessly-repeated process. The snake bites its own tail: mythical events recur in a timeless present, in the world of ritual and song.

Myth, ritual ... and revolution

The 'fathers-and-sons' theme is thus the crux of an ideological and political dilemma. If social justice is achieved through fundamental change, and if fundamental change means challenging patriarchal authority – an act associated, however distantly, with the crime of parricide – then social justice implies parricide. The thought itself is a 'miracle' carrying its own horror, a horror that Freud (in *Totem and Taboo, Moses and Monotheism*, and elsewhere) connects with the incest taboo.

Challenging the 'primal' father's will or arousing his jealousy carried threats of castration, for which the later, symbolic substitution was circumcision. Male circumcision, as part of the initiation rite, thus symbolizes the young man's preparedness 'to submit to the father's will, even if it imposed the most painful sacrifice on him' (Freud).

The possible ritualistic and mythic origins of the dilemma now become clear. Underlying the social protest in many of the ZANTAA plays – a protest reflected in the solidarity and fraternal spirit within ZANTAA itself – is the idea that someone is morally to blame for the way things are. Put crudely, for the young this means the old – not a socio-economic system, not neo-colonialism, not capitalism, but fathers, even forefathers. Ordinary patriarchal power means that men dominate women, fathers sons, and older men younger men.

Quasi-divine, absolute power, however, means that its possessor is responsible for everything, from the rising of the sun to the coming of the rains. Freud likens this absolutist model to a paranoid delusion: 'The model upon which paranoics base their delusions of persecution is the relation of a child to his father. A son's picture of his father is habitually clothed with excessive powers of this kind, and it is found that distrust of the father is intimately linked with admiration for him.' God is love; the wish to kill the father is the primal sin. The unconscious wish is therefore suppressed, re-appearing in its emasculated, masochistic form as the sacrifice of the son, and activating another culture myth: the death of the hero, part of the hero-martyr complex.

In other words, filicide and filial sacrifice, as recurrent themes, represent the guilty morror-image of a suppressed desire to eliminate the father, a kind of atonement as well as protest. In early Christianity, says Freud, 'men were acknowledging in the most undisguised manner the guilty primeval deed, since they found the fullest atonement for it is the sacrifice of this one son'. What better myth for short-circuiting revolutionary ambitions?

We have seen that in at least two plays father–son competition for (and opposition partisanship towards) women are introduced, while in *Tears of Musetambe* the symmetrical pairing of the two hunting fathers gives a hint of father–son rivalry for possession of the same girl. (Madzulo is *wrongly* thought to be escorting her as a sexual partner.) Freud's famous theory has the force of myth: the ruler of the primal horde was a violent, jealous father who kept all the females to himself and drove the sons away. Fraternal solidarity involves collective guilt, resulting in two taboos: against parricide and incest.

Another, more accessible explanation for the conflict of generations is the inequality of age distinctions in traditional African society, where older men control the allocation of resources, labour, and people, and accumulate household authority, ritual offices, and wives. Rivalries and antagonisms abound: polygamous fathers often nurse fears that their bachelor sons will commit adultery with their younger wives, while sons often resent the enormous power fathers wield over them with regard to marriage, journeys, working on the land, property, and ritual authority (Foner, 1984).

Witchcraft beliefs, says Foner, 'are closely related to inequalities between old and young', and 'do on occasion help to mute or forestall bitter age conflict'. Younger people 'find their subordination to the powerful and privileged old grating. Picturing old people as witches expresses their hostility'. The 'witchcraft' theme can therefore act as a safety-valve, releasing hostile, yet at the same time *ambivalent* emotions.[21] Just as in the plays of Bayete Nkosi, so among the Tiv of central Nigeria, 'influential elders by day were said to be witches by night'.

Towards integration or schism?

Looking at the fathers-and-sons theme as part of a dramatic and narrative structure, we note that at the end of a play death of the son is followed by punishment of, and/or repentance on the part of the father-figure, while near-death may be followed by punishment or a softening of the heart, a kind of 'conversion'.

At this point we can draw on Victor Turner's concept of 'social drama'. Primary public processes, says Turner (1974: 122), tend to generate myths, to the extent that even history 'repeats the deep myths of culture'. A social drama occurs within a community that shares the same values, and has four phases: a breach, a crisis, then redress, followed either by reintegration of the community or recognition of schism. One such 'public process' is 'the forwardness of youth versus the domineering elders' (1981).

Mechanisms for dealing with the crises vary, depending on the social inclusiveness of the crisis. Certain kinds require 'public ritual' involving 'a literal or moral "sacrifice", that is, a victim as scapegoat is offered for the group's "sin" of redressive violence'. Using the terms from Turner's fourfold 'process model', we could say that the social drama implied in the staged drama of the ZANTAA festival plays concludes more often with recognition of a schism than with reintegration.

The fathers-and-sons theme also finds expression in traditional oral narratives, which, as performances, contain many theatrical techniques. What Foner describes as factors mitigating conflict, such as the legitimation of age inequality in various folktales and myths, upward mobility, the genuine affection that can exist between fathers and sons, and strong kinship whereby the old act as protectors and patrons, are illustrated in this summarized version of a Kaonde folktale from the North-Western Province of Zambia: the 'new' theme in the ZANTAA plays has its roots in oral tradition.

> During a famine a father and his son went hunting. They built a shelter for drying meat and set off in different directions. The son came to a stream where six beautiful young girls were standing. Remarking on their beauty, he asked if he could marry one of them. They replied that he would have to marry all of them, but only if he killed his father. The son pondered this, then decided against it. The next day the father set off in the direction taken

by the son and reached the stream. He put the same question to the girls, who told him to kill his son. The father, excited at the prospect of so many beautiful girls for wives, decided to commit the deed. But that night the son observed his father's odd, short-tempered behaviour and took precautions. Foiled in his attempt, the guilty father felt ashamed. Next day the son felled and chopped a 'blood tree', made cuts in its bark and laid it on the ground, covering it with leaves to that it resembled a human body with fatal gashes. He told his father to hide, went off to inform the girls that he had killed his father, and returned. Soon afterwards, father and son saw six large flies settle on the tree and suck its 'blood', thus exposing the true identity of the 'girls'. Father and son then completed a successful hunt together and returned to their village, where the chief, after hearing the whole story, rewarded the son with half his domain. After that, the son became a wealthy ruler.[22]

In the ZANTAA plays, by contrast, we rarely see such upward mobility. In Greg Lungu's *The School Leaver's Notebook*, an orphaned school-leaver terrifies his guardian uncle when the latter reads what appears to be the boy's last testament (the 'sacrifice' theme again). But the boy manages to find financial security – not through patronage, but by selling his own art work on the market. Darius Lungu's frequently-produced short play, *The Mishanga Seller and the Graduate* (always done with improvisation and new material: scripts in Zambia are never sacred) shows a jobless school-leaver abandoning useless books for the illicit trade of his ironically better-off comrade.

At ZANTAA festivals, thirteen productions on average are by secondary schools and five are by primary schools, with the rest (about twenty) by various independent groups. One would like to know how much freedom school drama groups have, and what constraints are imposed on their choice of plays. My own impression is that this depends largely on the school, the attitude of the head, and the presence on the staff of a drama enthusiast. (Some school heads are extremely sensitive to 'critical' plays.)

In fact, hardly any of the 110 ZANTAA festival plays I saw dealt directly with school or school life, though the hierarchical relations of dominance and submissiveness within the school, and the influence of the ruling party UNIP (both through its school branches and the political education incorporated into the syllabus) have certainly had a 'conscientizing' (if not always desired) effect.

One thing is clear. The pyramidal structure of Zambia's education system, with its wasteful drop-out rate and its inability to sustain meritocratic expectations in a period of economic and social disintegration, is planting the seeds of its own dissolution: namely, an alliance between those who, in the 1960s, would have been members of the new middle class and the young members of a growing lumpenproletariat.[23] What Marjorie Mbilinyi (1979) says of Tanzania is beginning to apply to Zambia: an 'underdeveloped economy,' she says, 'cannot possibly absorb a "secondary school educated labour force", nor does society have the material resources to support such an education structure'.

Greg Lungu's *A Second Before the Storm* (Zanase, 1984), an apocalyptic play in the *Soweto* style about the coming nuclear 'storm', really alludes to *Africa's* holocaust, ecological, economic and social. Implicit in the fathers-and-sons theme is the view that under the present system Zambia's youth has no future. How, ideologically, artistically, and through drama, it is possible for theatre artists to evisage and work towards one, remains on the agenda.[24]

Notes

1 Wilhemina Kalu (1976), writing on the impact of urbanization on Ga adolescents, says of this behavioural convention: 'The relationship at home is so positive that the western phenomenon of teenage–parent friction and the generation-gap syndrome are not manifested . . . Talking to adults and arguing with them as if he and they were equals is considered totally disrespectful. One may dare to argue with appropriately selected adults, using a great deal of wit, humour, and diplomacy.'

2 Scudder and Colson (1980) note that the Zambian labour market had no difficulty in absorbing all Form V graduates from the Gwembe district up to 1967, and perhaps up to 1970. But in 1971, 30 per cent of the graduates were still unemployed six months after graduation.

3 Zambia's cultural heritage includes many kinds of ritual drama and dance drama in which religious, satiric, social, and morally symbolic characters are represented. Perhaps the two best examples are Nyau and Makishi, but in all the Zambian ceremonies a dramatic or paradramatic content is unquestionably there.

4 See John Reed (1984): 'For all the racial tensions that certainly existed, Northern Rhodesia was not a place in which a politically motivated Africanism was likely to develop .... Because of this history, Zambia has produced no fiction which could be called Africanist and no protest literature concerned with the injustices of the past.'

5 An example of this is radio drama, especially the plays of Julius Chongo and an enormously popular weekly programme in Bemba written by Mwansa Kapeya.

6 Tikwiza's patrons included businessmen, parastatal companies, and top government leaders, notably the President.

7 This was in an interview I conducted some months before Haggai Chisulo was killed in a car crash.

8 During Tikwiza's production of *The Cell* in November 1982, a government leader warned the vice-chairman by phone that unless certain changes were made in the play, party officials would have it taken off. The leader was reminded that the President himself had warmly endorsed the play in 1980. The production continued unhampered, but it marked the beginning of the end for Tikwiza.

9 *ZANTAA Newsletter*, Vol. 1, No. 2 (May 1982), p. 6–7.

10 In 1980 the members of Fwebena Afrika ('We Africans'), a Kitwe group led by Chibale Kalaba (playwright, schoolteacher and controversial letter-writer), took an oath in a Kitwe stream swearing 'to stay together in their desire to bring about an African cultural awareness' (*Theatre Magazine*, No. 1 (1985), p. 11). A few years later, after much infighting and factional squabbling, the group (re-named Africanist Dramatist Group) dwindled to relative insignificance, demonstrating once again the marginality of negritudist ideas in the Zambian context.

11 *ZANTAA Newsletter*, Vol. I, No. 3 (June 1982), p. 8.

12 *ZANTAA Newsletter*, Vol. II, No. 7 (Feb/March 1983), editorial.

13 ZANTAA festival plays have not, on the whole, tried to break down the conventional actor–spectator relationship. There is a danger that the environment of a competitive festival – usually a school hall with a captive audience – might lead to elitist conservatism. It should be borne in mind, however, that a play such as *Samala* is one kind of event when it is performed in an open space in a Kitwe compound, observed by a semi-literate, highly responsive, participating audience that includes dozens of noisy children, and another when it is performed in a school hall to an educated audience drawn from all parts of the country.

14 The only group to represent Eastern Province at the last two ZANTAA festivals. Bayete Nkosi originated in 1984 when four groups in Chipata, including one from the local Nursing School and another with the unusual name of Bafo ('Slaves' – in Ngoni tradition, descendants of war captives) collaborated on a theme for World Health Day. Out of a membership of sixty, only five are working, according to the group's leader, Benjamin Zulu. The rest are primary, secondary and college students, or are unemployed.

15 Obtaining playscripts is always difficult. Most groups have a 'resident playwright': Bayete's is John Mwale, a graduate of Chuonawe Secondary School and Chipata Teacher Training College, who took up drama in Kitwe. Where a play is already published (rare for ZANTAA, common in TAZ), duplicated scripts are generally used, based on typed – even, in some cases, originally handwritten – transcripts.

16 Where, under a system of matrilineal descent, the sister's son inherits, his patriarchal 'opponent' will be his mother's brother, or maternal uncle.

17 John Mwale, the author, told me that the play was based on an actual incident in which a female member of Bayete, who had won best actress award in the 1984 ZANTAA festival, was subsequently shot at by her father, and twice beaten by her brother.

18 'Mushanga' (plural: 'mishanga') is 'a stick', i.e., cigarette sold from packets by black-market vendors.

19 In Greg Lungu's *Oh My God* (Libala Secondary, 1985), Obi is told by his foster-parents that he is an adopted son. Stunned, he leaves home to find his 'real' parents. After meeting and almost escorting a prostitute in a bar, he discovers that she is his mother.

20 *ZANTAA Newsletter*, Vol. II, No. 7 (Feb/March 1983), p. 10.

21 For Freud, the psychological essence of totem and taboo is emotional ambivalence: the mixture of veneration and horror, desire and prohibition associated with objects carrying a mysterious and dangerous magical power'. The ambivalent attitude, says Freud, 'to this day characterizes the father–son complex in our children.

22 The original story was told to me by my wife Edith (née Kasanzale), who heard it as a child from her mother.

23 Cf. Guilbert Mudenda (1983) 'the economic crisis in the country has severely reduced the ability of the state to recruit and coopt large numbers of potential members of the various sections of the Zambian bourgeoisie. As a result, most of these people, especially the school dropouts and the lower sections of the petty bourgeoisie, are increasingly realizing that neocolonialism is not a viable alternative for Zambia's development.'

24 Any kind of alternative, or workers' theatre (e.g., the collaboration between strikers of the Metal and Allied Workers Union and the Junction Avenue Theatre group in South Africa) seems very far away. For fifty years Zambia's economy has depended almost entirely on copper, yet not one play about copper miners has, to my knowledge, ever been produced. In plays such as Darius Lungu's *Man in the Street* and Greg Lungu's *Song of the Shanties*, the workers are merely mouthpieces for abstract political slogans.

References

Martin Banham, *African Theatre Today* (Pitman, 1976).

Stephen Chifunyise, 'Triumph of a New People's Theatre', *Sunday Times of Zambia*, 4 January 1981.

Nancy Foner, *Ages in Conflict: a Cross-cultural Perspective on Inequality Between Old and Young* (Columbia University Press, 1984).

Sigmund Freud, *Totem and Taboo*, in *The Pelican Freud Library*. Vol. 13. (Penguin Books, 1985).

J. C. de Graft, 'Roots in African Drama and Theatre', *African Literature Today*, 8 (Heinemann, 1976), p. 1–25.

Wilhemina Kalu, 'The Impact of Urbanization on the Life Patterns of the Ga Adolescent', in Estelle Fuchs, ed. *Youth in a Changing World: Cross-Cultural Perspectives on Adolescence* (Mouton, 1976), p. 137–60.

Katete Kalumba, 'Working with the Rural Poor in Zambia' (Dept of Social Development Studies, University of Zambia, 1982).

Kabwe Kasoma, 'Is There Such a Thing as African Theatre?', paper written for the First International Colloquium/Workshop on the Social Role of Theatre in Africa (Lagos, 1978).

David Kerr, 'Didactic Theatre in Africa' (Dept of Literature and Languages, University of Zambia, 1980).

Marjorie Mbilinyi, 'Secondary Education', in *Education for Liberation and Development: the Tanzanian Experience*, ed. H. Hinzen and V. H. Hundsdorfer (Unesco, 1979), p. 103–13.

Gilbert Mudenda, 'Class Formation and Class Struggle in Contemporary Zambia', in Bernard Magubane and Nzongola-Ntalaja, ed., *Proletarianization and Class Struggle in Africa* (Synthesis Publications, San Francisco, 1983), p. 95–118.

Dickson Mwansa, 'Zambian Political Theatre', *Index on Censorship*, II, 2 (1982), p. 33–5.

Dickson Mwansa, 'Theatre as a Tool for Communication', *IFDA Dossier*, 42 (1984), p. 24–32.

John Reed, 'Zambian Fiction', in G. D. Killam, ed., *The Writing of East and Central Africa* (Heinemann, 1984), p. 82–99.

Thayer Scudder, and Elizabeth Colson, *Secondary Education and the Formation of an Elite: the Impact of Education on Gwembe District, Zambia* (Academic Press, 1980).

Victor Turner, *Dramas, Fields, and Metaphors* (Cornell University Press, 1974).

Victor Turner, 'Social Dramas and Stories about Them', in *On Narrative*, ed. W. I. T. Mitchell (University of Chicago Press, 1981), p. 137–64.

24 The art of festival in Ghana

Herbert M. Cole

Many festivals in Ghana are 'total works of art' (*Gesamtkunstwerke*). They commonly involve countless minor artistic forms and actions (i.e., songs, dances, sculptures, etc.) which can be seen as distinct, but whose separate nature is subsumed in such festivals by the impact of the whole, a continuous and unified event often of surpassing beauty and rich cultural significance. This paper is an examination of the artistic principles manifest in such festivals, and will discuss the relationship of parts to one another and to the unified whole.[1] It will conclude with an interpretation of festival art and meaning.

First a definition: a festival is a relatively rare climactic event in the life of any community. It is bounded by a definite beginning and end, and is unified thereby, as well as in being set apart from and above daily life. Its structure is built up on a core or armature of ritual. The festival brings about a suspension of ordinary time, a transformation of ordinary space, a formalization of ordinary behavior. It is as if a community becomes a stage set and its people actors with a battery of seldom-seen props and costumes. Meals become feasts, and greetings, normally simple, become ceremonies. Although dependent upon life-sustaining rituals, the festival is an elaborated and stylized phenomenon which far surpasses ritual necessity. It often becomes the social, ritual, and political apotheosis of community life in a year. At festival time one level of reality – the common and everyday – gives way to another, a more intense, symbolic, and expressive level of reality.

Many festivals in Ghana occupy five days or a week; others are compressed into one or two days. Whatever the duration, they are events of great complexity, and often confusion, especially for an outsider. They invoke all available artistic media orchestrated to a common purpose at once spiritual and serious, playful and entertaining. It is in their nature to be meaningful on several levels and difficult to understand, though enjoyable even without a full understanding. They are affecting and appealing experiences to a child and a wise local priest or farmer or chief, to an educated accountant returned home for the celebration and to a stranger. The well-staged festival brings everyone into its ambience. These characteristics and others they share with more conventional works of art. Indeed, the same vocabulary used in describing or analyzing a sculpture, musical composition, or drama can be applied with equal validity to festivals. They have boundaries (i.e., 'frames'), compositions and rhythms; patterns, textures, tonality, themes, and contrasts. Motifs and variations occur within acts and scenes, tempos and moods are established leading to climax and resolution.

Odwira in Akropong

To amplify these ideas let us turn to a specific festival held annually by the Akuapem peoples in Akropong, seat of the paramount chief of some 55,000 Akuapem (Kwamena-Poh 1973: 3). This is Odwira, and it embraces several related purposes: thanksgiving; eating New Yam; sacrificing to ancestors and other deities; purifying the king and his people for a New Year; mourning the deaths of the past year; reaffirming political loyalties and allegiances, re-establishing the military order and social ties, and proclaiming the unity of a state organization. This rich, multi-levelled content is reflected in the structures and composition of the five-day event, and tends to characterize most festivals. Both artistic forms and their meanings in festivals are often so numerous, layered and overlapping that they are seldom if ever fully intelligible from any single vantage point. At least fourteen distinct ceremonies occur during the five days, some simultaneously; no single participant or observer would or could be present at all times.

To aid in visualizing the shape of the whole festival, I have reduced it to a schematic and interpretive form, a diagram of 'energy flow' as I was able to observe or reconstruct from native accounts (Fig. 24.1). Two complementary types of behavior are graphed: below the centre time-line is my view of the flow of ritual intensity in ceremonies either public or private; above the time-line, the intensity and elaboration of public display and spectacle. As may be observed in the diagram, 'ritual intensity' and 'display elaboration' are sometimes discontinuous, sometimes simultaneous and interdependent. Together they form what may be called an 'energy system' which ultimately calls upon virtually all the ritual and artistic resources of the Akuapem state. The development of several Western art forms – ballet or opera, for example – could be charted along a time-line in an analogous manner.

The festival proper begins with the clearing of paths from various points to the state capital and festival site, Akropong, so 'the gods may come and eat.' The event ends five days later, after a magnificent procession, with a grandiose formal gathering during which chiefs revalidate political ties and make final sacrifices. The five-day period is shaped by a rhythmic ebbing and flooding of energy, with a crescendo building to the climax of the final day. This schematic expression of time flow can be supplemented and cross-cut by another type of diagram, shown here in series (Figs. 24.2A–G), in which the spaces of the town and circulation through them may be visualized at selected periods of time from a bird's-eye view. Again simplified, these space/circulation patterns make graphic both the *formal* character of different events and the *contrast* of one activity to another. The specific events, somewhat arbitrarily chosen, are several of the more important private and public phases of the festival's development. The symbols on them are explained in the key, and each phase is identified by a letter on the lower part of the time-energy flow chart. It is useful, I think, to give an abbreviated account of the main events of the five-day festival period.

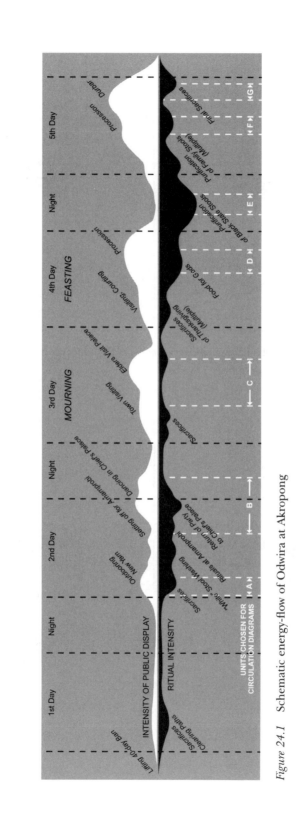

Figure 24.1 Schematic energy-flow of Odwira at Akropong

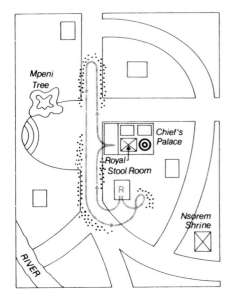

Figure 24.2A   'Outdooring' of New Yam.

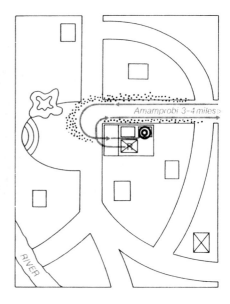

Figure 24.2B   Procession to Amamprobi.

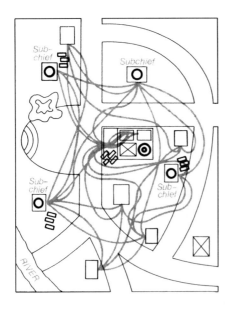

Figure 24.2C   Day of mourning.

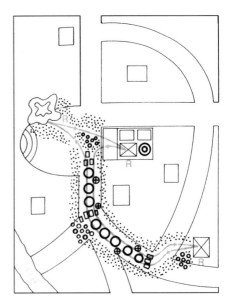

Figure 24.2D   Procession of sacrificial
foods to Nsorem shrine.

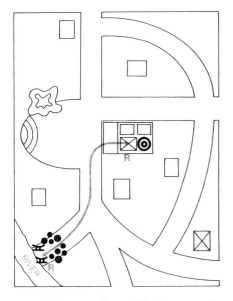

Figure 24.2E   Feeding of black ancestral state stools.

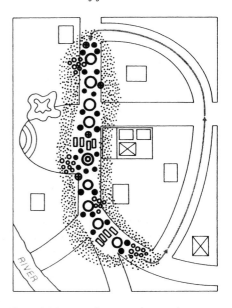

Figure 24.2F   Major state procession.

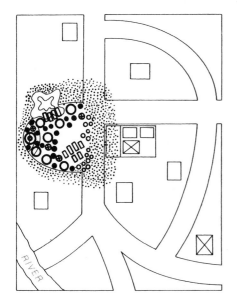

Figure 24.2G   Final Durbar.

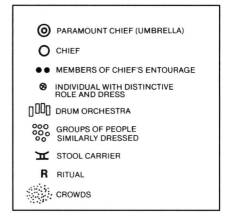

Figure 24A–G   Space/circulation diagrams of Odwira phases. Below, key to symbols used.

⊙	PARAMOUNT CHIEF (UMBRELLA)
○	CHIEF
●●	MEMBERS OF CHIEF'S ENTOURAGE
⊗	INDIVIDUAL WITH DISTINCTIVE ROLE AND DRESS
⫿⫿⫿	DRUM ORCHESTRA
°°°	GROUPS OF PEOPLE SIMILARLY DRESSED
⨌	STOOL CARRIER
R	RITUAL
⁖∴	CROWDS

Synopsis of Odwira

As if to prepare the community for an extraordinary event, priests impose a ban on drumming, dancing, and mourning forty days prior to Odwira. On Sunday before the Monday when the festival truly starts, one of the royal executioners (a clan that now has a largely ceremonial role, with police functions) shoots a gun into the air to lift the ban (Kwamena-Poh 1973: 150).

Monday

After preparatory sacrifices, pathways are cleared from and within Akropong to shrines, to the royal graveyard some miles distant, and to villages subject to the paramount chief of the Akuapem state. This 'path-clearing' has a more symbolic than practical value, especially in these days of greater commerce and mobility; lines of communication to ancestors, gods, and other men are opened that all may reaffirm the integrity of life under their living head of state.

Tuesday

After paths are cleared, the new agricultural year is officially opened. The yam crop, the yield of ancestral lands, is introduced to the gods and people by the town's senior elder. The 'outdooring' of New Yam (Fig. 24.2A) involves both non-public sacrifices and public display, the latter being a community-wide announcement of the former, including a kind of mock battle or race, when young men compete in kicking pieces of New Yam through the main street of Akropong. Little music and no dancing attend this unusual 'procession,' and its general tone is more athletic and martial than artistic or stately. At most, two or three hundred people are involved as participants and audience, and the spatial foci are first the house of the oldest living man in Akropong, and then a several-hundred-yard-long section of the town's main street. Clothing is for the most part non-distinctive.

Later the same morning an essentially private ceremony is held in one of the palace courtyards. This is the 'washing of "white" state stools'. It should be mentioned that for Akan peoples, stools mean far more than mere supports for the body; a person's soul is identified with his stool, and stools thus serve varied ceremonial functions. Those of particularly important dead leaders are ritually blackened, then enshrined, whereupon they serve as ancestral symbols. Five finely carved old stools, some made around 1850 or before,[2] are carried out by attendants and literally washed and cleaned in large brass basins with certain leaves and medicines mixed with water. Libations are poured, and clearly the stools are purified, although since they are domestic royal heirlooms rather than ancestral symbols (i.e. 'black stools'), the rite is neither secret nor as ritually intense as later stool ceremonies. Nevertheless, few observers were present.

The next event (Fig. 24.2B) – the procession of priests to the royal mausoleum at Amamprobi, three or four miles distant – begins quietly but distinctively. A solemn tone is set by mournful, measured beats on the executioner's drum. (This drum, incidentally, is a remarkable piece, carved in relief and covered with intricate brass repoussé.) A group of twelve to fifteen people, carrying sacrificial materials and leading a sheep (also for sacrifice), walk to the mausoleum. The group is led by the chief of the state executioners and includes the more important priests of the state (and town). I was barred from the rite itself (though not from the departure or return of the party), but was told that offerings were made at the graves of royal ancestors, and that a purifying, strengthening mixture was prepared from perpetual medicines at this site. This medicine and other paraphernalia, called 'Odwira,' recall state history because Amamprobi was the original Akuapem capital (ca. 1731) where sacred state symbols are kept. Brought to the current capital and king, these items and their corresponding rituals represent the purification and perpetuation of the state.

The rather triumphant return of this party draws crowds into the streets. Drumming and some spontaneous dancing converge on the small group as it brings the sacred Odwira medicine to the chief in his palace. In mourning costume the chief receives the party, and aided by the majestic state *frontomfrom* drums, much dancing ensues. The distinctive reds and blacks of mourning are appropriate dress for all in attendance at this crowded reception in the largest of palace courtyards.

Wednesday

The third day is devoted to public and private mourning. As the diagram (Fig. 24.2C) shows, there is much visiting throughout the town, with circulation patterns diffuse and random rather than strongly focussed. The activities of this day are repeated by all family heads and involve countless libations, prayers, and speeches remembering those who have died during the previous year. The mood is serious but festive, for Akan mourning involves much drumming, dancing, and drinking. Important elders, still in mourning costume, visit the paramount chief in the afternoon to pay him homage and to honour deceased members of the royal family.

Thursday

A similar pattern of intercompound visiting occurs during the fourth day, given over to feasting. This is a time of thanksgiving for life and health, a day on which townspeople promenade throughout Akropong in their best attire to show off the blessings they have received. Traditionally, too, this is a day of courting and making engagements. Family meetings are held to decide upon issues involving all its scattered members, whose attendance is all but mandatory. In many Ghanian festivals such feasts are dramatized in two particular ways. The first is the construction of special cooking hearths in public spaces adjacent to family compounds, in contrast to everyday sites inside. Such hearths are often artistically constructed at the beginning of a festival and ceremonially destroyed at its end.[3] The second, logically, is the preparation, ceremonious eating and distribution, to ancestors, passersby and the entire extended family, of distinctive and especially rich foods that are commonly not eaten during the rest of the year.

Such a focus on feasts, reiterated often during the festival period, is a universal aspect of such events, as the etymology of the English word 'festival' suggests.

By now the town is full of returned sons and daughters working and living elsewhere, and the atmosphere is buoyant and festive. The first of the week's two major processions occurs that afternoon, when young female representatives of all the chiefs carry sacrificial foods to a major shrine, Nsorem, on the outskirts of the town (Fig. 24.2D). The gods are honored and thanked and placated with these offerings, made by priests with a restricted audience inside the walled shrine. Crowds of people attracted by the colorful procession wait outside the enclosure; many dance and sing spontaneously to pass the time before the procession returns over its original route to the main plaza of Akropong opposite the king's palace. Further sacrifices are made at the impressive sacred tree there, *mpeni*, and still others are performed later and privately in the palace stool room.

This large procession included the 'sacrificial entourages' of some fifteen chiefs, each party made visible by its sheltering umbrella. Seven or eight musical groups took part and hundreds of people both lined the streets and followed entourages of their choice, the women often fanning with their 'covercloths' and thereby cooling and praising the heavily-laden food carriers, who occasionally stumbled, possessed by the spirits they were chosen to serve. Adding complexity and textural richness to the prescribed processional order and its core of essential participants, the 'audience' – now onlookers, now active participants – lent an air of informality and bustling interaction with the main actors. A considerable amount of unexpected, unprogrammed action – dance, gesture, song, and other random activity[4] – marked this procession, a contrast to the more formalized and larger procession of chiefs the next day.

Thursday night

The dramatic peak of ritual intensity followed this procession in the darkness of late evening, night and early morning, when the highly sacred state and royal 'black' ancestral stools were washed in the waters of the local stream (Fig. 24.2E). As I was not present during this time I will quote a colleague, Patricia Crane, who recorded her impressions of the event though she was also barred from the ritual itself: '.... The brilliance of display, the boisterousness [of previous events] were suddenly held in check by total silence, lack of movement, and non-visibility. For one evening out of the year there was an actual physical separation of the living and the dead, a spatial reversal. When the ancestral spirits are taken out of their shrine [the royal stool room], living inhabitants of Akropong must remain inside their homes. The noise of daily living ceased, giving way to the silence of the spirit.' At 9 p.m. a gong player moved through the town warning people to return home and extinguish lights. By ten o'clock it was eerily still and dark and the only sounds were executioners running and bombing rocks on the tin roofs of houses where occasional lights still burned. After half an hour, total silence and total darkness. Some hours later, perhaps 3 a.m., the blackened ancestral stools were taken by a priestly delegation to the stream, ceremonially washed, thereby purified, then 'fed' with the blood of a sacrificial sheep. About 4 a.m. the paramount chief greeted the returning stools and their entourage. Two shots were fired to announce that individual family stools should then be purified, and the royal ancestors – black stools – returned to their sanctuary.[5]

Friday

Begun with solemn and exclusively private rites, the fifth day blossoms later with a crescendo of dramatic public display and political panoply. The week's most majestic procession is mounted about noon (Fig. 24.2F). Colorful, gold-bedecked chiefs parade through the major town streets, hedged about by richly embellished members of their entourages. This procession was not held at Akropong during the Odwira I witnessed (1972) because the paramount chief was sick, but doubtless it would have been similar to others I have witnessed. Participants dress according to office or rank, in multiple variations on the theme of ceremonial finery. The procession reveals the splendor of displayed political power and wealth in stately movement. A thunderous drum or horn orchestra follows nearly every chief, while each entourage vies with the next in grandeur, elegance, and the size of its following. Scores of gold-leafed swords, staffs, flywhisks, and umbrella tops compete with sumptuous cloths, patterned bodies, elegant hair-styles, and luxurious gold and bead jewellery. Swaying, twirling umbrellas mark chiefs, linguists and swordbearers, and some chiefs are borne aloft in stately palanquins, expressing their superiority. Royalty and common people are bound together, however, by exaltation and common purpose. The display – activated by drum rhythms, horn blasts and song, made expressive by gesture and dance – captivates, entertains and dazzles; all townspeople, commoner and chief, old and young, are swept into its aura, caught by its majesty. But its multiple meanings are by no means lost. The social order is manifest in the dress and behavior of all participants, whether on-lookers or actors.

The procession is in turn measured and orderly or wildly active, transported by vibrant dances, as commanded by drummers. The parade ends at the main town plaza, opposite the chief's palace, where chiefs and nobles sit in state, their king and paramount centered at the highest position under his double umbrella, with lesser chiefs and officials carefully placed according to tradition and rank (Fig. 24.2G).

If the procession is the active, *popular* event which maximizes the public visibility of royalty and allied groups (i.e., priests, warriors, executioner clan, voluntary associations, musical bands and so forth) and which stimulates the 'audience' to become participants, then the hierarchically disposed and sedentary durbar is the cool and formal *political* event which binds the state into a cohesive unit. Socio-political display (the procession) terminates in real but nonetheless symbolic transactions between chiefs on behalf of their people (the durbar). Oaths are sworn, speeches given, and drinks are distributed to important people. Formal behavior prevails. Being spatially focussed rather than circulating through a mile or more of town streets amid thousands of people, the durbar reaches a smaller public – despite the large size of the plaza and the attendant crowds – and energy focusses on reciprocal expressions of loyalty and allegiance among the chiefs in the state organization. Yet these interchanges – expressed in speeches, prayers, dances, gestures and drummed proverbs – represent the solidarity of the renewed, purified state and its leaders, supported on the one hand by ancestral and other spiritual sanctions and on the other by the people at large. 'The edges of the years have met,' runs a local New Year's maxim, and the cosmos, embracing all Akuapem people is renewed and thus ready for the trials and triumphs of the year now beginning.

Form and content

Clearly one cannot separate the significance and content of such a festival from the complex orchestration of artistic media marshalled to express and reinforce such meanings. Indeed the multiplicity of art forms and processes supports the many levels and types of content. Such intricate interweavings of artistic patterns emphasize the importance and depth of the event, as well as present the onlooker/analyst with a profusion of elements and structures. In short, the festival is a complicated and often subtle art form. The fact that a festival may occupy several days rather than a few hours, like the performed arts in our culture, detracts not at all from its flow and unity in the minds of local people. In African ideas of time, events can be interrupted (e.g. by sleep) and discontinuous but still linked in purpose and therefore whole. The very length of such a work of art indeed serves to underscore its uniqueness in the ceremonial calendar and thus its centrality in the life of the community.

Structural elements

Certain structural elements that cross-cut both phases of the festival and its component arts (i.e., music, sculpture, dance, etc.) can be seen as devices which unify the entire event. Hierarchy, repetition, and variation are among the more important. Each of these, too, can be visualized both synchronically and diachronically. Thus a visible *hierarchy* of participants is clearly expressed in the formal seating of chiefs and others at the final durbar (Fig. 24.3). The double umbrella of the paramount chief is the apex of a pyramid comprised of lesser chiefs and their entourages; this entire structure in turn rests upon the broad foundation provided by the people at large, the 'supporting audience.' To this synchronic view, however, must be added the 'hierarchy of activities' during the five-day period, the apex being the final procession and durbar, the crowning events in a mounting flood of energy and intensity – both of artistry and of meaning. The 'energy flow' diagram can thus be taken as a diachronic view of hierarchy.

Many other hieratic structures are present, too, as might be expected in a socio-political organization such as that of the Akuapem in which a strong centralized leader is supported by varied levels of more or less specialized roles and groups. Thus the majestic spatial hierarchy of the durbar scene is echoed, in miniature, by that of a single chief seated or walking under his umbrella with his linguist and other members of his small entourage. The larger, 'linear' hierarchy of a state procession is made up of a linked series of smaller hieratic groups,

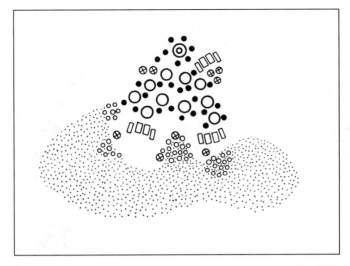

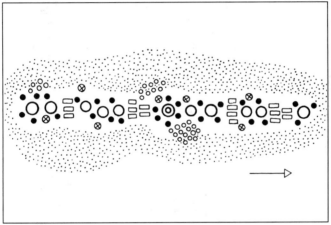

Figure 24.3   Hierarchy diagrams. (*Top*) Sedentary (durbar).
(*Bottom*) In motion (procession).
See key to Figure 24.2.

individual chiefs and their parties, with varied ancillary individuals and groups forming the 'sub-base' and the vast audience the base itself. The identities and distribution of main actors in an analogous New Year's festival procession (in Awutu) was accurately recorded (Fig. 24.4).

The principle of *repetition* follows logically, since each layer in a hierarchy, save the top, is composed of repeated or similar elements of varied character. Repetition, moreover, may be a still more fundamental component of festival structure than hierarchy. Virtually everything is repeated on different levels: rituals, including prayers, libations, sacrifices, and honorific gestures; musical performances; dance; isolable sculptures such as golden staffs, stools, swords and other items; processions; feasting; assemblies and speeches; ceremonial dress,

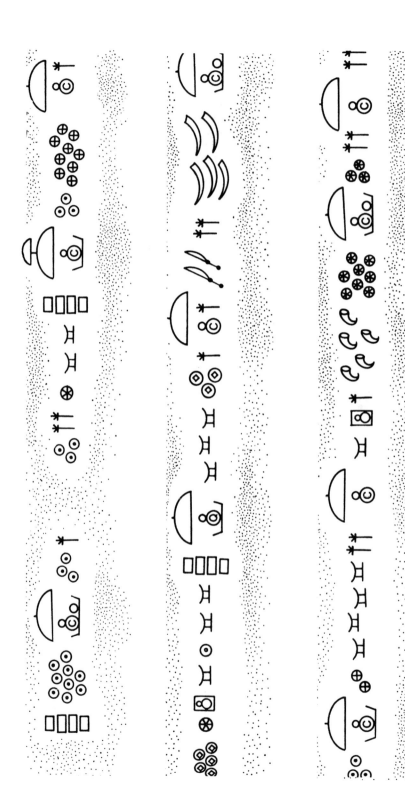

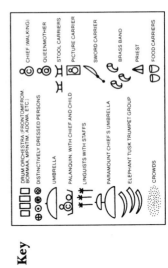

Figure 24.4 Awubia festival procession at Awutu.

Key

DRUM ORCHESTRA (FRONTOMFROM BOMMAA, MPINTIM, ADOMA, ETC.)

DISTINCTIVELY DRESSED PERSONS

UMBRELLA

PALANQUIN, WITH CHIEF AND CHILD

LINGUISTS WITH STAFFS

PARAMOUNT CHIEF'S UMBRELLA

ELEPHANT TUSK TRUMPET GROUP

CROWDS

CHIEF (WALKING)

QUEENMOTHER

STOOL CARRIERS

PICTURE CARRIER

SWORD CARRIER

BRASS BAND

PRIEST

FOOD CARRIERS

jewellery, body painting and hairstyling. Public events are repetitious, as are private ones; spatial and temporal patterns recur throughout the week and a good many events are repeated simultaneously in scores of family compounds throughout the town (Fig. 24.2C). Clearly, too, repetitions in visual patterns and artistic processes are expressions of content, that is, they reflect the socio-political and spiritual realities of a complex state and social organization, including the needs of ordinary people to act out their support of the power structure.

All such repetitions, moreover, involve the principle of *variation* to greater or lesser degrees. No two chiefs or priests dress or embellish themselves identically nor do their entourages include exactly the same numbers of people or the same decorations. Chiefs and many other participants wear different 'costumes' for as many different occasions. No two orchestras among the twelve or more present are the same either in make-up or in the musical pieces played. A number of men may dance in series to praise the king, but each dancing style is of course individual. Examples could be multiplied. Spatial and temporal variations and contrasts are of greater importance still in establishing the rhythmic progress of festival development. A plaza is now empty, then filled; one procession is small and another large; circulation is now random, later focussed along a prescribed route; one day is for mourning, the next for feasting. And in any one event, especially a major public one, there are dozens of individuals or groups whose personal ornamentations and actions are distinctive among roles. Visual, auditory, and kinetic variations are nearly impossible to count and document as a major event such as a state procession. The onlooker would have to be in a dozen places at once with eyes in the back of his head. If slides or videotape recordings are made from a distance, then of course individual variations are lost, though the textural richness and artistic depth and multiplicity of the whole are recorded fairly well, and its unity is apparent.

When repetitions and variations are multiplied, as they so often are in a festival, the principle of *elaboration* comes into play. Sights and sounds and motions, nearly all of which are stylized and thus removed from their daily counterparts, proliferate and thereby give an impression of enormous wealth and diversity. Like much of the music heard, the festival itself is polymelodic and polyrhythmic. The fabric of the whole comes from the complex interweaving of literally hundreds of disparate threads – elements that overlap, change, merge, move, and rest. The *ensemble* principle – a whole comprised of interrelating parts – is present in nearly all festivals.

Pars pro toto

Yet our interest in the whole should not obscure the significance of each element, however small, for it is often a microcosm, as well as being necessary to the existence of the whole. In this regard we may briefly consider what Allegra Fuller Snyder (1972) calls 'the dance symbol.' Whether a single dance gesture made by one person or an entire performance by many, dance often symbolizes and supports a people's world view. Akuapem (and much African) dancing does just that. A dancer who rolls his arms inward, then stretches his right arm out to the end beats of the music, is saying: 'If you bind me with chords, I shall break them to pieces' (Nketia 1963: 160n). Dozens of similarly meaningful gestures are made by both performers and their audience during the course of a dance. Festival dancing to state orchestras can refer to historical events, reinforce ritual actions, express the subservience of a sub-chief, the grief of mourners or the ferocity of a warrior. There would, of course, be no dance without music, and with neither of those arts present it is difficult to conceive of a festival at all. Professor Snyder believes that the dancer, internally, experiences 'transformation,' through which he 'experientially builds a bridge between physical reality and conceptual reality' (1972: 221). The dancer becomes something more, or 'other' than his ordinary self. Though his actions are of course real, he has created an illusion. Many other minor acts and arts could be cited to reinforce this point. A chief's linguist with his sculptured staff serves both to separate that chief from his audience and link him to it. The chief understands very well the voice of the visitor; the linguist is thus an essential (ideological) but unnecessary (practical) intermediary. He is at once minor in any transaction but most significant in expressing the nature of the transaction. He is somehow real but at the same time illusory.

Illusion and transformation

The festival too is simultaneously real and illusionistic: a transformation of the lives and spaces of a town for the brief duration of the ceremonial period. With ordinary life suspended, the community acts out its ultimate concerns. Yet the actors play *themselves*, validating and communicating their own traditional and up-dated ideas of what is important in the world. The people are also their own patrons, ordering a work of art necessary to their existence, a work that is executed communally by the very same 'artists,' that is the patrons! The shrines, and the foods fed to gods and ancestors, too, are real. We can ask if the gods really *eat* only if we ask if a Catholic priest really changes wine to the blood of Christ.

The 'play element' is very much present, as it is in all ritual, contributing to the transformation and the illusion embodied in the festival (Huizinga 1950). Both *recreation* and *display* are important characteristics of such events, and those words, broken down, reinforce ideas of both play and illusion, a central aspect of play; 're-*creation*' suggests the cosmic renewal of the New Year, while 'dis*play*' emphasizes the special, conventionalized character of festival activity, which stands apart from normal behavior. 'Re-*presentation*' stresses the creation, again, of a particular cosmic event, 'when the edges of the years meet,' when New Yam, a kind of eucharist, is presented to the gods and the people. Despite the varied non-spiritual embellishments of the festival, it remains a sacred performance rooted in and dependent upon ritual. Thus the festival, a *holiday*, is also a '*holy* day,' when gods and ancestors are invited to partake in this blessing which people may enjoy only through their beneficence. And, as Huizinga says, '... with the end of play [festival/ritual] its effect is not lost; rather it continues to shed its radiance on the ordinary world outside, a wholesome influence working security, order and prosperity for the whole community until the sacred play-season comes round again' (1950: 14).

The uniqueness of festivals

Any work of art – and a festival – is its own lowest common denominator. It cannot be reduced or compressed without being changed into something else. The festival is therefore an irreducible unity with an elaborate temporal and spatial composition and practically infinite numbers of component parts. As in a pointillist painting, each minor unit, each act and object contributes to the impact of the whole. To emphasize the visual arts, such as sculptured staffs or personal adornment, at the expense of verbal, kinetic, and musical arts is to misunderstand the complex but unified orchestration of all art forms which constitute the festival itself. Indeed the relationships among these varied forms give a particular festival its special character, just as components vary. Each festival is unique by virtue of the way in which its 'ensemble' is composed and what particular elements and meanings are stressed. Some Nigerian and Cameroon festivals emphasize masquerades, others architecture. In still others, for example Kalabari festivals analyzed by Horton in several publications, dance and music may be emphasized locally more than verbal or sculptured forms, though the latter are certainly present.

In Ghana, too, there are many local variations. The Homowo festival of Ga peoples in and near Accra lacks the conscious visual emphasis of most Akan festivals. In the parts of two Homowo I have witnessed, too, far less spatial and temporal order was perceptible than in Akuapem or Ashanti counterparts. Among the Ga, the ritual process seems to receive greater stress than formalized display, and much activity seems random and spontaneous. Ga processions, for example, lay less stress on measured pace, rhythmic repetition, and hierarchy than Akuapem, Ashanti or Fanti processions. Fanti festivals, in general, seem to fall between the Ga and Akuapem examples cited here in precision of spatial and temporal organization, as well as in self-conscious visual display of such things as ceremonial dress. Such variations can perhaps be attributed to differences in the socio-political organizations of the three peoples, though this suggestion must remain tentative pending further research.[6] In any case, there is much to be learned from a cross-cultural structural comparison of festivals, though it is too early to draw any definite conclusions.

Festival variation in a single town

The four or more annual festivals in any one community can also be usefully compared to one another, for each has its special character and artistic emphasis. Those of Anomabu, a coastal Fanti town, may serve as a brief example. Some are indeed 'less artistic' than others, laying greater stress on family rituals with repeated but localized celebrations, or on social interaction and recreation, than on display. This latter is true of the Ahoba festival in which amorphous crowds of people follow drummers and singers throughout the town. Intended to rid the community of all evil, the 'energy system' of this two-day event has a random spontaneous quality in contrast to the more self-conscious displays of state and military (Asafo) festivals held in Anomabu at different times of the year. An analogy in poetry is the contrast between blank verse and the more controlled sonnet form. While Anomabu royal festivals are analogous to Odwira – hieratic, highly formalized spatially and well-organized temporally – its Asafo ceremonies are far more democratic displays of large, distinctively dressed military groups which compete with one another in dancing, singing, flag twirling, and performing various skits. While gold and sumptuous multicolored *kente* cloths are the visual magnets in state events, those of Asafo emphasize masses of contrasting, bright uniforms. While the elitist gold-covered staff can be seen as a symbolic leitmotif at royal events, the colorful, embroidered flag, of cheaper, more common materials, is the Asafo counterpart. It is possible, then, to see variations and even a kind of 'structural hierarchy'[7] of festivals in a single community, each festival distinct not only in content but in artistic expression.

Conclusion

The artistic impact of a festival stems not from isolated artistic forms or actions but from the formally orchestrated interaction of all the aesthetic resources of a community. A varied and rhythmic interplay of smaller and larger events establishes a direct flow of energy which engulfs the people and transports them – through the mystery of ritual, the majesty of power and the magnificence of display – to a transcendent plane. Serious play builds an illusion of the world more controlled and more perfect than men actually find it. The festival is thus relief and catharsis and hope, a spatial and temporal pocket in workaday lives; people in the richest of clothes eat the richest of foods and turn talking into prayer and song, walking into dance. The stylized artistry of transient festival life points up the essentially non-artistic character of constant daily behavior. With work and other normal activities suspended, people transform their community into an intensified idealized world of communion among gods and men. Peace and order prevail, and the atmosphere is charged with promise.

Life and art interpenetrate, creating a dynamic interplay, a dialogue between reality and illusion, man and god, form and meaning. Returning to Odwira in Akropong, we can visualize these tensions through the metaphor of 'call and response':

- dancers respond to the urgent call of drumming;
- food-carrying messengers respond, swaying and bending to the calls of spirits possessing them;
- women, cooling and praising with fanning cloths, respond to the call of these spiritually-laden messengers;
- sub-chiefs respond to the political call of their paramount;
- the festival itself is a response to the call of spiritual and social renewal.

Life itself, throughout the year, is a spacious 360-day round of meaningful social and spiritual activities. But humdrum and ordinary daily life needs to be recharged and renewed. The formalized and charged atmosphere of the five festival days works this revitalization, isolating and dramatizing life's meanings in artistic form. Expressive acts, in the festival, *become* symbols of life and beget still more artistry, and multiple works of art cascade together through the week, climaxing at the durbar.

The artistic energy system of the unified whole stems from man's need to construct a symbolic and idealized world, a model capable of crystalizing and dramatizing those aspects of life which, in any given community, are so crucial to its health and continuity. It is clear that no work of art, other than a festival, is equal to the task of projecting all these meanings in virtually simultaneous form. Festivals, then, are the most important and complex and beautiful works of art in southern Ghana.

Notes

1 The research on which this paper is based was carried out under a National Endowment for the Humanities Fellowship in 1972–73. I am grateful for its financial support, as well as to the University of California, Santa Barbara, for a Summer Faculty Fellowship, an Academic Senate Research Grant, and on my two-months' re-visit to Ghana in the summer of 1974, a Creative Arts Fellowship.

I am of course very grateful to countless people in southern Ghana for their cordial hospitability, as well as for their cooperation and information. Although in communal works of art such as festivals it may be unfair to single out individuals, I would nevertheless especially like to thank Nana Kwame Fori II, the Omanhene of Akropong in 1972; Nana Amonu X, Omanhene of Anomabu; the Awutu Odefoy; the Omanhene of Abeadze Dominase, Nana Kwabu Ewusi VI. Other Ghanians to whom I am grateful: Mr. Ohene-Asante, Senior, Mr. Kofi Ohene-Asanti, and Mr. Adi Darko, all of Akropong Akuapem, and Mr. George Osign of Awutu.

The Los Angeles Ethnic Arts Council's symposium, 'African Perspective – New Directions' (Spring 1974) enabled me to work up many of the ideas in this paper. My symposium talk included ten minutes of videotape which I believe made many arguments more clear than still photographs are able to do. I gave another version of this paper to Professor Allegra Fuller Snyder's seminar on dance in the spring of 1974, and I would like to thank her and the students present for their helpful comments.

My own students at UCSB have been instrumental in my thinking on the subject beginning with a seminar on 'festivals as works of art' in 1970 and continuing through fieldwork in the summer of 1974. Three students read earlier versions of this paper and made important suggestions for its improvement: Patricia Crane, Michael Coronel, and Doran Ross. My ideas, too, have been influenced by a UCSB art history M.A. thesis (unpublished) by Patricia Crane, 'Odwira, a Drama of the Ashanti' (1971), and an important doctoral dissertation on Northern Edo (Nigeria) festivals by Jean Borgatti of UCLA.

2 One stool had two brass bells of European manufacture attached, and one of these has the cast-in legend, 'Amor vincit omnia, A.D. 1650.' There is, of course, no reason to assume that the date on the bell and that of the stool are coeval.

3 Such hearths may have been present in Akropong, but were not actually observed by the author until 1974, when they were very much evident in closely analogous festivals among Awutu and Fanti peoples. Artistic motivations are evident in the sculptural motifs rendered: varied three-dimensional letters of the alphabet or numerals, stools, hearts, and numerous other carefully finished and apparently abstract shapes which are entirely different from the normal household three-stone hearth, which cannot in any way be called artistic.

4 'Unprogrammed' actions may actually be 'expected' in a festival, for as an essential part of its nature, it is a *popular* event involving the whole community. Because 'core' events are necessarily visible and thus meaningful to a fairly limited audience, numerous supplementary 'events' are provided by the people themselves both to

entertain them and to weld them to the *main* event, which at once causes this activity and is enriched by it. In this light we can see food and trinket sellers as actually 'necessary' elements in a festival's overall design.

5 I gratefully acknowledge Patricia Crane's sensitive observations of these and several other events in the Odwira at Akropong in 1972.

6 Ga peoples are traditionally far more democratic or egalitarian than Akuapem (and Ashanti), while Fanti combine hieratic socio-political structures on the Ashanti model with the egalitarian tendencies of power vested in military organizations (Asafo) and thus fall somewhere between.

7 I am indebted to Doran Ross, who has done valuable fieldwork among the Fanti, for pointing out the hieratic nature of festivals in a single town.

Bibliography

Coomaraswamy, Ananda K. 1956. *Christian and Oriental Philosophy of Art*. New York.

Kwamena-Poh, M. A. 1973. *Government and Politics in the Akuapem 1730–1850*. Longman, London.

Kyerematen, A. A. Y. 1964. *Panoply of Ghana*. Praeger, New York.

Langer, Suzanne K. 1953. *Feeling and Form*. Scribners, New York.

Huizinga, Johan, 1950. *Homo Ludens: A Study of the Play Element in Culture*. Beacon Press.

Nketia, J. H. Kwabena. 1962. *African Music in Ghana*. Northwestern University Press, Evanston.

—— 1963. *Drumming in Akan Communities of Ghana*. Nelson, London.

—— 1965. *Ghana – Music, Dance and Drama*. University of Ghana, Legon.

Snyder, Allegra Fuller. 1972. 'The Dance Symbol' in *The Dimensions of Dance Research; Anthropology and Dance*. Cord, New York (mimeographed copy).

Index